USING THE
IBM
PS/1

ROB KRUMM

ADVANCED COMPUTER BOOKS

MIS: PRESS

© 1991 by Management Information Source, Inc.
P.O. Box 5277
Portland, Oregon 97208-5277

First Printing
ISBN 1-55828-072-3

Printed in the United States of America

TRADEMARKS

IBM PS1, IBM DOS, and Proprinter XL are trademarks of the IBM Corporation
Works, MS-DOS, and Windows are trademarks of Microsoft Corporation
Prodigy is a trademark of Prodigy Information Service
Compuserve is a trademark of Compuserve Information Service
WordPerfect is a trademark of WordPerfect Corporation
Lotus 1-2-3 is a trademark of Lotus Development Corporation
Eaasy Sabre is a trademark of American Airlines
LaserJet is a trademark of Hewlett-Packard Corporation

For Carolyn,
Without you none of this would be possible—or necessary.
Your turn again,
every 35 books seems fair.

Contents

Contents

SECTION II. PROJECTS

Contents

Contents

Introduction

The goals set for this book require it to be more than just a reference manual or a list of tips. Instead, this is an educational book designed to be used in conjunction with the hardware and software found in the IBM PS1.

Using the PS1. This book is designed to provide the information and experiences necessary to tap into the power of the PS1 computer.

Computer Use Skills. In addition, this book is designed to teach you the skills and concepts required to put your PS1 computer to work for you in business, school, hobbies, or other activities.

In order to achieve these goals the book is organized into three Sections.

Section I. PS1 Basics

The first three chapters serve as an introduction to the terms and concepts involved with computers—specifically the IBM PS1. While it is probably possible to operate a computer without having an understanding of how it works and how it is organized, the author believes that having some familiarity with these ideas will deepen and enrich all of the other operations you perform with the computer.

Section II. Projects

Once you have become acquainted with the basic organization of the PS1, Section II provides a series of projects that will teach how to use the various software applications provided with the PS1. This section contains complete, step by step instructions starting with simple tasks, such as creating a letter with a word processor, and continuing to more powerful tasks, such as creating a budget using spreadsheet modeling. It is important to understand that the projects are not merely designed to teach you how to complete the task, e.g., type a letter, but to educate you about the advantages of using a computer and how you can employ that power to improve your projects. This section contains all the keystrokes and mouse operations needed to complete the project, as well as numerous illustrations to which you can compare your results.

Section III. Beyond the Basics

Section III provides information that goes beyond the use of the basic PS1 hardware and software. This section explains how you can add programs of your own, such as popular applications like WordPerfect, Windows, or Lotus 1-2-3. It also demonstrates the use of various types of printers and system configuration options.

HANDS ON ACTIVITIES

The style of writing in this book is dictated by one simple idea. People learn by doing. In educational circles this approach is called the discovery method. This method believes that true learning is always based on actual experience with the subject. If you want to learn to dance you can't do it by just watching other people dance: at some point you have got to get up on your own two feet and move around.

Logic then dictates that you can only become an effective computer user by actually using the computer. Most of the information contained in this book is in the form of interactive, hands on operations. By carrying out the activities discussed here, you will gain a working knowledge of the computer hardware and software.

Of course, you don't need a book to get experience with the computer. All you need is to turn on the machine and spend some time with it. The purpose of this book is to provide a structured experience. A structured experience is one that leads you in the direction of knowledge and understanding, rather than simply random experiences. In fact, all of education, when it's done correctly, from pre-school to graduate school, involves providing a structured experience for the student.

Most computer books are divided into two types. Reference books discuss concepts in a general manner without giving a great number of specific examples. Tutorial books contain lists of keystrokes, shortcuts, or tips but often lack the conceptual framework for you to fully understand why you perform the operation. This book uses a dual track approach—a detailed discussion of the concepts interwoven with the step by step instructions. This means that a discussion of the concept behind an operation will be located at the place in the text where you are carrying out that operation, in order to complete a project. In other words, the how (the operations) and why (the concepts) are blended together into a single experience.

It is the author's belief that this approach is the best one for helping people integrate computers into their lives, which after all, is the reason for buying a computer like the PS1.

PS1 Basics

Chapter 1

Operating the PS1

T his chapter, along with Chapters 2 and 3, is designed to introduce you to the PS1 computer and teach you the concepts and terms you will need to know in order to operate the computer effectively.

This chapter will discuss basic operations, terms, and concepts related to the PS1 computer.

COMPUTER TERMS AND CONCEPTS

How much do you need to know about the workings of a computer in order to use it? One commonly used analogy is made between using a computer and driving a car. The analogy states that most people only need or want to know enough to drive a car—they don't need or want to know how it works. This attitude towards computer use is misleading and flawed in several important respects.

Goals. When you learn to drive a car you already know the goal that you have in mind, because you already know what a car is used for and what it can do. When you begin to work with a computer it is not possible to know in advance all of the things you can or want to do with it. Computers, unlike cars, are not dedicated to any one task. Instead, computers can perform an almost unlimited variety of tasks. Thus, part of the process of learning about a computer is learning about all of the different things that it could possibly do. No one knows in advance all the things they will end up doing with their computer. That is why it is such an important and powerful tool.

Interactive. When a car is driven, it generally doesn't matter who is doing the driving. The way the car is operated is independent of the particular driver, e.g., the gas pedal is always the same for every driver. Computers, on the other hand, have an interactive quality. The choices and preferences made by the individual using the computer has a direct result on the final product. In fact, no two people use the same computer in exactly the same way. This means that learning to use a computer can never be simply a matter of memorizing procedures, because using a computer requires you to make innumerable choices, which will seldom be exactly the same twice. The best way to learn to use a computer is to learn concepts that will help you make intelligent choices, based on your unique needs and preferences.

Growing into your Computer. Handling most industrial machines becomes routine and tedious once you have gotten familiar with their operation. The computer, conversely, will appear richer and more powerful as you become more familiar with its functions and features. As you learn more about the computer you will find new features and new ways to use old features. Put another way, computers bring out the creativity in individuals, unlike most machines that require boring, rote operations, e.g., driving for hours on a freeway.

For these reasons, this chapter will cover in some detail computer concepts and terminology as related to using the PS1.

PS1 Hardware

One of the most interesting and revealing concepts associated with computers is the distinction between *hardware* and *software*. Hardware is usually defined as the physical parts that make up the computer itself. Figure 1-1 shows the four basic components that make up the PS1 computer system.

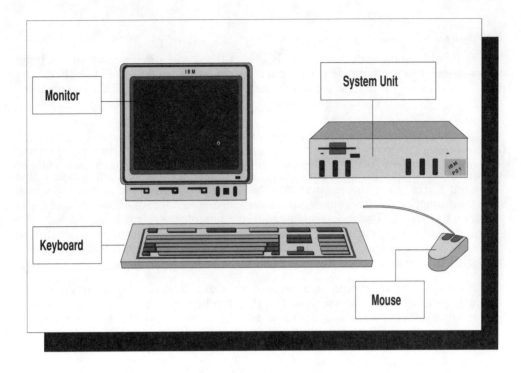

Figure 1-1. Four Basic Hardware Components of the PS1.

Monitor

The monitor or screen is built from the same basic components that are used to build televisions. Like a TV, the monitor displays information in the form of text or pictures. The main difference is that a TV receives its information from a remote source —the TV station—while the monitor receives its information from the system unit of the computer. The monitor is important because it is the primary means by which the computer provides you with information.

System Unit

The system unit is the part of the system that contains the actual computer, along with other electronic components. All the other components of the system are connected to the system unit in one way or another, so they can transmit or receive information generated by the system unit. The system unit contains the processor, the internal memory, the disks, and the modem.

Keyboard

The keyboard, along with the mouse, is one of the devices that allows you to input information into the computer. Computer keyboards contain all of the characters found on typewriter keyboards, plus a number of special keys that have meaning only within the context of computer operations.

Mouse

The name *mouse* is derived from the appearance of the device, which vaguely resembles a rodent with a long thin tail. The mouse provides an alternative to the keyboard for entering information into the computer. Unlike the keyboard, which enters information in the form of text, the mouse enters information by pointing at items on the screen. The mouse is linked to the computer system in such a way that as it is moved on the surface of the table or desk, a pointer on the screen will also move in a corresponding direction. The mouse also has two buttons that can be used to convey information to the computer.

A fifth optional component is a printer. Printers produce paper copies of the information displayed on the screen. The PS1 can be connected to a wide variety of printers from IBM or other manufactures. For details about printers see the section in this chapter entitled "Printers."

PS1 Software

The PS1 is different than most computers in that the hardware and software are sold as a single unit. Traditionally, computers are sold with only a minimum of software—usually just enough to get the computer turned on. The idea was that the owner of the computer could then purchase the software they liked separately. This approach is common in other areas of technology. For example, stereo equipment is usually sold in one store, and records, tapes, and compact disks, which are used in the stereo, are sold in a different store.

However, the separation between hardware and software sales creates certain problems that are particularly troublesome for new users.

Too Many Choices

The variety of software available to computer users is one of the best features of computers. A single computer can teach children how to read the alphabet, improve SAT scores, or produce a doctoral thesis. Unfortunately, this incredible variety is usually overwhelming to new users. Without experience new users often buy the wrong type of software, or software that is too complicated for their knowledge.

Installation

One of the hardest aspects of software usage is *installation*. Installation is the process by which computer information purchased in a store is transferred to your computer system. What is so hard about installation? The answer is that in the last 12 years most of the computers that have been sold do not have exactly the same type of equipment. For example, there are at least four major types of color screens available: composite, CGA, EGA, and VGA. Each one requires that the software operate slightly differently. Software that works with a wide variety of devices can be confusing to install, since many new users aren't sure about the technical names for the items they have.

The PS1 avoids these problems by supplying high quality software already installed. The software included with the PS1 is:

IBM DOS 4.00

IBM DOS is the operating system of the computer. The operating system is the program that coordinates and organizes all of the parts of the computer system. Operating system programs, such as IBM DOS 4.00, are distinguished from applications in that operating systems do not perform normal work tasks like typing a letter or adding a list of numbers. All operating system tasks are related to computer operations only. For this reason IBM DOS is usually considered an advanced subject and not discussed in basic books. However, some understanding of DOS is necessary for all computer users. This book will include that basic information.

Prodigy

Prodigy is a software application that links your computer, through normal telephone lines, to a remote computer service. By connecting your computer to the Prodigy service, you can use your computer for shopping, news and entertainment, weather, and more. All PS1 computers are supplied with a free three month subscription to Prodigy, as well as the hardware (called a modem) and software needed to connect to the service.

Microsoft Works

Works is a broad-based productivity software application that includes word processing, spreadsheet modeling, database management, and telecommunications features.

With these programs already installed and ready to run, you can begin to use your PS1 immediately.

HARDWARE AND SOFTWARE

If hardware refers to the physical components of the computer, what is software? The best way to answer this question is to use an analogy of a different type of activity—singing a song. The process of singing, like the process of computing, has two very definite parts roughly analogous to hardware and software.

In singing, the hardware is the physical means by which sounds are produced, i.e., the throat, vocal cords, air in the lungs, etc., that make it possible for a human being to produce sounds. If a person lacked any of these physical parts, e.g., if a cold prevented his/her vocal cords from vibrating, he/she would be unable to sing.

However, even when all the physical parts are present and in working order, there is still no guarantee that a song can be sung. What is required is something that you can't see, feel, or touch: the knowledge of how to sing, as well as a song to sing. This information plays the same function in singing as software plays in computing. A software program supplies the computer with the knowledge to carry out a task, such as the ability to multiply or divide numbers.

In order to accomplish a task, hardware and software must be present and working properly together. Neither part by itself is sufficient, but both parts are necessary for a computer system to function.

Hardware and software represent broad classifications. In working with the PS1 it is useful to breakdown these classifications into more detailed components.

The System Unit

The system unit the is the heart of the PS1. It contains almost all the electronic components of the system. All the other parts of the system—the screen, keyboard, mouse, and, if available, the printer—are connected to the system unit by means of a cable.

The system unit contains a variety of important computer parts. Keep in mind that most of the parts are contained within the system unit's box and cannot be seen without opening the case. Figure 1-2 shows the system unit.

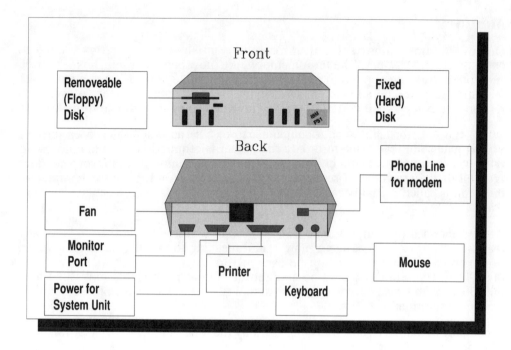

Figure 1-2. PS1 System Unit.

Disks

The PS1 is supplied with one 3.5 inch floppy disk drive and an optional 3.5 inch hard disk drive. Note that the hard disk cannot be seen while the front panel is in place. A small amber indicator on the right side of the panel lights up when the hard disk is used.

Ports

The back of the system unit contains the *ports* used to connect parts to it. On the left side is the port for the monitor cable, as well as the power cable from the monitor that supplies the system unit with power. In the center is a parallel printer port used for connecting the system to a printer. On the right side are two circular ports used for the keyboard and the mouse. In addition to those ports, in the upper right corner of the back panel is a phone jack used to connect the system's built-in modem to a normal telephone line.

Memory

One of the most important and unfortunately misunderstood terms related to computer use is *memory*. The term memory, like most computer terms, is borrowed from other uses and applied to computers in a figurative way. Since computers are machines, they don't really remember anything. When the term memory is used with reference to computers it describes the way in which computers store information.

What type of information can a computer store? The answer, which may surprise you, is that computers can store only one type of information: numeric values. In fact, the only numbers that it can store are 0 or 1. Everything that the computer does is based on the recording of sequences of the numbers 0 or 1. Information stored in this form is called digital because at base it is composed of number patterns made of 0 and 1.

At first, the idea of digital storage using only 0 or 1 seems too limited to be of any real use. The trick is to assign a more useful meaning to specific patterns of digits. For example, the letter A might be assigned to a sequence that looks like this: 00010001. The letter B would be a slightly different pattern that looks like this: 00010010. In this manner you could use digital storage to record an almost unlimited amount of information.

A computer's memory capacity is measured by the total number of digits it can hold. By tradition digits are counted in groups of eight, e.g., 10101010. This group is called a *byte*. The byte is the basic unit of measurement used for computer memory. Table 1-1 shows commonly used units of memory measurement.

Table 1-1. Units of Memory Measurement.

Unit	Number of Byte(digits)
byte	1(8)
kilobyte(KB)	1,024(8,192)
megabyte(MB)	1,048,576(8,388,608)

When you purchase a computer you will find that many of the components are rated by their memory capacity. For example, the PS1 can be equipped with either 512 kilobytes or 1 megabyte of memory. Selecting 1 megabyte doubles the amount of memory in the computer.

Types of Memory

Computer memory is probably the least understood of all computer terms. The primary source of the confusion is that every computer system has several different types of memory, each with a different function and a different set of characteristics.

In order for the system to function properly, each type of memory must play its proper role. To know how much of each type of memory you should have, you need to understand the different types and functions. The PS1 contains four different kinds of computer memory: internal RAM memory, disk storage, ROM, and CMOS.

Internal RAM Memory

This is the most important type of memory in the computer system. The name RAM stands for *random access memory*. It is called random because the computer system can directly change the value of any digit in the memory without disturbing any of the other digits. For this reason all the creations and revisions of information done on your computer use RAM memory as the storage area. The primary weakness of RAM memory, and this is an important weakness, is that it requires a constant source of electrical current in order to maintain the information. Within a small fraction of a second after the electricity is cut off, the RAM memory is erased completely, losing the information that was stored in it forever.

Disk Storage

If your computer contained only RAM memory, all your work would be lost as soon as you turned off the computer. This constant loss of data would make long term use of the computer impractical. The solution is to add a second type of memory to the computer system: disk storage memory. Disks are composed of the same material that is used for audio and video tapes. The advantage of this type of storage is that once information is placed on a disk it will remain there permanently, or until you specifically erase it, no matter how many times you turn the computer system on and off. The disadvantage of disk storage is that the information is stored in large blocks that cannot be easily rearranged or modified.

ROM

ROM stands for *read only memory*. ROM memory is used to add information to the system that will never need to be changed. For example, the start up screen that appears when you turn on your PS1 is stored in ROM memory. It cannot be erased or changed because it is built into the electronics of the computer. Because ROM cannot be easily changed or modified, only that information that is unlikely to ever change is stored in ROM.

CMOS

CMOS memory is a special form of RAM designed to work with a very small amount of electricity. The advantage of this type of RAM is that the data placed into CMOS can be stored for long periods of time, perhaps as much as 5 years, using long life batteries to supply power. CMOS memory combines the flexibility of standard RAM with the permanence of ROM or disk storage. CMOS memory is used to store information about the optional equipment installed in a given computer, such as the number and types of disks installed, the amount of internal memory available, and other items that might vary from one system to another.

In most computer systems the smallest amount of memory is the CMOS memory because it is the most expensive and requires battery power. The largest amounts of memory are found in the form of disk storage, because it is the least expensive and most permanent type of memory.

Types of Disks

Disks supply the permanent data storage component of the computer system. The PS1 can use two types of disks: floppy and hard.

Floppy Disk

All PS1 systems have one 3.5 inch *floppy* disk drive. The name floppy is a bit misleading since the 3.5 inch disks used with this drive are made of hard plastic. A more accurate name world be removable since you can remove and insert as many different disks as you desire into the floppy drive. The name floppy was used because the older 5.25 inch removable disks were made of soft plastic that could bend easily. Each 3.5 inch disk can hold a maximum of 1.44 megabytes of information.

Hard Disk

A hard disk is a high capacity disk drive that is installed into the computer as a single unit, disk, and drive, which cannot be removed from the machine. Hard disks can hold much more data than a floppy disk. The PS1's hard disk can hold 30 megabytes of information. In addition, the disk operates at a much higher rate of speed than do floppy disk drives, thus decreasing the amount of time it takes to save or retrieve data from the disk.

How the Different Types of Memory Are Used

The PS1 uses all four types of memory to create a useful computer system. For example, suppose you want to use Microsoft Works to type a letter (the task explained in Chapter 4 in Section II of this book). You begin with the PS1 startup screen.

Figure 1-3 shows how ROM, disk, and RAM memory are used when you load a program such as Microsoft Works. The first type of memory encountered is ROM. The PS1 startup screen image is stored in ROM memory, which is built into the PS1 system. When you select the Microsoft Works symbol from the startup screen the computer then accesses the disk locations in which a copy of the Works program is stored. The data from the disk is placed into RAM memory. Once placed in memory the computer can run the Works program.

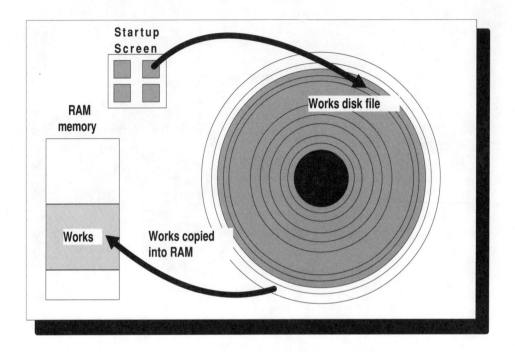

Figure 1-3. Memory Used when Loading Microsoft Works.

Note that only part of the memory is filled with the Works program. The remainder of the RAM memory is used to hold the data that you enter into the various parts of Works, e.g., word processing text.

Recall that RAM memory will not retain data of any sort when the computer is turned off. When you use a program for word processing or spreadsheet modeling, you will probably want to permanently store the information you have entered, rather than have it discarded. Data is saved by copying the user information entered into RAM memory into a file on the disk, as shown in Figure 1-4.

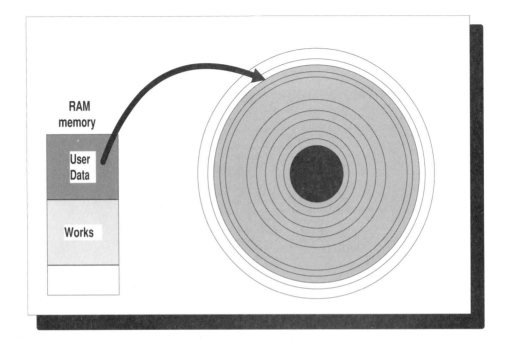

Figure 1-4. User Data Copied from RAM onto Disk File for Permanent Storage.

About RAM and Disk Capacity

The relationship between RAM memory and disk memory is very important to understand. Many computer users, even with years of experience, are not clear about the distinction between these two important types of memory. In the previous section, Figures 1-3 and 1-4 depicted how information is moved back and forth between the disk and the internal RAM memory. There are two important points to remember:

1. The size of the RAM memory determines the size or number of programs that can be running in the computer at any one time.

2. The size of the disk, hard or floppy, determines the total amount of programs and data that can be stored on the disk for use at some future time.

Disk Files

When information is stored on a disk, either hard or floppy, it is necessary to supply a name for each file. The type of names that can be given to a file is determined by the operating system of the computer. On the PS1, that operating system, IBM DOS 4.00, allows file names that are between 1-8 characters. The characters can be letters (A-Z), numbers (0-9), or some special characters, such as: ~, $, !, @, {, }, and (or).

The name can also have an optional three character file extension. The extension is separated from the file name by a period. The file extension is generally used to identify the type of file. Program files have either an EXE (executable program) or COM (command) extension. The extension DOC is usually, but not always, associated with word processing.

The following are examples of file names that might appear in a PS1 disk:

    WORK.EXE
    README.DOC
    COMMAND.COM
    AUTOEXEC.BAT

USING PS1 SOFTWARE

The next section of this chapter begins a hands on, step by step series of instructions that will introduce you to the PS1 and the software provided with the computer. The remainder of this chapter will introduce you to the PS1 operating system including IBM DOS version 4.0. Chapter 2 will introduce Microsoft Works, an application that can perform word processing, spreadsheet modeling, data base management, and communications. Chapter 3 will introduce you to using the Prodigy on-line service. As a PS1 buyer you are automatically entitled to use Prodigy free for three months.

Begin this section by turning on your computer.

The Startup Screen

When you first turn on the PS1, the computer displays its startup screen. This screen is the starting point for all your operations with the computer. The screen is divided into five parts: date/time display, information, Microsoft Works, Your Software, and IBM DOS. Figure 1-5 shows a diagram of a startup screen.

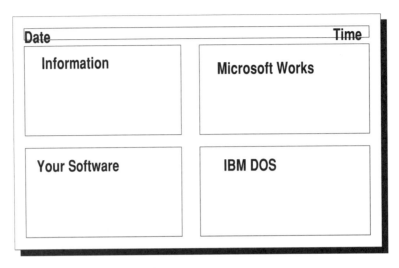

Figure 1-5. Diagram of Startup Screen.

Date/Time Display

At the top of the screen is a narrow box that displays today's date on the left side and the current time on the right side. The PS1 has a clock/calendar with a battery backup so that it will maintain the correct date and time even when it is shut off. Later in this chapter you will learn how to change the date or time settings should they need to be altered, e.g., for daylight savings time.

Information

When selected, this option leads you to the Prodigy system software which can be used to connect your computer to the Prodigy service and the IBM Users Club (part of Prodigy). This option also provides you with access to two programs designed to teach you about your computer: System Tutorial and Works Tutorial.

Microsoft Works

When selected, this option leads you to Microsoft Works. Works is a broad-based application that provides you with popular computer applications, such as word processing, spreadsheet modeling, data base management, communications, and graphing. In addition, because all these applications are contained in a single program you can combine information in interesting and useful ways.

Your Software

This option leads you to the PS1 *folder* system. The folder system is unique to the PS1. It is designed to provide a method by which you can access information stored on MS-DOS compatible disks. The folder system is a *shell* program. The term shell refers to a program that presents basic operating system information in an organized form. You will find that there are three different ways to interact with the operating system of the PS1, of which the folder system is only one.

IBM DOS

This option leads you to the IBM DOS (Disk Operating System) version 4.00. Like the folder system, DOS provides a means by which you can interact with the operating system of the computer to perform tasks such as copy information, deleting unwanted data or changing the time/date settings for the system. IBM DOS can function in two different ways: the IBM DOS shell and the command prompt. IBM DOS is not unique to the PS1. You can find versions of DOS that look and operate the same way on a variety of computers, from IBM and other manufacturers.

What is the difference between Your Software and IBM DOS? The remainder of this chapter will attempt to answer that question in some detail. In general, IBM DOS is the more powerful and more complicated of the two systems. The folder system provided under Your Software is designed mainly for finding and running computer programs other than the two applications (Prodigy and Works) supplied with your PS1 computer. IBM DOS provides commands that cover all areas of computer operations. Most users will only ever need to use a few of the basic operations in DOS, even though your PS1 comes with a complete set of DOS utility programs.

The Keyboard

Your PS1 system comes supplied with two methods of communicating with the computer: a keyboard and a mouse. The keyboard used with the PS1 is similar to the the type of keyboard used with a typewriter but with a number of additional keys, as shown in Figure 1-6.

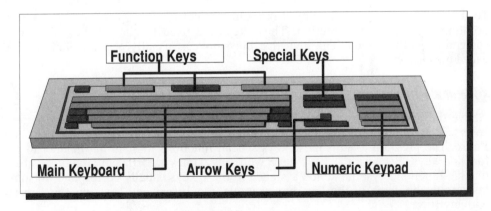

Figure 1-6. PS1 Keyboard.

21

You may wonder why a computer keyboard has so many keys. The answer is that computers can perform an almost unlimited number of tasks. One method of telling the computer you want to perform a task is to press a key that corresponds to that action. By adding more keys to the keyboard you increase the number of different instructions you can give to the computer just by pressing a key.

Main Keyboard

The main keyboard has a typewriter style layout. The primary differences are the addition of two special keys labeled [Alt]-alternate and [Ctrl]-control. These keys are used in a similar manner as the [Shift] keys; that is, they do not produce a character when they are typed. Instead, these keys are used in combination with other keys. This means that on the PS1 keyboard there are four possible ways to use each key:

1. Type the key by itself
2. Hold down [Shift], type key
3. Hold down [Alt], type key
4. Hold down [Ctrl], type key

Function Keys

On the top row of the keyboard are 12 keys labeled F1, F2, F3, etc. These keys are called *function* keys and they are used to enter commands into the program that you are working with. Despite their name these keys have no particular function. Each program that you work with will assign its own meaning to the function keys. However, over the past decade since the IBM PC was introduced, some of the function keys have become associated with certain actions, e.g., F1 is the Help key. However, every program is free to define the function keys in whatever way it chooses.

Arrow Keys

To the right of the main keyboard is a cluster of four keys, each with an arrow pointing in a different direction. These keys are used to change the position of something on the screen. The item that they move is usually a small blinking line called the *cursor*.

Special Keys

Above the arrow keys you will find a cluster of keys with the following names: **Insert**, **Delete**, **Home**, **End**, **Page Up**, **Page Down**, **Print Scrn**, **Scroll Lock**, and **Pause**. The program assigns these keys special functions in a similar manner to the function keys. Because the keys have words as names rather than simply numbers like the function keys, the action assigned to these keys usually correspond, in some fashion, to the name of the key. For example, the **Insert** key has something to do with inserting.

Numeric Keypad

On the right side of the keyboard is a numeric keypad similar to those found on calculators. This keypad is different from a calculator keypad in that it has keys, words, and arrows, in addition to numbers. This means that each key has two functions. The function of the key is controlled by the **Num Lock** key. When the **Num Lock** key is on, the keys on the keypad operate as number keys. When the green light labeled Num Lock is lit, the **Num Lock** key is on. When the Num Lock is off, the keys function according to the word or arrow labels. The keys with arrows have the same function as the keys in the arrow key cluster. Note that the names of the keys are abbreviated, e.g., **Page Down** is **Pg Dn**, **Insert is Ins**.

You may wonder why there are two sets of arrow and special keys. The answer is that the original IBM PC keyboard did not have separate arrow and special keys. Even though the PS1 keyboard has these additional keys, the dual function of the keypad is maintained in order to keep the PS1 compatible with programs and users who are used to the older style keyboard.

The **Num Lock** key is a toggle. Each time you press the key it changes from on to off or from off to on.

Keystroke Conventions

Since this book discusses in detail how to use your PS1, you will find that throughout the book you will be instructed to enter keystrokes. Keystroke instructions in this book will follow the conventions shown below.

Special keys will be enclosed in [], e.g., **[End]**, **[Pg Up]**, **[F1]**. The Enter key will be represented by **[return]**. The arrow keys will appear as **[left]**, **[right]**, **[up]**, and **[down]**. For example, below is an instruction that tells you to type in the word "hello" and then press **[return]**:

```
hello [return]
```

As mentioned, you can combine any key with the **[Shift]**, **[Alt]**, or **[Ctrl]** keys. The instruction shown below tells you to press and hold down the **[Alt]** key, and while holding it down, press the letter A. Once you have pressed A you should release both keys:

```
[Alt-a]
```

Key combinations can also include functions or special keys. The instruction below tells you to hold down **[Shift]** and then type **[F10]**:

```
[Shift-F10]
```

In addition to these special keystrokes, the [Shift] key is used to enter upper case letters A through Z. You can lock the keyboard into all upper case letters by pressing the [Caps Lock] key. Like [Num Lock], this key toggles between on and off each time it is pressed.

The Mouse

The mouse is a device that you can use to point at and select items on the screen by moving the mouse on the table. The mouse, as shown in Figure 1-7, has two buttons, left and right.

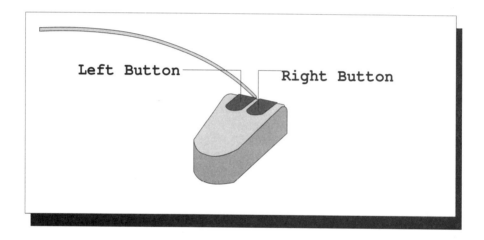

Figure 1-7. Mouse with Left and Right Buttons.

There are three actions you can perform with the mouse: pointing, clicking/double clicking, and dragging.

Point

Pointing with the mouse refers to moving the mouse pointer. This is done simply by moving the mouse on the table. As shown in Figure 1-8, the mouse pointer on the screen will move in the same direction as you move the mouse on the table. This movement allows you to point at any object, text, or graphic on the screen.

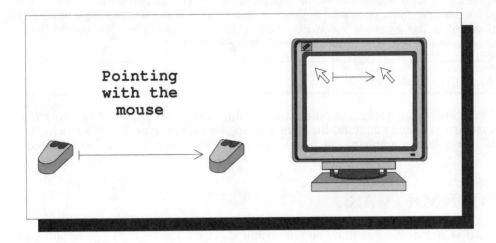

Figure 1-8. Pointing with the Mouse.

Click/Double Click

Clicking the mouse refers to pressing down and then releasing one of the mouse buttons. The term click is used to describe this action since the mouse buttons issues an audible click when they are pressed and released. For the most part, clicking refers to clicking the left mouse button. Some programs also make use of clicking the right mouse button. A double click refers to clicking the mouse button twice in rapid succession. Programs that employ double click operations keep track of the amount of time between clicks. If two clicks occur within a specified time period, a small fraction of a second apart, they are treated as double clicks. Otherwise the clicks are treated as two single clicks.

Drag

Dragging the mouse is the same as pointing, with the addition that you press and hold down one of the mouse buttons while you are moving the mouse on the table. The drag ends as soon as you release the mouse button.

In this book instructions requiring the mouse will begin with point, click, double click, or drag to indicate the action. If the action is a click or a drag, the button, left or right, will be enclosed in parentheses. For example, the instruction below tells you to point the mouse at the word "file", which appears somewhere on the screen, and click the left mouse button:

Click(left) on **File**

Mouse instructions often work in groups. The instruction below tells you how to perform a drag. First you point the mouse at the place on the screen where the drag is to begin, in this example the word "data." Then press down the left mouse button and drag the mouse pointer to the word "management":

Point at *data*
Drag(left) to *management*

If the item you are asked to point at, click on, or drag to, is part of the program's command or menu structure, the item will appear in bold type in the instruction. If the item is text or numbers which you entered into the program, italics will be used.

YOUR SOFTWARE

The first area of the PS1 that you will examine is the section labeled Your Software. This section is designed to help you store and execute software programs other than those provided with the PS1 (Prodigy, Works and IBM DOS) which have their own sections on the startup screen.

Select Your Software using the mouse:

Click(left) on **Your Software**

When you make this selection the PS1 screen changes to display the PS1 folder system, as shown in Figure 1-9. The folder system display consists of several parts: drives, current directory, open folder, other folders, and commands.

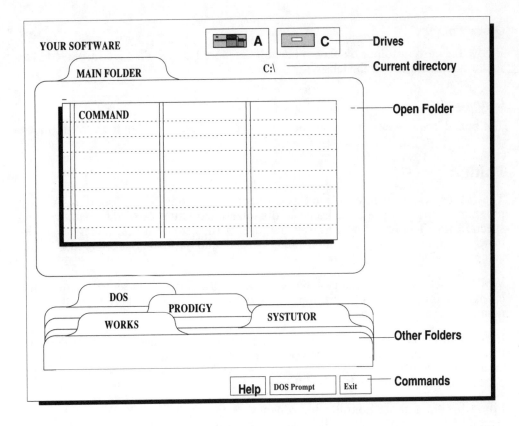

Figure 1-9. Folder System Display.

Drives

A symbol will appear for each drive in the system. If you have a floppy drive system only the A symbol will appear. Hard drive systems will display an A and a C symbol.

Current Directory

This is the name of the DOS current directory. You will learn more about the DOS directory system as you continue in this chapter.

Open Folder

This display shows you the contents of the current folder. The tab of the folder shows the folder name. The names of the programs contained within the folder are listed below.

Other Folders

Below the current folder display, other folders stored on the disk are displayed. The folder names appear on the tabs.

Commands

The boxed items represent commands which can be executed from the current folder.

Folders

The folder system was described as an operating system shell program. A shell program is one that presents the basic organizational structure of the computer in a special form. The folder system uses the idea of files stored in file folders as a way of representing the way in which files, in particular programs, are stored on your computer's disks.

While a shell program changes the way the information is presented, it does not change the fundamental organization of the computer system. That remains the same no matter what type of shell you are using.

In order to understand how the folder system is used, it is necessary to understand the ideas and concepts used by the operating system to store files. If you are working on a system that has only a floppy disk, the system of file storage is quite simple because all the files on each disk will be listed in the main folder displays.

Filing becomes more complicated when you have a hard disk. Why? The main reason is the large number of files that can be stored on a hard disk. For example, a floppy disk will typically hold 20 to 40 files. On the other hand, a hard disk can easily hold over 1,000 files. Listing all the files in one list is practical for 20, 30, or even 40 files. However, a list of 1,000 files is much to large to be useful.

The problem with long lists of files has less to do with computers than with the way in which people read and remember information. A person looking at a list of 20 or 30 names will have no trouble picking out a particular name. But if the list were much longer, say 300 names, the task would be more difficult and the person reading such a list would be more prone to making a mistake. As the list gets longer it becomes harder and harder to use efficiently.

How can you avoid long lists if the disk hold hundreds or thousands of files? The answer is to create a system by which the one long list of files can be broken down into smaller groups. For example, you might break a long list of names into groups-based alphabetical order. Instead of one long list, you would have 26 shorter lists, one for each letter in the alphabet. When you wanted to locate a name you would first select the list which corresponds to the first letter in the name. Your search would then concentrate on just the names in that group.

Of course, alphabetical organization is only one possibility to divide and organize lists. It might be more meaningful to group items based on other characteristics such as the state or city in which people live. Suppose that you had a large list of names and addresses that needed to be organized. You might first divide the list by state so that you had one group for each state. With a very large number of names you might want to go further and create subgroups within the state for the major cities. For example, you might have main groups for New York, New Jersey and Pennsylvania. The Pennsylvania group could be divided into Pittsburgh and Philadelphia subgroups.

Organization, such as the type described above, in which a given list of items is divided into groups, which can then be further divided into subgroups and so on, is called a *hierarchy*. A common example of a hierarchy is an outline with heading, subheading, and sub-subheadings.

IBM DOS, the operating system of the PS1, supports a hierarchical system of file storage. The system is based on the idea of folders. At the highest level is the Main Folder. Every disk, hard or floppy, has a Main Folder. The Main Folder can be used for two purposes: listing program files and listing additional folders.

List Program Files

The Main Folder will display the names of program files. The Main Folder of a floppy disk will usually display the names of all the programs on that disk, if any. On a floppy disk system, when you select Your Software, the Main Folder displays the names of all the program files on the disk that is currently inserted in the floppy drive, if any.

List Additional Folders

The Main Folder can also be used to show the names of any additional folders on the disk. On hard disk systems the Main Folder will show four folders, DOS, PRODIGY, SYSTUTOR, and WORKS, supplied with the PS1 hard disk. The purpose of these additional folders is to divide the files contained on the hard disk into groups based on function. The PRODIGY folder contains all the files needed to access the Prodigy service. The WORKS folder contains the files needed for Microsoft Works. Dividing the files into groups based on function helps organize the large amount of information on the hard disk better than simply having everything dumped into the Main Folder.

In theory floppy disks can also have additional folders. However, since the amount of information that a floppy disk can hold is rather limited, compared to a hard disk, most floppy disks have only a Main Folder.

Running Programs from the Folder System

When you select Your Software from the startup screen the folder system begins by displaying the Main Folder of the current disk. If you are using a floppy only system the folder uses the disk in drive A, if any. If you have a hard disk system the folder is the Main Folder of the hard disk.

The purpose of the folder system is to allow you to run programs other than those built into the startup screen. When you use the folder system you can perform the following operations: open a folder, run a program, or use folder system commands.

Open Folder

You can open any of the additional folders shown on the screen by clicking (left) on the folder tabs.

Run a Program

You can run any of the programs listed on the open folder by clicking (left) on any of the names on the list. If the list contains more than 24 names, you can scroll the list up or down by clicking on the Page Up or Page Down boxes that appear on the open folder.

Folder System Commands

At the bottom of each display are boxes that represent folder system commands, as shown in Table 1-2.

Table 1-2. Folder System Commands.

Command	Function
Close Folder	closes the current folder
Help	displays information about system
DOS Prompt	activates DOS system prompt
Exit	exits the folder system
[Esc] key	exits current folder display.

Keep in mind that you should use the DOS **Prompt** command only if you are familiar with direct entry of MS-DOS or IBM-DOS commands from operating other computers. Once you select the DOS Prompt option you will remain at that level until you enter the DOS command **EXIT**, which will return you to folder system.

It is important to keep in mind that the folder system does not explain the meaning or use of the program names that appear on its display. For example, you might see names listed in the Main Folder such as AUTOEXEC or COMMAND. What is the purpose of these programs? Why or when would you want to execute them? The folder system does not supply information that would answer these questions. The folder system is based on the assumption that you know the names of the programs and understand what they will do when you select them. Of course, there is nothing to stop you from selecting by clicking (left) any program which is listed. It is not recommended that you try this random approach, since the results of some programs can have a permanent effect on your computer system. You should only execute programs with which you are familiar or have additional information, such as that found in this book, that explains how to use the various programs.

Running the CHKDSK Program from the Folder System

As an example of how to use the folder system you can execute the DOS command **CHKDSK**. The program named CHKDSK, called "check disk", is a DOS utility that can provide statistical information about disks and also performs some standard maintenance operations.

If you have a hard disk system, the CHKDSK program is located in the DOS folder. Open the DOS folder by using the mouse:

Click(left) on *DOS*

The folder system changes the display to show the contents of the DOS folder.

If you are using a floppy disk system, insert the Operating disk from the set of IBM DOS disks. Display the folder for this disk by clicking the drive A symbol:

Click(left) on *drive A symbol*

Examine the list of programs shown on the folder display. You should find the name CHKDSK listed. Note that the names appear in alphabetical order listing across each row and the down to the next.

To execute a program listed in the folder, click(left) on the program's name:

Click(left) on **CHKDSK**

When you select a program for execution, the folder system displays a new screen which is used to start a selected program, as shown in Figure 1-10. The screen displays the name of the program and a box which allows you to enter any options for the program. As with the function of the program itself, you must already know what options, if any, are available with the selected program and how you would specify those options. The Help function in the folder system explains the folder system itself not the program you have selected.

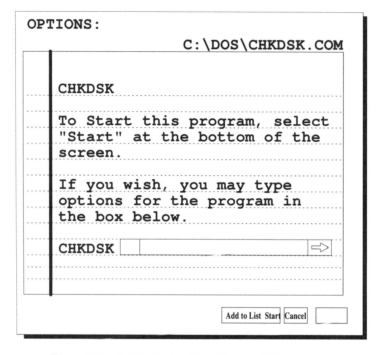

OPTIONS:

C:\DOS\CHKDSK.COM

CHKDSK

To Start this program, select "Start" at the bottom of the screen.

If you wish, you may type options for the program in the box below.

CHKDSK

Add to List Start Cancel

Figure 1-10. Folder System "Start Program" Screen.

You can execute the program by pressing **[return]** or clicking on the **Start** command at the bottom of the screen:

Click(left) on **Start**

The CHKDSK program will generate a screen that lists information about the current disk, as shown in Figure 1-11. The information provides a statistical summary of the disk and RAM memory in the computer.

```
Volume MAIN FOLDER created 05-12-1990 1:59a
Volume Serial Number is 125C-08FD

 30976000 bytes total disk space
    73728 bytes in 3 hidden files
    20480 bytes in 7 directories
  9269248 bytes in 334 user files
    22528 bytes in bad sectors
 21590016 bytes available on disk

     2048 bytes in each allocation unit
    15125 total allocation units on disk
    10542 available allocation units on disk

   655360 total bytes memory
   544176 bytes free


Press Enter ( ◄┘ ) or mouse button to return.
```

Figure 1-11. Current Disk Information.

Total Disk Space

This value shows the total number of characters of storage available on the disk.

Hidden Files

Some disks will have special files that do not appear on lists of files. These are called *hidden files*. Hidden files have special system functions and are not directly accessible by users.

Directories

A directory is the DOS terminology for folders. This line tells you the total number of folders on the disk.

User Files

User files count the number and the space used by normal disk files.

Bad Sectors

Most hard disks, and some floppy disks, will contain defects that make some sections of the disk unusable. The operating system avoids errors by marking these areas as bad and subtracting their space from the usable disk space.

Bytes Available on Disk

The total amount of space available for use on the current disk.

Bytes in Each Allocation Unit, Allocation Units on Disk and Available Allocation Units on Disk

These values describe the technical details behind the way that disk space is allocated. The allocation unit is the minimum amount of space used for each file, e.g., 2,048 on a hard disk, 1,024 on a floppy disk. The entire disk space is divided by that unit into allocation units. If you multiply the number of allocation units by the allocation unit size you will match the value for total disk space.

Bytes Memory and Bytes Free

These values measure internal RAM memory of your computer. They do not measure disk space. The first value is the total amount of memory installed in the computer which is available to the operating system, either 524288 for a 512K system or 655360 for a 1 Megabyte system. The second figure is the amount of that memory that is not being used at the moment. Note that some of the computer's memory is always in use even when you are just running the folder system.

When you have completed viewing the information, return to the folder system by pressing [**return**] or clicking(left):

Click(left)

The computer returns to the folder system screen showing the files in the current folder.

If you have a 1 megabyte system you may be wondering why the CHKDSK program shows only 655,360 for the total size of the memory. 1 megabyte should be equal to 1,048,576. What happened to the missing 393,216? The missing memory is caused by a built in limitation of the IBM DOS 4.00 operating system. This limitation was placed into DOS when it was created for the first IBM PC in 1981. At the time most personal computers used a maximum of 64,000 bytes of memory. The IBM PC multiplied that limit by 10 assuming that in the future no personal computer would require more than 640K (655,360) bytes of memory. The operating system designed for that computer was also designed for that limit. Over the past decade the hardware used in the IBM PC has been replaced by systems that can use vastly greater amounts of memory. However, software development is a different story. All the popular software applications that interested people in using personal computers was designed to run under the DOS operating system. This meant that even though you could install more memory in the computer, you would still use the software designed for a maximum of 640K. The result is that even in a computer such as a 1 megabyte PS1, DOS remains blind to this additional memory.

In Section III of this book you will learn how to customize the PS1 to use this additional memory for special tasks.

Running Programs with Options

Many programs allow you to designate options which change or alter the way they function. Of course, what these options are and how you access them is something the folder system assumes you already know. As an example, the CHKDSK program can be used to generate a list of all the files contained on a disk, hard or floppy. You can generate this list by specifying the /V option. The V stands for verbose since this option causes CHKDSK to list the names of each file it counts when summing up the statistics for the disk.

Select the CHKDSK program from the folder list:

```
Click(left) on CHKDSK
```

Type in the option:

```
/v
```

Execute the program with the /V option:

```
Click(left) on Start
```

This time the program lists all of the files in all of the folders on the disk before it shows the statistical summary. If you are using a hard disk system the list will show several hundred files. Return to the folder display:

```
Click(left)
```

The list of files scrolled very quickly—too quickly for it to be readable. If you have a printer attached to the computer you can use another option to print a copy of this command. Make sure your printer is connected and turned on, ready to print, before you attempt the next command:

```
Click(left) on CHKDSK
```

Type in the option:

```
/v>prn
```

Execute the program with the /V option:

```
Click(left) on Start
```

This time the program shows a blank screen but sends the information to your printer. When the printing is complete you return to the folder display.

Adding a Command to the Main Folder

If you have a hard disk system, you can use the folder system command **Add to List** to add a program stored in any folder on the disk to the Main Folder display. This option is handy for placing frequently used programs in the Main Folder so that they are easy to locate and use. This option applies mainly to software programs that you add to the PS1 after you have purchased the computer. However, you can use any of the supplied programs, such as the CHKDSK utility, as an example.

Display the start screen for CHKDSK:

```
Click(left) on CHKDSK
```

Instead of starting the program, use the **Add to List** command to place the name of the program in the Main Folder:

```
Click(left) on Add to List
Click(left) on Ok
```

The CHKDSK program now appears as an option on the Main Folder display. Exit the folder system:

```
Click(left) on Exit
```

Return to the folder system:

```
Click(left) on Your Software
```

When the computer shows the Main Folder display, the **CHKDSK** command appears on the list.

You can remove a program from the list by using the **Remove from List** command. Begin by selecting the program you want to remove:

```
Click(left) on CHKDSK
Click(left) on Remove from List
Click(left) on Ok
```

The program is removed from the Main Folder program list. Keep in mind that this operation does not erase a program from the disk. It merely deletes the program name from the Main Folder display. Also note that you cannot remove a program from the Main Folder list if that program is actually stored in the main folder. When you select a program that is stored in the Main Folder the **Remove from List** command will not appear at the bottom of the screen.

Exit the folder system:

Click(left) on **Exit**

Notes for DOS Users on the Folder System

If you have worked with versions of MS or IBM DOS on other computers the folder system represents certain limited aspects of DOS. The folders correspond directly to DOS directories. Selecting a folder is the same as using the DOS command **CD** (change directory).

The folder system display does not list all files. Rather, it lists the names of those files that have one of three specific file extensions: COM, EXE, or BAT. In DOS these files can be directly executed from the operating system. The folder system does not display or use other disk files, such as data files, text files, or program support files because these files do not have one of the three specified extensions.

The folder system is designed to create a menu system of programs by placing the names of the programs on the Main Folder list. You cannot perform operations such as file copying or deleting with the folder system. The next section discusses the use of the IBM DOS shell program which has a much wider range of operations than the folder system.

THE IBM DOS SHELL

The IBM DOS option displayed on the startup screen of the PS1 activates the IBM DOS 4.00 shell program. As mentioned before a shell program is one that presents operating system information in a special form or style. The folder system represents a shell with the limited purpose of executing programs stored on the floppy or hard disk which are not part of the startup screen options. The folder system is unique to the PS1. The IBM DOS shell program is a much more powerful shell that provides you with a much wider range of options than the folder system. The style and layout of the IBM DOS shell is not unique to the PS1. It can be found on any computer running IBM or Microsoft DOS 4.00 or higher. If you are already familiar with the DOS 4 shell program from using another computer system, you will find that the

IBM DOS option on the PS1 works exactly the same way.

Activate the IBM DOS shell program:

Click(left) on **IBM DOS**

The computer loads the IBM DOS shell program and displays the main DOS screen, as shown in Figure 1-12. The screen is divided into four basic parts: title bar, menu bar, group menu, and function key commands.

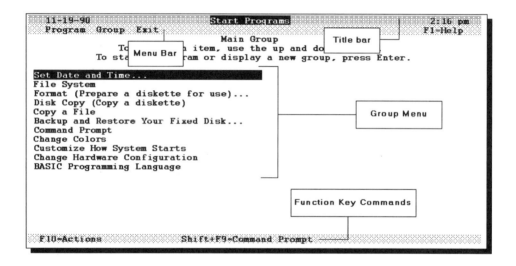

Figure 1-12. IBM DOS Screen.

Title Bar

The top line of the display shows the current date and time as well as the title of the display. The Start Programs screen is always the first displayed when you enter IBM DOS.

Menu Bar

The menu bar is used to access commands. The bar lists the names of command menus available at this time. The menu bar displays pulldown menus, which list the commands under each category that appears on the menu bar.

Group Menu

The group menu is a list of specific actions which can be executed by pointing at the names and clicking. Group menus are not automatic. They must be created through a process that specifies in detail what command or group of commands to execute for each item on the menu. The current menu was supplied with the PS1 to help you work with your computer. This menu can be modified or even replaced if desired. Section III of this book will detail how to customize the DOS group menus.

Function Key Commands

The bar at the bottom of the display lists shortcut function key commands that can used to execute specific actions. The **[F10]** key activates the menu bar. The **[Shift-F9]** combination activates the DOS prompt mode. Note that using the DOS prompt mode requires a prior knowledge of DOS commands. If you enter the DOS prompt mode you will remain in that mode until you enter **EXIT [return]**.

Using the Main Group Menu

The Main Group menu lists 11 options that can be selected using the keyboard or the mouse. The **[up]** and **[down]** keys will move the highlight up and down on the menu. Pressing **[return]** will execute the selected menu option. If you use the mouse, you can execute a command by double clicking (left) on the command you want to perform.

Set Date and Time

This option allows you to change the time and date settings for the computer. You would use this to adjust the computer's clock/calendar for changes in daylight savings time, etc.

File System

This option accesses the DOS file system. With this option you can perform operations such as copy, deleting, and renaming files.

Format (Prepare a Diskette for Use)

This option allows you to prepare a floppy disk for use in the system. Most floppy disks are unusable directly from the box. Once purchased you must format the disk in order to use it in your PS1. Using an unformatted disk will generate an error. Note, as a safety precaution, you cannot format your hard disk with this option.

Disk Copy (Copy a Diskette)

This option allows you to create a duplicate a floppy disk. Note that the disk on which you want to place the copy must be formatted before you use it to make a duplicate.

Copy a File

This option allows you to create a copy of a specific file.

Backup and Restore Your Fixed Disk

This option allows you to create a backup of all the files on your hard disk. You must format a sufficient number of floppy disks, before you use this command. You can estimate the number of floppy disks needed by dividing the total amount of hard disk space used by files by the capacity of your floppy disks (720,000 or 1,400,000 bytes). You can find out the total amount of disk space in use by using the **CHKDSK** command as discussed in the previous section on the folder system.

Command Prompt

This command activates the DOS prompt mode. This option has the same effect as the **[Shift-F9]** command.

Change Colors

This option allows you to change the colors used by the DOS shell program.

Customize How System Starts

This option allows you to customize the startup procedure used by the PS1. See Section III for details about customization of the PS1 system.

Change Hardware Configuration

Use this option to reconfigure the system's setup in the computer's memory if you add new equipment to your PS1, e.g., adding a hard disk to a floppy disk system.

BASIC Programming Language

This option activate the BASIC programming language. Once activated the basic language will remain active until you enter the command **SYSTEM [return]**. In order to use BASIC you must have a prior knowledge of BASIC language commands and operations.

Suppose that you wanted to reset the time in the PS1 clock. Select the Set Date and Time option:

Click(left) on **Set Date and Time**

The screen display changes to reveal the Set Date and Time menu. This menu has two options, Set the Date and Set the Time. Select the Set the Time option:

Click(left) on **Set the Time**

DOS displays a rectangle in the lower right area of the screen, as shown in Figure 1-13. This rectangle is called a dialog box. A dialog box is a box displayed by a program in response to a command. The dialog box allows you to enter specific details or make selections required to complete the command. Not all commands have dialog boxes. Dialog boxes are used with commands that require the user to specify information or options without which the command cannot be completed. In this case you must enter the new time to which you want the system's clock reset. The dialog box displays information about the entry that is needed. Here, an example of the format for the time entry is shown, e.g., 2:51 pm.

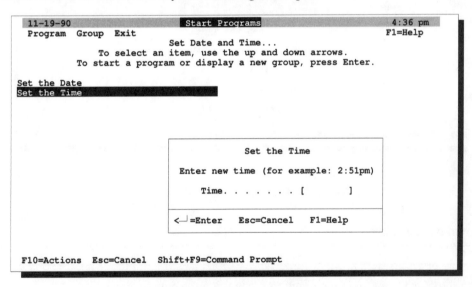

Figure 1-13. Dialog Box Displayed for Set Time Option.

The [......] area is called a text box. This is the area in the dialog box in which you can enter the required information.

The dialog box also displays three commands that you can use. The **[return]** key enters the new time into the system's clock/calendar. The **[Esc]** key will cancel the command and return you to the previous menu. The **[F1]** key will display help. Select the Help option by entering:

```
[F1]
```

DOS displays another box that explains more about the operation specified by the current dialog box, as shown in Figure 1-14.

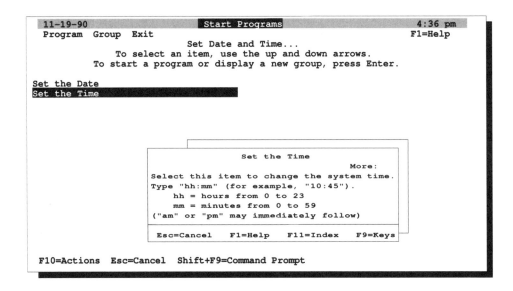

```
 11-19-90                    Start Programs                  4:36 pm
  Program  Group  Exit                                      F1=Help
                          Set Date and Time...
                 To select an item, use the up and down arrows.
               To start a program or display a new group, press Enter.

 Set the Date
 Set the Time


                    ┌───────────────────────────────────────────┐
              ┌─────┤              Set the Time                  │
              │                                         More:     │
              │   Select this item to change the system time.     │
              │   Type "hh:mm" (for example, "10:45").            │
              │      hh = hours from 0 to 23                      │
              │      mm = minutes from 0 to 59                    │
              │   ("am" or "pm" may immediately follow)           │
              │                                                   │
              │   Esc=Cancel    F1=Help    F11=Index    F9=Keys   │
              └───────────────────────────────────────────────────┘

  F10=Actions  Esc=Cancel  Shift+F9=Command Prompt
```

Figure 1-14. Help Displayed for Dialog Box.

To remove the help box enter:

```
[Esc}
```

Return to the Main Group menu without changing the date by entering:

```
[Esc](2 times)
```

Using the Shell Menus

In order to exit the DOS shell and return to the startup screen you will need to use the menus. The **[F10]** command activates the menu bar. You can also activate the menu bar by clicking on the menu bar item you want to access. In this case you will want to use the Exit menu:

┌───┐
│ Click(left) on **Exit**   │
└───┘

When you select one of the items from the menu bar, the program displays a rectangle below the item, called a pulldown menu, as shown in Figure 1-15. This menu list the commands that fall under the selected item. In this case there are two commands, **Exit Shell** and **Resume Start Programs**. The first command on the menu, **Exit Shell**, is highlighted.

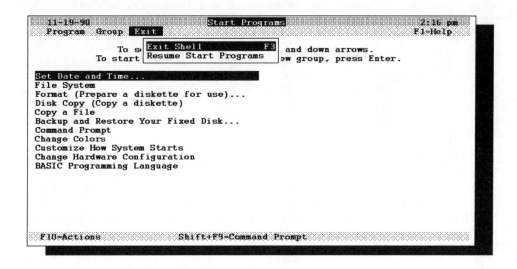

Figure 1-15. Pulldown Menu Displayed.

The **F3** on the same line as **Exit Shell** indicates that the [**F3**] function key is a shortcut for this command. This means you can Exit the DOS shell program without using the menus if you press [**F3**]. Select the Exit Shell command from the pulldown menu:

┌───┐
│ Click(left) on **Exit Shell**   │
└───┘

The DOS shell program is terminated and you return to the startup screen.

SUMMARY

This chapter covered some of the basic terms and concepts associated with computer use. It also introduced three of the basic elements of the PS1: the startup screen, the folder system, and the IBM DOS shell program.

Hardware. Hardware refers to the physical aspects of the computer. A computer is not a single machine but a number of different devices that work together to form a computer system. The PS1 has four basic pieces of hardware: the system unit, the monitor unit, the keyboard, and the mouse. The system unit contains the RAM memory, the disk units (hard and floppy), and other essential elements in the system, including the modem used for telecommunications.

Software. Software refers to the information stored in the computer system that tells the computer how to operate. The PS1 comes with several software programs installed for use on the PS1 system. The programs are Microsoft Works, Prodigy, and IBM DOS 4.00. In addition, the PS1 has a built in startup screen which automatically appears each time you turn on the computer. All operations on the PS1 begin from the startup screen.

RAM Memory. RAM memory is installed inside the system unit of the computer. This memory is also called internal memory. RAM memory is used to hold all the programs and data information needed for the computer to perform a function, such as word processing. All the work done on your computer must first be stored in RAM memory. However, RAM memory can retain information only as long as it is supplied with a constant flow of electricity. When the computer is turned off, the RAM memory is wiped clear.

Disk Storage. Disk storage refers to the process by which information is copied from the internal RAM memory, which will lose data when the electricity is turned off, to a disk that can retain the information permanently regardless of how many times the computer is turned on or off. The PS1 can use both floppy (removable disks) and hard (fixed) disks. Information stored on a disk must be given a file name that fits the limits imposed by the operating system.

The Startup Screen. The PS1 displays the startup screen each time the computer is turned on. The startup screen is built into the PS1 and cannot be modified. The screen has four options: Information (Prodigy and tutors), Microsoft Works, Your Software, and IBM DOS. Clicking any of the items activates that option.

Keyboard. The keyboard is one of two means of communication with the computer. In addition to a typewriter section the keyboard has special keys (**Home**, **End**, **Page Up**, **Page Down**, **Insert**, and **Delete**), arrow keys, functions keys, a numeric key pad, and the [**Alt**] and [**Ctrl**] keys that work in combination with the other keys.

Mouse. The mouse is a device that is used to point at items on the screen based on movement on the table. You can perform four operations with the mouse: point, click, double click, and drag. The mouse has two buttons. Most programs only use the left button but in some cases the right button is also used.

The Folder System. The option labeled Your Software activates the PS1 folder system. This system is designed to list the programs stored on the disk so that you can select them for execution. On hard disk systems programs files are grouped according to function in folders. To execute a program you must first open the folder in which it is contained and then select the name of the program you want to execute from the folders list of programs. Floppy disks usually list all their files in a single folder, although occasionally a floppy disk will contain folders as well. The folder system is unique to the PS1.

The IBM DOS Shell. This program is part of the MS or IBM DOS system. It can be found on any computer that uses MS or IBM DOS 4.00 or higher. The primary purpose of the shell is to organize IBM DOS operations in the form of group menus and dialog boxes. The PS1 is supplied with a menu of 11 DOS functions. The options can be selected from the Main Group menu. You can expand or modify the menu system to add your own programs.

Chapter 2

How to Use Works

Your PS1 computer includes a multi-purpose software program called *Works*. Works is created by the Microsoft corporation, which is also the creator of the DOS 4.01 operating system supplied with your PS1. The Works program provides four different types of computer applications combined into one program. This chapter shows you how to use Works. The major areas are: word processing, spreadsheet modeling, database management, and communications.

Word Processing. Word processing deals with the creation of text documents from simple one page letters to multi-page reports or papers containing hundreds of pages. Word processing is the most commonly used type of computer application, since almost any activity requires the creation of some type of document.

Spreadsheet Modeling. The term *Spreadsheet Modeling* refers to the most commonly used type of program for performing mathematical calculations. Unlike pocket calculators that can work on only one operation at a time, e.g., add, subtract, multiply, or divide, computer applications can remember hundreds or thousands of numbers and calculations. All of the numbers and calculations needed to solve a given problem form a model of the problem from which the computer can produce an answer. Spreadsheet Modeling provides a unique way to learn and use all sorts of mathematical ideas, in particular, those that relate to money like to savings, loans, and taxes.

Database Management. A *database* is an organized store of information. A database management program helps you create, update, and search databases of your own design. Databases can hold information as varied as your Christmas card list to accounts receivable information.

Communications. Although the PS1 is supplied with software specifically designed to communicate with the Prodigy service, you can also use the modem built into the computer with the communications portion of Works to connect to other on-line services such as CompuServe, or to communicate with computers at work or school.

Because Works combines all four applications into one program there are added benefits. You can move information between various applications. For example, you could copy the results of a spreadsheet model into a report you were preparing. You can use the communications features to dial phone numbers stored in the database. You can even use spreadsheet values to create pie charts or line graphs.

In Section II of this book you will find a series of detailed projects that teach you how to use and understand the manifold parts and features of the Works program. However, before you begin to work through these projects, it is a good idea to get familiar with the basic structure of the Works program.

The purpose of this chapter is to help you get familiar with the following concepts used in the Works program.

- •Menus bars
- •Pulldown menus
- •Menu selection keys
- •Command letter keys
- •Mouse operations
- •Dialog boxes
- •Options boxes
- •Text boxes
- •List boxes
- •Command buttons
- •File lists
- •Using Works help

STARTING WORKS

When you turn on the PS1, you can use the image in the upper left corner of the startup screen to start the Works program.

Click(left) on *Microsoft Works*

When the Works program is loaded you will see a screen display that looks like the screen shown in Figure 2-1.

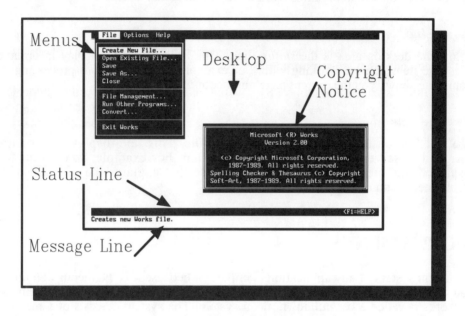

Figure 2-1. Opening Works Screen Display.

The display consists of five separate parts: menus, copyright notice, desktop, status line, and message line.

Menus

The line at the top of the screen and the rectangle in the upper left corner of the screen are the Works program *menus*. A menu is a list of commands or operations that you can perform. Works uses a system of menus referred to as a *bar/pulldown* menu system. In this system the top line of the screen always shows a menu bar. The bar lists the major categories of operations available in Works at the current time. In this case the bar lists three categories: File, Options, and Help. The rectangular box below File is the pulldown menu for that category. The box lists the actual commands and operations related to the main topic of File.

Copyright Notice

When you first start Works the copyright notice is displayed to inform you of the copyright on this software.

Desktop

The large blank area in the center of the screen is called the desktop. It is in this area that your work, e.g., word processing or databases, will appear. The term desktop is used to make an analogy between the way work is organized on the computer screen and the way you would organize work on top of an actual desk.

Status Line

Below the desktop area is the *status* line. This line is used to display information about the item you are working with. For example, if you are word processing, the status line shows you the current page number and type font.

Message Line

The last line on the screen is the message *line*. This line displays information designed to serve as a reminder or explanation. For example, when a menu is displayed, the message line contains a phrase that explains the function of the highlighted menu option.

WORKS MENUS

The menu system of any application is important because it is the menus that present you with the commands and operations available in the application. The system used in Works is called a bar/pulldown menu system. The system consists of a menu bar that is always displayed at the top of the screen and rectangular boxes (pulldown menus) that can be displayed for each of the items on the menu bar.

The menu bar serves as an outline of the commands available at the current time. The menu bar does not list actual commands. Instead, each word on the menu bar represents a category of commands which you might want to use. The menu bar has two very important advantages. First, it is always visible so that you can access one of the menu categories anytime you desire. Second, the list of command categories will change when you change activities. This means that the bar will read differently when you are word processing than it will if you are building a spreadsheet model.

When you first start the Works program only three items, File, Options, and Help, appear on the menu bar. In addition, the pulldown menu for File is automatically displayed.

Browsing the Menus (Keyboard)

How you use menus will vary greatly depending upon your amount of experience with the Works program. When you have become experienced with the program you will probably know which menus contain the commands you like to use. However, when you first learn how to use the program, you will probably not recall or know where in the menu system the commands you want to use are located.

One of the main advantages of a menu bar/pulldown menu system is that you can browse through the menus using the mouse or the arrow keys. Browsing allows you to explore all the options available without having to make a selection.

Begin exploring the menus using the arrow keys. If you look at the menu currently displayed on the screen you will notice that the File and Create New File are displayed as light letters on a black background. These are called *highlights*. The **[left]** and **[right]** arrow keys will move the highlight across the menu bar. The **[up]** and **[down]** arrow keys will move the highlight in the pulldown menu box up or down.

For example, you can move the highlight to the **Open Existing File** command by entering:

```
[down]
```

When you move the highlight in the pulldown menu, the highlight in the menu bar does not move. If you look at the message line (the bottom of the screen) you will see that the message has changed to read "Opens existing Works file." This message is designed to explain what the currently highlighted command will do should you select it.

If you use **[left]** or **[right]** arrow keys you will move the highlight on the menu bar. Enter:

```
[right]
```

When you move the highlight on the menu bar, the program closes the previous pulldown menu and opens the pulldown menu that corresponds to the newly highlighted category. In this case, the commands listed under Options are displayed. Works automatically highlights the first item on the pulldown menu when you open it. Display the Help pulldown menu by entering:

```
[right]
```

If you move past the left or right ends of the menu, the highlight jumps to the opposite end of the bar. For example, entering **[right]** again will take you back to the File menu. Enter:

```
[right]
```

If you want to exit the pulldown menu without selecting a command, use the **[Esc]** key. Enter:

```
[Esc]
```

The pulldown menu is removed from the screen leaving only the menu bar at the top. Note that none of the items on the menu bar is highlighted.

Alt Combination Keys

At the moment the menu bar is inactive. This means that none of the items on the bar nor any pulldown menus are displayed. In order to use or simply browse the menus you must activate the menu bar. This can be done using the [**Alt**] key in one of two ways: [**Alt**] and [**Alt-letter**].

[Alt]

Pressing and releasing the [**Alt**] key will activate the menu bar by placing a highlight on the first category on the bar.

[Alt-letter]

Works designates one letter in each of the words as the command key. For example, the letter **F** is the command key for File. You can access the File pulldown menu with the [**Alt-f**] combination keystroke. (Recall that to enter a combination keystroke the [**Alt**], [**Shift**], or [**Ctrl**] keys are pressed and held down while you press and release the letter key.)

Activate the menu by entering:

```
[Alt]
```

The program places the highlight on File but does not display the pulldown menu for that item. In addition, the items on the menu bar now show one letter in each word in bright white. These letters are the command letters for each of the items, e.g., **O** for Options and **H** for Help. Keep in mind that the first letter is not always the command letter since some menus have more than one item that begins with the same first letter.

How can you display the pulldown menus? The answer is that you can do so by either pressing [**down**] to display the menu for the highlighted item or entering the command letter for the desired item. Display the Help menu by entering:

```
h
```

The program shows the Help menu. Deactivate the menu system by entering:

```
[Esc]
```

Now that you are familiar with the command letter keys for the items, you can take a shortcut route to any menu by entering its [Alt-letter] combination when the menus are inactive. For example, go directly to the Help menu by entering:

```
[Alt-h]
```

The [Alt-letter] combination takes you to the desired menu with a single keystroke. Which is the best method? The answer is up to you. When you are unsure you can browse the menu system or when you know what, you want you can go directly to it. This type of flexibility is one of the strong points of the pulldown menu system.

Deactivate the menu bar by entering:

```
[Esc]
```

Browsing the Menus (Mouse)

You can use the mouse to activate and deactivate the menu bar.

Activate

Click (left) on the menu bar item to activate that pulldown menu.

Deactivate

Click (left) on any part of the screen except the menu bar or pulldown menu.

Suppose that you wanted to activate the Help menu using the mouse. Perform the following mouse operation:

```
Click (left) on Help
```

The Help pulldown menu is opened. You can select any of the other menus by performing the same action:

```
Click(left) on File
```

Deactivate the menu system by clicking anywhere on the screen other than the bar or pulldown menu:

```
Click(left) on the desktop area
```

The menus are deactivated. Which is the best method, mouse or keyboard? The answer usually has to do with where your hands are when you want to issue a command. If you are typing you might want to use the keyboard method so that your hands don't leave the keyboard. Conversely, if the mouse is convenient, the mouse selection method would be more favorable. As you work with Works you will evolve habits with which you feel the most comfortable.

PULLDOWN MENUS

The pulldown menus contain the commands and operations available in Works. Display the File menu using the mouse:

Click(left) on **File**

The program displays the file pulldown menu, as shown in Figure 2-2.

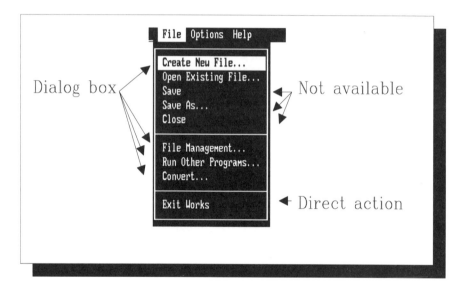

Figure 2-2. File Pulldown Menu.

If you examine the menu closely, you will see that there are two different ways in which the commands are displayed on the menu.

Active

The active items on the menu are displayed in black letters with a single bright white letter indicating the command key for that item. These items are the active items from which you can make a selection. Among the active items there are two kinds: dialog box and direct action.

Dialog Box. If the command name is followed by three periods(...), selecting this command will display a dialog box. Dialog boxes are used by commands that require special, detailed information in order to be completed. When the command is selected, a box will appear in the center of the screen into which you can enter the details or select the options you desire. For example, the **Create New File** command is a dialog box command because the three periods appear after the name.

Direct Action. If there are no periods following the command name, the command will execute as soon as it is selected. For example, the Exit Works option will execute as soon as you select it.

Unavailable

Some of the items on a menu will appear in gray, without a command key highlight. The reason for this appearance is that these commands, although part of the Works program, cannot be executed at the current time. For example, the Save option is unavailable because there is nothing on the desktop which needs to be saved. If there were, this item would appear as an active item.

Selecting a Command (Keyboard)

Suppose you wanted to select the command **File Management.** To use the keyboard you would do so in two ways: arrow-return and command letter.

Arrow-Return

Use the arrow keys to move the highlight to the command you want to select and press **[return].** The highlight will automatically skip over any items that are unavailable.

Command Letter

Each of the items on the menu displays a command letter key in bright white. You can select the option by typing that command letter. Note that when the pulldown menu is displayed you do not have to hold down the **[Alt]** key when entering a command letter.

In this case the command letter for the **File Management** command is **F.** Enter:

```
f
```

The program executes the selected command, resulting in the display of the File Management dialog box, as shown in Figure 2-3.

Figure 2-3. File Management Dialog Box.

Once a dialog box is displayed you can cancel the command with the **[Esc]** key. Enter:

[Esc]

The menu system is deactivated.

Selecting a Command (Mouse)

You can use the mouse to execute the a pulldown menu command. Display the File Management dialog box:

Click(left) on **File**
Click(left) on **File Management**

You can cancel the dialog box by using the mouse to click on the word "<cancel>". "<cancel>" will always appear in the lower right corner of any dialog box:

Click(left) on **<cancel>**

The menus are deactivated.

Dialog Boxes

As discussed previously, some Works commands can be directly executed from the pulldown menus, while others marked with three periods display dialog boxes when they are executed. Dialog boxes allow you to specify settings and options needed to carry out various commands. The heart of the Works command system is the use of dialog boxes. In order to use Works you need to understand how dialog boxes are organized.

Use the mouse to display the Options pulldown menu:

Click(left) on **Options**

This menu lists two interesting options: Calculator and Alarm clock. The calculator option displays a box that functions like a pocket calculator. This feature allows you to do calculations without having to have a calculator next to your computer. The Alarm clock option allows you to set alarms that will pop up while you are using works.

Select the **Alarm clock** command by the command key for that option, A:

a

The command reveals a dialog box for the Alarm clock command, as shown in Figure 2-4.

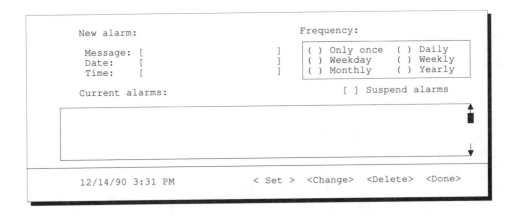

Figure 2-4. Alarm Clock Dialog Box.

This dialog box is a good example of dialog box organization because it contains all of the different elements found in dialog boxes.

Text Box

A text box is used to enter information that must be typed into the dialog box. This information can be text or numeric values. Since you can enter anything into a text box these are the items in a dialog box that are most likely to contain errors. Take care to enter information that is appropriate to the function of the text box. For example, if the label on the text box is "Date" you should enter a valid date in the month/day/year format, as shown in Figure 2-5.

```
Message:  [.......................]
Date:     [.......................]
Time:     [.......................]
```

Figure 2-5. Text Box.

Option Box

Option boxes contain a list of alternative settings for a given option. Each alternative has a ( ) in front of the option, as shown in Figure 2-6. The option that is currently active has a large black dot inside the ( ). The options in an option box are mutually exclusive. This means that only one of the items can be selected at a time.

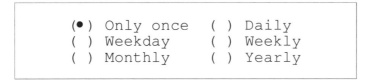

```
(•) Only once    ( ) Daily
( ) Weekday      ( ) Weekly
( ) Monthly      ( ) Yearly
```

Figure 2-6. Option Box.

Check Box

A check box is used for settings that can be either on or off, as shown in Figure 2-7. A [ ] appears in front of each check box. If the [ ] is empty the option is off. If an X appears in the [ ] the option is on.

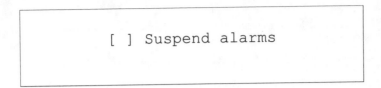

Figure 2-7. Check Box.

List Box

The function of a list box is similar to that of an option box with the exception that the number of items in a list box will vary from time to time. List boxes are used primarily for lists of user-defined items, such as file names or directories. In the Alarm clock dialog box the list box shows the alarms, if any, that have been set, as shown in Figure 2-8. The list box has a scroll bar on the right side which can be used to scroll through a list of items. This list is too long to be displayed in the box at one time.

Figure 2-8. List Box.

Command Buttons

At the bottom of the dialog box, separated from the other elements by a horizontal line, are two or more command buttons as shown in Figure 2-9. Command buttons are enclosed in < > brackets. The command buttons, unlike the other dialog box elements, will cause the program to perform some action as soon as it is selected. The two most common command buttons are < **OK** >(save the dialog box and execute the settings) and < **cancel** >(close the dialog box and discard the settings). The Alarm clock dialog box uses the buttons **<Set>, <Change>, <Delete>** and **<Done>**. In this case **<Done>** functions like < **OK** >.

```
┌──────────────────────────────────────────────────┐
│                                                    │
│   < Set >    <Change>    <Delete>    <Done>        │
│                                                    │
│                                                    │
└──────────────────────────────────────────────────┘
```

Figure 2-9. Command Buttons.

All dialog boxes have a default command button. If you look at the command buttons in the bottom of the dialog box you will see the brackets, < >, of one of the command buttons displayed in bright white as is the case with the **< Set >** command button in this example. When you press the **[return]** key in the dialog box, Works automatically executes the currently selected command button.

Filling in Text Boxes

Information is entered into text boxes by using the keyboard. In the Alarm clock dialog box the cursor is initially positioned in the message box labeled "Message."

This box is used to enter the text of the message that should appear when an alarm is displayed. In this case, enter the following text. Do not press **[return]** at the end of text:

```
┌────────────────────────────────────────────────────────────┐
│ Pick up Joey from school                                     │
└────────────────────────────────────────────────────────────┘
```

Note that Works allowed you to enter a message that was longer than the text box. In this example, the program scrolled the text to the right to allow you to continue entering text.

In a dialog box pressing **[return]** does not advance the cursor to the next text box or other option. Recall that pressing **[return]** in a dialog box executes the selected command button. To move to the next or previous item in a dialog box use the **[tab]** or **[Shift-Tab]** keys. Enter:

```
┌────────────────────────────────────────────────────────────┐
│ [Tab]                                                        │
└────────────────────────────────────────────────────────────┘
```

Enter the date of the appointment. Enter today's date in the same format, as shown below:

```
┌────────────────────────────────────────────────────────────┐
│ 10/14/90 [Tab]                                               │
└────────────────────────────────────────────────────────────┘
```

To enter the time, input a time that is five minutes from the current time, e.g., if the time is 2:45 enter 2:50:

```
┌────────────────────────────────────────────────────────────┐
│ 2:50 PM                                                      │
└────────────────────────────────────────────────────────────┘
```

Options Boxes

In the current dialog box the Frequency setting is controlled by an option box. The Frequency option box lists six different ways in which to set an alarm. The default setting, marked by a black dot, is Only Once, meaning that the designated alarm should ring only once and then be discarded.

The are two ways to change the selected option in an option box ,using the keyboard: [Tab]/[Arrow] keys and command letters.

[Tab]/[Arrow] keys

Use the [Tab] key to move the cursor to the option box. Once the cursor is positioned in the option box the arrow keys will move the cursor and the black dot to any of the options. When the black dot is positioned on the desired option, press [Tab] to move to the next item in the dialog box.

Command Letters

Each option in the option box is assigned a unique command letter that appears in bright white. You can select an option by combining the command letter with [Alt], e.g., [Alt-m] for Monthly. Note that if the cursor is positioned inside the option box you select an option by typing the command letter with or without [Alt].

In this example you might want to set the alarm as a daily alarm. Use the [Tab]/[Arrow] key method. First use [Tab] to advance the cursor to the Option box:

[Tab]

Now that the cursor is positioned in the option box, use the [right] key to change the setting from Only once to Daily.

[right]

The dot, indicating the selected option, moves along with the cursor. However, in considering the options you realize that the Weekday option would be more appropriate, since school is not in session on the weekends. This time use the mouse to make your selection. You can select an item in an option box by clicking on any part of the option text:

Click(left) on **Weekday**

The dot indicator moves to the options, Weekday, which was selected with the mouse.

Command Buttons

The command buttons, which appear below the line at the bottom of the dialog box, are used to execute specific actions. The alarm you have specified is not actually set until you use the < Set > command button. You can perform that operation with the keyboard or the mouse. Since command buttons are always located at the bottom of the dialog box it is usually easiest to use the mouse to execute a command by clicking on the appropriate button. Set the specified alarm by clicking on the < Set > button:

Click(left) on < Set >

The < Set > command button, like all command buttons found in dialog boxes, immediately carries out some action. In this instance that action was to copy the information entered in the text boxes into the Current alarms list box, creating an active alarm, as shown in Figure 2-10.

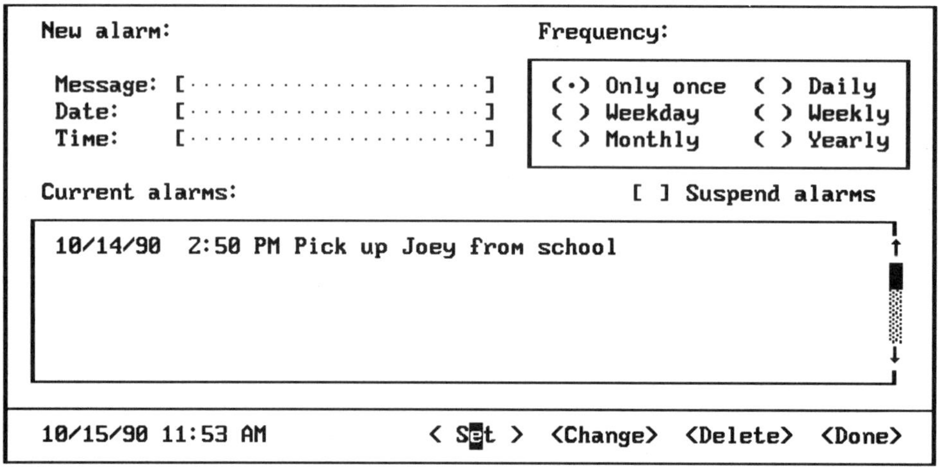

```
 New alarm:                          Frequency:

    Message:  [··················]    (·) Only once  ( ) Daily
    Date:     [··················]    ( ) Weekday    ( ) Weekly
    Time:     [··················]    ( ) Monthly    ( ) Yearly

 Current alarms:                              [ ] Suspend alarms

   10/14/90  2:50 PM Pick up Joey from school                    ↑




                                                                 ↓

    10/15/90 11:53 AM           < Set >   <Change>  <Delete>  <Done>
```

Figure 2-10. Alarm Entered with < Set > Command Button.

Once you set an alarm, the setting in the option and text boxes return to their default settings ready for you to enter another alarm, if desired.

Using Check Boxes

The current dialog box contains one check box option labeled Suspend alarms—it can be on (when it is checked) or off (when it is not checked). By default, the Suspend alarms options is off, i.e., no X appears between the [ ] next to the option name. Each time you click on a check box item you toggle its setting from on to off or off to on:

Click(left) on **Suspend alarms**

Works places an "X" inside the brackets next to the option. By turning on this option you will suspend any of the set alarms that appear in the list box. Toggle the setting to off by repeating the mouse operation as shown below:

Click(left) on **Suspend alarms**

The "X" is now removed from the brackets indicating that this option is turned off.

Using List Boxes

The current dialog box contains a list box labeled Current alarms. A list box is similar to an option box with the exception that the items listed in the box are user-defined items which will vary from computer to computer. The items in options boxes, because they are part of the Works program, will be the same on all computers.

You can select any of the items that appear in a list box by clicking on any part of the item. Select the "Pick up Joey from school" alarm using the mouse:

Click(left) on *Joey*

The program highlights the entire entry. In addition, the text and options boxes are reset to the values that you entered when you created the alarm. One other change is that two of the commands buttons, **<Change>** and **<Delete>**, change from inactive (gray) to active (black with a bright white command letter.)

Command buttons often have a direct link with items in list boxes. The command buttons will usually operate on the select item in the list box. For example, if you use the **<Delete>** button, the program will delete the highlighted alarm:

Click(left) on **<Delete>**

The alarm setting is removed from the dialog box. The list box is empty once again, indicating that there are no alarms set in the system.

You can leave the dialog box, and return to the previous activity by selecting either the **<Done>** or **<OK>** buttons, which save the changes made in the dialog box, or the **<cancel>** button (if available) which discards the changes:

Click(left) on **<Done>**

The dialog box is removed from the screen and the program goes back to the opening desktop display.

USING FILES

As discussed in Chapter 1, your computer uses disks, either the 3.5 inch removable disks or the internal hard disk, to permanently store information in the form of disk files.

The Works program will use disk files to hold the information, word processing, spreadsheet, or database that you enter with the help of the Works program. When you need to select files from the disk, Works uses a special type of dialog box called the file selector box. Because working with files is so important, it is a good idea to look at the Works file selector dialog box in order to understand its meaning and its use. Display the File menu using the mouse, as shown below:

Click(left) on **File**

The **Open Existing File** command is used to load Works projects that have been stored on the disk. The PS1 is supplied with several example Works files. Select the command **Open Existing File**:

Click(left) on **Open Existing File**

The program displays the Works file selector dialog box, as shown in Figure 2-11. This dialog box contains the following elements: file to open, files, directories, open read-only, and <OK>/<Cancel>.

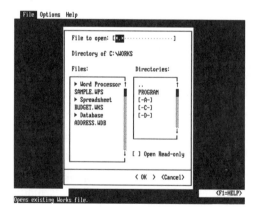

Figure 2-11. File Selector Dialog Box.

File to Open

This item is a text box which can be used to enter the name of a file. By default the text box contains *.*. The *.* is a special symbol that stands for all files (See Chapter 1, Wildcards, for details.) This means that Works will display all available file names in the Files list box.

Files

This option is a list box that shows the names of all the files contained in the current directory. Works divides the files into groups based on their typeword processing, spreadsheet, database, or other.

Directories

This option is also a list box. It lists the directories, if any, and disks available in the system.

Open Read-only

This option is a check box. When turned on, it prevents you from making any modifications to the files loaded into Works. When this option is off, files can be modified once they have been loaded.

< OK >/<Cancel>

The **< OK >** command button closes the dialog box and loads the file highlighted in the Files box, if any. The **<cancel>** button closes the dialog box without loading any files.

Loading a File

You can load one of the files listed in the Files box in the following ways: type filename, click/<OK>, and double click filename.

Type Filename

Type the full file name into the File to open text box and press **[return]**. Note that you must type the name exactly as it appears in the Files box, including the extension, e.g., sample.wps. Works treats upper and lower case letters the same so you are free to use whichever you feel comfortable with.

Click/< OK >

You can select a file using the mouse by Clicking (left) on the name of the file you want to load. This will cause Works to place a highlight on the selected file and automatically write in the filename in the text box. Once this has been done you can load the file by pressing **[return]** or Clicking (left) on **< OK >**.

Double Click Filename

A double click operation refers to clicking the mouse button twice in rapid succession. When you double click on a file name, the program loads the selected file from the disk.

The double click method is the easiest way to load a file. Keep in mind that if you are not used to double clicking the mouse button it may take some practice. If you wait too long between the clicks, the program treats them as two separate single clicks instead of a double click.

Load the SAMPLE.WPS file using the double click method.

Double click(left) on *SAMPLE.WPS*

WINDOWS

When you load a file from the disk, Works places the information in a window, as shown in Figure 2-12. In Works the term *window* refers to a rectangular box that encloses a word processing document, a spreadsheet model, or a database record. The SAMPLE.WPS is a word processing file supplied with your PS1.

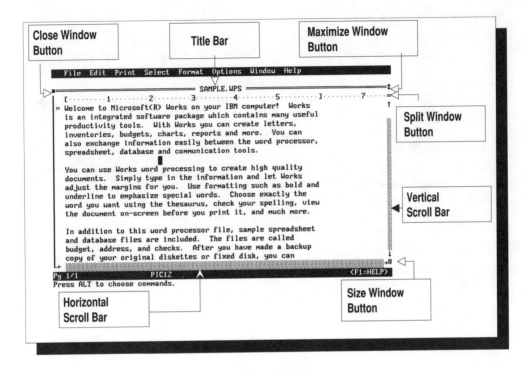

Figure 2-12. Works Window.

Each window that is displayed by Works has several distinct parts.

Title Bar (Move Button)

The top line of the window is the title bar. It displays the name of the file associated with the window. In addition, the title bar functions as a large button. You can move the window around the desktop by dragging the title bar with the mouse.

Close Window Button

This button is located in the upper left corner of the window. Clicking on this button causes the program to close the window. When a window is closed it is removed from the screen and all of the information contained in the window is removed from the computer's memory. If there is information in the window that has not yet been saved, a dialog box will appear asking you if you want to save the modified data or not.

Size Window Button

This button is located in the lower right corner of the window. Dragging this button changes the size of the window on the desktop. You can change height, width or both depending upon the direction in which you drag the mouse. When you release the mouse the window is resized to fit the selected dimensions.

Maximize Window Button

This button is found in the upper right hand corner of the window. If you click on this button the window is expanded to fill the entire desktop, i.e., its maximize size. If the window is currently maximized, clicking the maximize button will return the window to its previous size.

Split Window Button

This button is located just below the Maximize button. When you drag this button vertically, the current window can be split into two separate panes. The panes allow you to view two non-adjacent parts of the information contained in the window. For example, you could view the beginning of a long letter in the top window pane and the closing in the bottom pane.

Scroll Bars

On the left and right sides of the window the borders are not lines but gray bars called *scroll bars*. At the top of the vertical bar and at the left of the horizontal bar are black squares called the *scroll boxes*. At the ends of both bars are arrows which are called *scroll buttons*, left, right, up and down respectively. The scroll bars are used to handle files which contain more information than can be displayed within a single window. The bars allow you to scroll in any direction revealing different parts of the document. In any given document the entire scroll bar represents 100% of the width or length. The scroll box indicates the section of the document that is currently visible in the window.

Sizing a Window

You can change the size and shape of a window by using the mouse to drag the Size button. Recall that the term drag refers to pointing the mouse at an object, holding down the mouse button (usually the left button), and then moving the mouse while the button is held down. When you release the mouse button the drag operation is completed.

As an example, you can change the size of the current document window:

```
Point at the size button
Hold down the left mouse button
```

When you hold down the mouse button while the mouse is pointed at the size button, the border of the window changes to a thin line. This indicates that the sizing mode is active. You can now alter the size of the window by moving the mouse while continuing to hold down the left mouse button:

```
Drag towards the upper left corner of the window
```

As you drag the mouse, the thin line border of the window changes size to reflect the new size of the window, as shown in Figure 2-13.

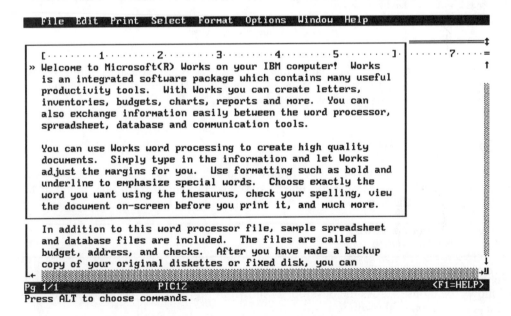

Figure 2-13. Outline Changes as Mouse is Dragged.

```
Release the mouse button
```

When you release the mouse button, the window is resized to fit the size indicated by the outline, as shown in Figure 2-14.

69

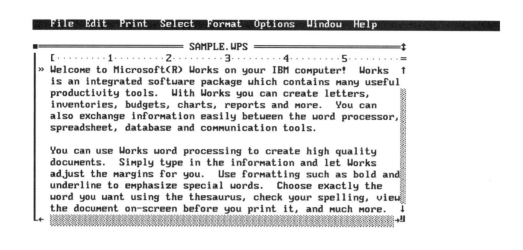

Figure 2-14. Window's Size Altered.

Keep in mind that when you change the size of the window you are not altering the information contained within the window in any way. The window, as indicated by its name, is simply a way to view the information.

Moving a Window

You can change the location of the window on the desktop by dragging the *title bar*. Recall that the title bar is the top line of the window which shows the name of the file displayed in the window:

> Drag(left) the *title bar* down
> Release the mouse button

When you drag the title bar, an outline, which is the current size of the window, follows the mouse across the desktop, as shown in Figure 2-15. The outline indicates the new location of the window.

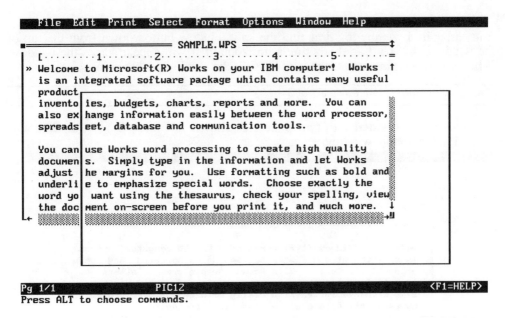

Figure 2-15. Outline Shows Where Window will be Moved.

When you release the button the window is redrawn at the new location.

Zooming a Window

You can zoom a window so that it fills the entire desktop by clicking on the maximize button located in the upper right hand corner of the window:

Click(left) on the *maximize* button

The window is expanded to fill the entire desktop. The button functions as a toggle since clicking it a second time will return the window to its previous size and location:

Click(left) on the *maximize* button

Splitting a Window

Even when a window is expanded to maximum size, there may be more information in the file than can be displayed at one time. Window splitting allows you to display two non-adjacent sections of the information at the same time. This is useful in comparing or revising different sections of the same file.

You can split a window by dragging the split window button down from the top of the window. As you drag the button a horizontal bar will appear across the window. When you release the mouse the bar will split the window at that point:

Drag(left) the *split button* down about 2"

The window is divided into two panes, as shown in Figure 2-16. The cursor is located in the bottom window.

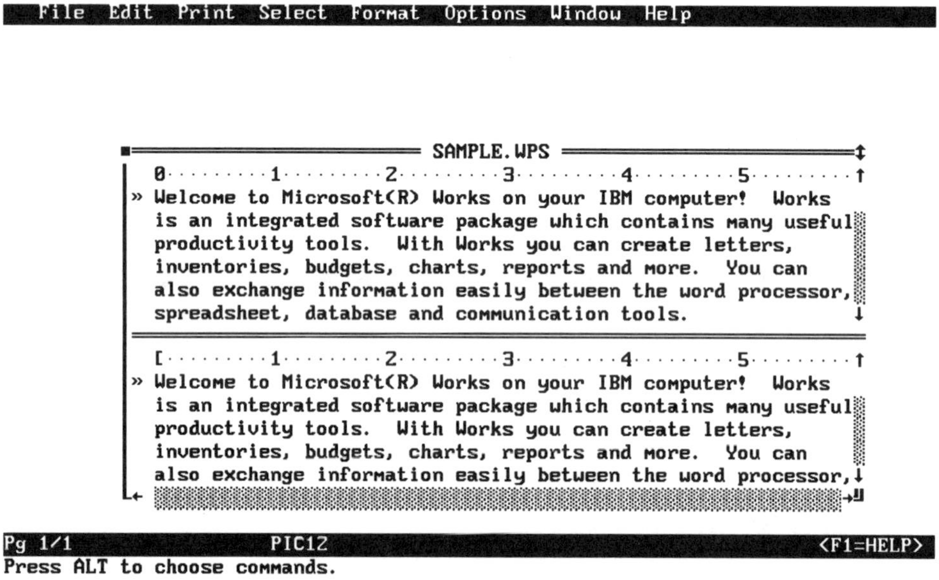

```
  File  Edit  Print  Select  Format  Options  Window  Help


       ▪══════════════ SAMPLE.WPS ═══════════════╪
       0········1········2········3········4········5········↑
    »  Welcome to Microsoft(R) Works on your IBM computer!  Works
       is an integrated software package which contains many useful
       productivity tools.  With Works you can create letters,
       inventories, budgets, charts, reports and more.  You can
       also exchange information easily between the word processor,
       spreadsheet, database and communication tools.          ↓

       [········1········2········3········4········5········↑
    »  Welcome to Microsoft(R) Works on your IBM computer!  Works
       is an integrated software package which contains many useful
       productivity tools.  With Works you can create letters,
       inventories, budgets, charts, reports and more.  You can
       also exchange information easily between the word processor,↓
   ←▪                                                       →▪

Pg 1/1                      PIC12                        <F1=HELP>
Press ALT to choose commands.
```

Figure 2-16. Window Split into Two Sections.

At first, both windows show the same part of the document. However, you can scroll the windows through the information, independently of one another. Move the cursor to the end of the document by entering the following keystroke:

[Ctrl-End]

The two windows now show different sections of the same file. You can remove a split by dragging the split button back to the top or down to the bottom of the window. The difference is that when you drag the button to the bottom, the section in the top window remains, while if you drag the button to the top, the bottom window remains, as shown below:

Drag(left) the *split button* to the top of the window

The bottom pane is removed and the window displays the information in a single pane.

Using the Scroll Bars

The scroll bars, located on the left and bottom sides of the window, enable you to change the section of the file displayed in the window. This process is called *scrolling*.

The bars act as symbols that represent the relationship between the information visible in the window at the current time and the total amount of information contained in the file. The entire bar, vertical or horizontal, represents the entire length or width of the document. The black scroll box shows what section of the information is currently displayed in the window. In this example, the scroll boxes are at the top of the bars indicating that you are looking at the upper left corner of the file's information.

The bars function on a proportional basis. For example, if you wanted to display the middle of the file, you would move the scroll box to the middle of scroll bar. The scroll box is moved by dragging with the mouse:

```
Drag(left) the vertical scroll box
to the middle of the bar
```

When you release the mouse, the section of the file which appears in the window changes to match the relative location of the scroll box.

You can click (left) on the scroll arrows that appear at the ends of the scroll bars to scroll one line at a time through the document:

```
Click(left) on the down scroll arrow
```

The text scrolls down one line:

```
Click(left) on the right scroll arrow
```

The window scrolls one character width to the right.

Closing a Window

You can remove a window from the desktop by clicking on the close button found in the upper left hand corner of the window:

```
Click(left) on the close button
```

The window is removed from the screen. Note that if you had made any changes to the contents of the window, Works would have displayed a dialog box with the question "Save changes to: SAMPLE.WPS" with three command buttons: **<Yes>** to save the changes, **<No>** to discard the changes and **<cancel>** which cancels the closing of the window.

USING WORKS HELP

In order to provide reference information while you are working, Works contains a Help system. You can access the help system in two ways: the help menu and **[F1]**.

The Help Menu

You can access help by selecting the Help menu from the current menu bar. Help is always the last option on the right side of the menu bar.

[F1]

You can also access help by pressing the **[F1]** key. The **[F1]** key is useful because it allows you to get help even when the menu bar is not available, such as when a dialog box is displayed on the screen. The help information displayed when **[F1]** is used is context sensitive. This means that the information displayed relates to the activity you are performing when you press **[F1]**. For example, if you have the Open Existing File dialog box on the screen, help for that topic will be displayed.

Access help by entering:

```
[F1]
```

The program displays the help screen for the topic "File Create New File" command, as shown in Figure 2-17. This is because the menu highlight was positioned on that command when you pressed **[F1]**.

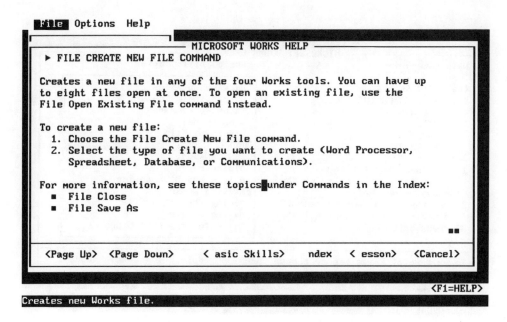

Figure 2-17. Context Sensitive Help Screen.

Once help is active, you can change topics by using the help index. Display the indent by using the **<Index>** command button:

Click(left) on **<Index>**

The help index screen is displayed, as shown in Figure 2-18. The index consists of option buttons on the left side of the screen that allow you to select the general topic for which you want help. The default selection is the Basic Skills topic. On the right side of the screen is a list box that lists the individual topics.

You can select a help screen for display by double clicking on the topic in the list box you want to see.

2 How to Use Works

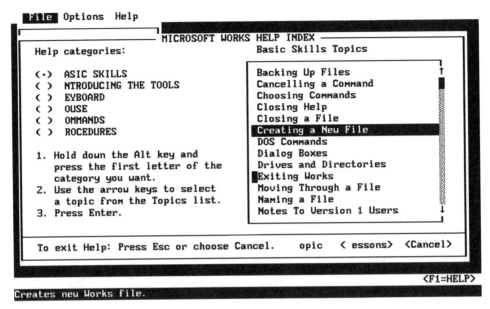

Figure 2-18. Help Index Screen.

Suppose you wanted to know more about the use of the mouse. Begin by selecting the Mouse option from the category option buttons:

Click(left) on **MOUSE**

When you select mouse, the topics in the list box change to match the selected category. Select the topic called "Using the Mouse":

Double click(left) on *Using the Mouse*

The help for that subject is displayed. You can exit help and return to Works at any time by using the **<Cancel>** command button or entering the **[Esc]** key. Enter:

[Esc]

The help screens are removed and you return to Works.

Exiting the Program

When you are done working with Works you can exit the program by selecting Exit Works from the File menu:

> Click(left) on **Exit Works**

The program is terminated and you return to the PS1 startup screen.

SUMMARY

The purpose of this chapter has been to help you gain a familiarity with the basic structure of the Works program. That basic structure includes the following concepts.

Menus. Commands and operations in Works are selected by means of the menu system. The menu system consists of a menu bar that appears at the top of the screen and pulldown menus that expand from the menu bar to list the commands grouped under each menu bar category.

Desktop. The area below the menu bar and above the status and message lines is the desktop. It is in this area of the screen that you Works windows will appear.

Mouse. The mouse can be used to make selections using three mouse operations: click, double click and drag. Clicking(left) on items in the menu bar and pulldown menu selects those items and executes the command for which they stand.

Command Keys. Each item on the menu bar and any subsequent pulldown menu has one letter assigned as the command key. The command key letters appear in bright white so that they are in contrast to the rest of the text on the menus. The command keys for the menu bar items appear when you press the [**Alt**] key. The command letters for pulldown menu commands appear when the menu is displayed. You can directly display a pulldown menu by entering the command key for that menu in combination with [**Alt**], e.g., display the File menu by entering [**Alt-f**]. Selection of commands on pulldown menus can be made using the command letters with or without [**Alt**]. All of the items displayed within dialog boxes (with the exception of items in list boxes) can also be selected with [**Alt**] command key combinations.

Dialog Boxes. Commands that require special values, text, or settings, display a dialog box. The box allows you to fill in the information needed or select from the options available for the selected command. Dialog boxes can contain text boxes, option boxes, check boxes, list boxes, and command buttons. Command buttons, which appear at the bottom of the dialog box, immediately perform an operation when they are selected.

Files. Information entered into the Works program is stored in a permanent form in files on the disk. Each file is given a name by the person who creates it and an extension, added by Works, which indicates the type of information stored in the file. Information can be loaded from disk files into Works using the file selection dialog box associated with the **Open Existing File** command.

Windows. When information is created or retrieved in Works it is placed into a window. Each file created or opened is placed into its own window. The size and location of the window can be changed using the size button and title bar respectively. The maximize button expands the window to fill the entire desktop. The split button can be used to divide one window into two panes. Each pane can display a different part of the same file. The horizontal and vertical scroll bars are used to change the section of the document which is displayed in the window.

Help. Works contains a system of help screens that provide reference information about the program. The screens can be accessed from the Help menu or by pressing **[F1]**. Pressing **[F1]** displays the help screen that is related to the activity you are performing. This is called context sensitive help.

Chapter **3**

How to Use Prodigy

P rodigy is an *on-line* computer service. The term "on-line" refers to a process
by which you use your computer to access information stored on and
programs running on another computer. In the past, such links between
computers at different locations required special data communications lines.
Today, computers can be connected using existing telephone lines. This means that
home or office computers can gain access to large computer databases. Your
personal computer can become part of a vast network of computer information and
services. This chapter introduces Prodigy.

The Prodigy program supplied with your PS1 computer is used to connect your
computer, by means of telephone communications to the Prodigy network of
computers and computer services. Prodigy is different from traditional on line
services in three ways.

Graphical Display. Most on-line services communicate using text characters only.
The advantage of this approach is speed, since text is the simplest type of
information you can communicate across a telephone link. Prodigy uses a graphical

displays, including color and pictures, which is more interesting to look at than simple text. However, the amount of information displayed on the screen at any one moment is less than could fit if standard text was used. Also, the speed at which it can be changed and updated is much slower than using text. The graphical displays require you to use Prodigy software to connect to the service. Text-based services can be accessed with any telecommunications program.

Cost. Most on-line services charge you by the minute for the time you are connected to the service. They may also add special fees for individual services that you access while connected. These services also change more for daytime connection than they do for nighttime connection. Prodigy changes you a flat fee for an entire month no matter how much or how little you use the service.

Advertisements. In order to defray the cost of running a service that does not charge for connect time, Prodigy sells advertising space to various businesses. These ads appear at the bottom of the screen displays that appear as you move through the various Prodigy services.

When you use PS1 with Prodigy software to connect to the Prodigy network you are linking your computer to large main frame computers that operate the Prodigy service, as shown in Figure 3-1.

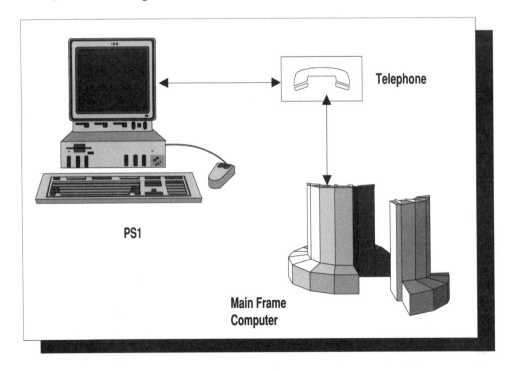

Figure 3-1. Prodigy Connects You to Main Frame Computers.

The connection is made using a device called a *modem*. The word modem is short for a modulator/demodulator, a device that converts digital values into sound (modulator) or sound into digital values (demodulator).

The PS1 includes a 2400 baud modem. The baud rate tells you the number of digital values that can be communicated per second. The higher the baud rate the faster information can be exchanged using the modem. Telephone communication is one of the slowest operations performed by your computer. For example, most printers receive information at 9600 baud or faster.

Note that in addition to using the modem to connect to Prodigy, you can use the 2400 baud modem to connect to any computer that communicates at 2400 baud or slower speeds such as 300 or 1200 baud. Microsoft Works can be used to connect your modem with other services such as CompuServe, discussed in Section III of this book, or your office computer.

In order to access Prodigy you must know your Prodigy password. The password is included in the Prodigy kit included with your PS1.

In addition you will need the Phone Book pamphlet to find the phone number of the Prodigy network closest to where you live. On the cover of this pamphlet is a sticker that tells you the network symbol. You will need to enter this symbol when you sign on to Prodigy first the first time.The phone numbers of the Prodigy network nodes are listed by state and within the state, by city. Find the nearest phone number to your location and make a note of it.

PRODIGY SOFTWARE VERSION

The Prodigy service can only be accessed if you are running the Prodigy software. Other on-line services such as CompuServe use standard text displays so that you can access the service with any telecommunications program such as Microsoft Works or CrossTalk.

Prodigy is much more dependent on the software you are running in your computer than other on-line services. The information that the Prodigy service sends through the telephone lines to your computer cannot be understood by a standard telecommunications program. Instead, the Prodigy data must be combined with the information stored in the Prodigy software and in special files on your computer's disks in order to create the screen displays.

For that reason many of the features of Prodigy will only function if you have the correct version of the Prodigy software. When the PS1 was introduced in the Fall of 1990 the Prodigy Software included with the computer was version 1.5. In November of 1990 Prodigy issued an update to its software, version 2.01, which included several significant features such as support for using your mouse and access to an on line encyclopedia.

In this book, the discussion on setup of Prodigy will assume that you are working with the pre-November 1990 version supplied with the PS1. Since Prodigy will mail you updated software once you have signed on as a member, the remainder of the book will discuss features added to the 2.01 version released in November 1990.

HOW PRODIGY WORKS

The main advantage Prodigy has over traditional on-line services is its use of graphics images. Traditional on-line services such as CompuServe display only text and cannot use color or pictures to enhance their displays. Conversely, the use of graphics and colors requires a much larger amount of data for each screen displayed. This means that it takes longer to send color and graphic images over the phone line than it would simple lines of text.

In order to improve the performance of Prodigy, the program uses your disk space to store many of the pictures and images used by the Prodigy service. The Prodigy software creates, maintains, and expands two files, STAGE.DAT and CACHE.DAT. The purpose of these files is to store elements of Prodigy screen displays locally so that Prodigy can cut down on the amount of information that has to be received over the phone line.

For example, when you want to display a weather map, Prodigy stores the outline of the map, i.e., the national or regional map on the disk in the STAGE.DAT file. Only the details of the forecast need be sent over the phone line in order to accurately update the weather information. The screen display that you see is a combination of stored and transmitted images. Many of the text displays that appear on Prodigy are stored in the CACHE.DAT file. This enables you to flip back and forth in an article without requiring Prodigy to resend the entire article. In Section II of this book you will learn how you can take advantage of the data stored in CACHE.DAT with Microsoft Works.

ACCESSING PRODIGY

To access the Prodigy service you must first connect your computer's modem to a working phone line. Use the phone cord included with the PS1. Plug one end into a wall jack and the other into the modem port on the back panel of the system unit. (This section assumes that you are working with a version of Prodigy earlier than 2.01.)

Select the Information option from the PS1 startup screen:

Click(left) on **Information**

The startup screen changes to displays a box that lists four options that are available under information. This is shown in Figure 3-2.

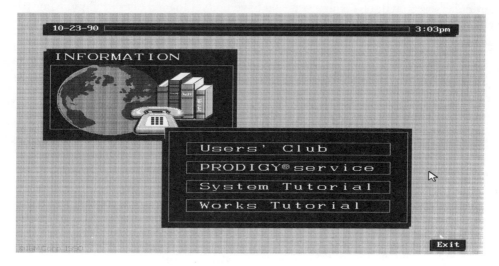

Figure 3-2. Information Option Box.

User's Club

This is a special part of Prodigy setup for use by PS1 users. In order to use the club you must first sign on to Prodigy.

Prodigy

This option accesses the Prodigy service.

System Tutorial

This is a program that provides information about the use of the PS1. The modem is not needed for this option and it does not tie up the phone line if the modem is already connected.

Works Tutorial

This option runs a program that teaches you about using Microsoft Works. The modem is not needed for this option and it does not tie up the phone line if the modem is already connected.

Select the Prodigy option:

Click(left) on **Prodigy Service**

When the Prodigy program is loaded the screen changes to display a screen entitled "THE BEGINNING OF SOMETHING BIG", as shown in Figure 3-3. Note that this particular screen will be displayed if you have not yet logged onto Prodigy. After you have made your initial log on you will begin Prodigy with a different screen display.

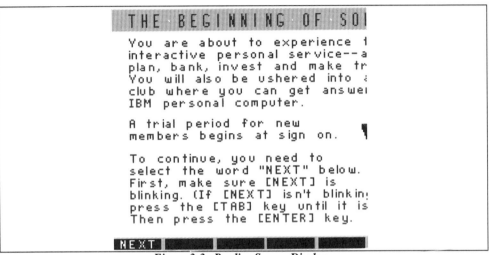

Figure 3-3. Prodigy Screen Display.

Prodigy Commands

The Prodigy program is controlled by selections made from the menu bar at the bottom of the screen display. The bar is divided into eight parts, some of which contain commands words. The initial display screen shows the commands **NEXT**, **HELP** and **EXIT**.

One of the items on the bar, in this case **NEXT**, is blinking. The blinking item is the currently selected menu option. Pressing [**return**] will activate the select menu option. If you want to select a different option from the menu bar you can move the blinking highlight using the [**Tab**] or [**right**] keys to move to the right or the [**Shift-Tab**] or [**left**] to move to the left.

You cannot use the mouse while Prodigy is active.

Execute the **NEXT** command by entering:

[return]

Move to the next screen by again entering:

```
[return]
```

Setting Up Prodigy

The first time that you use Prodigy you will set up the program for future use. The first question posed by the software is the type of phone service that you have: Pulse or Tone. Most push button phones use tone dialing. If you have a phone with a rotary dial you should leave the highlight on the default option, PULSE. All other users should select TONE by entering:

```
[down] [return]
```

The next item of information need by Prodigy is the network code symbol. This symbol is a single letter found on the sticker pasted to the front of the Phone Book pamphlet. Enter your code letter (the letter Z is used as an example):

```
z [return]
```

The next screen asks you to enter the Prodigy service access number you want to use. This is the phone number, found in the Phone Book pamphlet of the nearest city to your location. Note that you should type in only the digits of the phone number with no punctuation such as dashes. For example, if the local access number is 930-0525 you would enter 9300525. Enter your access number (9300525 is entered as an example):

```
9300525 [return]
```

The information you have entered will now be recorded on the disk. Prodigy will automatically use this information each time it is activated.

Sign-On

Up to this point, the modem has not been activated. All of the operations have been contained within the computer system. The next step is to have the modem dial the access number and initiate the sign on procedure.

To sign on to Prodigy you will need the ID and Password contained in the white envelope enclosed with the Prodigy start up kit. To process the sign-on enter:

```
[return]
```

The screen shows two options: Sign on and Change the phone information. The Change the phone information option would be used if you moved your computer to another location and wanted to sign onto Prodigy from there.

Select Sign-on by entering:

```
1 [return]
```

The programs displays the Prodigy sign on screen. Enter the ID number supplied with your Prodigy kit. The following is an example:

```
abcdefg [return]
```

Next enter the password. The following is an example:

```
passwd
```

When you enter your password the screen shows * instead of the characters you type. This prevents people from learning your password by looking at your screen while you sign on. Complete the sign-on by entering:

```
[return]
```

The program responds with the message "Dialing the PRODIGY service." When the computer has successfully connect to Prodigy, the Welcome screen will be displayed.

The first time you sign on, Prodigy will ask you to fill out billing information. Note that you are entitled to three free months of Prodigy when you purchase a PS1 computer. Continue by entering:

```
[return]
```

The next screen allows you to fill in the billing information. The entry below is a sample:

```
Mr [return]
Walter [return]
Q [return]
LaFish [return]
1250 Pine Street [return] [return]
Walnut Creek [return]
CA [return]
94598 [return]
415-943-1200 [return]
```

Confirm that the information you have entered is correct by entering:

```
[return]
```

Next, Prodigy asks for personal information such as your date of birth and sex. This entry is optional:

```
09/13/51 [return]
m [return]
[return]
```

Each Prodigy membership can include up to five users at the same location. You have the option to add other names to your sign-on if you desire. When you have added all of the users you desire, continue by entering:

```
[down] [return]
```

Prodigy will display a summary for the information you have entered. Confirm that this information is correct by entering:

```
[return]
```

The next step in signing on is to accept the Prodigy service agreement. This agreement is found in the startup kit and contains the legal parameters under which Prodigy operates. If you have read and understood the agreement enter:

```
[return]
```

The final step is to create your own password to replace the password supplied with Prodigy. This is not necessary, but it is easier to remember a password that you have created. Keep in mind that if you forget your own password you will have to get another Prodigy kit in order to sign on again. The password can be 4 to 10 characters and you can use letters or numbers. Note that Prodigy passwords do not distinguish between upper and lower case letters. Enter your password (the word "password" is used as an example):

```
password [return]
[return]
```

You have now completed your sign-on.

HIGHLIGHTS

The next screen that appears is the Highlights screen, as shown in Figure 3-4. The Highlights screen is the first screen that will be displayed each time you connect to Prodigy.

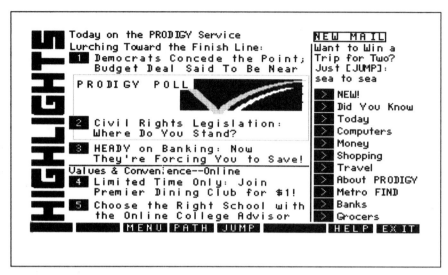

Figure 3-4. Prodigy Highlights Screen.

The screen is actually composed of four different parts.

Today's Highlights. The left side of the screen list 5 special items that have been selected by the Prodigy service as the highlights of the day. Each item is assigned a number, 1 through 5. The first item is usually a new item. Items 2 and 3 are special news items, columns, or a Prodigy user opinion poll. The last two items are usually new services or products offered through Prodigy. The information in this column changes each day.

Main Topic Menu. On the right side of the screen is the main menu for the service. It lists the main items, New, Did you know, Today, Computers, Money, Shopping, Travel, About Prodigy, Metro FIND, Banks and Grocers. These items will remain the same each time you sign onto Prodigy. At the top of this column is usually a reminder of a contest or promotion being offered through Prodigy.

Action Menu. At the bottom of the screen you will see the action menu bar. This bar lists the commands you can execute from the current screen.

Mail Box. Prodigy offers an electronic mail messaging service. If any electronic mail has been posted to your mailbox since your last sign on, a message, New Mail, will flash in a box at the top of the Main Topic Menu column. When you first sign on to Prodigy the New Mail message will automatically flash. This is because the Prodigy service automatically sends you mail as soon as you sign on.

Selecting Actions

Each Prodigy screen presents you with information, which can be read, and action commands, which can be selected. The action commands on a Prodigy screen can appear within the text area of the display and at the bottom of the screen on the menu bar.

Screen Commands

Screen commands are items that appear within the text information on the screen and relate specifically to the information on the current screen. The letters, numbers or symbols used to select various action appear in reverse color, black characters on a white background.

Menu Bar

At the bottom of the screen, Prodigy displays a bar that will contain command words. These command words, **NEXT, BACK, JUMP, MENU, PATH**, etc., are actions that apply to the Prodigy service as a whole not just to the current screen.

Special Keys

Some of the special keys on the PS/1 keyboard are assigned to Prodigy commands, as shown in Table 3-1.

Table 3-1. Special Keys and Actions.

Action	Key
Back	[Pg Up]
Find	[F8]
Guide	[F5]
Help	[F1]
Index	[F7]
Jump	[F6]
Menu	[F9]
Next	[Pg Dn]
Path	[F4]
Review List	[F10]
ViewPath	[F3]

Mouse

If you have version 2.01 of the Prodigy software you can select an item on the screen by double clicking(left button) on the menu number, word, or symbol you want to select. Using the mouse is by far the fastest way to make selections on Prodigy.

One of the action commands on the screen is surrounded by a flashing box. The box indicates the command action that will be executed if you press **[return]**. You can move the flashing selection box around the various actions on the screen or on the menu bar using the arrow keys or the **[Tab]** key.

In addition, if the action commands are numbers you can jump the flashing box to that item by typing the corresponding number on the keyboard. Also, action commands that are words, e.g., PRINT, can be selected by typing the first letter of the word. Keep in mind that this rule has two exceptions. First, some Prodigy screens have open areas for the entry of information. If the cursor is positioned in such an entry area, all typed letters and numbers are entered as part of the text of the entry rather than jumping to a corresponding action command. The second exception is when two or more action commands begin with the same letter, only the first item with a given letter will be selected. In these cases use the arrow keys to move to the desired command.

Note that moving the flashing selection box does not activate a command or option. You must still enter **[return]** in order to activate the command.

In this case you can use the Exit command to sign off. If an option or command contains a word, e.g., **Menu, Print, Exit**, you can select that option by entering the first letter of the word. To select the **Exit** command enter:

```
e [return]
```

Prodigy clears the Highlights screen and shows the Exit screen. The first option, End Session, is flashing indicating that it is the default selection. Complete sign off by executing option 1 by entering:

```
[return]
```

The PS1 returns to the startup screen.

USING PRODIGY

Once you have signed on to Prodigy and selected your new password, you are ready to begin using the features of the system.

Quick Sign-On

Once you have signed on to Prodigy you can set up a quick sign-on option that will speed up the process of logging onto the Prodigy service. Start Prodigy by selecting Information from the startup screen:

```
Click(left) on Information
```

Select the Prodigy Service:

```
Click(left) on Prodigy Service
```

The standard Prodigy sign on screen appears. This screen lists three options which are as follows: sign-on, change phone information, and create or change the sign-on shortcut list.

Sign-On

Sign-on Prodigy by manually entering your ID number and password.

Change Phone Information

Use this option to change the Prodigy access number if necessary.

Create or Change the Sign-On Shortcut List

This option provides a shortcut way to enter Prodigy.

In most cases you will want to take advantage of the shortcut method. Select option 3:

```
3 [return]
```

The sign-on screen can hold the names of up to 6 people. By adding your name to the list, you will create a new option that will appear on the sign on menu showing your name. You can then select your name from screen in order to access Prodigy. Add your name to the list by entering:

```
[return]
```

Type in your name and your ID number (not your password.) Enter (for example):

```
Walter [return]
aaaa22b [return]
[return]
```

When you have entered your name a box will appear on the screen. This box allows you to enter your password as part of your personal sign on. It is important to keep in mind that adding your password to the sign on shortcut eliminates the need for you to enter the password in order to gain access to Prodigy. This means that anyone can use your sign-on without having to know the password. This removes much of the security from your Prodigy account. If you are confident that your account will not be compromised you can add your password to the shortcut. When you do so you can sign onto Prodigy with a single keystroke.

On the other hand, if you require the highest level of security do not add your password. Keep in mind that a person using your shortcut sign-on cannot learn what your password is. This means that if you want to reactivate your password you can do so by deleting you shortcut sign on from the list.

If you choose to include your password as part of the sign-on enter (for example):

```
passwd [return] [return]
```

If you don't want to include your password enter:

```
[Tab] (2 times)
[return]
```

Return to the sign on menu by selecting the MENU option.

```
m [return]
```

Note that there is another problem that can arise when you use automatic sign on. Since you no longer need to enter your password each time you log on to Prodigy, you may have a tendency to forget what the password is. If you ever need to manually sign on to Prodigy you may find that you no longer know your password. You may want to store the password in a secure place if you are using automatic sign on.

ELECTRONIC MAIL

One of the most interesting and powerful features available through Prodigy is electronic mail. Each user that signs on to Prodigy establishes an electronic mail box in which other users can place messages. Conversely, you can send messages to other people using Prodigy. Electronic mail also allows Prodigy or merchants who sell through Prodigy to send messages to and receive messages from you. The term E-mail is a popular name for electronic mail.

Note that your name will not appear on the member list, available to all Prodigy users, unless you use the MEMBER LIST option to sign up. If you don't sign up you name will not appear on the list. You can still receive mail from users who know your ID number (not password). This allows you to avoid unsolicited mail.

When you first sign on to Prodigy you will automatically be sent mail on a weekly basis from the Prodigy service. When you sign onto the service, a message will flash

NEW MAIL in the upper right corner of the screen if you have received any mail since your last sign on. If you have just completed the sign on as discussed in the previous section, your NEW MAIL will be flashing at this time.

You can access Prodigy mail by entering:

```
[return]
```

The Prodigy message center screen is displayed as shown in Figure 3-5. The screen lists up to four messages at a time. Each message displays five items of information.

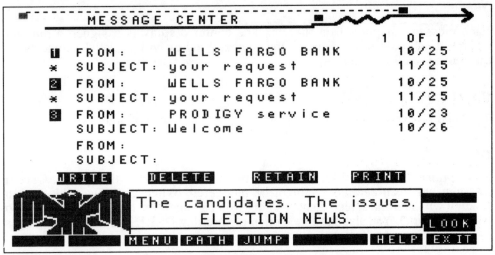

Figure 3-5 . Prodigy Message Center Screen.

From

This item displays the name of the person or company sending the message.

Subject

The subject is an option phrase that describes the contents of the message. If the message is new mail, i.e., mail that has not been read before, an * will appear below the message number. If no * appears, the message is an old message that has not been deleted from the system. When a new message is read, Prodigy removes the * from its display.

Date Sent

This date, which appears across from FROM, shows the date the message was sent.

Date Deleted

Below the date sent is a second date. This date shows when the message will be automatically deleted from the Prodigy system. Note that you can select, using the message **OPTIONS** command, to extend the retention period an additional 14 days.

Message Commands

The message center displays five commands that can be used to manipulate the messages displayed in the message center.

Number

Each message displayed on the message center display is assigned a number command 1 through 4. If you select the number, Prodigy will display the contents for the message on the screen.

WRITE

The **WRITE** command is used to create and send a message of your own.

DELETE

This option allows you to delete one or more messages from the system. Once a message has been deleted it cannot be recovered. When you select this option Prodigy will alter the screen display so that you can mark the messages to be deleted with the letter D. You also have the option of choosing **DELETE ALL** which purges all of your messages from the system.

RETAIN

This option allows you to extend the retention period of one or more messages for an additional 14 days. If you select this option you can mark messages that you want to retain with the letter R or select RETAIN ALL to extend the period of all current messages.

PRINT

This command sends a copy of the message center display to the printer. Note that this option prints the list of messages you see on the screen, not the contents of the messages themselves. Printing an entire message can be done when you are displaying the on the screen. (See Options under the next topic).

Reading Messages

You can select any of the messages listed on the screen to read by typing the number of the message. For example, to read the first message, typically a welcome from the Prodigy service, enter:

```
1 [return]
```

If you are using version 2.01 of the Prodigy software you can use your mouse to make the selection:

```
Double Click(left) on 1
```

Prodigy displays the text of the selected message. In the upper right area of the screen the current page number and the total number of pages for the message will be displayed, e.g., 1 OF 3. If the message contains more than a single page you can display the next page by entering the page number or by using the **NEXT** command. The **[Pg Dn]** and **[Pg Up]** keys can be used in place of the **NEXT** and **BACK** commands. Enter:

```
[down] (2 times)
[return]
```

Note that once you position the flashing cursor to the **NEXT** command it will remain there until you move it again. This means that you can continue to page through the message by pressing [return]. The **BACK** command can be used to move back to the previous page of the message.

In addition to reading the message the following commands are available while reading a message: **reply**, **delete**, **next mail**, and **options**.

REPLY

This command takes you to the message writing screen and automatically addresses the message to the person who sent you the mail.

DELETE

Marks this message for deletion from the system.

NEXT MAIL

This command skips to the first page of the next message, if any, in the message center.

OPTIONS

This command displays a box which contains two commands: **PRINT** and **RETAIN**. The **PRINT** command on this menu prints the full text (all pages) of the current message. The **RETAIN** command retains the message for an additional 14 days. Press [**Esc**] to exit the options menu.

Note that when you print information from Prodigy, the program does not issue form feeds at the end of each item. This means that your printer will not advance to the next sheet of paper but will stop immediately after the last line has been printed. If you are using a laser-type printer, this means that the printer will not print anything if the text is less than a full page in length. In order to advance the paper in a standard printer or to feed the page on a laser printer you must use the Form Feed buttons on the printer.

When you have completed reading your message, return to the Message Center screen by using the **MENU** command:

```
m [return]
```

Advertising On Prodigy

Below the message window you will see a display that advertises some product or feature of the Prodigy service. You will find that the Prodigy service will display an advertisement at the bottom of most screen displays. Like commercial television, Prodigy offers low cost access, a single monthly fee, to its on-line service. Prodigy pays for the services by selling advertising which appears at the bottom of each screen display. This contrasts with more traditional on-line services such as CompuServe that do not include ads but charge a fee based on the amount of time you spend logged onto the service.

All ads display the **LOOK** command. You can select the **LOOK** command by entering l [**return**]. The command actives the ad and displays more information about the item being advertised. As an example, select the LOOK option from the current display:

```
l [return]
```

The ad expands to cover the full screen. Some ads are linked with other services on Prodigy such as shopping, home banking, etc., and may display menus of its own.

Returning to the Previous Screen

When you use the **LOOK** command to access information from a screen ad, you will probably want to return to the screen you were working on when you selected to look at the ad. In order to return to that screen you must use two Prodigy commands.

JUMP

The **JUMP** command is one of the most important in Prodigy. **JUMP** provides a means of moving from one section of the Prodigy service to another. The **JUMP** command appears at the bottom of every screen in Prodigy and can be accessed by enter the letter J.

ZIP

The **ZIP** command, which appears only in the JUMP menu box, will return you to the last Prodigy screen you had been using before you selected an ad:

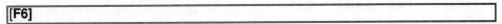

The **JUMP** command displays a special menu box that overlays part of the current screen display, as shown in Figure 3-6.

```
Type JUMPword:
┌─────────────────────────────────┐

or select command:
┌────────────┬──────────────────┐
│ FIND       │ REVIEW           │
├────────────┼──────────────────┤
│ GUIDE      │ VIEWPATH         │
├────────────┼──────────────────┤
│ INDEX      │                  │
├────────────┼──────────────────┤
│ ZIP        │ >READ MAIL       │
├────────────┼──────────────────┤
│ TOOLS      │ >HIGHLIGHTS      │
├────────────┼──────────┬───────┤
│ UNDO       │ >ADS     │>[ESC] │
└────────────┴──────────┴───────┘
```

Figure 3-6. The JUMP Menu.

There are two ways to use the JUMP menu: **JUMP**word and **JUMP** commands.

JUMPword

Each section of Prodigy has a unique name. The name is the JUMPword for that item. You can jump to a specific area of Prodigy from any other area by entering the desired JUMP word into the entry box.

JUMP commands

The menu also contains a list of **JUMP** commands which perform special functions related to finding and displaying specific topics within Prodigy. For example, the **HIGHLIGHTS** command returns you to the Highlights screen which appears when you first sign on to Prodigy.

In this case you want to use the **ZIP** command. **ZIP** returns you to the last Prodigy screen used before you selected an ad. Enter:

```
[down] (4 times)
[return]
```

Or use the mouse:

```
Double Click(left) on ZIP
```

The commands returns you to the Message Center screen display. You can return to the Highlight screen, the one that appears when you first sign on to Prodigy by selecting the HIGHLIGHTS option in the Jump menu. Display the jump menu by entering:

```
[F6]
```

Or use the mouse:

```
Double Click(left) on JUMP
```

Select HIGHLIGHTS from this menu. Enter:

```
[Tab] (2 times)
[down] (3 times)
[return]
```

Or use the mouse:

```
Double Click(left) on HIGHLIGHTS
```

USING THE JUMP COMMAND

The **JUMP** command is the most important command in the Prodigy system. It is with the **JUMP** command that you can directly access any of the features of Prodigy. It also contains commands that help you locate features in Prodigy.

The JUMP menu, Figure 3-6, is the key to Prodigy. The menu can be accessed any time you see JUMP displayed on the menu bar at the bottom of the screen.

The JUMP menu contains 12 commands.

FIND

This command will generate a list of all Prodigy features that are rela. ed to a topic or key word which you enter. For example, if you enter the word "camera," Prodigy will displays a list of features that are related to that word. The feature list is divided into categories such Features, Reference, Clubs and Goods. For camera, PHOTO NEWS would appear under Features while CR(Consumer Reports) CAMERAS would appear under reference. The Goods list will show all merchants on Prodigy that carry goods related to your specified topic.

REVIEW

This command displays a list of the previous features you have accessed during the current session. **REVIEW** allows you to quickly back track to a feature that you have already used during the current session.

GUIDE

The GUIDE is a system of tree structured menu from which you can access Prodigy features. A tree structured menu system begins with a main menu from which other menus will branch. Each branch may in turn branch to more detailed menus. At the end of each series of branches is a feature. The main menu of the GUIDE divides all of Prodigy's features into six categories: News & Features, Living, Shopping, Money, Travel, and Computers. If you select News & Features, Prodigy then displays the News & Features menu which contains Information, Newsroom, Business, Sports, Weather, Consumer, and Extra Extra.

VIEW PATH

The **VIEW PATH** command displays your personal PATH list. A PATH list is a list of Prodigy features which you frequently like to access. The PATH list works in conjunction with the **PATH** command. Each time you select the **PATH** command from the menu bar at the bottom of a Prodigy screen, you automatically jump to the next item on your PATH list. VIEW PATH displays the PATH list as a menu from which you can randomly select a feature. Note that when you first sign on to Prodigy a PATH list is automatically generated for you. Later in this chapter you will learn how to delete the automatic PATH list and create one of your own.

INDEX

This command is used to browse the index of Prodigy features. When you select this command Prodigy positions you at the current topic in the index, e.g., HIGHLIGHTS if you are currently at the HIGHLIGHTS screen. You can search the index list by entering one or more letters of a topic. Prodigy will jump to the first item in the list that matches or is close to the entered characters.

COPY

This command will copy the text of the current feature to your printer. This command is not available on all Prodigy screens. If COPY does not appear in the JUMP menu and there is no PRINT option on the screen you cannot print the item. Note that Prodigy disables the **[Print Screen]** key on your keyboard while Prodigy is running.

READ MAIL

This command jumps you directly to the message center so that you can read your electronic mail.

TOOLS

This command jumps you to the Tools menu. This menu allows you to modify your personal information such as your address, credit card information, and password.

HIGHLIGHTS

This commands jumps you directly to the HIGHLIGHTS screen.

UNDO

This has the same function as REVIEW in that it lists the previous topics selected during the session.

ADS

This command allows you to directly access the any of the ads that appear on Prodigy.

ESC

Pressing the **[Esc]** key cancels the JUMP menu and returns you to current screen.

The JUMP menu offers four different ways to access Prodigy features. They are: by subject, topic name, and by personal preference.

By Subject

The **FIND** command allows you to locate items based on a subject such as cameras, video, books, etc.

By Topic

GUIDE command allows you to move through a series of menus by selecting topics. The tree structured menus move from the general (e.g., Sports) to specific topics (e.g., NFL standings).

By Name

The INDEX command allows you to browse an alphabetical list of Prodigy topics.

By Personal Preference

The **PATH** and **VIEWPATH** commands allow you to create a personal list of Prodigy features.

Exit the JUMP menu by entering:

```
[Esc]
```

Using the FIND Command

The **FIND** command searches Prodigy for a list of all of the features that are related to a key word which you enter. To use the **find** command, display the JUMP menu. Enter:

```
[F6]
```

or:

```
Click(left) on JUMP
```

Select the **FIND** command from the JUMP menu:

```
[Tab] [return]
```

or:

```
Click(left) on Find
```

Prodigy displays the FIND screen. There are two ways to use the FIND screen.

Where Can I FIND

At the top of the screen is an entry box into which you can enter a word that represents the topic you want to search for.

WORD LIST

At the bottom of the FIND screen is a command labeled **>WORD LIST**. This command will displays an alphabetical list of topic which relate to one or more features in the Prodigy service. The word list option is useful when you are not sure what you want to look for.

As an example, enter "pets" as the topic you want to search for:

```
pets [return]
```

Prodigy now searches for all of the features in the service that relate to pets. When the search has been completed Prodigy displays a list of the features that relate to the search topic. The features are organized under the headings Features, Reference, Clubs, Goods, and Goods and Services.

You can use the list as a way to jump to any of the topics listed. For example, suppose that you wanted to access the PETCARE GUIDE. Select that option by entering:

```
Tab] [return]
```

Prodigy jumps to the Petcare Guide feature. Once you are located at the feature you can follow the menus to access information stored in this area, in this case the Petcare Guide and Petcare Column.

Prodigy stores a copy for the FIND list so that you can return to this list to access another option listed under your selected topic. To return to the list, display the JUMP menu once again:

```
[F6]
```

Select FIND:

```
[Tab] [return]
```

When Prodigy displays the FIND screen you will see that a new option appears at the bottom of the screen labeled Prior FINDlist. Selecting this option will return you to the last find list you requested avoiding the need to wait for Prodigy to search for the topics a second time. Display the previous find list by entering:

```
[Tab] (5 times)
[return]
```

The selection highlight is flashing on the last selection you made from this list, PETCARE GUIDE.

You can use the **PRINT** command displayed on this menu to print a copy of the items on the find list. Printing the provides a lists of JUMP words that you can use during another session without having to perform another search.

Use the JUMP menu to return to the HIGHLIGHTS screen. Enter:

```
[F6]
[down] (4 times)
[Tab] [return]
```

Using the GUIDE Command

Another way to locate information on Prodigy is through the use of the **GUIDE** command. The GUIDE is a series of tree structured menus which list topics and features in Prodigy. A tree structured menu system begins with a main menu that lists the major topics. If you select a topic from the main menu, the program will then display a submenu that lists in greater detail all of the topics that fall under the selected heading. This process may continue for several layers. Each submenu reveals in more detail the choices that fall under the previous heading. At the end of each series of menus and submenus is a Prodigy feature. Conversely, all Prodigy features are located at the end of one or more branches of the menu structure.

The GUIDE allows you to browse through Prodigy features by moving from a general topic to more specific subtopics. The GUIDE menu system is like a table of contents in which all of the features of the Prodigy service are organized according to topic. The GUIDE menus are accessed through the JUMP menu. Enter:

```
F6]
[down] (2 times)
[return]
[
```

Prodigy displays the main GUIDE menu as a pop-up menu which cover part of the Prodigy screen, as shown in Figure 3-7. The menu lists the main topic division in Prodigy.

Figure 3-7. Main GUIDE Menu.

You can select any of the items that appear on the GUIDE menu or press **[Esc]** to cancel the display and return to the current Prodigy screen. Select Living by entering:

[down] [return]

Prodigy overlays the Living menu on top of the main menu, as shown in Figure 3-8. The items on this menu are all subcategories of Living.

Figure 3-8. Living Menu Overlays GUIDE Menu.

Select Health by entering:

```
[down] (5 times)
[return]
```

Health displays a menu of features relating to Health. Choose Psychology Today (Psyc Today) by entering:

```
[down] [return]
```

When you make this selection the menus disappear since you have reached the end of a branch. Prodigy now displays the current screen for Psychology Today.

When you activate the guides from a screen other than HIGHLIGHT, the menu that appears is the branch at which you are located. Display the GUIDE by entering:

```
[F6]
[down] (2 times)
```

The three levels of menus, Guide, Living, and Health appear on the screen. You can move backwards by using the **[Esc]** key. For example, suppose you wanted to change to Travelog. Enter:

```
[Esc]
```

The Health menu is removed and you return to the Living menu. Select Travelog:

```
[down] [return]
```

Choose the Mobil Travel Guide. Enter:

```
[down] [return]
```

The menus disappear again leaving you at the end of a different branch.

Return to the HIGHLIGHT screen. Try this on your own. The correct command can be found under Exercise 1.

Creating Your Own Path

The PATH feature of Prodigy enables you to quickly check your favorite Prodigy features each time you access the service. When you first sign on to Prodigy the service creates a path for you. Once you have worked with Prodigy for a while you can create a path of your own.

To create your own path, display the current path list, the one created for you by Prodigy, by using the **VIEWPATH** command on the JUMP menu. Enter:

```
[F6]
[down] (2 times)
[tab] [return]
```

Prodigy displays a menu entitled Your PATHlist. This is the list furnished by Prodigy which begins with Weather, Headlines, Market Update, etc., as shown in Figure 3-9.

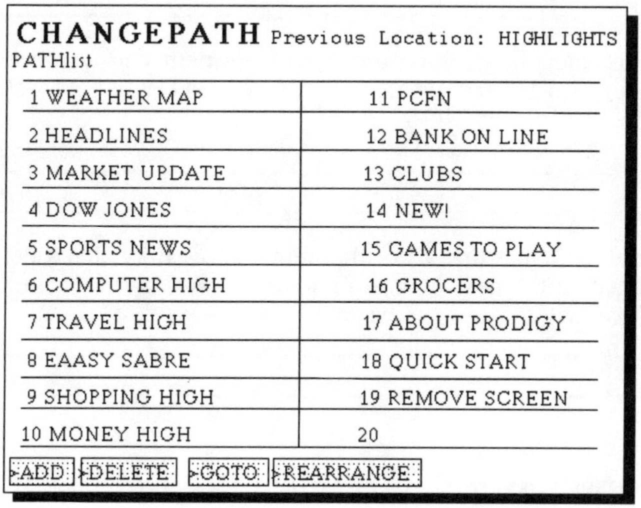

```
CHANGEPATH Previous Location: HIGHLIGHTS
PATHlist
┌─────────────────────┬──────────────────────┐
│ 1 WEATHER MAP       │ 11 PCFN              │
│ 2 HEADLINES         │ 12 BANK ON LINE      │
│ 3 MARKET UPDATE     │ 13 CLUBS             │
│ 4 DOW JONES         │ 14 NEW!              │
│ 5 SPORTS NEWS       │ 15 GAMES TO PLAY     │
│ 6 COMPUTER HIGH     │ 16 GROCERS           │
│ 7 TRAVEL HIGH       │ 17 ABOUT PRODIGY     │
│ 8 EAASY SABRE       │ 18 QUICK START       │
│ 9 SHOPPING HIGH     │ 19 REMOVE SCREEN     │
│ 10 MONEY HIGH       │ 20                   │
└─────────────────────┴──────────────────────┘
 [ADD]  [DELETE]  [GOTO]  [REARRANGE]
```

Figure 3-9. PATHLIST Display.

At the bottom of the menu is the **CHANGEPATH** command. This command allows you to modify the path list. You can add new items, delete items you don't want, and change the order of various items. Enter:

[End] [left]

Prodigy displays the CHANGEPATH screen. The screen is divided into 20 slots each of which contains a JUMP word that takes you to a Prodigy feature.

Removing Path Items

Items 3 and 4 on the PATH list are MARKET UPDATE and DOW JONES. Of course, not everyone is interested in the stock market. You can use the **DELETE** command to remove items from the PATH list. Select the **DELETE** command by entering:

```
[tab] [return]
```

You are asked to enter the position number of the item you want to remove. In this case that number is 3 to remove item #3 on the PATH list, MARKET UPDATE. Enter:

```
3 [return]
```

The item is removed. Note that all of the items below the deleted item move up one item. This means that the next item to remove, DOW JONES is now #3. Repeat the process to remove that item:

```
[return] 3 [return]
```

Adding a New Item

Suppose that you wanted to add the PET CARE guide to your path list. Select the **ADD** command by entering:

```
[left] [return]
```

Selecting ADD displays two more options. Previous Location systematically selects the last Prodigy feature used before you selected CHANGEPATH. That feature is displayed at the top of the screen. In this example that feature is the HIGHLIGHTS screen. This option make it easy to add the feature you are currently working on to the PATH list.

The **OTHER LOCATION** command allows you to select any location in Prodigy for addition to the PATH list. To add PET CARE to your path list you will need to use OTHER LOCATION since that is not the previous location. Enter:

```
[down] [return]
```

Enter the name of the feature you want to add:

```
pet care [return]
```

Prodigy checks to see that your entry is a valid jump word. If it is valid, Prodigy then displays a prompt that asks you what space on the path list should the new feature be inserted. Assume that this feature is an important one for you. Place it in position 4 following SPORTS NEWS:

```
4 [return]
```

PET CARE is now the fourth item on your path list.

Changing the Path List Order

Suppose that you liked to see sports news before regular news. In the current Path list HEADLINES comes before SPORTS NEWS. You can use the **REARRANGE** command to change the sequence of the items already on the path list. Select the **REARRANGE** command by entering:

```
Tab] (3 times)
[return]
```

Enter the position of the item you want to move. In this case that is item #3 SPORTS NEWS:

```
3 [return]
```

SPORTS NEWS is temporarily deleted from the path list. Prodigy then prompts you to enter the new position for SPORTS NEWS. Enter:

```
2 [return]
```

The items are rearranged on the path list.

Note that you can cancel all of the changes you have made to the path list by selecting the **CANCEL CHANGES** command that appear at the bottom of the screen after you have made a change to the path list.

Using the Path List

The path list can be put to use by issuing the PATH command. When you issue the **PATH** command, Prodigy jumps to the first feature on your path list. Each subsequent **PATH** command moves down to the next item on the path list and perform a jump to that location. The first item on the path list is WEATHER. If you enter the **PATH** command you will jump to the WEATHER feature. Enter:

```
[F4]
```

The WEATHER map screen is displayed showing today's weather. Jump to the next feature. Recall that this is now SPORTS NEWS due to the modifications you made to the path list in the previous section:

```
[F4]
```

The SPORTS NEWS feature is displayed.

Moving Around the Path List

In order to operate the **PATH** command, Prodigy keeps track of the items on the PATH list which you have used. If you lose track of what the next item on the path list is or where you are in the path list for the current session, you can find out what the next path item will be by displaying the path list with the **VIEWPATH** command.

Prodigy allows you to access specific commands on the JUMP menu directly from a Prodigy screen without first having to call up the JUMP menu. This is done by typing the first letter of the JUMP menu option you want to execute. Table 3-2 shows the **JUMP** menu commands and corresponding letters.

Table 3-2. Jump Menu Commands.

Letter	Command
F	JUMP FIND
R	JUMP REVIEW
G	JUMP GUIDE
I	JUMP INDEX

To directly execute the **VIEWPATH** command from a Prodigy screen display enter:

```
v
```

The highlight in the JUMP menu is positioned on **VIEWPATH**. Select that command by entering:

```
[return]
```

The VIEWPATH shows that the next item to be brought up by PATH will be HEADLINES. It is possible to change the sequence of path movements by moving the highlight on the VIEWPATH menu to a different location on the list. For example, suppose that you want to continue working through the path list starting at TRAVEL HIGH (highlights). Move the selection highlight to that JUMP words and execute the JUMP from that location:

```
[down] (3 times)
[return]
```

Prodigy jumps you to the TRAVEL HIGH screen. If you enter PATH now what will appear. Enter:

```
[F4]
```

Prodigy jumps you to EAASY SABRE, the next item on the list following TRAVEL HIGH. You can use this technique to continue the path sequence at any path item you desire. For example, by using VIEWPATH to jump to the first item on the list restarts the path sequence at the beginning.

Exit Prodigy by entering:

```
e [return] [return]
```

SUMMARY

This chapter discussed the basic techniques and concepts involved in using the Prodigy service.

Prodigy. Prodigy is a software program that connects the PS1 to the Prodigy service by means of the modem included in the PS1. When connected to Prodigy you can access a wide variety of information services and merchants who provide goods and services through Prodigy.

Sign-On. Connecting your computer to Prodigy requires a procedure called sign-on. During sign-on you must enter your Prodigy ID number and your password. You can automate the sign-on process by creating a user sign-on shortcut. However, automatic sign-on shortcut eliminates the password protection offered by Prodigy.

Electronic Mail. You can use the Prodigy service to send and receive messages from other Prodigy users or parts of the Prodigy system. The message NEW MAIL appears on the HIGHLIGHTS screen whenever you have new mail posted.

JUMP. The **JUMP** command provides a means by which you can access various parts of the Prodigy system. Each part of the system is assigned a JUMP word. Entering the JUMP word takes you to that specified area of Prodigy. The JUMP menu also includes other commands that allow you to find and access Prodigy features in different ways.

FIND. The **FIND** command locates all of the Prodigy features that relate to a key word which you select. FIND enables you to determine which Prodigy features might contain the information in which you are interested.

GUIDE. The GUIDE is a series of tree structured menus that organize all of the features of Prodigy according to topic. You can use the GUIDE menus to find a specific topic by making selections from the menus moving from general to specific topics.

INDEX. The INDEX is an alphabetical list of all of the JUMP words in the Prodigy system. You can browse this list in order to locate items you want to access.

PATH. The **PATH** command is used to access your personal list of Prodigy features. The **VIEWPATH** command allows you to view, select from and modify your personal list of features. The **PATH** command will displays the next item on your path list each time it is executed.

EXERCISES

Exercise 1

Return to the HIGHLIGHTS screen:

```
[F6]
[down] (4 times)
[tab] [return]
```

Section II

Projects

Chapter 4

Writing a Letter

T his chapter introduces the basic concepts and features of word processing. Word processing can be used to produce documents as single as a one page letter or as complicated as a college research paper.

Word processing offers a number of advantages over other forms of document production such as hand or type writing.

Editing. One of the primary sources of frustration in writing by hand or even using a typewriter is that mistakes are easy to make but almost impossible to correct. In many cases, a mistake requires the writer to rewrite the entire page or even the entire document.

Creating a document with a word processor eliminates this frustration because any mistake, large or small, can be corrected quickly and simply with the same techniques used to enter text. Once corrected, the document appears as if the error never existed. Editing can also be used to rearrange words, phrases, sentences, or paragraphs with just a few keystrokes.

The most important benefit of editing is that because writers can easily correct and revise their text, they are encouraged to refine and improve their writing. By eliminating much of the frustration associated with handwritten or typewritten documents, word processing helps the writers improve not only the form but the content of their documents.

Reference Tasks. The Works word processor includes built-in spell check and thesaurus options. The spell check option finds spelling mistakes in the document and suggests corrections. The thesaurus displays lists of synonyms for words that you have used in the document. The synonyms help you expand the vocabulary used in the document.

Formatting. Formatting refers to the way that text is arranged on the page. You can add special accents to text such as bold type, italics, or underlines. Text can be centered automatically and paragraphs can be indented in various ways. In addition, Works allows you to draw lines and boxes around your paragraphs to create sophisticated document layouts.

In this chapter you will learn how to perform editing, reference tasks, and formatting using the Works word processor. It is important to keep in mind that the purpose of this project, as with all projects in this book, is not simply to produce the end product, e.g., a letter, but to provide a structured experience that will help you discover how the power of your computer can be put to use. If approached in this way, creating even a simple, one page letter (the project for this chapter) can teach you a great deal about what the Works word processor can do and do for you.

Note

If you have not worked with Works before you might want to go back to Chapter 3 and work through the section entitled "Accessing Works" to learn more about the basic structure of Works, its menus, and other conventions before you begin this project.

STARTING THE WORD PROCESSOR

The first step in creating a document is to activate the Works word processing mode. Begin by selecting Microsoft Works from the main system menu:

Click(left) on *Microsoft Works*

Figure 4-1 shows the Works logo.

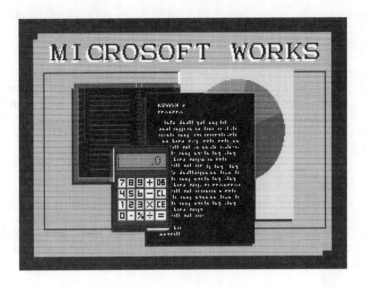

Figure 4-1. The Works Logo.

The PS1 system menu loads the Works program into the memory of the computer. When the program is loaded it displays the File menu, as shown in Figure 4-2.

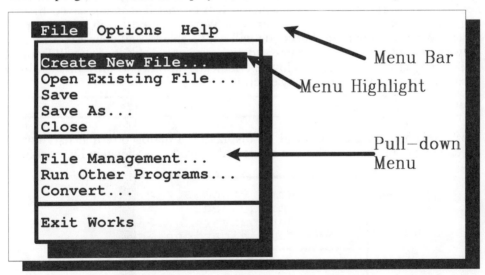

Figure 4-2. Works Display File Menu.

The Works menu system consists of two parts: the menu bar and the pulldown menu.

Menu Bar

The top line of the displays is the menu bar. This line lists a series of words each of which is a major category of the commands and operations you can carry out in Works. The items listed on the menu bar will change depending upon what type of work window, if any, is currently active. When you first start Works, the menu bar lists only three items (File, Options and Help) because no work windows have been created or used.

Pulldown Menu

When you select one of the items on the menu bar, Works displays a box called a pulldown menu. This box contains a list of commands and operations, related to the selected topic, from which you can choose. When you first start works the File menu is automatically displayed and the first item on that menu **Create New File** is highlighted.

In order to create a word processing document you must use the File menu command **Create New File** to create a word processing window into which you can enter the text of your document. Technically speaking, the use of the word File in the command name is misleading. The information you enter into a window doesn't actually become a file, i.e., data permanently stored on the disk, until you specifically command Works to Save the document. This point is worth noting because any work entered into a window will be lost if it is not saved first. For example, suppose you create a letter with Works when a storm causes a power failure. When you return to Works you will not be able to find your text since it was only entered into the screen window and not saved as a disk file. You will learn later in this project how to save windows periodically in order to prevent such losses. Create a new document window by entering:

```
[return]
```

Works responds to the command by displaying a dialog box that lists the four different types of windows that can be created in Works, as shown in Figure 4-3.

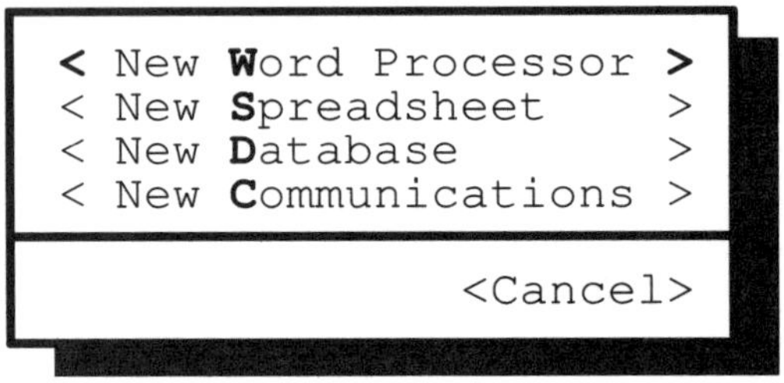

```
< New Word Processor >
< New Spreadsheet    >
< New Database       >
< New Communications >

                <Cancel>
```

Figure 4-3. Dialog Box Lists Type of Windows that can be Created.

118

In this project you want to create a Word Processor window. Before you make your selection it might be useful to consider how you know that you want to use a word processing window for this project. Word processing is used for entering text (non-numeric) information that is organized in lines, sentences, and paragraphs. In this case it might seem obvious that typing a letter is a word processing task. But suppose you wanted to create a family budget. While it would be possible to enter this information into a word processing window, the fact that a budget contains numeric values and is not organized in sentences or paragraphs suggest that another type of window, e.g., a spreadsheet, would be a better choice.

Works automatically places the cursor on the New Word Processor option. You can select this option by entering:

[Return]

Works displays the a word processing window on the screen, as shown in Figure 4-4. The menu bar displays five additional topics (Edit, Print, Select, Format, and Window) in addition to three (File, Options, and Help) that were on the first menu bar display.

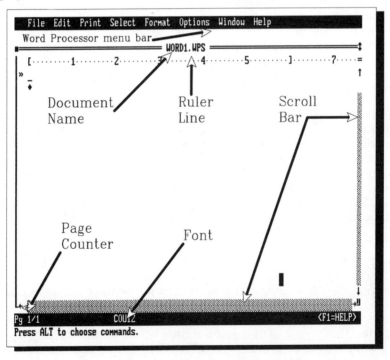

Figure 4-4. Word Processing Window.

The top line of the word processing window is the title bar which shows the name of the document contained in the window. Works automatically assigns temporary name to each new window you display. The temporary name for word processing documents is WORD followed by a number (1, 2, 3, etc.) with a three character extension, .WPS. The WPS identifies the document as a word processing type window.

Below the title line is the *ruler* line. The ruler line helps you relate space on the screen to space on the printed page. The [marks the location of the left margin while the] marks the location of the right margin. The numbers on the ruler line represent inches from the left margin. For example, the number 3 appears at a position that is inches from the left margin. Between the numbers are dots. Each dot stands for 1/10 of an inch. For example, the fifth dot after the number 1 would be 1.5 inches from the left margin.

Note that the number 6 is missing because the](right margin) is located at that position. This also tells you that Works sets the maximum width for the any line of text at 6 inches. You will see later how Works uses the margins to perform various tasks such as centering and paragraph line wrapping.

At the bottom of the window is a line that contains two items. The left item tells you the current and total page numbers as a fraction. For example, Pg 1/1 tells you that you are on page 1 of a 1 page document. Pg 3/7 would tell you that you were looking at page 3 of a 7 page document. Since you can only view about 20 lines of text at a time, the page indicator is useful in help you figure out what portion of the document you are viewing.

To the right of the page indicator, is the *font* name. The word font is borrowed from the printing profession. A font is a family of characters that are formed using a particular style of lettering. Font families have names that reflect the style of the lettering or the creator of the style. By default, Works sets the font type as Pica 12 point. Points are a unit of measurement commonly used by printers. 1 point is equal to 1/72nd of an inch. 12 point text prints 6 lines of text per vertical inch. This style and size of lettering, or a close equivalent, is supported by almost all computer printers. (For a detailed background on fonts and point sizes see Chapter 2).

Editing Text

When you first display a new word processing window there are three small marks that appear in the upper left corner of the window. The first is a >> symbol; the symbol marks the beginning of the document. Next to that symbol is a blinking _. This is called the *cursor*. The cursor shows where in the document any new characters will be inserted. The last symbol is a diamond shaped symbol that appears below the cursor. This is the end of document marker.

The beginning and end of document markers will always appear at the beginning and the end of the document, respectively. Since the new document does not contain any text, the beginning and end markers are displayed one after the other. As text is added to the window the markers will become separated.

The cursor, unlike the markers, is not fixed at any one position in the document but can be moved to any point in the document. This allows you to insert new characters at any location in the document, not just at the end or the beginning.

Entering text is simply a matter of typing the characters, words, and sentences you desire to add to your document. Begin by entering the name of the person to whom the letter will be sent:

Miss K. Flynn

As you type in the characters, the cursor moves along with the text. The cursor is now positioned to the right off the last character you typed.

Suppose that you decide instead of using an initial for the first name, you want to use the full first name, i.e., "Kerri "instead of K. If you were using a typewriter you would probably have to discard the page you started and begin on a new page. However, word processing allows you to perform editing. At its most basic, editing consists of two operations: inserting and deleting.

Insert

Inserting text means adding characters to the existing document. The trick to inserting text is that the word processor will automatically move all of the text to the right of the insertion point to make room for the new characters.

Delete

Deleting characters accomplishes two things. First, the characters are removed from the document and second, all of the text to the right of the deleted character is closed up to make the text look as if the deleted character had never been there in the first place.

These two operations alone can save you a tremendous amount of time, effort, and frustration.

Moving the Cursor

Both insert and delete depend upon the cursor being positioned at the correct point in the document. There are two ways to move the cursor.

Keyboard Movement

When in the word processor, the keys listed in Table 4-1 will change the position of the cursor.

Table 4-1. Cursor Movement Keys.

Cursor Movement Keys Function	Key
Left one character	[left]
Right one character	[right]
Up one line	[up]
Down one line	[down]
Left one word	[Ctrl-left]
Right one word	[Ctrl-right]
Up one paragraph	[Ctrl-up]
Down one paragraph	[Ctrl-down]
Beginning of line	[Home]
End of line	[End]
Beginning of document	[Ctrl-Home]
End of document	[Ctrl-End]

Mouse

You can position the cursor by pointing the mouse at any character in the document and clicking the left mouse button.

Which method is best? There are several factors that go into the decision about how you should move the cursor at any given moment. As a general rule, movement over small areas can be quickly done with keystrokes. Movement over large areas is probably better carried out with the mouse. Another factor is the way that you type. People proficient at touch typing may feel that moving their hand from the keyboard to the mouse wastes time. On the other hand, since a single mouse click can position the cursor at any location on the screen, the mouse is often faster than repeating an arrow key 10 or 20 times.

In this case use you want to position the cursor on the period following the letter K. Use the keyboard method to move the cursor. Enter:

```
[Crtl-left]
```

The cursor moves to the beginning of the previous word, the letter F in Flynn. Next, move two more characters to the left by entering:

```
[left](2 times)
```

The cursor is in the correct position for inserting text following the letter K.

Inserting Text

The Works word processor will automatically insert new characters at the current cursor position. Fill in the full name by entering:

```
erri
```

The full first name has been inserted, as shown in Figure 4-5, and the cursor is now positioned under the period following the first name.

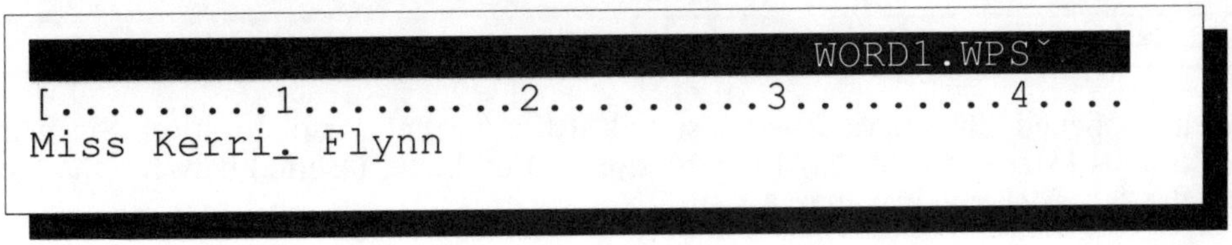

```
                                        WORD1.WPS˘
[..........1.........2.........3.........4....
Miss Kerri. Flynn
```

Figure 4-5. Text Inserted at Cursor Position.

Deleting Text

The period, under which the cursor is now located, no longer belongs in the text since the initial K has been expended to the full name "Kerri." There are two keys which can be used to delete individual characters from the document, as shown in Table 4-2.

Table 4-2. Delete Keys and Functions.

Delete Function	Key
Delete at cursor position	[Del]
Delete previous character	[Backspace]

Since you want to delete the character at the current cursor location—the period, enter:

```
[Del]
```

Note that when you delete the character, all of the text to the right of that location closes up to eliminate the space that previously occupied that the deleted character.

123

You can make as many editing changes as you desire. Suppose that you want to change "Miss" to "Ms." First, position the cursor on the character you want to delete. This time use the mouse to move the cursor:

Click(left) on *i* in *Miss*

The cursor is moved to the location of the click(left). Delete the "i" and the "s" by entering:

[Del](2 times)

To complete the editing you need to add a period. Enter:

.(period)

What happened? The period was inserted at the current cursor location. Since the cursor was located on the "s," the period ended up being inserted between the "M" and the "s", as shown in Figure 4-6.

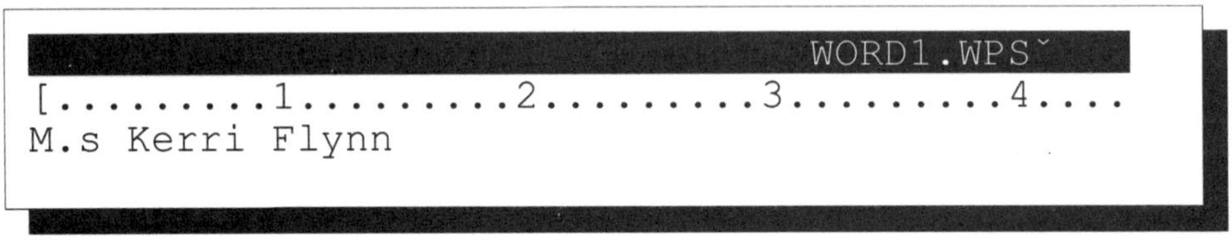

```
                                          WORD1.WPS˘
[.........1.........2.........3.........4....
M.s Kerri Flynn
```

Figure 4-6. Character Inserted at the Wrong Location.

It is important to remember that you must position the cursor to the correct location before you insert or delete text. Correct the mistake you have just made by entering:

[Backspace]

Move the cursor past the "s" by entering:

[right]

Now insert the period in its proper location. Enter:

.(period)

By using insert and delete, along with cursor movement, you have been able to change the text from the way it was entered in Figure 4-5 to the way it looks in Figure 4-7. The simple keystrokes used to make these changes are the single most powerful feature in any word processor because they allow for the correction of any mistake in the text of the document. Editing allows you to make those corrections with the least number of keystrokes possible.

```
                                              WORD1.WPS˜
[..........1.........2.........3.........4....
Ms._Kerri Flynn
```

Figure 4-7. Original Text Edited.

STARTING A NEW LINE

You have now entered all of the text that is necessary for the first line of the address block of your letter. Recall that an address block consist of several short lines of text: one for the name, one for the street address and another for the state, city and zip code. To start a new line you must move the cursor to the end of the line and enter one of two keys: new line or new paragraph.

New Line

The **New Line** key is **[Shift-return]**. This keystroke is used to start a new line within the same paragraph. For example, an address block is really a single paragraph with three or more short lines.

New Paragraph

The **[return]** key begins a new paragraph.

What is the difference between a new line and a new paragraph? If you were using a typewriter there would be no reason, nor any way, to distinguish between a new line and a new paragraph. But in the Works word processor there is a subtle but significant difference. If you have a series of short lines that function as a related group, e.g., an address block, the lines should be ended with **[Shift-return]** rather than return. You will see later in this project why this distinction is important. Move the cursor to the end of the line by entering:

[End]

[End]
[Shift-return]

125

Enter the next two lines of the address:

> **University of Massacusetts[Shift-return]**
> **Amherst, MA 07550**

Since this is the last line in the address block you can end the paragraph with a paragraph ending keystroke, **[return]**:

> **[return]**

Inserting the Date

The next item to enter is the date of the letter. One way to enter the date is to simply type in the date manually. However, if you want to place today's date in the document you can automatically insert the date using a Works word processor command. The PS1 is equipped with a built in clock/calendar. Many programs, such as Works, can access the time and date information generated by this clock. The command which inserts the date is found on the Edit menu. Display the Edit menu using the mouse:

> **Click(left)** on **Edit**

The program displays the Edit menu. This menu lists commands related to document editing, as shown in Figure 4-8. The menu is divided into four commands: **undo**, **cut and paste**, **insert**, and **documentation**.

Figure 4-8. The Edit Menu in the Word Processing Mode.

Undo

This command restores accidentally deleted text.

Cut and Paste

These commands allow you to rearrange existing text. You will learn more about them in this chapter.

Insert

This section contains commands that insert special non-text items into the document. The command that inserts the date is included in this section.

Documentation

This section contains commands that create special effects (footnotes, bookmarks) used in formal documents such as research papers.

The **Insert Special** command is used to add special items to the text of the document. Select this option with the mouse:

Click(left) on Insert Special...

Figure 4-9 shows the INSERT SPECIAL dialog box.

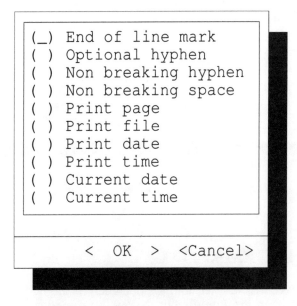

```
(_) End of line mark
( ) Optional hyphen
( ) Non breaking hyphen
( ) Non breaking space
( ) Print page
( ) Print file
( ) Print date
( ) Print time
( ) Current date
( ) Current time

      <  OK  >  <Cancel>
```

Figure 4-9. The Insert Special Dialog Box.

Works displays a dialog box that lists all of the special items that can be inserted into a document. Four of the items in this dialog box are related to the insertion of time and date information.

Current Date and Current Time

These options insert the current date (mm/dd/yy format) or time (hh:ss format) into the document at the current cursor location. Once entered, the date or time remains the same unless you change it by editing.

Print Date and Print Time

These options insert a date symbol (*date*) or a time symbol (*time*) into the document at the current cursor location. When the document is printed, Works automatically replaces the symbols with the current date or time. This means that the date or time information in the printed document reflects the date and time when the document was printed rather than the date and time when it was created.

Select the Current Date with the mouse:

```
Click(left) on Current date
Click(left) on OK
```

Works inserts the date, e.g., 10/8/90, into the document. Keep in mind that this date is treated from this point on as text, meaning that it can be edited just like any other characters in the document. The automatic date insertion is simply a convenience. The text should look like Figure 4-10.

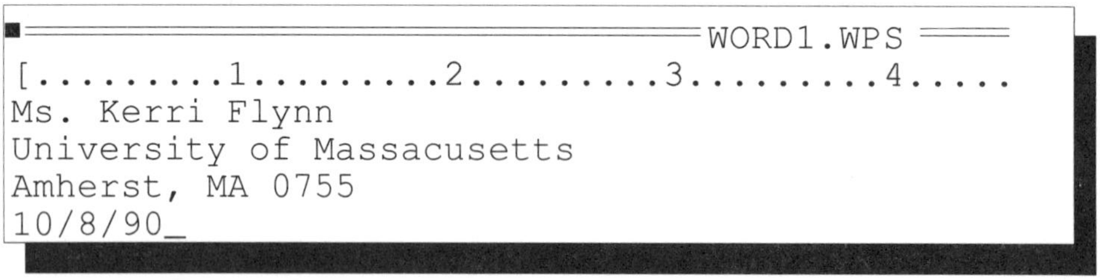

```
■ ══════════════════════════WORD1.WPS ═════
[.........1.........2.........3.........4.....
Ms. Kerri Flynn
University of Massacusetts
Amherst, MA 0755
10/8/90_
```

Figure 4-10. Date Inserted into Document.

PARAGRAPH FORMATTING

The date that you have just inserted into the document is aligned on the left margin of the window and is on the line directly below the previous paragraph, i.e., the address block. The appearance of the document could be improved if you made changes in the format of the paragraph. For example, you might want to have a blank line inserted before the new paragraph. It is also customary to center the date between the margins.

Both of these suggested changes affect the format of the paragraph. The format refers to the manner in which the text of a paragraph is arranged on the page. The arrangement of any paragraph of text in a Works document depends on four basic qualities possessed by any paragraph: indents, spacing, alignment, and flow.

Indents

An indent is space added to the left or right sides of a paragraph which narrow the length of the lines in that paragraph, as shown in Figure 4-11. Works can set separate values for the left and right paragraph indents as well as an indent that affects only the first line of the paragraph.

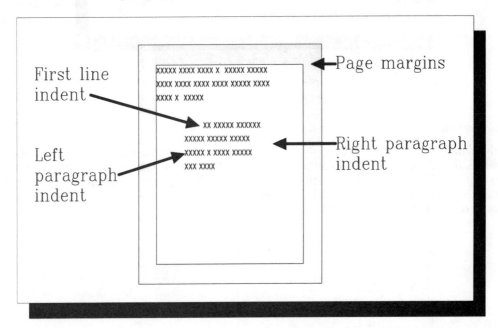

Figure 4-11. Paragraph Indents.

Spacing

While indents control the horizontal arrangement of the text, the spacing settings control the vertical arrangement of the text, as shown in Figure 4-12. Works allows you to specify the line spacing—the amount of space between each line of a paragraph and the amount of space before or after each paragraph.

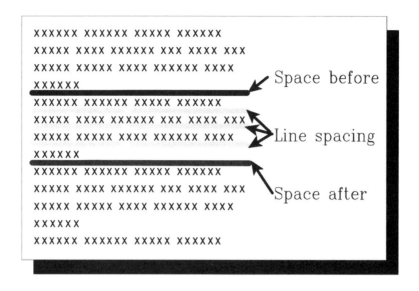

Figure 4-12. Paragraph Spacing.

Alignment

Most lines of text do not fill the total number of characters that can fit on a line. This means that there is usually some blank space at the end of each line. You can select to align the lines of text on the left margin, the right margin, or centered between the margins, as shown in Figure 4-13. Justified text inserts blank space between words in order to align the text on the left and right margins evenly.

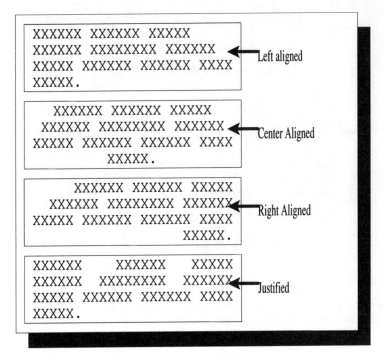

Figure 4-13. Paragraph Alignment.

Flow

Flow refers to how paragraphs are treated if they happen to fall at the bottom of a page. Works will normally fit as many lines of text on a page as permitted by the page margins. The Works option Don't break paragraph will ensure that the entire paragraph will be printed on the same page. If it cannot fit at the bottom of the current page it will be moved to the top of the next page. The Keep this paragraph with the next option ensures that the current paragraph will print on the same page as the next paragraph. This option is useful when you want to keep two closely associated paragraphs on the same page, e.g., a table and the table caption.

When you first begin a new document, Works uses the settings in Table 4-3 for each paragraph.

Table 4-3. Default Paragraph Format Settings.

Default Paragraph Format Settings	
Left indent	0"
First line indent	0"
Right indent	0"
Line spacing	single
Space before	none
Space after	none
Alignment	left
Breaks within paragraph	yes
Keep with next	no

There are two ways to change the format of a paragraph.

Format/Indents & Spacing Dialog Box

This dialog box contains settings for all of the paragraph formatting options available in Works. The dialog box has the advantage of showing all of the current settings in a single display. This method enables you to make as many formatting changes as you like with a single command.

Shortcut Formatting Keys

Most of the commonly used formatting options can be applied to a paragraph by using special **[Ctrl+character]** key combinations, as shown in Table 4-4. These key combinations help you quickly apply common paragraph attributes without having to display the dialog box.

Table 4-4. Paragraph Formatting Shortcut Keys.

Function	Key
Indent left 1/2"	[Ctrl-n]
Undo left indent	[Ctrl-m]
Hanging indent 1/2"	[Ctrl-h]
Undo hanging indent	[Ctrl-g]
Single space	[Ctrl-1]
Double space	[Ctrl-2]
1-1/2 space	[Ctrl-5]
Left alignment	[Ctrl-l]
Right alignment	[Ctrl-r]
Center alignment	[Ctrl-c]
Justified alignment	[Ctrl-j]
1 line before paragraph	[Ctrl-o]
0 lines before paragraph	[Ctrl-e]
Return to default settings	[Ctrl-x]

In this case you want to make two formatting changes: add one line before the paragraph and center alignment. Display the INDENTS & SPACING dialog box by using the mouse:

Click(left) on **Format**
Click(left) on **Indents & Spacing**

The program displays the INDENTS & SPACING dialog box which contains all of the paragraph formatting settings, as shown in Figure 4-14.

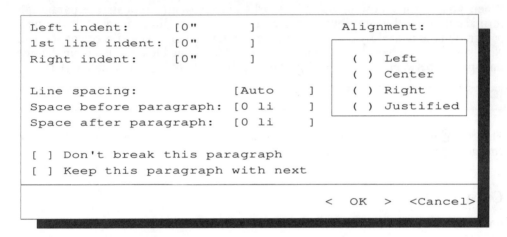

```
Left indent:        [0"       ]          Alignment:
1st line indent:  [0"       ]
Right indent:      [0"       ]           ( )  Left
                                          ( )  Center
Line spacing:                [Auto     ]  ( )  Right
Space before paragraph:  [0 li    ]  ( )  Justified
Space after paragraph:   [0 li    ]

[ ]  Don't break this paragraph
[ ]  Keep this paragraph with next


                                        <  OK  >  <Cancel>
```

Figure 4-14. Indents and Spacing Dialog Box.

Begin by changing the alignment to center by using the mouse:

Click(left) on **Center**

You can move around the dialog box by using the **[Tab]** and **[Shift-tab]** keys. Move the cursor to Space Before Paragraph by entering:

[Shift-Tab](3 times)

Enter the number of lines that should be inserted before the paragraph:

1

You can conclude the dialog box editing by clicking on **OK** or simply pressing **[return]**. In this instance use the **[return]** key:

[return]

When the dialog box is removed from the screen the date is centered between the margins. Keep in mind that centering is relative to the margins not the center of the window. Begin a new paragraph by entering:

[return]

When you begin a new paragraph, Works automatically repeats the paragraph formats used in the previous paragraph. In this case that means that the new paragraph is separated by one line from the previous paragraph and is center aligned. Now you want to change the alignment back to left aligned text but maintain the one line spacing between paragraphs. You can use the shortcut key combination **[Ctrl-l]**:

[Ctrl-l]

The cursor returns to the left margin indicating that the alignment format has been changed from center to left aligned text.

Copying Text

Enter the salutation of the letter:

Dear[spacebar]

The next word in the letter should be the name of the person to whom the letter is addressed. In most cases you would simply type that name into the document. However, since the purpose of writing this letter is to explore word processing features, there is another way to get the name entered. Recall that the name of the person is already entered as part of the address block. This means that you can copy the name from the address block into the greeting. While a short name such as "Kerri" is just as easily typed as copied, in this case you will use the copy method in order to learn how it is done.

The first step in the copying process is to select the text you want to copy. *Selection* in Works refers to highlighting a block of two or more characters. Selection can be performed in several ways, either with the keyboard or the mouse.

In general, mouse selection is usually the fastest and simplest method. For example, if you right click on any word in the document, Works highlights the word. Highlight the word "Kerri " using the mouse:

Right click on *Kerri*

A highlight is placed on the word "Kerri " plus the space immediately following the word. Recall that the **Copy** command is found on the Edit menu. Create a copy of the highlighted word using the mouse:

Click(left) on **Edit**
Click(left) on **Copy**

When you make a copy of a highlighted section of the document, Works stores that copy in a special area of the memory designated as the *clipboard*. The clipboard is used by Works to temporarily hold items, such as text being moved or copied. Keep in mind that text stored in the clipboard is not visible on the screen. How can you retrieve this text? If you look at the last line on the screen display you will see that Works displays the message "Select new location and press **ENTER**. Press **ESC** to cancel." The message tells you that you can place a copy of the text currently stored in the clipboard by moving the cursor to the desired location and pressing [**return**]. In this case that location is at the end of the document. You can jump to that position by entering:

[Ctrl-End]

Insert the text from the clipboard by entering:

[return]

The word "Kerri" is inserted next to "Dear". While this may seem like a lot of trouble to go through just to copy one word, it is because the concept and method is new to you. With a little practice you will soon find that it is quite easy to copy a word, phrase, or even a paragraph or two instead of entering the text again manually. Continue entering text by completing the greeting:

[End] [backspace]
,(comma)
[return]

Note that because Works automatically included the space following the word "Kerri" when you highlighted the block, it was necessary to delete that extra space from the end of the line. If you had continued to add text to the line instead of adding a comma, then the space would have been left in the document.

PARAGRAPH TEXT

Up to this point in the document you have entered only short lines of text. You have now reached the point where you will type the body of the letter. This text is *paragraph format* text. This means that you will want to type lines of text that are as wide as the margins will permit. If you were using a typewriter you would have to be very careful not to type too close to or past the right margin. But when you are using a word processor this concern is unnecessary. The program will automatically advance the cursor to the next line when you have filled the line you are typing on. This feature is called *line wrap*. With line wrap you don't have to be concerned with the length of each line. You simply type all of the text you want to include in the paragraph. Only when you have entered the last sentence in the paragraph is it necessary to enter **[return]** to end the current paragraph and start another.

Enter the following paragraphs. Keep in mind that the length of the lines as they appear in this text do not mean that you need to enter a **[return]** after every line. You can simply continue entering text until you reach the end of the paragraph:

> **This letter is the first project I am creating on my new**
> **computer. I just unpacked it a few hours ago and I am**
> **already using it and having a lot of fun trying to figure**
> **out what this thing can do. [return]**

As you enter the text, the program automatically starts a new line whenever it is necessary. Also notice that because you set the paragraph format to include a blank line before each paragraph, the spacing between paragraphs is automatically added each time you press **[return]** to start a new paragraph. Add another paragraph to the document:

> **I suppose your are wondering why I, of all people, should**
> **have bought a computer. To tell the truth I'm not exactly**
> **sure myself. [return]**

The screen should look like Figure 4-15.

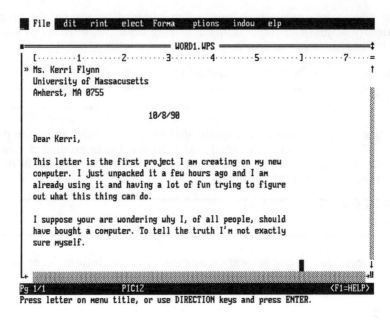

Figure 4-15. Document Window with Paragraph Text.

Delete and Undo

Deleting text from a document does not mean that you have permanently lost the text. Works always saves the last section of delete text in a special area of the computer's memory. If you change your mind, Works can use this information to restore the document to its previous condition.

For example, you might think that the previous paragraph might flow better if the phrase "of all people " was removed. Position the cursor with the mouse in the word I:

Click(left) on I

Move the cursor to the comma that follows that word:

[right]

Delete the phrase from the text by entering:

[Del](16 times)

Note that when you remove text from a line within a paragraph, the program will automatically adjust the line endings. In this case the number of lines in the paragraph was reduced from 3 to 2.

Move the cursor to the beginning of the next paragraph:

```
[Ctrl-down]
```

Suppose that when you reread the text you change your mind about the deletion of the phrase. You can recall the deleted text with the **Undo** command found on the EDIT menu or by using the shortcut command [**Alt-backspace**]. Undo the deletion using the mouse to select the command:

```
Click(left) on Edit
Click(left) on Undo
```

The text is restored to its appearance prior to the deletion. Keep in mind the following point about the use of **Undo.**

Last Deletion Only

The **Undo** command will restore only the last deletion made. When you delete text you remove any text currently in the Undo memory area and replace it with the current deletion.

Deletions Formed by Consecutive Keystrokes

When you delete more than one character at a time, all of the characters deleted can be restored with **Undo**. In the example, 16 characters were deleted and then restored. However, the deletion is not consider consecutive if you enter any other key except [**Del**]. For example, suppose that you enter [**Del**] eight times, moved the cursor to the right and then continue deleting eight more times. Works would undo only the last eight characters deleted. The eight characters deleted before you moved the cursor would be lost because they belong to a prior deletion group.

Cursor Position

When text is restored with **Undo**, it is restored to the exact location in the document from which it was deleted, regardless of the current cursor position. In the previous example, the cursor was positioned at the end of the paragraph when the text was restored to the first line of the paragraph. Also note that following an **Undo** operation, the cursor will have been returned to the place in the text where the deletion was made.

Return the cursor to the end of the text by entering:

```
[Ctrl-down]
```

Scrolling

Continue the document by adding a third paragraph:

> **The computer that I got has a color screen, a keyboard and a mouse.**

What happened to the screen display? When you entered the word "mouse "all of the previous text seems to have disappeared. Why?

The answer is that there is a limit to the amount of text that can be displayed in the window at any one time. In order to allow you to create documents which are much larger than the window itself, the program will scroll the text up or down within the window. In this case, when your cursor moved onto the new line, the first window full of text was scrolled up displaying a blank window on which you could continue your document.

How can you tell that the current window display is simply part of a larger document? The answer can be found in the scroll bar display on the right side of the window, as shown in Figure 4-16. The scroll bar represents the size of the entire document. Within the bar is a highlighted box called the scroll box. The box represents the location of the cursor within the document. In the current example, the scroll box is located near the bottom of the scroll bar. This tells you that your current cursor position is near the end of the document. While only the word mouse is currently visible, you can infer from the scroll bar display that you are viewing only a small part of a larger document.

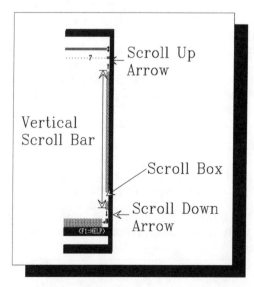

Figure 4-16. Vertical Scroll Bar Display.

You can use the mouse and the scroll bar display to change the portion of the document displayed in the window. Notice the arrows that appear at the top and bottom of the scroll bar. Clicking (left) those arrows will scroll the document display up or down within the window:

```
Click(left) on the up scroll bar arrow
```

The mouse action causes the program to scroll upwards revealing the beginning of the current paragraph. Scroll upwards again:

```
Click(left) on the up scroll bar arrow (2 times)
```

As you scroll the display upwards, the scroll box also moves upwards on the scroll bar. The location of the scroll box is synchronized with the portion of the document displayed in the window.

The scroll box itself can be used to scroll the display by using the mouse to drag the box up or down the scroll bar. Recall from Section I that drag refers to holding down the mouse button while you move the mouse. For example, to scroll the display to the top of the document you can drag the scroll box to the top of the bar:

```
Point at the scroll box
Drag(left button) to the top of the scroll bar
```

When you release the mouse button, Works scrolls the window to the top of the document. Where is the cursor? When you scroll the display with the mouse, Works maintains the current cursor position, even if that position is no longer visible within the window. In the current example, the cursor position is still located following the word mouse at the end of the document. If you were to enter a keystroke on the keyboard, the program would automatically scroll back to the cursor position and insert the character at that point. For example, if you enter [spacebar] that space will be placed after the last sentence in the document:

```
[spacebar]
```

The character is inserted at the last cursor position before you scrolled the display within the window. Complete the paragraph by entering:

```
I also have a modem and a hard disk drive. The modem
allows me to connect with other computer through ordinary
telephone lines. [return]
```

Indents

You have now reached the end of the body of this letter. The next step is to enter the closing of the letter:

Very truely yours,

How should you complete this line (should you enter **[return]** or **[Shift-return]**)? In this case, the line you have typed is really the first line in a group of related lines called the closing. Although it is a short line of text (one that does not fill the width between the margins), it is not a paragraph unto itself. This means that you should end the line **[Shift-return]** but not the paragraph **[return]**:

[Shift-return]

Since you will probably sign the letter by hand, add some blank lines to the closing to leave room for your signature:

[Shift-return](2 times)

Complete the closing by entering the following:

Carolyn Q. LaFish Your loving Auntie

You might have noticed that the closing paragraph is aligned on the left margin of the document. While this is acceptable in many cases, some people prefer to indent these lines from the margins. This can be easily done with Works using the formatting shortcut key combination **[Ctrl-n]**. Each time you enter **[Ctrl-n]**, the left indent of the current paragraph is increased by 1/2 inch.

The command causes the entire paragraph to indent 1/2 inch from the left margin. Note that because all of the lines in the close are part of the same paragraph, **[Shift-return]** endings, all of the lines in the close are affected by a single command. The other paragraphs in the document are not affected by the command because paragraph formatting change effect only the paragraph in which the cursor is currently located. Increase the indent by another 2 inches by entering:

[Ctrl+n](4 times)

If you find that you have indented too far you can undo the indent in 1/2 inch increments using **[Ctrl-m]**. In this case you can remove 1 inch of the current indent by entering:

[Ctrl-m](2 times)

The text in the window looks like Figure 4-17.

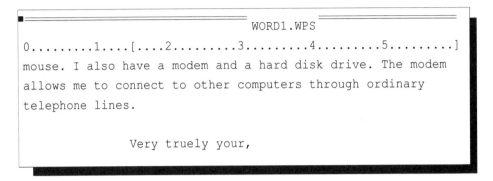

```
=============================== WORD1.WPS ===============================
0........1....[....2.........3.........4.........5.........]
mouse. I also have a modem and a hard disk drive. The modem
allows me to connect to other computers through ordinary
telephone lines.

               Very truely your,
```

Figure 4-17. Closing Indent from Left Margin.

CHECKING SPELLING

Even in the simplest document you may find need of the reference features of the Works word processor. The reference features are the **Spell Check** and **Thesaurus** (synonyms) commands found on the Options menu.

The most important feature is the **Spell Check**. You should always use this option to catch typos or spelling mistakes before you print a document. Begin a spell check of the current document:

Click(left) on **Options**
Click(left) on **Check Spelling**

Because the cursor is currently located at the end of the document, Works displays a dialog box that asks if you want to return to the top of the document in order to begin the spell check, as shown in Figure 4-18.

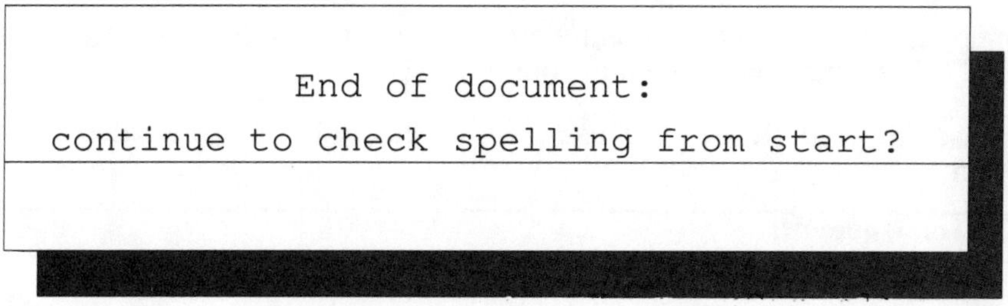

Figure 4-18. Start Spell Check Dialog Box.

Begin the check from the top of the document:

Click(left) on **OK**

The program returns to the beginning of the document and displays the first word in the document that cannot be found in the Works dictionary, the word "Kerri". The word which is considered a mistake is placed into the dialog box so that you can edit the text in order to correct the spelling. In addition the dialog box lists six options: Change All, Change, Ignore All, Ignore, Suggest, and Add.

Change All

This option corrects the current mistake and automatically repeats the correction if the same mistake is encountered again in the document.

Change

This option makes the current correction only.

Ignore All

This option tells the program to ignore the current mistake and any other of occurrences of the same mistake. This option is used to skip over names or special words in the current document.

Ignore

This option tells the program to ignore only the current word.

Suggest

This option causes the program to list possible correct spellings of the current mistake.

Add

This option is used to add the current word to the dictionary. This is useful for names or special terms which occur often in your writing.

In this case the word "Kerri " is a name which should be skipped. Select the Ignore All option:

Click(left) on **Ignore All**

The next mistake is also a name:

Click(left) on **Ignore All**

The next word is actually a mistake, Massacusetts. You can have the program display of suggested corrections by using the **Suggest** command:

Click(left) on **Suggest**

The program lists three acceptable spellings for the name of the state, as shown in Figure 4-19. The first spelling is the one most commonly used. That spelling is automatically copied onto the Replace line.

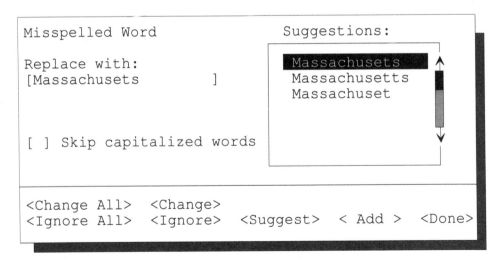

```
Misspelled Word                    Suggestions:

Replace with:                      Massachusets
[Massachusets          ]           Massachusetts
                                   Massachuset


 [ ] Skip capitalized words


<Change All>   <Change>
<Ignore All>   <Ignore>   <Suggest>   < Add >   <Done>
```

Figure 4-19. Suggested Corrections Appear in Dialog Box.

Replace the misspelled word with the correct spelling:

Click(left) on **Change**

The program makes the correction in the text and proceeds to the next questionable word. This word is also a name, the name of a city:

Click(left) on **Ignore All**

The next problem word is modem. Modem—short for modulator/demodulator—is the type of technical term that may not be found in the dictionary. You may want to add this term to your dictionary so that Works will not consider this word a mistake in the future:

Click(left) on **Add**

Next the word "truely" is encountered. Suggest correct spellings:

Click(left) on **Suggest** Click(left) on **Change**

Ignore the next two words because they are both names:

Click(left) on **Ignore All** (2 times)

When the entire document has been checked a dialog box appears with the message "Spelling check finished". End the spelling check:

Click(left) on **OK**

Limits of Spelling Checks

It is important to understand that the spell check feature locates misspelled words by comparing the words in the document to a dictionary file included with the program. This process locates all words in the document that are not included in the dictionary file. Many words, such as proper names of persons, places, or things, will be treated as mistakes because that are not include in the dictionary file. Since the number of words in the dictionary file is limited to about 100,000 words, unusual or technical terms will also be treated as mistakes even though they may be spelled correctly.

When such words are displayed in the Spell Check dialog box you must skip the words with the **Ignore** or **Ignore All** command.

On the other hand, a spell check does not guarantee that your document is without errors. Mistakes in grammar, e.g., using "their" instead of "they're" or using "he don't " instead of "he doesn't," would not be treated as mistakes because even though the words are used incorrectly, they are spelled accurately. As helpful as a spell check is in catching errors, it cannot substitute for careful proofreading.

The best course of action is to use the Spell Check to locate all of the obvious errors before you take the time to carefully read through your document.

Scrolling with the Keyboard

In addition to scrolling the display with the mouse and scroll bar you can use the **[Pg Up]** and **[Pg Dn]** keys to scroll up or down one window at a time. However, when you use the keyboard to scroll, the position of the cursor in the document is changed. Enter:

```
[Pg Up]
```

The document scrolls up one window. The cursor remains in the same relative position in the window, i.e., two lines from the top and 1.5 inches from the left margin. However, since the text in the window is different the cursor is now positioned on the word "just " instead of "Auntie".

Thesaurus

The Thesaurus can be used to display list of words with similar meanings to the words you have used in your document. The lists help you improve your writing by suggesting words that might be used in place of the word you used originally. Figure 4-20 shows the thesaurus dialog box.

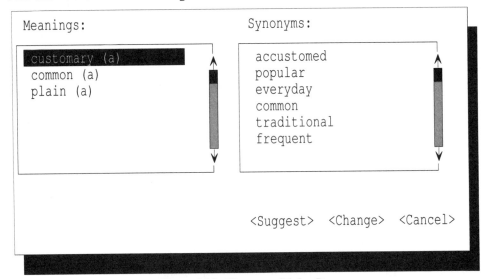

Figure 4-20. Thesaurus Dialog Box.

For example, suppose you wanted to replace the word "ordinary " with a synonym. Begin by placing the cursor on the word you want to look up:

```
Click(left) on ordinary
```

The **Thesaurus** command is found on the Options menu:

```
Click(left) on Options
Click(left) on Thesaurus
```

Works displays a dialog box, as shown in Figure 4-20, which shows two lists of words. The box on the left lists the main categories of meaning of the selected word. Each word in this list is designated as a part of speech by a letter enclosed in parentheses, e.g., (n) for noun, (v) for verb, (a) for adjective or (o) for other parts of speech. The box on the right lists synonyms for the highlighted word in the left box.

In this example, the selected word "ordinary" could be used to mean either customary, common, or plain.

In this case the word "ordinary" is used in the sense of "plain", i.e., a "plain" telephone line, nothing special required. To display a list of synonyms for "plain ", highlight that word in the left box using the mouse:

```
Click(left) on plain(a)
```

The Synonyms box displays the words "commonplace" and "homely". It displays the synonyms for "common". Try this on your own. You will find correct command at the end of the chapter under Exercise 1.

The Synonyms box shows a list of words that are similar in meaning to "common". You can replace the word currently in the text, "ordinary", with any of the words in the Meanings and Synonyms boxes by clicking on the desired replacement and then left clicking on Change.

If you want to explore a particular synonym more closely you can use the Suggest option. When Suggest is selected the program looks up that word in the Thesaurus and displays meanings and synonyms based on that word instead of the word used in the document.

For example, the last word in the current synonym list is "conventional". A "conventional " telephone line has the correct meaning but the word "conventional " sounds a bit formal for a personal letter. To explore words related to "conventional" use the Suggest option:

```
Click(left) on conventional
Click(left) on Suggest
```

The boxes now show meanings and synonyms for "conventional". Note that one of the meanings of "conventional " is "ordinary", the word that you started with.

In this case, the word "standard" would probably be a good replacement for "ordinary":

```
Click(left) on standard
Click(left) on Change
```

The word "standard" replaces "ordinary" in the document.

Limits of the Thesaurus

It is important to keep in mind that the Thesaurus is not a substitute for a dictionary. The Thesaurus helps remind you of words, whose meaning you already know, that are related to a given word. The Thesaurus cannot tell you the exact meaning or usage of a given term. It can only suggest the use of words because they fall into a similar category as the selected word. You will find that from time to time you will need to use an actual dictionary to find the meaning or shades or meaning of certain unfamiliar words.

SAVING AND PRINTING

Saving and printing are two activities that have a similar function; they both copy the information contained in the document window to a different media. Saving copies the information from the window into a file on the disk. Printing copies the text from the window onto the paper inserted in your printer.

Which should you do first? The Works program does not care whether you print or save first. However, as a general rule you should save the document you are working on from time to time in order to avoid losing your document in the case of an accident with your printer or a power failure. Once a document has been saved in a disk file, it can always be loaded into a window again and then edited or printed. If you only print your document but do not save it as a disk file, you will have only the printed copy left.

Saving a Document (To Hard Disk)

The **File Save** command transfers the information in the current document window to a file on the disk. This process creates a permanent copy of the document which can be used or modified at some later time. Information stored in disk files remains in the computer system after you exit the program or turn off the computer. The information will stay on the disk until you specifically delete it, e.g., by using the **File Management Delete File** command.

The first time you use the **File Save** command with a new document, you must assign the document a file name. This name will be used to identify the document file from that point on. The name you select will appear in the title bar where WORD1.WPS currently appears.

Once a document has been assigned a file name, the program will update the disk file with any additions, changes or deletions made in the document window each time you use the **File Save** command. Note that if you make changes but do not save the file, the disk file will contain the last saved version of the document.

The type of names that can be used for disk file names must follow these rules:

1. The file name can be 1 to 8 characters in length.

2. You can use letters A-Z, numbers 0-9, or special characters such as !@#$%^&(){}-_.

3. You cannot use space as part of the file nor can you use any of the following special characters:.(period),(comma):(colon);(semicolon)/\"'[]|<>=+

All files created from word processing windows are automatically assigned a file extension .WPS which identifies them as Works word processing files.

Making up file names is a bit of an art because it is by the file name that you will recognize (or fail to recognize) the document you stored on disk. It is usually a good idea to try to develop a system by which you can come up with file names that have some consistent meaning. For example, when you are storing letters you might use the a four letter abbreviation for the person to whom the letter is being sent and a four digit code for the date of the letter. A letter sent to "Kerri " on 10/8/90 would have a file name of KERR1008. Of course, there are may possible ways to organize file names. It is important to use names that will help you remember what is in the file. Names such as LETTER would be too vague to help you recall the contents of the file.

Save the current document by using the **File Save** command:

```
Click(left) on File
Click(left) on Save
```

The program displays the SAVE FILE dialog box, as shown in Figure 4-21. The name of the file is entered on the line labeled Save file as:. By default the temporary file name assigned to window when it was created, WORD1.WPS, appears highlighted on that line.

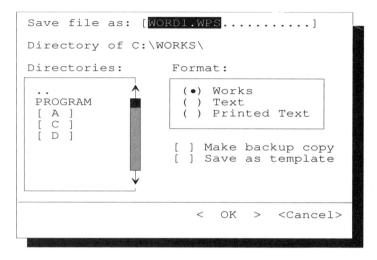

```
Save file as: [WORD1.WPS..........]

Directory of C:\WORKS\

Directories:          Format:

  ..                   (•) Works
PROGRAM                ( ) Text
[ A ]                  ( ) Printed Text
[ C ]
[ D ]
                       [ ] Make backup copy
                       [ ] Save as template


                           <  OK  >  <Cancel>
```

Figure 4-21. The Save File Dialog Box.

Replace the default file name with your own file name. Note that it is not necessary to enter the .WPS extension since Works will add that to the file name automatically. In this case enter:

kerr1008 [return]

The program will copy the information contained in the current window into a disk file called KERR1008.WPS. As soon as that is done, it will take a brief second, the name in the title bar at the top of the window will change to KERR1008.WPS indicating that the save operation has been successfully completed.

It is probably a good idea not to wait until you complete a document before you save it. There are many times when your work will be interrupted. As a rule, you should save the document each time you leave the computer. This ensures that you can recover your document should something or someone disrupt the session while you are away from the machine.

Printing a Document

If the document text is complete you can create a printed copy, assuming that you have a printer correctly attached to your computer. (See Chapters 1 and 3 for information about printers.) If you do not have a printer skip this section and continue at "Closing a Window".

Printing operation are carried out from the Print menu:

Click(left) on **Print**

The program displays the Print pulldown menu, as shown in Figure 4-22. The menu has three sections: normal printing (plus special print options such as printing label), commands for inserting page breaks and running headings, and printer setup.

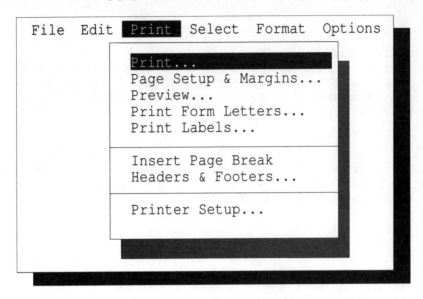

Figure 4-22. The Print Pulldown Menu.

In this case select the Print option for normal printing:

The program displays the PRINT dialog box, as shown in Figure 4-23.

```
Number of copies: [1    ]

[ ] Print specific pages
    Pages: [            ]

[ ] Print to file
    File name: [          ]

[ ] Draft quality

              <Print>   <Cancel>
```

Figure 4-23. The Print Dialog Box.

The most important item in the dialog box is the setting for the number of copies to print. The default value is one copy. The other options are: printing specific pages, printing to file, and draft quality.

Print Specific Pages

If your document contains more than one page you can use this option to print a specific range of pages. For example entering 2:5 would print pages 2 through 5. If you entered 2,5 the program would print page 2 and page 5, skipping pages 3 and 4. You can combine individual pages with ranges. For example, 2,10:15 would print page 2, skip to 10, and print 10 through 15.

Print to File

This option is used when you do not have a printer available. You can select to send the printed output to a disk file. The file can be used with another computer that has a printer but does not have a copy of Works.

Draft Quality

Some printers, such as the IBM Proprinter XL, will print a low quality, high speed draft. Select this option to speed up the printing process when you are not concerned with quality. Note that not all printers have a draft mode. If your printer does not a draft mode then this option is ignored.

Print the document by selecting the Print option in the dialog box:

```
Click(left) on Print
```

The document is printed and the program returns to the document window.

Closing a Window

Saving or printing a document does not remove the document window from the screen. The document window will stay active until you exit the Works program or explicitly close the window. This enables you to work on several documents at the same time, since each is displayed in its own document window.

When you no longer want to work with a given document you can close the window using the keyboard or mouse. The **Close** command is found on the File menu.

The mouse method is even easier than the keyboard method because each window has a special button in the upper left corner of the window, as shown in Figure 4-24.

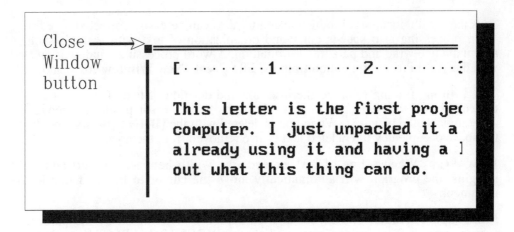

Figure 4-24. The Close Window Button.

Close the document window using the mouse:

Click(left) on **the Close button**

The window is removed from the screen display and the program once again displays the File pulldown menu. Keep in mind that if you have not saved the document before you closed the window, Works would have displayed a message box asking if you wanted to save any changes made to the document since it was last saved.

Exit Works by selecting the Exit Works option from the File menu:

Click(left) on **Exit Works**

You have now completed your first word processing project.

SUMMARY

In this chapter you have learned the basic skills need to create, edit, save, and print most documents. While the Works word processor has additional features to offer, the commands discussed in this chapter form the basis of all word processing operations.

Word Processing. Word processing is used to create documents in which text is organized in paragraphs. Word processing eliminates the problems and frustrations associated with document product since mistakes can be easily corrected by editing. Word processing also speeds entry and organization of text with features such as automatic line wrap and paragraph formatting. A word processing window is created with the Word Processing option from the **File Create New Window** command.

Text Editing. Editing refers to the insertion and deletion of text. Text is inserted at the cursor position. All of the text to the right of the cursor position is moved to accommodate the new text. When text is deleted with the **[Del]** or **[backspace]** keys, the space occupied by the deleted text is also removed from the document.

Line Wrap. When a line of text exceeds the width between the left and right margins, the program will automatically move the cursor to the next line in the document.

Paragraph Formats. The layout of a paragraph is determined by the paragraph format settings. The settings are found on the INDENTS & SPACING dialog box found on the Format menu. Paragraph formats fall into four categories: indents from the left and right margins; spacing before, after, or between lines of a paragraph; alignment of text on the left or right margins, centered between the margins, or justified; and how paragraphs are treated if they fall at the end of page. When you start a new document Works applies the default settings to all new paragraphs.

Shortcut Keys. Works allows you to apply specific formatting settings by using special shortcut key combinations.

Indents. Paragraph indents reduce the width of the lines by moving the text in from the left or right margins.

Spell Check. This program checks the spelling of the words in your document by comparing them to the words in the dictionary file. When a mistake is encountered you can request that the program display a list of correct spellings. The **Check Spelling** command is located on the Options menu.

Thesaurus. The Thesaurus can be used to find alternatives for words used in your documents. The **Thesaurus** command is located on the Options menu.

Saving. Text entered into a document window is stored in a permanent form until the text is saved in a disk file using the **File Save** command. Files must be assigned a unique file name of 1 to 8 characters. A file extension of .WPS is automatically added to all word processing files.

Printing. The text of the document can be sent to a printer by using the **Print** command. You have the option of making more than one copy of the document if desired.

Closing Windows. Clicking on the close window button in the upper left hand corner of the window will remove the window form the screen. If the text has not been saved, Works will ask you if you now want to save or discard the text or changes to the text.

EXERCISES

Exercise 1

Display synonyms for the word "common":

Click(left) on *common*

Chapter 5

Formatting a Letter

This chapter will show you how to expand the power of word processing by formatting text and paragraphs, and copying, cutting, and pasting. The skills discussed in Chapter 1 enable you to create, correct, and update documents. The text in the letter consisted of two types: short line and full text paragraphs.

Short Line Paragraphs. Short line paragraphs consist of lines of text. None of these lines is long enough to reach the right margin of the page requiring you to enter a line ending command, [**Shift-return**] at the end of each line, with the exception of the last line in the group which was ended with a [**return**]. An address block is an example of a short line paragraph.

Full Text Paragraphs. These paragraphs contained one or more sentences which create lines that filled the page between the left and right margins. In these paragraphs the line endings were automatically inserted by the program. A [**return**] was entered only once, at the end of the paragraph.

The goal of this chapter is to add to those basic skills some of the more sophisticated features and commands available in Works word processing. These features will allow you more flexibility in editing and formatting. They can help you produce a variety of text layouts which can be used to present information in forms other than short line or full text paragraphs such as those created in Chapter 4. This chapter will show you how to:

- •Retrieve an existing document
- •Cut, Copy and Paste text
- •Format characters (bold, underline, etc.)
- •Format paragraphs (indents, borders)
- •Perform multiple window operations

You will learn these skills by writing another letter which will contain a more varied and interesting assortment of paragraph styles and forms. Begin by loading the Works program in the usual manner:

> Click(left) on the *Microsoft Works* symbol

TEXT AND PARAGRAPH ENHANCEMENTS

Begin this project by creating a new word processing document. Note that creating a new word processing document requires you to select the first item on the file menu and then the first item in the following dialog box. This means that pressing **[return]** twice, after you have started Works, will open a new word processing window. Enter:

> **[return]***(2 times)*

The letter written in Chapter 4 was an informal letter. For example, the person writing the letter did not create a letter head at the top of the page that identified the source of the letter. This is fine for a personal letter but more formal letters such as business correspondence usually require such a letter head.

Begin this letter by entering the information required for the letter head:

> **LaFish Enterprises [Shift-return]**
> **Carolyn Q. LaFish [Shift-return]**
> **1250 Pine Street [Shift-return]**
> **Walnut Creek, CA 94598**

Centering

In order to make the letter heading stand out from the rest of the document these are several modifications and enhancements you can make to the text and the paragraph. The most obvious is to center the lines between the paragraphs. In Chapter 4 you learned how to center paragraphs using the shortcut command, **[Ctrl-c].** But suppose you don't recall the shortcut key. You can always find the commands you need by browsing the pulldown menus:

Click(left) on **Format**

The **Center** command found midway down the menu, will center the current paragraph:

Click(left) on **Center**

All of the lines in the paragraph are centered between the margins. Keep in mind that the lines operate as a group because of the **[Shift-return]** used at the end of each line. If you had placed a **[return]** at the end of each line, Works would treat each line as a separate paragraph and center only the line on which the cursor was positioned. This is the primary advantage of using the **[Shift-return]** to create short line paragraphs.

Text Formats

When you type in text Works assumes that you want the character to print as normal text. However, from time to time you may want to enhance the printing of a word or a phrase so that it stands out from the rest of the text. If you were using a typewriter, the only method available to accomplish this is the use of an underline. Like the typewriter, Works can also underline text. In addition, you can also specify bold and italic printing styles. What is possibly even more important, these text formats can be added to or removed from any part of the document. As with inserting and deleting text, the word processor allows you to change your mind as much as you like without getting stuck with something that you don't like.

For example, in the current address block you might want to change the text format of the first line, LaFish Enterprises, from normal to bold text. Adding text formats to existing text requires a two step process: selecting text and choosing format.

Select Text

Before you can apply a format, such as bold, you need to indicate what part of the document you want to alter. This is done by highlighting the characters, words, or paragraphs that you want to change. You can highlight text using either the keyboard or the mouse.

Choose Format

Once you have highlighted the text you want to change you can then apply the desired format, e.g., bold or underline, using the pull down menus or the shortcut key commands for the desired format.

The two-step method used by Works is called an object oriented command structure. In other words, most Works operations are point and shoot commands. Pointing refers to the highlighting process which indicates the object, i.e., the section of the document that is to be changed. The shoot step is the selection of the command from the menu. Traditionally computer software has been command oriented. In command oriented systems, you first select the command and then tell the computer where to apply that command. The consensus today among computer users is that object oriented programs are much easier to use and understand.

Selecting Text with the Mouse

One of the best uses for the mouse is to select sections of the document for highlighting. The mouse can be used to make selections in two ways: clicking and dragging.

Clicking

You can select an item by clicking the mouse at a specific location on the screen, as shown in Table 5-1.

Table 5-1. Clicking.

Mouse Action	Highlight
Drag(left)	character by character
Drag(right) on word	word by word
Drag(left) in left margin	line by line
Drag(right) in left margin	paragraph by paragraph

Dragging

If you drag the mouse you will highlight as many items as you cover during the drag, as shown in Table 5-2. For example, if you drag the mouse over 3 characters the highlight will cover those three characters.

Table 5-2. Dragging.

Mouse Action	Highlight
Drag(left)	character by character
Drag(right) on word	word by word
Drag(left) in left margin	line by line
Drag(right) in left margin	paragraph by paragraph

In this example you want to highlight the first line of the address block. You can highlight a single line by clicking (left) in the left margin area opposite the line you want to highlight. The left margin area is the space between the left edge of the window and the "[" that indicates the margin on the ruler line, as shown in Figure 5-1.

Figure 5-1. Click or Drag Mouse in Left Margin Area to Select Lines and Paragraphs.

Use the click(left) method to highlight the first line. Point the mouse at the left margin opposite the first line of the text, as shown in Figure 5-1. Then select the line by clicking:

Click(left) in margin opposite *Lafish Enterprises*

Works automatically highlights the entire first line. You can now apply any format to this text.

Applying a Text Format

To change the text to bold, you can use the **Bold** command on the Format menu or the keyboard shortcut command **[Ctrl-b].** Use the **menu** command:

Click(left) on **Format**
Click(left) on **Bold**

The highlighted text changes to bold text. The bold text is indicated by a slight thickening of the characters. In addition to the on screen appearance of the text, Works displays the letter B on the status line. The status line display is important because not all of the attributes Works can add to text appear on the screen exactly as they will print. The status line display shows you the actual formatting of whatever text the cursor or highlight is positioned on. Note that when you apply a text format, no change is made in the highlighting. The entire first line remains highlighted and will continue to be highlighted until you select a different part of the document, move the cursor, or begin inserting new text.

The fact that the highlight remains positioned on the text even after you have issued a command is very useful. It allows you to add or change the attributes of the same textwithout having to highlight it again. For example, suppose you wanted the text to be both bold and underlined. You can add the underline attribute to the currently highlighted text by using the menu command **Format Underline** or the shortcut key **[Ctrl-u]**. Enter:

```
[Ctrl-u]
```

The program adds an underline to the text. Also, the status line shows the letters "BU" to indicate that the text is bold and underlined.

Removing Text Attributes

One of the advantages of word processing is that attributes that are added to text can also be removed without disturbing the document. For example, suppose that you change your mind and want to remove the underline from the text. In Works you cannot directly remove a text attribute. Instead you would return the text to plain text and then reapply only the bold attribute. Change the text back to plain text by selecting the **Plain text** command from the Format menu (or the shortcut **[Ctrl-spacebar]**):

```
Click(left) on Format
Click(left) on Plain text
```

Both the underline and bold format have been removed from the text. Add the bold format, this time, using the keyboard shortcut **[Ctrl-b]**:

```
[Ctrl-b]
```

The text has been changed to bold only once again. Note that all of these operations have taken place without altering the location of the highlight.

Drag Highlighting

Clicking the mouse is designed to highlight one unit of text (a word, line or paragraph) at a time. If you want to include several items, i.e., a group of consecutive words, lines, or paragraphs, you would drag the mouse instead of simply clicking.

Suppose that you wanted to change the last three lines of the address block to italic text. The last three lines of the paragraph do not constitute a specific unit of text, i.e., a word, line or paragraph. You can select this text by dragging the mouse over the text. You could drag (left) over the text to highlight word by word or drag (left) down the margin to highlight line by line. Since you want to include three entire lines dragging in the margin would be the fastest way to highlight the desired text:

```
Point at the left margin opposite Carolyn
Drag(left) down to Walnut Creek
```

Note that once you begin to drag(left) in the margin the highlight advances by whole lines. This ensures that you have included all of the text on these lines in the highlight. Apply italics to these lines. Italic text is printed with a slant to the right:

```
Click(left) on Format
Click(left) on Italic
```

The highlighted lines now appear as italic text. The status line shows I to indicate italic text.

Paragraph Borders

Another way to make a paragraph stand out from the rest of the document is the addition of paragraph borders. A paragraph border is a line drawn around the paragraph. Works allows you to add border lines above, below, and on the left and right of the paragraph. If you select outline, a box is drawn around the entire paragraph. You can also specify the type of line to use in drawing the border: normal (single line), bold, or double line. Add a border to the letter head paragraph:

```
Click(left) on Format
```

At the bottom of the format menu is the Borders option. The program displays the Borders dialog box, as shown in Figure 5-2.

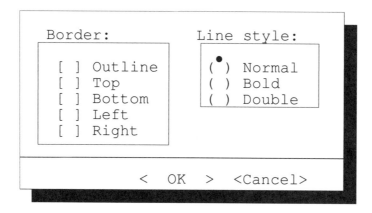

Figure 5-2. Borders Dialog Box.

To place a box around the letter head paragraph select the Outline check box:

Click(left) on **Outline**
Click(left) on **Ok**

The program draws a border around the entire paragraph, as shown in Figure 5-3. Note that when you perform paragraph format operations, the cursor or highlight can be located on any part of the paragraph. The command will affect the entire paragraph regardless of the cursor or highlight location.

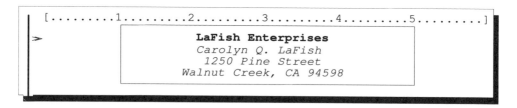

Figure 5-3. Border Drawn around Paragraph.

Border and Indents

When an outline or other type of border is drawn around a paragraph, the length of the lines is determined by the margins of the paragraph, not the length of the text. In the current example, you can see that the outline box extends across the entire width of the page between the left and right margins even though the lines of text are too short to reach the margins.

Suppose you want to draw the box so that the left and right sides were closer to the text which is in the center of the page. If you indented the paragraph one inch from the left and right margins, the sides of the box would be drawn in one inch on each side.

Display the Indents & Spacing dialog box:

Click(left) on **Format**
Click(left) on **Indents & Spacing**

Enter one inch indents for the left and right:

[Tab] [Tab]
1 [return]

The program adjusts the width of the border outline to fit the indent margins of the paragraph.

Returning to Normal Paragraph

You have now completed the formatting of the letter head section of the document. You can now begin the actual text entry. Move the cursor to the end of the paragraph by entering:

[Ctrl-down]

Create a new paragraph by entering:

[return]

What has happened? When you pressed **[return]** Works create a new paragraph with the exact same formatting (italic text, outline border, one inch indents) as the previous paragraph. However, in this case you only want the first paragraph on the page to have those unusual attribute. How can you return to the normal type of paragraph?

Works provides two formatting commands, **Plain Text** and **Normal Paragraph** that will reset the selected text or paragraphs to the default settingsplain text and not paragraph formatting. You can select those commands from the Format menu or use the shortcut keys **[Ctrl-spacebar]** and **[Ctrl-x]** respectively. Since returning to a normal paragraph is a common command learning the shortcut key method is probably a good idea. Enter:

[Ctrl-spacebar] [Ctrl-x]

The paragraph is now back to the default settings for Works word processing text. You should remember this combination since you can use it to remove any unwanted formatting that you encounter.

CUT, PASTE, AND COPY

One of the most important differences between word processing and typing is that in word processing you can make use of text which you have typed before. Works allows you to cut or copy text from one location in a document or even another document window and paste it into a different location or document window.

For example, suppose that you wanted to send a letter to someone to whom you had already written. Instead of typing in the address block again, you could copy it from the existing document. Conversely, now that you have created a letter head for your correspondence, you might like to copy that paragraph into other letters.

Works enables you to exchange information between different documents by allowing you to have multiple document windows open at the same time.

Opening an Existing Document

The first task will be to copy the address and salutation from the document you created in Chapter 4 into the current document. In order to perform that operation you must first open a document window for that file:

Click(left) on **File**
Click(left) on **Open Existing File**

The file selection dialog box appears. You should find, listed under Word Processor, the file name KERR1008.WPS. Open the document using the double click method:

Double click(left) on **KERR1008.WPS**

When the program opens the KERR1008.WPS file it creates a new window into which it places the text from that document. The new window is placed in front of the WORD1.WPS window in which you had been working, as shown in Figure 5-4. Works stacks the document windows on the desktop. Note that the KERR1008.WPS window is slightly smaller than the WORD1.WPS window so that the new window does not completely cover the previous window.

If you look closely at the title bars you will notice that there are some differences in appearance. The title bar of the KERR1008.WPS window is brighter than the WORD1.WPS title bar. Also, KERR1008.WPS shows a double line across the title bar while the other window has only a single line. The difference in appearance is used to indicate which of the windows is the active window. The active window, in this case KERR1008.WPS, is the one in which the cursor is position. Any text entered or commands issued effect the active window only.

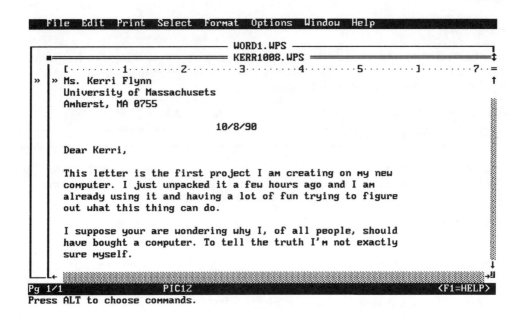

```
  File  Edit  Print  Select  Format  Options  Window  Help

                    ══════════ WORD1.WPS ══════════
                    ══════════ KERR1008.WPS ═══════════════
     [········1········2········3········4········5········]········7··=
 »  » Ms. Kerri Flynn                                                  ↑
      University of Massachusets
      Amherst, MA 0755

                    10/8/90

      Dear Kerri,

      This letter is the first project I am creating on my new
      computer. I just unpacked it a few hours ago and I am
      already using it and having a lot of fun trying to figure
      out what this thing can do.

      I suppose your are wondering why I, of all people, should
      have bought a computer. To tell the truth I'm not exactly
      sure myself.

 Pg 1/1                    PIC1Z                            <F1=HELP>
Press ALT to choose commands.
```

Figure 5-4. Two Document Windows Open on the Desktop.

Switching Active Windows

When you have more than one window open on the desktop you will need to change the active window from time to time. There are three ways in which you can change the active window which are described as follows:

The Windows Menu

Unlike most of the menus in Works, the contents of the Windows menu changes so that it can list the names of the windows currently open on the desktop. The windows are listed at the bottom of the menu in the order in which they were created or opened. The windows are assigned command numbers beginning with one. You can activate any open window by selecting it from the windows menu.

[Ctrl-F6]

This key will activate the next window each time it is pressed. When the last open window has been activated pressing the key again will activate the first open window again.

Click(left)

You can activate any window visible on the desktop by clicking the left mouse button on any part of the window. If a window is completely covered by another window you cannot use the click method.

Activate the WORD1.WPS window using the click method:

Click(left) on **WORD1.WPS**

The WORD1.WPS window is activated. This means that the program moves the window forward so that its contents are visible on the screen. Because this window is larger, it obscures the KERR1008.WPS window temporarily.

Since you cannot see the KERR1008.WPS window you must use either the Windows menu or **[Ctrl-F6]** to activate the window. Enter:

[Ctrl-F6]

The active window is switched to KERR1008.WPS.

Copy Between Windows

The KERR1008.WPS window is currently active. Suppose that you want to copy the address block from this document into the new letter you are creating. Highlight the address block paragraph using the mouse. Notice that in order to select an entire paragraph you must use the right mouse button:

Click(right) in the left margin next to *Ms. Kerri...*

You can place a copy of the highlighted text into the clipboard using the Copy command found on the Edit menu or by using the shortcut key command **[Shift-F3]**. Recall that the clipboard is an area in the memory used for temporary storage of text being cut or copied. Use the shortcut command to copy the text:

[Shift-F3]

When the text is copied to the clipboard you see this message: "Select new location and press ENTER. Press ESC to cancel." In this case, the new location for the text is in a different document window. Activate the WORD1.WPS window with the mouse:

```
Click(left) on WORD1.WPS
```

The program activate and displays the WORD1.WPS window. Note that the cursor position in this window has not changed. Insert the copied text into this document by entering:

```
[return]
```

Use the shortcut command to add a line of blank space before the paragraph:

```
[Ctrl-o]
```

The new document now contains the address block copied from the other document window, as shown in Figure 5-5.

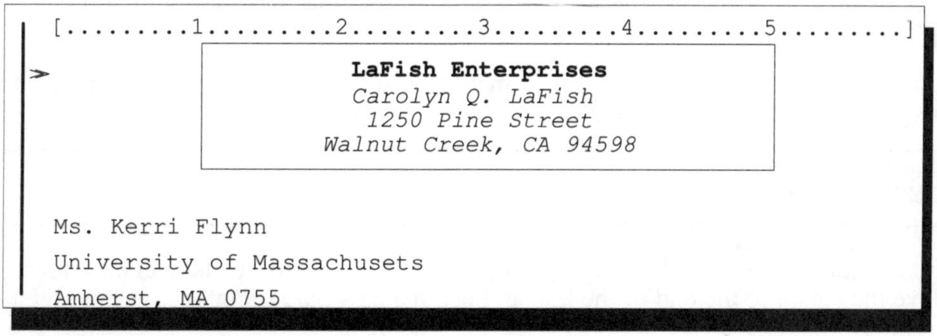

```
  [.........1.........2.........3.........4.........5.........]

>                       LaFish Enterprises
                        Carolyn Q. LaFish
                         1250 Pine Street
                       Walnut Creek, CA 94598


      Ms. Kerri Flynn

      University of Massachusets

      Amherst, MA 0755
```

Figure 5-5. Text Copied from Another Document Window.

Date Codes

The next part of the letter will be the date line. Format this paragraph for one line of blank space before and center alignment using the shortcut keys. Try this on your own. You will find the correct command at the end of the chapter under Exercise 1.

In the previous chapter you used the **Insert Special** command to insert the current date as kept by the system's built in clock/calendar. That command inserted date text into the document. But suppose that you don't intend to finish this letter on the same day that you start writing. In fact, there might be a delays of several days before you actually complete and print the letter. Instead of inserting the date text, you can insert a date print code. A print code is a special symbol, *date* which appears in the text. When the document is printed, Works substitutes the current date, i.e., the date when the document is printed, in place of the code.

You can insert a date code by selecting the Print date option from the Insert Special dialog box (Edit menu) or use the shortcut command **[Ctrl-d].** Enter:

```
[Ctrl-d]
```

The date code is inserted into the document. Keep in mind that although the code looks like text it is really a special symbol. Typing the characters * d a t e * will not create a date code symbol.

Undoing Formats

The **Undo** command found on the Edit menu can be used to undo the effects of commands, such as text or paragraph formats, as well as text insertions and deletions. For example, suppose you add a box to the current paragraph. Try this on your own. You will find the correct command at the end of the chapter under Exercise 2.

If you change your mind about the formatting use the Undo command to return the paragraph to its previous format:

```
Click(left) on Edit
Click(left) on Undo
```

The outline is removed from the paragraph and it returns to its previous format. Move the cursor to the end of the line and begin a new paragraph:

```
[End] [return]
```

APPLYING FORMATS

When you are using a word processor such as the Works word processor you are perform two different levels of activity: editing and formatting.

Editing

Editing refers to all of the operations that affect the text of the document: insert, delete, undo, copy, spell check, etc.

Formatting

Formatting refers to operations that arrange, organize, and enhance the text: line spacing, alignment, indents, bold, italics, etc.

Up to this point you have performed both tasks more or less at the same time. This means that as you enter text, you apply the text and paragraph formats desired immediately after you entered the text.

While this method works perfectly well, it might be useful to consider a different approach in which you separate the two tasks.

Text Entry

First, enter all of the text of the document. This allows you to concentrate on the actual text without getting distracted by formatting issues.

Document Layout

Once the text has been entered, edited and spell checked, you then go through the document a second time and decide how it should be formatted.

This two stage approach has the advantage of having the full text of the document entered when you apply the formats. You can then see exactly how various formats affect the text you have entered.

Instead of entering text for a new letter, save time by copying the paragraphs you entered into the KERR1008.WPS document. Switch to that window using the Windows menu:

Click(left) on **Windows**

The Windows menu is displayed in Figure 5-6. Note that at the bottom of the menu all of the open documents are listed by window (or file) name.

Figure 5-6. Windows Menu Lists Active Open Windows.

Select the KERR1008.WPS document:

```
Click(left) on KERR1008.WPS
```

The KERR1008.WPS window is now active.

Extending a Highlight

Begin by highlighting the salutation paragraph:

```
Click(right) in the left margin next to Dear...
```

Suppose that you decide that you want to highlight more than just the current paragraph. Normally, if you move the mouse or the cursor you remove the current highlight because the program assumes you want to change the highlight to some other part of the document. However, Works includes a command called **Select Text** found on the Select menu. This command turns on the select mode. When the select mode is active moving the cursor with the mouse or the keyboard will extend instead of changing the highlight.

Turn on the select mode with the mouse:

```
Click(left) on Select
Click(left) on Text
```

The select mode is now active. The status bar show EXT indicating that cursor movements will not extend the current highlight. For example, if you click the mouse on any part of the text, you will extend the highlight to that location:

172

```
Click(right) on project
```

The highlight now extends from Dear to project. Moving the cursor with the keyboard will have the same effect. Enter:

```
[down]
```

The highlight extends down one line. Enter:

```
[Ctrl-down]
```

The highlight now covers two paragraphs. In this case you will want to extend the highlight to include all of the rest of the text in this window. Use the keyboard command **[Ctrl-End]** to jump the cursor and the highlight to the end of the text:

```
[Ctrl-End]
```

Copy the highlighted text using the shortcut command **[Shift-F3]**:

```
[Shift-F3]
```

Switch to the WORD1.WPS window using the Windows menu. Try this on your own. You will find the correct command at the end of the chapter under Exercise 3.

Paste the copied text into the window by entering:

```
[return]
```

Cut and Paste

A variation on copying text is *cut and paste*. In cut and paste the highlighted text is copied into the clipboard and removed from the document. When you press **[return]** the text is inserted back into the document at a new location. This operation is handy for rearranging words, sentences or paragraphs without having to delete and retype text.

For example, the first paragraph in the body of the letter contains two sentences. The first states that they are creating a letter on their computer. The second states that they have just bought a new computer. The paragraph might be improved if the order of the sentences were reversed placing the two thoughts in the correct time sequence, i.e., first, you buy the computer, and then you use it.

Move the cursor to the first sentence in that paragraph:

```
Click(left) on letter
```

The shortcut key for the *select mode*, **[F8]**, has some special uses when you are highlighting word processor text, as shown in Table 5-3.

Table 5-3. Uses of [F8].

To Highlight	Press
Current word	[F8]*(2 times)*
Current sentence	[F8]*(3 times)*
Current paragraph	[F8]*(4 times)*
Entire document	[F8]*(5 times)*

To highlight the current sentence enter:

```
[F8](3 times)
```

You can cut the text from the document using the **Move** command on the Edit menu or the shortcut key **[F3]**. Enter:

```
[F3]
```

Move the cursor to the location in the text where you want the highlight sentence to be placed. In this case move to the end of the paragraph by entering:

```
[Ctrl-down] [left] [return]
```

The sentence is removed from the beginning of the paragraph and placed at the end. However, because the sentence which was moved was the first sentence in the paragraph, you need to insert a space in front of the sentence once it has been moved to its new location. Enter:

```
[spacebar]
```

Formatting Multiple Paragraphs

The paragraphs that you have copied from the KERR1008.WPS document are written in a block style. Each paragraph begins at the left margin and is separated by a blank line from the previous paragraph.

Another style of writing eliminates the blank line before the paragraphs. Instead the beginning of each paragraph is marked by an indent. This style of formatting has the advantage of using less blank space on a page thus allowing more text to be entered per page.

Suppose that you wanted to change the format of this letter to the indented style. The change in style can be accomplished using the Indents & Spacing dialog box. However, in this case the paragraphs to be formatted have already been entered.

Under normal circumstances paragraph formatting commands effect only the current paragraph. This would mean that you would have to repeat the formatting operations for each of the paragraphs.

However, there is a shortcut. If you issue a formatting command while a section of the document is highlighted, the format will be applied to all of the paragraphs contained (fully or partially) in the highlight. Begin by highlighting all of the paragraphs from the current paragraph to the end of the document. Move the cursor to the beginning of the current paragraph:

```
[Ctrl-up]
```

Shift Key Highlighting

You have already learned several ways to highlight areas of the document. Still another method is the [Shift] cursor move approach. In Works, if you hold down the [Shift] key while entering cursor movement commands, the program will extend the highlight just as it would if the select mode were active.

For example, the [right] key moves the cursor one character to the right. But if you combine the [right] key with [Shift] you will highlight one character at a time:

> **Note**
> Recall that the PS1 has two sets of arrow keys one of which appear as part of the numeric keypad on the right side of the keyboard. If you are using the arrow keys on the numeric keypad the NUM Lock must be off if you want to use the [Shift] extend method.

```
[Shift-right]
```

Instead of moving the cursor to the right, the program highlights the current character. Repeat the keystroke:

```
[Shift-right]
```

The highlight is extended one character to the right. The method works with all basic cursor movement keys. For example, the [End] key moves the cursor to the end of the current line. If you add the [Shift] you will extend the highlight to the end of the line. Enter:

```
[Shift-End]
```

The **[Ctrl-down]** combination moves the cursor to the end of the current paragraph. Even though this command is already a combination, you can add the **[Shift]** to it in order to extend the highlight to the end of the paragraph making the command **[Shift-Ctrl-down]**. This type of keystroke is entered by holding down the **[Shift]** and **[Ctrl]** keys first and then pressing **[down]**. Enter:

[Shift-Ctrl-down]

You can extend the highlight to the end of the document by adding **[Shift]** to the **[Ctrl-End]** command. Enter:

[Shift-Ctrl-End]

The highlight is extended to the end of the document. Note that when you extend the highlight in this manner most of the text is scrolled off the window display. Recall that using the mouse on the scroll bar will scroll the display without changing the cursor or highlight position:

Click(left) on up button on the vert. scroll bar*(14 times)*

Since each click scrolls the text up one line, 14 clicks reveal 14 lines of highlighted text in the window. Note that in this instance the selection is too large to be displayed entirely in a single window.

First Line Indents

Now that the text is highlighted, any formatting commands issued will affect all of the highlighted text. To change any part of the paragraph formatting, display the Indents & Spacing dialog box:

Click(left) on **Format**
Click(left) on **Indents & Spacing**

Note

The dialog box is displayed with all of the settings blank in contrast to the usual display in which the current settings are displayed. This is because the highlighted text contains paragraphs with different settings so that no one dialog box could give an accurate picture of the formats contained within the highlight.

The style you want to apply to the highlighted text is one in which the first line of each paragraph is indented 1/2 inch there is no extra space between paragraphs. In addition you might want to use the justified alignment style so that the paragraph have an even right margin.

To create an indent on the first line of each paragraph you need to enter the size of the indent in the 1st line indent text box:

[Tab]
.5

Next, specify 0 inch space before each paragraph:

[Tab] *(3 times)*

Set the alignment as justified and save the changes:

Click(left) on **Justified**
Click(left) on **Ok**

All of the paragraphs contained in the highlight are formatted according to the new settings, as shown in Figure 5-7, which changes the letter from a block to an indented style.

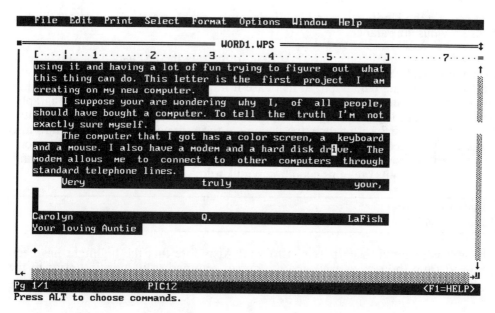

Figure 5-7. Multiple Paragraphs Formatted with One Command.

However, there is a problem. The last paragraph in the text—the closing of the letter—looks very strange. The words in two of the lines are spread across the margin width separated by large gaps of blank space. Why? How can it be corrected?

The reason for this odd appearance is the use of the Justified alignment style on a short line paragraph. The justified alignment style works nicely for text paragraph such as those in the body of the letter. The program adds spaces in between the words on the line to ensure that the line ends with a letter rather than blank space creating an even right margin. Justification does not affect the last of the paragraph which ends with a [return].

However, when you have a short line, ended with [Shift-return], the justified style will usually distort the appearance of the text because it inserts too many spaces between the words in order to fill the entire line.

You can see that application of the new format to the last paragraph in the document is a mistake. At this point you have to alternative ways to proceed which are:

Reformat the Last Paragraph

This approach leave the new format in place and requires you to then change the format of the last paragraph in order for its text to be displayed properly.

Undo the Multiple Paragraph Format

You can use the **Undo** command to eliminate the new formatting and return the text to its previous appearance.

Which method should you choose? At first, formatting the last paragraph might seem to be the logical choice. However, it is possible that you don't recall what format was used for the closing paragraph. In that case it might be better to restore the original formats with **Undo** and then apply the new style to only the body text paragraphs. The Undo method is usually the safest course to take when you have made a formatting error since it restores the document to its previous condition. **Undo** also gives you the freedom to experiment with different types of formatting. If you don't like the effect, as is the case in this example, you can simply Undo the command. Restore the text to its previous condition with **Undo:**

```
Click(left) on Edit
Click(left) on Undo
```

The text is restored to its previous format. Also note that the highlight has been removed from the text as well and the cursor returned to its position prior to the highlight.

Repeating Format Commands

Now that the text has been restored to its previous style you can apply the indent style to only those paragraphs in the body of the letter. Format the current paragraph to the indent style:

```
Click(left) on Format
Click(left) on Indents & Spacing
```

```
[Tab]
.5
[Tab] (3 times)0
0
```

```
Click(left) on Justified
Click(left) on Ok
```

The current paragraph is now formatted for the indent style. But wasn't it a mistake not to have highlighted all three paragraphs before you set the format? The answer is that Works provides a special keystroke command, **[Shift-F7]**, that will repeat the last formatting command. You can use **[Shift-F7]** to apply the same format to another part of the document without having to use the dialog box again. For example, to format the next paragraph with the same settings as the previous paragraph you would move the cursor to the next paragraph and use the **[Shift-F7]** repeat command:

```
[Ctrl-down] [Shift-F7]
```

Format the third body text paragraph:

```
Click(left) on The computer...
```
```
[Ctrl-down] [Shift-F7]
```

All three paragraphs have the correct format. The **[Shift-F7]** repeat command enabled you to format all three without having to return to the dialog box even though you did not highlight the paragraphs before you entered the formatting settings. The **[Shift-F7]** repeat command is not consecutive and therefore cannot be contained in a single highlight. Keep in mind that **[Shift-F7]** will repeat the last copy or format command issued.

Last Paragraph Format

If you look closely at the last paragraph in the letter, the closing, you will notice that the lines appear to be centered, rather than indented. You can check the format settings of any paragraph by placing the cursor in that paragraph and displaying the Indent & Spacing dialog box:

Click(left) on *Carolyn*
Click(left) on **Format**
Click(left) on **Indent & Spacing**

The dialog box shows that the paragraph is center aligned with no indents. Recall that the current alignment is indicated by the option in the Alignment box which had the black dot next to it. Exit the dialog box:

Click(left) on **Cancel**

How did this happen? The answer involves a quirk in the program that occurs when you paste text onto the end of a document. Recall that in the last formatted paragraph, the date code, in the WORD1.WPS document was formatted as center aligned before you pasted in the text from the KERR1008.WPS document . When you pasted in the text from the other window, Works attached the current format to the past paragraph in the pasted text since that was the current format in the document at the time. Ideally, the program ought to have maintained the paragraph format used in the original document but as you can see that is not the case.

Copying Formats

How can you resolve this problem? One method would be to return to the KERR1008.WPS window and use the Indent & Spacing dialog to display the format used in that document for paragraph. Then switch back to WORD1.WPS and apply that format to the closing paragraph.

The **Copy Special** command, located on the Edit menu allows you to copy text or paragraph formats without having to copy the actual text or paragraph. You can use this command to format text or paragraphs using an existing format as a model. In the current example, you already have the text of the closing entered into the document. All that is missing is the paragraph format.

Switch to the KERR1008.WPS window:

Click(left) on **Windows**
Click(left) on *KERR1008.WPS*

Place the cursor in the paragraph that has the format you want to duplicate:

> Click(left) on *Auntie*

Instead of using the **Copy** command use **Copy Special**:

> Click(left) on **Edit**
> Click(left) on **Copy Special**

Return to WORD1.WPS:

> Click(left) on *WORD1.WPS* title bar

The cursor is still positioned in the closing paragraph. Enter:

> **[return]**

The program displays a dialog box, as shown in Figure 5-8, that provides the option of copying either the text or paragraph format. The default is paragraph format.

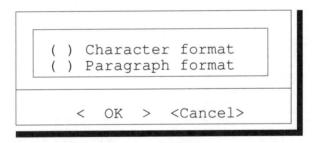

```
( )  Character format
( )  Paragraph format

    <  OK  >  <Cancel>
```

Figure 5-8. Dialog Box with Two Format Options.

Complete the operation by entering:

> **[return]**

The paragraph format changes to the indented format copied from the other document. Copying formats, either text or paragraph, is very important because it allows you to use existing formats, either in the current document or in other windows as models. You can use the **Copy Special** command to quickly format a new document by using formats you have already established with previous documents. This saves you time and improves the consistency of your document since the same styles appear in all of your documents.

You have now completed your second document. Use the Close button to save and put away both of the open documents:

Click(left) on Close button

Works shows a dialog box that shows command button for saving or discarding the text in the WORD1.WPS window. Save the text in a disk file:

Click(left) on **Yes**

Enter a valid file name, one to eight characters, for the new document. Keep in mind that this name must be unique. If you give this document the same name as an existing document, the new document file will erase the old document. In this case the name will be KERR1030 in keeping with the naming system created in the previous project. Enter:

KERR1030 [return]

Close the KERR1008.WPS window:

Click(left) on Close button

Note that when you closed this document no dialog box was displayed. Works will only display the save dialog box only when a window contains new or revised text.

If you are done working you can exit Works:

Click(left) on **Exit Works**

If you want to go on to the next project, leave the program running. The next project will introduce the use and concepts of spreadsheet modeling.

SUMMARY

This chapter illustrated two important concepts that expand the power of word processing: text and paragraph formats and copying, cutting, and pasting.

182

Text and Paragraph Formats. You can enhance the appearance of text and paragraphs by adding special effects such as bold or italic text or paragraph borders.

Copy, Cut, and Paste. Works contains a number of commands that allow you to create text and formats by using existing documents or sections of documents. You can use Copy Special to copy the formatting, text or paragraph, from one area to another without having to duplicate the text.

The special techniques discussed were:

Text Formats. The style of text can be enhanced with bold, underline, or italic printing. These options can be used individually or combined, e.g., bold italic or bold underlined text.

Paragraph Borders. Works can draw single, bold or double lines at the top, bottom, left, or right sides of paragraphs. The outline option encloses a paragraph in a box. The width of the box is determined by the paragraph indents, if any.

Selecting Text. Text and paragraph formats can be applied to specific sections of the text by selecting the desired text before you apply the formatting commands. Once the text is selected, any formats are applied to all of the highlighted text.

Keyboard Selection. You can select text using the keyboard. The **[F8]** key can select text into two ways. First, pressing **[F8]** once activate the select mode. In this mode all cursor movements made with the keyboard or mouse will extend the current selection instead of moving the cursor. If **[F8]** is pressed more than once it will select the current word, sentence, paragraph or document respectively.

Mouse Selection. Selections can be made with the mouse using both buttons and click or drag operations, as shown in Table 5-4.

Table 5-4. Mouse Selection.

Mouse Action	Highlight
Click(right) on word	one word
Click(left) in left margin	one line
Click(right) in left margin	one paragraph
Drag(left)	character by character
Drag(right) on word	word by word
Drag(left) in left margin	line by line
Drag(right) in left margin	paragraph by paragraph

Shift Key Selection. You can select using cursor movement keys by combining the key combination with **[Shift]**.

Windows. Each document, created or opened, is placed into its own window. Each new window created is slightly smaller than the previous window so that the title bars can be seen when the windows are stacked on top of one another. You can change the active window by clicking on the window (if visible), selecting the window name from the Windows menu or using **[Ctrl-F6]** to rotate through all the open windows. Information and formats can be copied or cut from one window to another enabling different document to exchange text and/or formats.

Cut, Copy, and Paste. These operations enable you to move or copy text from one location to another in the same document or into documents in different windows.

Copy/Repeat Formats. Multiple format operations can be carried, in addition to highlighting, by using the **Copy Special** or **Repeat Format ([Shift-F7])** commands. **Copy Special** copies the text or paragraph format of the current selected item to the indicated location. The repeat command, **[Shift-F7]** repeats the last format command and applies it to the current selection.

EXERCISES

Exercise 1

Format paragraph with 1 blank line before and center alignment:

```
[Ctrl-o] [Ctrl-c]
```

Exercise 2

Add a border outline to the current paragraph:

```
Click(left) on Format
Click(left) on Border
Click(left) on Outline
Click(left) on Ok
```

Exercise 3

Switch windows:

```
Click(left) on Windows
Click(left) on WORD1.WPS
```

Chapter 6

Budgeting Expenses

T his chapter introduces the use of spreadsheet models to address tasks which require mathematical calculations. However, it is important to understand that spreadsheet modeling is more than just a type of computerized calculator. It is a very special approach to the entire field or mathematical and arithmetic problem solving.

In Chapters 4 and 5 you saw how word processing not only provides a better way to type but creates an environment in which you take a whole approach to writing changes because of the abilities presented by the word processor. Because the word processor eliminates the frustrations and dead ends associated with writing text by hand or on a typewriter, the entire process of writing is changed. Revision and changes can be made quickly and without problems. Text can be moved and copied between documents to avoid reentry of text. Formatting can add professional touches to any document.

Similarly, spreadsheets have many conceptual as well as technical advantages over doing math with paper and pencil or even electronic calculators. Traditional math education stresses calculation skills such as the memorization of addition and multiplication tables. However, the connection between problem solving in the everyday world and the technical skills associated with arithmetic are poorly established and lead to a situation where students can pass arithmetic tests without having the faintest idea of how to apply mathematical concepts to solving problems.

Computer spreadsheet programs approach math in a different manner. The key concept in spreadsheet operations is that of the model. The goal of any spreadsheet is to create a model of some real world activity, e.g., earning and spending money or borrowing to purchase a home, in which a number of different items work together to make up the final result. When you create the spreadsheet model, you have created a computer simulation of the activity which can be used to examine the consequences of various courses of action.

A model consists of three parts: items, labels/values, and relationships.

Items. Rather than starting with arithmetic, a model begins with the layout of all of the items involved in the activity. For example, if you plan to purchase a house the price of the house, your monthly income, the amount of the down payment, the interest rate on borrowed money, etc. are all items which determine whether or not, or under what circumstances, you can make the purchase.

Labels/Values. Each item in the model is expressed as a *label* and a *value*. A label is a word or phase that identifies the meaning of the item in the model. A value is a numeric value assigned to a given item. For example, the amount required for a down payment might have a label that reads Down payment and a value of $15,000. While the use of labels with values may seem like common sense, most methods of mathematical problem solving separate labels, which explains the meaning of the various numbers, from the arithmetic side of the problem. In practice this causes people to lose track of the meaning of the calculations they perform. By uniting these two elements into one model, spreadsheets overcome the key intellectual problem involved in practical applications of math.

Relationships. The most powerful element in modeling is the ability of a model to link the value of one item to another. For example, down payments are often linked by means of a percentage to the price of the house, e.g., the down payment is 10% of the selling price of the house. When you add items to your model you can establish relationships between various items based on the way in which they are linked together in the real world. Once complete, your model will be able to show you the effect on the overall model of any change in any of the elements in the model. For example, suppose the down payment was changed to 15% of the selling price. The model, due to the relationships that link the various items, can immediately update the values to reflect the impact of this change.

Modeling shifts the emphasis on math away from the mechanical skills of calculation towards the more important and powerful skills needed to express relationships between items. Put another way, traditional math stresses adding, subtracting, multiplying and dividing. Modeling stresses the more important skill of knowing when and where you should apply math operations such as adding, subtracting, multiplying, and dividing in order to solve everyday problems.

In the next series of projects, you will learn how to create simple but useful models with Works. You will also learn how to use the concepts of modeling in solving all sorts problems from everyday tasks like budgeting to important financial decisions such as purchasing a home or academic problems related to math and science education.

The example used in this chapter will be a spreadsheet that helps you estimate the overall costs of an activity, e.g., planning a party. When you plan an activity for business, leisure, or education, there are always costs associated with the activity. In this chapter you will learn how spreadsheet modeling can help you effectively estimate and plan the costs of any type of activity.

CREATING A SPREADSHEET WINDOW

If you have exited Works at the end of the last project, begin this project by loading Works:

Click(left) on *Microsoft Works* symbol

If you have just completed the last project, display the File menu:

Click(left) on **File**

In either case the screen will now show the File pulldown menu. Select the **Create New File** command:

Click(left) on **Create New File**

The program displays the dialog box that lists the four different types of new files that you can create. In Chapters 4 and 5 you created word processing windows. This time select the New Spreadsheet option:

Click(left) on **New Spreadsheet**

The Spreadsheet Window

Works displays a window on the desktop in Figure 6-1. In many respects this window is organized in the same way as the word processing windows created in Chapters 4 and 5. The window has title and scroll bars as well as the close, size and maximize buttons. The title bar shows the name assigned to the new spreadsheet window, SHEET1.WKS. Spreadsheet windows are name by default SHEET plus a number. The WKS extension marks a file as a spreadsheet in contrast to WPS which marks word processing files.

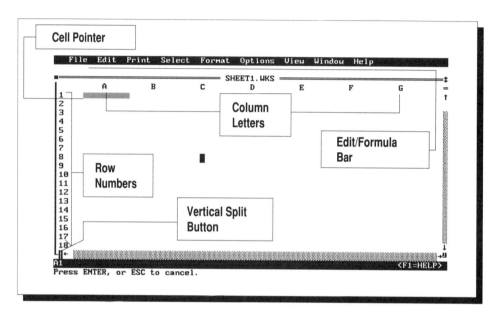

Figure 6-1. Spreadsheet Window.

However, there are some aspects of this window that are different from word processing windows and unique to spreadsheet windows.

Column Letters/Row Numbers

The most obvious difference between a word processing and a spreadsheet window is the presence of the column letter and row number bars at the top and left of the window. These bars indicate that spreadsheet windows, unlike word processing windows, are highly structured. The window is really a grid of small blocks called cells arranged in rows and columns so that they cover the entire worksheet window, as shown in Figure 6-2. Each cell is given an address name based on the columns and row in which it falls. For example, the cell in the upper left corner of the window is in column A and row 1. Its address is A1.

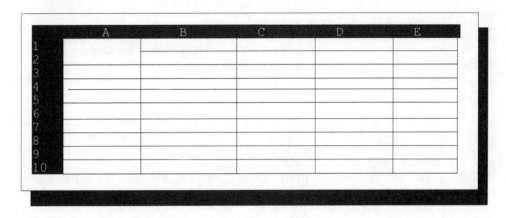

Figure 6-2. Spreadsheet Window is a Grid of Cells Arranged in Rows and Columns.

Cell Pointer

When you look at the spreadsheet grid a highlight appears in the upper left corner of the window. This highlight is called the *cell pointer*. The cell pointer performs a function which is similar to the cursor in a word processing window in that it indicates the part of the spreadsheet has been selected. Like the cursor, the cell pointer can be moved using the keyboard or the mouse. The cell pointer indicates the active cell. The address of the active cell will appear on the left side of the status line. When you first open a spreadsheet window the address of the cell pointer is A1, i.e., the first column and the first row of the window.

Edit/Formula Bar

When a spreadsheet window is active, an additional bar appears on the desktop. The bar appears below the menu bar when ever a spreadsheet window is active. This bar called the edit or formula bar. When you make entries into spreadsheet cells,the information appears on the edit or formula bar as you enter it into the cell.

Vertical Split Button

Both the word processing and spreadsheet windows have horizontal slip buttons (upper right corner) which can be used to divide the window into two panes. Spreadsheet windows have an additional button (lower left corner) which can be used to split the window vertically. This means that a single spreadsheet window can be split into four separate panes.

The Origin of the Term Spreadsheet

You might wonder where the name spreadsheet came from. The source of the term spreadsheet is from accounting. Financial accounting is one of the achievements of the Renaissance when the basics of trade and finance, so important to our modern society, first appeared.

By tradition, financial accounts were written so that each separate account was placed into separate columns on the page. Writing amounts in separate columns has the advantage of doing two things at once. Not only was the value recorded but its position in a specific column classified the transaction. For example, if cloth was purchased the amount was written in the Cloth column. On the other hand, a purchase of leather would be placed in a different column. This approach saved time, since there was no need to write cloth or leather over and over again. It also improved accuracy because totals for each classification could be found by adding down the columns. This avoid the need to try to pick out specific items, e.g., cloth purchases, from a long list that included other items.

This type of record keeping required a special, wide paper that could be unfolded to display more columns than on ordinary pages. This paper was called "spreadsheet paper" because it could be unfolded into a wide sheet when needed and refolded for storage. The name spreadsheet was applied to the current type of program because computer screen is divided into a series of columns and rows similar in appearance to spreadsheet paper.

It is important to understand that while the appearance of a spreadsheet window is similar to spreadsheet paper, its functions and abilities are very different. In fact, a more accurate name for this type of application would be a modeling program. However, the spreadsheet name, for better or worse, has stuck. In this book the term spreadsheet model is used to indicate both the common name and the more accurate reference to modeling.

SPREADSHEET ENTRY

The project in this chapter is a budget. A budget is a type of plan used to estimate how much money you have to spend and what you want to spend it on. The goal of any budget is to arrive at a balance between the money you expect to have and the cost of the items you expect to purchase or put away for savings. Balancing a budget requires you to think carefully about all of the items involved and make decisions about where the money can best be used. As you will see, creating a budget in a spreadsheet window provides some very special features which help you see the consequences of decisions before they actually take place.

Suppose that you are asked to plan a party for a group or organization to which you belong. In order to get things organized you will have to figure out how much all of the items required for the party will cost. Once you know the total cost you can use that value to figure out how to raise the money to pay for it. You might simply divide the cost among all of the people who want to attend or, if the party is open to the public, figure how much you should charge for a ticket.

You will see in this project just how helpful a spreadsheet can be in planning any activity that involves using money.

Moving the Cell Pointer

The cell pointer is the highlighted block that is currently positioned on cell A1. You can change the position of the cell pointer using keyboard or mouse. For example, the arrow keys move the cell pointer one cell in the specified direction. Enter:

```
[down]
```

The cell pointer moves down one row to cell A2. Note that A2 now appears on the status line. The [Tab] and [Shift-Tab] keys can be used in place of the [right] and [left] keys respectively. Enter:

```
[Tab](3 times)
```

The cell pointer moves three columns to the right to cell D2. The [Pg Dn] and [Pg Up] keys will move the cell pointer one full screen down or up. Enter:

```
[Pg Dn]
```

The cell pointer appears to have remained in the same place. That is true in the sense that it is still positioned in the second row and the fourth column in the window. However, the row numbers on the side of the window show that the row number is now row 20. The spreadsheet is actually far larger than the window. As you move up and down, the window will scroll to reveal other rows and columns.

The [Ctrl-Home] combination will return the cell pointer to A1 no matter what the current location. Enter:

```
[Ctrl-Home]
```

You can position the cell pointer with the mouse by clicking the mouse on any cell in the spreadsheet:

```
Click(left) on D9
```

The cell pointer will jump to the cell location which was clicked. Note that when you are attempting to click on an empty cell in the middle of the window you may encounter some difficulty in determining the row and column location. Use the status line display to check the cell address to be sure that you are in the right location.

The Size of the Spreadsheet

How many rows and columns are contained in a spreadsheet window? You can find out by using [Ctrl] in combination with the arrow keys. Enter:

[Ctrl-right]

The cursor jumps to cell IV9. Column IV is the 256th column in the spreadsheet. The first 26 columns are numbers A-Z. The columns after that have two letter, AA, AB, AC, etc. until they reach IV. Check the number of rows. Enter:

[Ctrl-down]

The cell pointer jumps to IV4096 indicating that row 4,096 is the last row in the spreadsheet. Return to the top of the spreadsheet by entering:

[Ctrl-Home]

The spreadsheet contains 256 columns and 4,096 rows: a total of 1,048,576 cells. Can you really use over a million cells? The answer is no. While the spreadsheet has the ability to account for all of those cells, the information entered into each cell uses up internal RAM memory. Since the PS1 has a maximum of 1 megabyte of internal RAM memory, which must be shared among DOS, Works and your spreadsheet, it is not possible to utilize all of the possible spreadsheet cells. However, you have more than enough memory for most non-professional tasks. (See Chapter 1 for details about RAM memory).

Entering Labels

While spreadsheet programs are primarily designed to perform math operations, it is very important to understand the role played by labels. A label is a word or phrase entered into a cell. These words serve to identify the meaning of the numbers that will appear on the spreadsheet. Without labels, a spreadsheet would simply be a list of meaningless values.

The first step is to figure out what items you will need for the party. Begin with a list of the food items. Enter a label that will serve as a heading for the topic of food:

Food

When you enter text into a cell Works displays the text as you type in two places: in the cell and on the edit line, as shown in Figure 6-3.

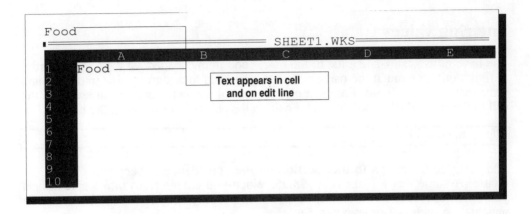

Figure 6-3. Text Entered in the Cell and the Edit Line.

You can complete the entry in two ways: complete and complete and advance.

Complete

If you press [**return**] at the end of the entry the text is placed into the cell and the cell pointer remains on the current cell.

Complete and Advance

In many cases you will be entering a series of items down a column or across a row. You can complete an entry and advance to the next cell by using the [**left**], [**right**], [**up**], or [**down**] keys instead of [**return**]. You can complete an entry with the mouse by clicking on the next cell into which you want to make an entry.

In this case move down to cell A2 by entering:

```
[down]
```

The cell pointer advances to cell A2 while the word "Food" appears in cell A1. Enter the following list of food items for the party:

```
Pizza [down]
Soda [down]
Chips [down]
Cake [return]
```

Entering Values

You have now established a list of the basic food items needed for the party. In order to figure out how much the party will cost, you need to assign a value in dollars and cents to each of the items. For example, the cost of a pizza should be entered into the cell to the right of the word "pizza." Position the cell pointer by using the mouse:

Click(left) on cell B2

The cell pointer jumps to the location on the spreadsheet where you clicked the mouse. Assume that a pizza costs $8.95. When you enter values into a spreadsheet you enter only the numbers and a decimal point, if needed. You do not enter punctuation such as $ or commas. Enter:

8.95 [down]

A six pack of soda will cost about $2.95. Enter:

2.95 [down]

Enter the values for a bag of chips and a cake:

1.99 [down]

You have now entered a list of items, labels and values, into the spreadsheet. The screen should look like Figure 6-4.

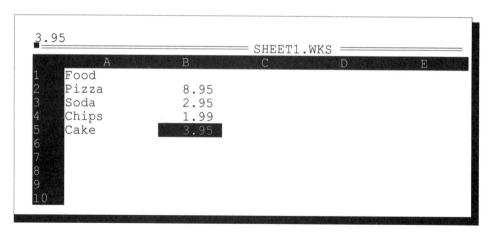

Figure 6-4. Labels and Values Entered into Spreadsheet.

Creating a Formula

The spreadsheet you have created so far assumes that you will be buying only one of each item. That is probably not the case. Suppose that you wanted to have 3 pizzas for the party. What would be the cost? That value can be calculated by multiplying the value of each pizza—$ 8.95— by the number of pizzas you order.

You can add this information to your model. You can use column C to hold the values that represent the quantities of the items. Start by entering the number of pizzas:

Click(left) on cell **C2**

Enter:

3 [return]

You now have the cost of each pizza entered into B2 and the number of pizzas entered into C2. In order to find out the total cost of all three pizza you must create a formula. A formula is a mathematical statement that relates various parts of the spreadsheet. In this case you know that the values in cells B2 and C2 are related by multiplication. If you create a spreadsheet formula that indicates this relationship to Works, the program will calculate the formula and display the results in a spreadsheet cell.

The first step in creating a formula is deciding where in the spreadsheet you want the answer to appear. You can place a formula in any empty cell on the spreadsheet. In this example, you might want to place the formula in cell D2, the cell to the right of the cells that are being multiplied:

Click(left) on cell **D2**

When you want to enter a formula into a spreadsheet cell you must activate the formula entry mode. This is done very simply by entering an equals sign (=) as the first character in the formula. The equals sign (=) is used because the formula will determine what value appears in the cell. Enter:

=

With the equals sign entered you are ready to enter the actual cell formula. Formula can contain three types of items, cell references, arithmetic operators and numbers.

Cell References

A cell reference is the address of a cell on the spreadsheet that contains a value you want to use in your formula. In this example cells B2 and C2 contain values needed

195

in order to obtain the total cost of the pizzas. You can enter a cell reference in three different ways.

Manual Entry. Manual entry refers to simply typing in the column letter/row number address of the cell you want to reference, e.g., B2.

Keyboard Highlighting. When the formula entry mode is active you can use the arrow keys to move the highlight to the cell you want to reference. As you move the highlight, Works enters the cell address of the highlighted cell into the formula.

Mouse Highlighting. Clicking the mouse on a cell while the formula mode is active causes Works to insert the address of the highlighted cell into the current formula.

The keyboard and mouse highlighting methods are usually faster and more accurate than entering the cell references manually because you use the highlight to indicate the cell you want to reference instead of trying to visually determine the columns and row location of the value.

Arithmetic Operators

Works recognizes 5 basic mathematical operators and uses the symbols in Table 6-1 to represent them.

Table 6-1. Arithmetic Operators.

Operation	Symbol
Addition	+
Subtraction	-
Multiplication	*
Division	/
^	exponential

Numbers

You can enter a numeric value directly into a formula if necessary. This option should be used only when the value in the formula is a standard unit of measurement such as 24 for the number of hours in day. In most cases it is best to place numeric values in individual cells and refer to them with cell references. The formula you are about to write for the first value is the cost of an individual pizza. That value is located in cell B2. You can select that cell by clicking the mouse on the value, 8.95, as it appears in the cell:

```
Click(left) on cell B2(8.95)
```

When you click on the cell, Works writes the address, B2, on the edit bar which now reads =B2. The next step is to tell Works what operation(+, -, * or /) you want to perform on this value. In this case the operation is multiplication. Enter:

*

When you enter a mathematical operator such as * for multiplication Works returns the highlight to the cell in which the formula is being entered. The formula now reads =B2*. The formula means "cell D2 is equal to the value in cell B2 multiplied by." You can see that the formula is an incomplete statement. You need to add another cell reference in order to tell Works what to multiply the value by. That other cell is C2, which contains the number of pizzas you want to order:

Click(left) on cell C2(3)

The formula now reads =B2*C2. This formula is now complete since it expresses the relation between the values that will result in the answer you are looking for. To complete the formula and calculate the answer press [**return**]:

[**return**]

When you complete the formula the program will calculate the value of the formula, as shown in Figure 6-5. Note that while the cell shows the total cost of the pizzas, the edit line shows the formula, =B2*C2, is used to arrive at the value.

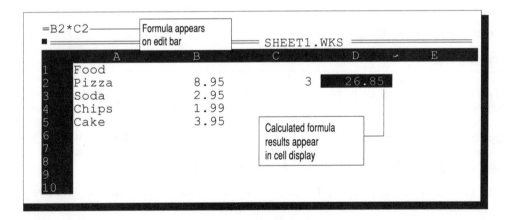

Figure 6-5. Recalculating the Value.

Recalculation

Suppose that at this point you decide you really need 4 pizzas instead of 3. Place the cell pointer on the cell that contains the number of pizzas. This time use the keyboard to move the highlight:

```
[left]
```

You can replace the contents of a cell by entering a new value. Enter:

```
4 [return]
```

When you enter 4 the value in cell C2 changes to 4. However, that is not the only change. The formula in D2 is automatically updated to reflect the new values that appear on the spreadsheet. The ability of the spreadsheet to update formulas each time a value is changed on the spreadsheet is called recalculation. Recalculation makes sure that the formula sin the spreadsheet always accurately reflect the current values stored in the referenced cells. What is the cost of 32 pizzas? Try this on your own. You will find the correct command at the end of the chapter under Exercise 1.

Return to the original value for C2 of 3. Enter:

```
3 [return]
```

Now, suppose that you wanted to order more expensive pizzas, e.g., 11.75 each:

```
Click(left) on cell B2(8.95)
```

Enter the new value for the pizza:

```
11.75 [return]
```

The formula automatically recalculates updating the total to match the cell values referenced in the formula.Recalculation is one of the major benefits of spreadsheet models. It also points up the difference between mere calculation, as you would perform with a paper and pencil or even a calculator, and model building. If you were using a calculator to find the cost of the pizzas you would have to enter the entire formula each time, i.e., 8.95 X 3, then 8.95 x 4, etc.

The calculator would perform the calculation but it could not retain the structure of the formula or the raw values used to calculate the result.

A spreadsheet can perform the calculation just as a calculator does. But the spreadsheet goes beyond the calculator in that it retains the structure of the calculation, i.e., the formula and its supporting values in the referenced cells.

When you solve a problem with a calculator you solve one problem at a time. When you build a spreadsheet model of a problem, you actually solve all possible variations of the same problem.

Copying a Formula

You can apply the same approach to the other items in the food list. Enter the quantities of the other items needed for the party:

Click(left) on cell C3

Enter:

4 [down]
2 [down]
2 [return]

In order to calculate the total amounts for soda, chips and cake you need to place a formula like the one in cell D2 in cells D3, D4, and D5. One way is to enter a new formula into each of those cells. A better solution would be to have the program copy the original formula into all of the other cells in column D that require the same type of calculation.

The simplest way to duplicate the formulas is with the **Fill** command found on the Edit menu. The **Fill** command has two forms which can duplicate a formula down a column, **Fill Down** or across a row, **Fill Right**. In this case, you can use the **Fill Down** command to fill in cells D3 through D5 with the formula in D2.

The duplication process begins by placing the cell pointer on the cell that contains the formula you want to duplicate:

Click(left) on cell D2(35.25)

Before you issue a **Fill** command you must use the highlight to indicate the cells into which the copies should be placed. This is done by expanding the cell pointer highlight to cover a block of cells. The cell pointer highlight can be extended to cover a block of cells in three ways: **[F8], [Shift]+arrow**, and drag (left).

[F8]

The **[F8]** key activates the select mode. When active this mode causes the cell pointer highlight to expand when you use the arrow of the **[Tab]** key.

[Shift]+arrow

You can extend the highlight without activating the select mode by combining the arrow keys with the **[Shift]** key. For example, entering **[Shift-down]** would extend the highlight to include the cell in the row below the current location.

Drag(left)

Dragging the mouse will expand the highlight to include all of the cells covered by the dragging mouse.

In this case use the **[Shift]** key method. Enter:

```
[Shift-down] (3 times)
```

The highlight now covers a block of four cells, D2 through D5. If you look in the lower left corner of the screen on the status line you will see D2:D5 displayed. This notation indicates that the all of the cells from D2 to D5 are currently highlighted. When a block of cells is contained in a single highlight it is called a range of cells.

When you want to use a **Fill Down** or **Fill Right** command to copy a formula, the formula that you want to copy must be the first cell in the range.

If that is not the case, Works will use whatever happens to be in the first cell in the range as the item to be copied. For example, if the first cell in the range is blank, Works will duplicate the blank cell down or across the range. This will have the effect of erasing any other values or formulas in the range.

When you have highlighted the correct range of cells you can then use the **Fill Down** command to duplicate the formulas:

```
Click(left) on Edit
Click(left) on Fill Down
```

The **Fill Down** command fills the highlighted range with duplicates of the formula in the first cell, as shown in Figure 6-6. Cells D3 through D5 calculate the totals for the food items listed on their respective rows.

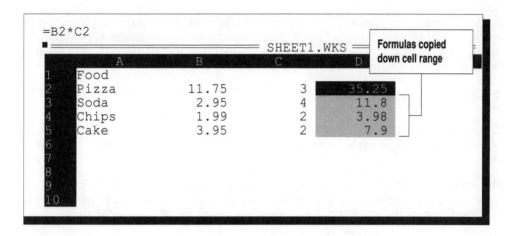

Figure 6-6. Formula Copied Down Column with the Fill Down Command.

The **Fill** command is an important tool in building and expanding the scope of models. In the current model you can see that each food item in the list requires the same type of calculation to arrive at its total cost. Without a way to duplicate the formula in D2, you would have to write a new formula for each item added to the list. This tedious process would discourage you from expanding the model because each new item would be as difficult to total as the first item. Instead, the spreadsheet makes it easy to duplicate the calculation made for the first item for any number of items added to the list. Duplication also insures that all of the formulas in the column are as accurate as the first formula eliminating errors.

The **Fill Down** command is a good example of how model building with a spreadsheet eliminates much of the repetitive, frustrating and tedious work normally associated with math problem solving. It allows you to work quickly enough so that you can continue to focus on the key relationships involved in the problem instead of getting lost in the details of calculation.

Functions

For the moment, assume that you have added all of the items to the food list which will be needed for the party. The last step is to add together all of the items to arrive at the grand total for the cost of food. What type of formula would you need to write in order to calculate that total?

The most obvious way would be to write a formula that added the contents of the four cells, D2 through D5, which contain food costs. Such a formula would look like this:

```
=D2+D3+D4+D5
```

While a formula like the one shown above would work correctly, it suggests that the longer the list of items to be added, the larger and more cumbersome the formula for adding that list would be. For example, if the food list was doubled to contain eight items, the size of the formula would also double like this:

```
=D2+D3+D4+D5+D6+D7+D9+D10
```

If this were the only way to add up a column of figures, the formulas needed for models with 10 or 20 items to total would be so complicated they would be almost useless.

The solution to this problem is the use of range-oriented functions. A function is a special term that can be used in a formula to represent a certain type of mathematical operation. For example, Works has a function called *SUM*. The SUM function is a shortcut method for calculating the sum of all of the values included in a range of cells. Because SUM is a range oriented function it is not necessary to list all of the cells that need to be added together. Instead, you can simply enter the address of the first and last cells in the range. In this example, the range of cells starting at D2 and ending at D5 would be written as D2:D5.

Cell ranges used with functions are always enclosed in parentheses. The formula needed to total the cell values from D2 to D5 would read:

```
=SUM(D2:D5)
```

The advantage of the function is that you do not have to write a formula with all of the arithmetic details spelled out. Instead you use functions to write out a shorthand instruction that tell the spreadsheet the type of arithmetic that needs to be performed. The range orientation of the function means that the size of the formula will not increase in size when you increase the size of the range. For example, if you added 100 more cells to the range the formula would read "=SUM(D2:D104)"—only one character longer than the previous formula.

In this example, place the total for food in cell D6:

```
Click(left) on cell D6
```

Enter the formula:

```
=sum(
```

Instead of typing in the cell range you can use the mouse to highlight the cells that you want summed:

Point at cell D2(35.25)
Drag to cell D5(7.9)

When you drag the mouse, Works writes the cell range indicated by the highlight onto the edit line as part of the formula. If you have performed the mouse operation properly, the formula now reads "=SUM(D2:D5". Complete the formula by adding the closing parenthesis:

) [return]

The formula using the SUM function calculates the total of all of the values contained in the selected range, as shown in Figure 6-7.

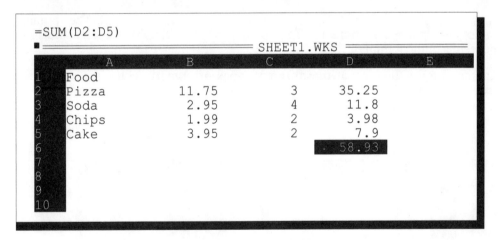

```
=SUM(D2:D5)
■                            SHEET1.WKS
         A           B          C          D          E
1   Food
2   Pizza        11.75         3       35.25
3   Soda          2.95         4       11.8
4   Chips         1.99         2        3.98
5   Cake          3.95         2        7.9
6                                      58.93
7
8
9
10
```

Figure 6-7. SUM Function Used to Sum a Range of Values.

What would happen if you decided to change some of the values on the spreadsheet? For example, suppose you bought chips that cost 2.49 a bag but eliminated one of the cakes. Make the changes:

Click(left) on cell B4(1.99)

2.49 [return]

Click(left) on cell C5(2)

1 [return]

After each change the spreadsheet updates all of the cells affected by the change and calculates new values. The grand total for food changes to 55.98.

UNDERSTANDING MODEL STRUCTURE

The spreadsheet you have created is a model because it demonstrates how various factors contribute to the overall cost of the party you are planning. If you change any of the factors, the model recalculates in order to insure that the values displayed are accurate.

When you look at the the values displayed on the spreadsheet, the structure that supports the values is not visible. All of the cells with values appear pretty much alike. However, you know from building this model that there are two very different types of cells present in the spreadsheet. One type of cell contains simple numeric values that appear on the spreadsheet exactly as they were entered. These values are called literals because the cell's contents are exactly what appears on the spreadsheet.

In contrast, other cells that display numeric values contain formulas. The formulas do not appear literally on the spreadsheet, e.g., =SUM(D2:D5), but instead display the results of the formulas.

Another way of looking at the different types of numeric cells is a distinction between the independent and dependent cells, as shown in Figure 6-8.

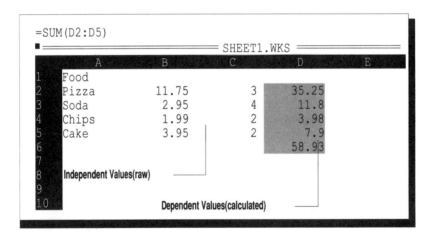

Figure 6-8. A Model Consists of Dependent and Independent Cells.

These cells are described as follows: independent and independent cells.

Independent Cells

Independent cells are cells whose values are not subject to calculation by other elements in the model. These values are the raw values with which you start the model. For example, cell C2 contains the number 3 which represents the the number of pizzas. In this model there is no mathematical reason why there should be three pizzas. The reason for using that value lies outside the model, e.g., you might recall a previous party at which 3 pizzas were ordered. The important point about independent values is that they represent your assumptions. The rest of the model is built upon the independent values.

Dependent Cells

These cells are one whose value can be mathematically determined based on the cell formula and the current values of the cells referenced by the formula. Dependent cells express relationships between other items (dependent or independent)

How do you know which cells on the spreadsheet are independent and which are dependent? If you were the person who created the spreadsheet you might remember which cells contained the formulas and which did not. The basic organization of the information would also give you a clue. However, the only sure way to find out is to move the cell pointer to each cell and compare the contents of the status line to the cell contents. If they are the same, the cell contains literal information, and if they are different, the cell contains a formula of some kind.

The status line inspection method will suffice most of the time. However, in cases where you want to get a better picture of your spreadsheet's structure you can use the **Show Formulas** command located on the Options menu to change the screen displays so that the spreadsheet cells show the same information as the status line:

```
Click(left) on Options
Click(left) on Show Formulas
```

Because showing formulas takes more space than showing the normal spreadsheet data, Works automatically widens the worksheet columns scrolling column D off the screen. Scroll the display by entering:

```
[right]
```

You can now see the formulas, as entered, appear in the cell locations on the spreadsheet in Figure 6-9.

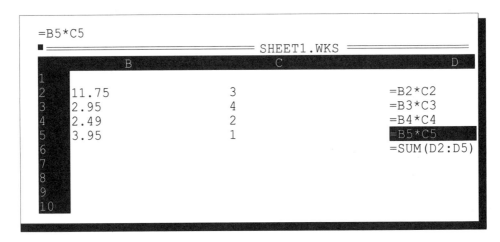

Figure 6-9. Formulas Displayed on Spreadsheet with Show Formulas Command.

Formula Adjustment

The **Show Formulas** command reveals something interesting about how this spreadsheet was built. If you look at the formulas in cells D2 through D5 you will see that while they are similar in that they multiply the values of one cell by another, the formulas are not identical. Recall that the formulas in cells D3 through D5 were not directly entered into the spreadsheet but created by using the **Fill Down** command.

You can see that the **Fill Down** command did not make literal copies of the original formula. Instead, the command modified the formula slightly for each duplicate of the original. If you look at the formulas you will see a definite pattern to these modifications. The column portion of the cell references remains unchanged throughout the range of formulas. On the other hand the row references increase by 1 for each row. This means that wile the formula in cell D2 referred to cells B2 and C2, the formula in D3 referred to B3 and C3.

Why were these modifications made? The answer is obvious if you think about what it would mean to copy a formula without making modifications. Placing exact duplicates of the ordinal formula, =B2*C2 into a series of cells would simply reproduce the same value throughout the range. This is not what you has in mind. What the **Fill Down** command was designed to do was to duplicate the relationship indicated by the formula not the literal formula itself. In order to maintain the relationship, the program adjusted the cell references in order to maintain the basic idea of the formula.

In this example the idea behind =B2*C2 was to multiply the value in column B, the cost of an item, by the value in column C, the quantity of that item. Since each row in the range has a different value for cost and quantity, the formula should have been adjusted to use the values on the row on which the formula appeared rather than always referring back to the original row, row 2.

The effects of the automatic modification of the formulas created the formulas that you needed even though you might not have recognized the need for adjustment when you issued the **Fill Down** command.

Return to the normal spreadsheet display by entering the **Show Formulas** command a second time:

```
Click(left) on Options
Click(left) on Show Formulas
```

```
[Ctrl-Home]
```

Improving the Model

What makes a good model? A good model is one in which you reduce the number of independent values to a minimum. Why would that be true?

When you increase the number of dependent cells in a spreadsheet model you place the burden of the work on the computer, which must calculate the values rather than on yourself, i.e., manual entry of long lists of numbers.

Second, more dependent cells means that you have been able to determine more relationships between values in your spreadsheet. In life, most activities are the result of many different relationships. If you can reflect those relationships mathematically in your spreadsheet model, you will have a model the provides more accurate and useful information.

For example, Figure 6-8 shows that only the values in column D are the result of calculated relationships. All of the other values are independent entries. Is this an accurate picture of how this model should work?

Probably not. For example, how would you decide how many pizzas to order? The answer to that question would be, "It depends on how many people will be at the party."

The answer to the question indicates that the quantity of items required for the party is not a number you pick out of the air but is, in fact, directly related to another value, that is, the number of people who will attend. the conclusion you must draw is that your model could be improved by linking mathematically the values in column C to other values that reflect the attendance at the party. In other words, the model would be more accurate if cells C2 through C5 were dependent rather than independent cells.Keep in mind that the relationship exists even though you may have no idea how many people will actually attend.

Inserting Columns and Rows

The next question to tackle is the method by which you can relate the quantity of each item to the number of people attending the party. One question you might ask is how many people can be fed by each item, e.g., how many people can be fed with one pizza, bag of chips, etc.? The answer to this question would require reference to previous experience. A pizza cut into eight pieces, might give four people two pieces each. You could make similar estimates for all of the items on the list.

Suppose that you wanted to place these values next to the cost of each item. You can do so by inserting a new column between column B and C. If you want to insert a column, highlight the column that is just after the position you want the inserted column to be placed. This means that if you want the new column inserted between B and C, highlight column C. You can highlight an entire column or row by clicking on the column letter or row number in the bars at the top and left sides of the window:

```
Click(left) on C
```

Works displays a highlight down the entire column. The **Insert Row/Column** command is found on the Edit menu:

```
Click(left) on Edit:
Click(left) on Insert Row/Column
```

Works inserts a new column C and moves all of the other columns to the right. The program used the current highlight, in this case a single column, as an indication of the type of insertion you wanted to make, i.e., a single column. Fill in the values for the number of people that can be fed with each item:

```
Click(left) on cell C2
```

Enter:

```
4 [down]
3 [down]
5 [down]
6 [return]
```

In addition to these values, you also need to add a value to the spreadsheet that represents the number of people expected to attend the party. While it is possible to place this value anywhere, it would be logical to place it at the top of the spreadsheet since all the other values depend upon that value.

Rows can be inserted in the same manner as columns. If you want to insert more than one row or column at a time, highlight more than one row or column before you issue the command. For example, to insert two rows at the beginning of the spreadsheet highlight rows 1 and 2 by dragging the mouse down the row number bar:

```
Point at 1
Drag(left) to 2
```

The first two rows of the spreadsheet should now be highlighted. Use the **Insert Row/Column** command:

```
Click(left) on Edit
Click(left) on Insert Row/Column
```

Enter the information about the attendance for the party:

```
Click(left) on cell A1
```

Enter:

```
People [right]
15 [return]
```

Adjusted Formulas

When you add or delete columns and rows to the worksheet you indirectly change the location of various items in the model. For example, inserting two rows at the top of the spreadsheet changes the location of the price of the pizza from cell B2 to B4. This is significant because you have previously written formulas that referred to a value in cell B2 which is now a blank cell. The cell that contained the formula has also been moved to a new location. What changes has this caused?

```
Click(left) on cell E4(35.25)
```

The edit line shows the formula =B4*D4. Recall that your original entry was =D2*C2. Works has modified the formula so that the formula refers to the same cells, relative to its new location, as it did before the rows and columns were added. The column and rows addresses have been changed in response to the modifications made on the spreadsheet using the same technique used to adjust formulas duplicated with the **Fill Down** command:

```
Click(left) on cell E8(55.98)
```

The formula for this cell, =SUM(E4:E7), has also been adjusted to its new location. The adjustments made by Works allow you to modify the Works without disrupting the relationships established by your formulas.

Assigning a Name to a Cell

Cell values are referenced in formulas by entering the column letter/row number address of the cell. In the current spreadsheet the address of the value that represents the number of people attending the party is B1. You will need to refer to that cell when you create formulas that relate the number of people to the amount of food needed:

```
Click(left) on cell B1(15)
```

When you have a cell that contains an important value which is often referenced in spreadsheet formulas, you might want to take advantage of a feature in Works that allows you to assign a descriptive name to a cell or range of cells. A descriptive name can be between 1 and 15 characters in length. The name can include spaces if desired. In this case name cell B2 people. The **Range Name** command is found on the Edit menu:

```
Click(left) on Edit
Click(left) on Range Name
```

When the program displays the Range name dialog box, the name "people" already appears in the text box. Why? The answer is that Works will automatically enter the label, if any, that appears immediately to the left of cell as a possible cell name. In this case cell A1 contains the word "people." Create the name by selecting the **<Create>** command button:

```
Click(left) on <Create>
```

The cell is assigned the name "people." This means that you can use the name "people "in a formula instead of the cell address B1. Conversely, any formulas that already referred to this cell will now show the name "people "instead of the cell reference to B1. Move the cell pointer to B3:

```
Click(left) on cell B3
```

Enter labels which will identify the columns:

```
Cost [right]
Can Feed [right]
Quantity [right]
Cost [return]
```

The next step is to place a formula in cell D4 that will use the new values for "People" and "Can Feed" to determine the quantities needed:

```
Click(left) on cell D4(3)
```

210

You can determine the number of items needed by dividing the number of people attending the party by the number that can be fed by each item. Start the formula entry by entering:

```
=
```

Select the cell that contains the number of people attending the party:

```
Click(left) on B1(15)
```

When you click on cell B1 Works write the name of the cell, People, onto the formula edit line. Enter the operation symbol for division:

```
/
```

Select the cell that contains the number of people that can be fed by one pizza:

```
Click(left) on cell C4(4)
```

Complete the formula by entering:

```
[return]
```

The formula reads =People/C4. When calculated, the formula shows that you will need 3.75 pizzas to feed the 15 people who will attend the party. Note that the cost of the pizza—cell D4—and the total costs—cell E8—update to reflect the change in the number of pizzas.

Rounding

The only problem with the formula you have just created is that you cannot buy .75 of a pizza. In this spreadsheet the values that appear in the quantity column must be whole numbers since you cannot purchase a partial pizza or bag of chips.

In order for the model to be useful the formula must calculate the nearest whole number needed. For example, 3.75 would logically mean that you need 4 pizzas. Works includes a function called ROUND() that can be used to round the value of a formula to the nearest decimal place.

The ROUND() function is a bit more complicated to use than the SUM() function in that it requires the use of more than one argument. An argument is the name given to the information enclosed with the parentheses of a function. For example, the cell range, E4:E7, used in the formula =SUM(E4:E7) is the argument of the SUM() function. The ROUND() function requires two arguments:

ROUND (*formula, number of decimal places*)

211

The formula argument in the current example would be People/C4. If you wanted to round to the nearest whole number you would enter a value of zero as the second argument—number of decimal places. The arguments in a function are always separated by commas. Keep in mind that the order in which the arguments in a function appear is significant. If the arguments are not written in the correct order, the formula will not calculate properly.

In this example, a formula that would round the quantity to the nearest whole number would be =ROUND(People/C4,0). The rounding would cause the values in the quantity column to round to the next highest whole number if the formula calculated a decimal portion equal to or greater than .5.

Note

In this example, the assumption is made that you only want to add the extra item if the decimal portion needed is more than half. Another way to approach this problem would be to add the extra item if there was any decimal portion at all, e.g., if the quantity value was 3.1 you would still order 4 pizzas. This type of rounding is called a ceiling calculation. A ceiling calculation adds a value just smaller than a half to the formula so that the rounded result will always be rounded to the next whole number if there is any decimal portion at all. The formula =ROUND(People/C4+.4999,0) would calculate the ceiling value rather than the rounded value.

Editing a Formula

Instead of entering a new formula into cell D4, you can edit the existing formula. Press **[F2]** or click on the edit line to activate the formula editing mode. You can insert and delete items on the edit line to make it possible to modify an existing entry or formula by re-entering the entire item. When you press **[F2]** the cursor is placed at the end of the current entry. You can use the **[left], [right], [Home],** and **[End]** keys to move the cursor back and forth on the edit bar. If you use the mouse to edit a formula, the cursor will be placed where you click. You can move around the edit line by clicking at different locations. In this example the instructions will use the keyboard method:

```
[F2] [Home] [right]
```

Insert the new function at the beginning of the formula:

```
ROUND(
```

Move the cursor to the end of the line and add the closing section of the formula:

```
[End]
,0) [return]
```

The ROUND() function causes the value of the formula to be calculated as the whole number 4 rather than the decimal value 3.75.

Shift Key Range Highlighting

Now that you have established the formula in cell D4 which relates the attendance at the party to the quantity of food required, you can copy the formula into cell D5 through D7 using the **Fill Down** command.

The last time you used **Fill Down** you highlighted the range of cells by dragging the mouse. A quick way to highlight a block of cells is to use the [**Shift**] key with either [**Ctrl- right**] or [**Strolled**]. These key combinations will extend the highlight to the end of the current range. The current range is all of the cells following the current cell until a blank cell is encountered. In this spreadsheet the next blank cell in column D is D8. Entering [**Shift-Ctrl-down**] will highlight all of the cells up to that point. Enter:

```
[Shift-Ctrl-down]
```

These key combinations are handy because they follow the pattern you have established in creating the model. They are especially useful when you have a model that is larger than can fit into the window display when dragging is not as handy.

Use the **Fill Down** command to duplicate the formula:

```
Click(left) on Edit
Click(left) on Fill Down
```

What is the result of the new formulas? In Table 6-2, if you look at the values in column D you will see that they do not seem to make sense. The quantities for soda and chips show zero, a clearly incorrect result. The cake quantity should be 3 (15/6 = 2.5), not 2.

Table 6-2. The New Formula.

Food	Price	Can Feed	Quantity	Cost
Pizza	11.75	4	4	47
Soda	2.95	3	0	0
Chips	2.49	5	0	0
Cake	3.95	6	2	7.9
				54.9

What is the cause of these errors? The answer can be found by examining the formulas that were actually created by the Fill Down command. Use the **Show Formulas** command to display the cell formulas in the spreadsheet window:

```
Click (left) on Options
Click(left) on Show Formulas
Click(left) on right arrow on the horz. scroll bar
```

Controlling Automatic Adjustment

Table 6-2 reveals the details of the formula created with **Fill Down**. If you examine the cell references in the formulas you will see the source of the problem. As with the previous **Fill Down** operation, the program has modified the row value of the cell references:

```
Quantity
=ROUND(People/C4,0)
=ROUND(B2/C5,0)
=ROUND(B3/C6,0)
=ROUND(B4/C7,0)
```

It is the modification that has caused the error. In the first formula, the value for the number of people is drawn from the "people" in cell B1. However, in the next formula in the column, Works has adjusted that reference to read B2. The problem is that B2 is blank. Therefore, instead of using the desired value of 15 in the calculation, the formula uses the value zero and creates the apparent error.

The formulas reveal that in some cases, Works automatically adjusts of cell references and distorts the intention of the formula. In this example, all of the formulas in column D should refer to the same cell, B1(named "people.") In order for the copying process to correctly duplicate the formula as you intended it, you need to find a way to prevent the program from adjusting the reference to cell B1(named "people.") This can be done by placing a $ before the cell reference. When Works encounters a $ in front of a reference it will not adjust that reference when the formula is copied. This means that if you enter the cell reference as $people it will remain exactly the same in all duplicates of the formula. Any cell references that do not have $ symbols will be subject to automatic adjustment.

Add the $ to the current formula:

```
Click(left) on the P in People on the edit line
```

Enter:

```
$
```

Note that the highlight is still covering cells D4 through D7. Repeat the **Fill Down** command:

Click(left) on **Edit**
Click(left) on **Fill Down**

The formulas are rewritten with $People appearing in all of the copies. The reference without the $, C4 in the original formula, is adjusted.

Quantity
=ROUND($People/C4,0)
=ROUND($People/C5,0)
=ROUND($People/C6,0)
=ROUND($People/C7,0)

To see the effect of the new formulas return the window to the normal spreadsheet display by entering:

Click(left) on **Options**
Click(left) on **Show Formulas**

The cells now show the correct values for the quantities. Those values in turn are used by the other formulas in the model to arrive at the total cost of food for the party. The current model shows that 15 people require $81.07 worth of food.

In spreadsheet terminology a cell reference within a formula that uses the $ symbol to avoid automatic adjustment is called an absolute reference. The cell references that are automatically adjusted are called relative references. Keep in mind that the $ used in cell formulas has nothing to do with the use of $ as the dollar sign indicating a dollar value.

How do you know if a cell reference in a formula is absolute or relative? Absolute references occur when you want to relate a list of items to a single value. In this model, the number of people at the party is a single value used by many different formulas. On the other hand, relative references occur when you are comparing lists of values. The formulas in column E multiply items from two lists, columns B and D, in which each row contains a different pair of values to be used for the calculation. Keep in mind that the difference between absolute and relative references has meaning only when you copy a formula from one cell to another. You need to analyze the type of relationship your formulas imply in order to know when adjustment should or should not take place.

All formulas should contain at least one relative reference since making duplicates of a formula with all absolute references would not add any new values to the spreadsheet.

What If Analysis

The model you have created now links together, by a series of values and formulas, the number of people attending a party to the cost of food for that party. This allows you to perform what if analysis. For example, what if 25 people attended the party; how much would the food cost?

The answer can be found by entering the value and allowing the model to generate the answer. Move the cell pointer to B1 by entering:

[Ctrl-Home] [right]

Enter the new value for attendance:

25 [return]

The model uses the new value to generate values for all of the formulas arriving at a new total for the cost of the food, as shown in Figure 6-10.

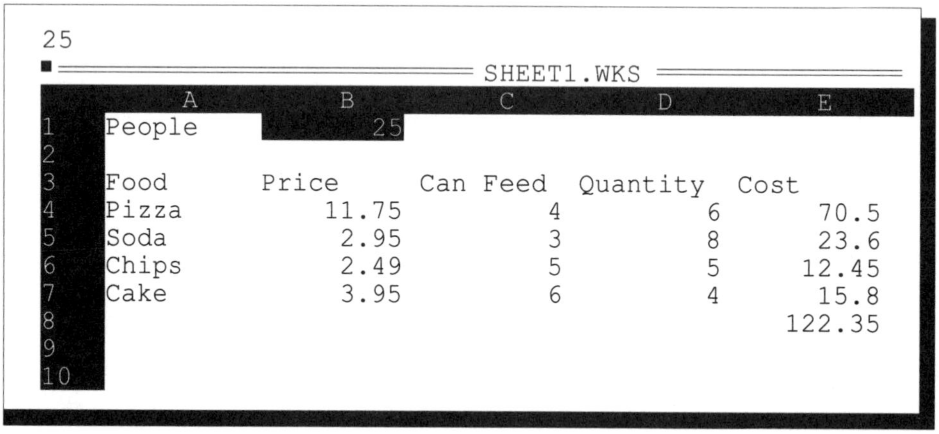

```
25
■                                        SHEET1.WKS
          A           B           C          D          E
 1 People            25
 2
 3 Food         Price      Can Feed   Quantity   Cost
 4 Pizza        11.75          4          6        70.5
 5 Soda          2.95          3          8        23.6
 6 Chips         2.49          5          5       12.45
 7 Cake          3.95          6          4        15.8
 8                                                122.35
 9
10
```

Figure 6-10. Model Relates People to Food Costs.

Unlike other methods of calculation, a spreadsheet model, such as the simple one you have created, can be used to explore an unlimited number of possibilities. Change the model to show the what if result of 5 people:

5 [return]

Models do not simply solve problems. When you create a model you create a tool which can be used to generate information. In this case you have created a tool that relates two values through a series of formulas. The key to model building is to be able to express real life situations in terms of mathematical relationships.

Save the spreadsheet as a disk file using the **Save** command on the File menu using the name "PARTY" as the file name:

```
Click(left) on File
Click(left) on Save
```

```
party [return]
```

Close the window:

```
Click(left) on the Close button
```

If you are done working you can exit Works:

```
Click(left) on Exit Works
```

If you want to go on to the next project in Chapter 7 leave the program running. The next chapter will deal with enhancements that you can make to the appearance of the spreadsheet.

SUMMARY

This chapter covered the basic concepts used to create and use spreadsheet models.

Spreadsheet Windows. A spreadsheet window has a column letter bar at the top and a row number bar on the left side of the window. When a spreadsheet window is active, an additional bar appears at the top of the screen. This is the edit/formula bar which is used for entry and editing of cell labels, numbers or formulas.

Spreadsheet Models. Spreadsheet models are the most common form of math calculation used on a computer. Unlike calculators, spreadsheets solve problems by building systems of relationships rather than one time calculations. The structure of the model should reflect the real life relationships involved in the problem you are trying to solve.

Independent and Dependent Values. Models contain two types of values. Independent values are literal values which are entered into the model as givens or basic assumptions whose value is determined by factors outside the scope of the model. Dependent values are those that are determined by relationships within the model as expressed by the math formulas used in the spreadsheet. Effective models have a high percentage of dependent values that are generated by the spreadsheet formulas. A high percentage of independent values suggests that you have not determined many relationships between the values and have made only limited use of modeling to solve a problem.

Cells. The spreadsheet is composed of individual rectangles called cells. A cell can hold a text label, a literal numeric value, or a formula that calculates a value. Each cell has a unique address consisting of its column letter and the row number, e.g., A1 or IV4096.

Labels. A label is a text entry placed in a cell. Labels have no numeric value but serve to identify the meaning of the values that appear on the spreadsheet.

Formulas. A formula is a mathematical expression that calculates the value of the cell in which it is stored. All Works spreadsheet formulas begin with an =. Formulas can contain symbols for addition(+), subtraction(-), multiplication(*), division(/) and exponentiation(^). You can reference a value stored in another cell by entering the cell address, e.g., A1, in the formula.

Recalculation. Each time an entry is made or changed the spreadsheet formulas are recalculated to reflect the effect of the new or modified value.

Duplication of Formulas. A single formula can be duplicated to fill a range of cells below or to the right the formula cell using the **Fill Down** or **Fill Right** command. When formulas are duplicated, Works will automatically adjust the cell references in the formula relative to the location of the duplicate formula.

Absolute and Relative References. Duplication of cell formulas does not create exact duplicates of the original cell formula. Works adjusts cell references contained in the formula so that the formula retains the same relative relationship with the cell in the spreadsheet. An absolute cell reference is marked with a $. When a cell is copied absolute references are not adjusted. Absolute references are use to refer to a value which is used to analyze a list of different values.

Ranges. A range is a block of cells. Ranges are designated by using the first and last cell address separated by a colon, e.g., B2:B5. Ranges allow you to refer to large blocks of values without having to specify each individual cell.

Functions. A function is a special word that Works recognizes as an instruction to carry out a special calculation. The SUM() function calculates the total value of the values in a range of cells. The ROUND() function calculates the rounded value of a formula. Functions use () to enclose one or more values called arguments. Different functions require differ types and numbers of values.

Range Names. You can assign a one to fifteen character name to a cell or range of cells. All references to the cell will show the name rather than the cell address. Descriptive names are often easier to work with than cell address since the range name suggests the purpose and meaning of the value contained in the cell.

EXERCISES

Exercise 1

Calculate the value of 32 pizzas:

```
32 [return]
```

Chapter 7

Spreadsheet Enhancements

This chapter continues with the basic spreadsheet model created in Chapter 6. The goal of this chapter is to learn how the information contained in the PARTY.WKS spreadsheet file can be enhanced in order to make a more professional presentation.

Spreadsheet models provide a unique approach to solving math related problems. They are particularly useful in helping you foresee the effects of various decisions on future outcomes. In Chapter 6 you used the spreadsheet to estimate the cost of food required for a party attended by a specified number of people. The modeling characteristic of the spreadsheet allowed you to link, though a series of relationships, the number of people attending the party to the total cost of the food required for that number of people. By changing the value used to represent the number of people attending, the model was able to reveal instantly the effect that would have on the overall cost, something that would not be possible with ordinary means of calculation.

Once you have used the spreadsheet model to arrive at a solution, you may need to present that solution to others in the form of a printed document. With that consideration in mind, there are a number of different ways in which the information can be enhanced in order to make the data more easily understood by others. For example, suppose that the party you were planning was being sponsored by a club or organization to which you belong. You would need to present your spreadsheet data to the organization so that they could decide how to raise the money needed for the event.

In this chapter you will learn how to enhance your spreadsheet in the following ways.

Format Cells. You can control the appearance of numbers in terms of the number of decimal places and the use of punctuation.

Text Enhancements. You can apply text enhancements such as bold or italic print to spreadsheet cells. In addition, you can change the alignment of text, the width of columns and add special effects such page numbers to the printed spreadsheets.

Page Setup. You can add page headers and footers to your printed spreadsheet, insert page breaks at specific locations, print a selected range of pages or a selected section of the spreadsheet .

RETRIEVING A SPREADSHEET

The tasks in this chapter require the use of the spreadsheet, PARTY.WKS, which was created in Chapter 6. Load the spreadsheet using the **Open Existing File** command found on the File menu:

```
Click(left) on File
Click(left) on Open Existing File
Double click(left) on PARTY.WKS
```

The file is loaded into a spreadsheet window. Note that the cell pointer's position in cell B2 is in the same position it occupied when you saved the spreadsheet. This is different than word processing. When you open a saved word processing file the cursor is positioned at the beginning of the document regardless of where the cursor was positioned when the document was saved.

Having the cell pointer's position saved as part of the spreadsheet file is often handy when you want to change some of the assumptions in the spreadsheet. In this case the cell pointer is positioned on the key value of this spreadsheet—the number of people attending the party. Change the value from 5 to 15:

```
15 [return]
```

The model instantly recalculates the costs of food for the party to a total of $81.07.

CELL FORMATS

One issue that comes up when you are working with spreadsheet models is the concept of *numeric* formatting. If you look at the values in column E, the Cost column, you will notice that the number of decimal places varies with the values that are calculated for the cells. The current display in Figure 7-1 shows that the pizza costs 47 with no decimal places while the rest of the values show two decimal places.

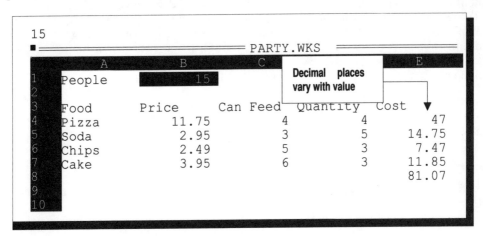

Figure 7-1. Decimal Places Vary with Values.

Why do the decimal places vary? The answer is related to the mathematical concept of *significant* digits. Significant digits are the part of a number which contains the actual mathematical value. For example, a value written as $47.00 has two significant digits, 47. The other characters, $ .00, do not add anything to the mathematical value of the number. The extra characters are used to make reading the numbers easier even though they don't change the mathematical meaning.

Normally, Works will display only the significant digits of a value entered into a cell or calculated by a cell formula. In the current example, the value in E4 is exactly 47 so that no decimal places are needed. Recalculate the spreadsheet by entering:

```
50.00 [return]
```

Note that even though you typed in 50.00, Works displays only the significant digits in that value, 50. The value in E1 changes to 152.75, a value with two significant decimal places. On the other hand cells E6 and E7 show values (24.9 and 31.6) that require only a single significant decimal place.

However, displaying only the significant digits of values can make a spreadsheet display difficult to read. When a person reads rows or columns of figures, they may have trouble understanding the value of the numbers if the columns are not aligned vertically by place value. When Works uses its normal significant digit display, the horizontal location of the decimal point may vary from row to row. In column E the decimal point is the third character from the right in cells E4 and E5, but changes to the second character from the right for the remainder of the column.

It is interesting to note that inconsistent positioning of the decimal point makes it harder for a human to read the value accurately. This fact indicates that the way in which information is presented, visually on the page, does have an effect on how well the information contained on the page is communicated to the reader. For example, if a column of values was written so that all of the values began with a $ and ended with two decimal places, even though the values might be zeros, the reader would assume that these were monetary values. They would also be able to pick up easily the dollar portion of the numbers from the cents portion.

Works allows you to designate a numeric format for a cell or group of cells. The format instructs the program about the way in which the values should be displayed. Works supports six different types of numeric formats.

General

This format is the normal, significant figure only format used by Works. Example: 1000

Fixed

This format allows you to display a fixed number of decimal places regardless of the significant digits. Example: 1000.00

Currency

This format operates like Fixed but adds a $ before the value and inserts comma separators for values over 999. Negative values are enclosed in parentheses. Example: $1,000.00

Comma

This format is the same as currency but without the $. Example: 1,000.00

Percent

This format converts a decimal value to a %. The value is multiplied by 100 and a % sign is placed to the right of the value. Example: a value of .1 would display as 10%

Exponential

This format uses the conventions of scientific notation to display numbers. The format is used when working with scientific or engineering application which use very large or very small numbers. Example: the distance between the Earth and the Sun is 93,000,000 miles. In exponential notation the number would be displayed as 9.3E+07

In this example you might want to apply the Currency format to the values in columns B and E since they represent dollar values. You can apply a format to one cell at a time or use the highlighting methods to apply a format to a block of cells with one command. Begin with the values in column B:

```
Click(left) on cell B4(11.75)
```

Highlight the values in that column by entering:

```
[Shift-Ctrl-down]
```

Display the Format menu:

```
Click(left) on Format
```

The six numeric formats are listed at the top of the menu. Select the Currency format:

```
Click(left) on Currency
```

When you select any format except General, a dialog box appears so that you can specify the number of decimal places to the right of the decimal point that should appear. If you want dollar and cents you would use the default value 2. If you wanted only the dollar portion to show you would enter 0. You can specify between 0 and 7 decimal places for any format. In this case accept the default value of 2 decimal places by entering:

```
[return]
```

The format changes the appearance of the values in column B, as shown in Figure 7-2.

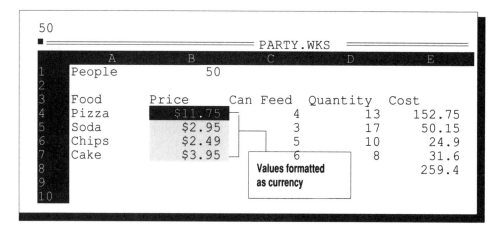

Figure 7-2. Currency Applied to Values.

Apply the same format to the values in column E:

Click(left) on cell E4(152.75)

Highlight the values in column E:

[Shift-Ctrl-down]

Apply the format to the highlighted cells. Recall from Chapter 5 that the **[Shift-F7]** repeats the last command issued. That same principle applies to spreadsheet operations. You can use **[Shift-F7]** to apply the Currency format because it was the last command you issued:

[Shift-F7]

The currency format adds zeros to the ends of the numbers that appear in cells E5 through E7 which causes the values to align vertically in decimal place columns. This makes it much easier to read the numbers in the columns. Change the value for pizza to $9.00:

Click(left) on cell B4($11.75)

9 [return]

Because this cell is formatted as currency with two decimal places, a single digit value—9—is displayed with two decimal places, 9.00, with a $. Numeric formats create displays that are consistent in their appearance regardless of the number of significant digits entered. Move the cell pointer to B5 and enter the value for soda that has one decimal place:

```
[down]
2.9 [return]
```

This time the format pads the appearance of the value with an additional decimal place so that the format is consistent with the other cells.

Using Cell Names

Another value that might be useful to calculate is the cost per person of the food for the party. This can be calculated by dividing the number of people attending, cell B1, by the total cost of the food, cell E8. Create a cell name, "Food Costs" for E8. Try this on your own. You will find the correct command under Exercise 1 at the end of the chapter.

Once you have named the cell, move cell pointer to A9 and enter a label:

```
Click(left) on A9(blank)
```

```
Cost/Guest [right]
```

The cell pointer is now on B9. Use the range names "People" and "Food Costs" to enter a formula that calculates the cost per guest:

```
=food costs/people [return]
```

The use of cell range names often makes it simpler to compose formulas because the text of the formula directly resembles the meaning of the calculation. In this case the formula literally reads "food costs divided by people". Compare that to a formula that reads =E8/B2. The range names create a much more meaningful formula. One big advantage of formulas that use names is that the formula itself reminds you of what you had in mind when you wrote the formula. This may not seem very important at the moment. However, if you return to this spreadsheet in several months chances are that cell address like E8 or B2 won't mean much but that terms like "food costs" and "people" will have meaning. The extra effort taken to create names for important cells or cell ranges will pay off later on in a significant way.

Format Rounding

The formula entered into cell B9 calculates a value of 4.456 as the cost per person. Apply the currency format to this cell since the value represented by the formula is a dollar amount:

```
Click(left) on Format
Click(left) on Currency
Click(left) on <Ok>
```

The appearance of the value changes to $4.46. What has happened to the additional decimal place that Works originally calculated? If you look at the value displayed in the cell, it appears that Works has rounded the value calculated by the formula to the number of decimal places specified in the cell format. Since the third decimal place to the right contained the digit 6, Works rounded the cents portion of the value up from 45 to 46.

You can see that cell formats can cause a rounding effect when the value in the cell has more significant decimal places than the cell format specifies. How is the rounding effect implemented by a cell format different than the ROUND() function used in Chapter 6? The answer may seem a bit technical but it is important to understand the difference. The ROUND() function changes the actual value of the cell. The rounding caused by a cell format effect only the appearance of the cell. The cell's value still contains all of the decimal places.

An experiment can make this difference clear. If you look at cell B9 it appears to have a value of $4.46. Suppose that you write a formula in another cell—B10—that doubled the value of B9, that is 2 times 4.46 should be 8.92. Create the formula in B10 and see if you get the results you expect. Enter:

```
[down]
=2*
```

Use the arrow keys to point at the cell you want to reference:

```
[up] [return]
```

The value that appears in B10 is 8.912 slightly less than the 8.92 you might have expected. Apply the same currency format to this cell so that the display will be consistent:

```
Click(left) on Format
Click(left) on Currency
Click(left) on <Ok>
```

The formatted cell show $8.91, one cent less than it should. The reason is that the when the formula uses the value in B9 it uses the actual value 4.456, not the displayed value of $4.46, when it calculates the value of the formula. This explains the apparent one cent error.

The ROUND() function could be used to resolve the apparent error. If you multiply the ROUND(B9,2) by 2 you will get a result that matches the displayed values exactly. Note that the key is to specify the same number of decimal places in the ROUND() function as you have selected for the cell format.

Which approach is correct? It depends on your needs. In most cases the occasional discrepancy between the formatted appearance of the spreadsheet values and the actual values stored in the cells is insignificant. This means that you can use cell formats to enhance the appearance of values without taking the trouble to add ROUND() functions to all the formulas.

However, certain specific uses of spreadsheet (formal business accounting or scientific calculations) might require a spreadsheet whose appearance exactly matched its actual value. For example, accounting ledgers must balance exactly to the penny. For most users this type of precision is not needed and you can proceed using the formats without ROUND() functions.

Erasing a Cell

The formula you have just written was an experiment used to explore an idea. At this point you will want to erase the formula from the spreadsheet. The [[**Del**] key will clear the formula, label or value from the cell on which the cell pointer is positioned:

```
[Del]
```

The formula is removed from the cell. Note that [**Del**] removes only the contents of the cell. The format, in this case currency (2 decimal places) remains. If you enter another value or formula into the cell it will be displayed using that format. Enter:

```
1 [return]
```

The value is formatted as currency. The format will stay in force in a cell. You can also clear a cell or a highlighted range of cells using the menu version of the [**Del**] key, **Edit Clear**:

```
Click(left) on Edit
Click(left) on Clear
```

Note that [**Del**] effects only the cell pointer cell even if a range is highlighted. **Edit Clear** affects all highlighted cells.

Alignment of Text

Most of the items entered into the spreadsheet's cells do not fill the entire width of the cell. Instead the item is aligned to one side or the other of the cell. By default Works will align text tables on the left side of the cell and value or formulas items on the right side of the cell. This approach works well in most cases. If the results of this default approach are not satisfactory you can use the **Style** command on the Format menu to change the alignment to always left, right, or center. The same dialog box also offers options for adding bold, underline, or italics printing to cells.

The most common use of the **Style** command to change alignment is the case of column headings. If you look at the column headings entered into row 3 you will see that the text aligns to the opposite side of the cell from the values in the column. These headings would be easier to associate with the values that appear below them in the column if they were centered or aligned to the right side of the cell.

You can change the alignment of the current cell or range of cells using **Format Style**. First, select the cells which need an alteration in their alignment. By selecting the cells before you issue the command you can change a block of cells with a single command:

```
Click(left) on cell B3(Price)
```

```
[Shift-Ctrl-right]
```

Note that cell A3 was not included in the range because the items in column A are all text labels which are aligned to the left edge of the cell. Enter the **Format Style** command:

```
Click(left) on Format
Click(left) on Style
```

The dialog box shown in Figure 7-3 contains three parts: alignment, styles, and locked.

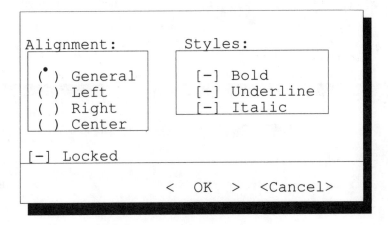

Figure 7-3. Format Style Dialog Box.

Alignment

This option selects the alignment within the current cell width. The default is general-left for labels and right for values or formulas. Note that unlike the general option, which treats values and labels differently, the other three options maintain the selected alignment regardless of what is entered into the cell.

Styles

This option adds enhancements to the cell's display such as bold, underline, or italic printing.

Locked

The locked option is used in conjuncation with the **Protect Data** command found on the Options menu. When **Protect Data** is selected all cells that have been assigned a locked attribute will be protected from editing changes. This allows you to protect key cells from accidental changes. Keep in mind locked cells are not protected unless **Protect Data** is turned on. If **Protect Data** is off, locked cells behave exactly like unlocked cells.

Select right alignment:

Click(left) on **Right**
Click(left) on **<Ok>**

The selected range of cells nows displays the column headings aligned to the right edge of the cells, as shown in Figure 7-4.

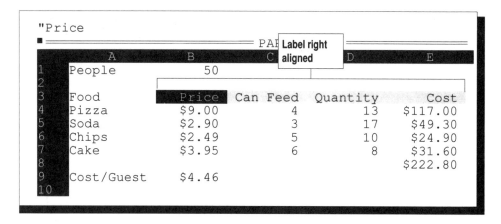

Figure 7-4. Column Heading Labels Aligned Right.

You can add text enhancements such as bold, underline, and italics to the data displayed inside cells. Add bold and underline to the column headings. In this case you will want to add cell A3 to the selected range:

[Home] [Shift-Ctrl-right]

Add the bold and underline attributes to these cells:

Click(left) on **Format**
Click(left) on **Style**
Click(left) on **Bold**
Click(left) on **Underline**

When you click on any of the enhancement options the "-" in the check boxes change to X's indicating that the specified attribute is being added to the selected range of cells. Complete the application:

Click(left) on **<Ok>**

The text in the selected cells now appears as bold, underlined text.

Removing a Text Enhancement

Suppose that in looking at the current spreadsheet you decide that you don't need the bold attribute. Removing a text enhancement from a spreadsheet cell is a bit trickier than performing the equivalent operation in word processing. The reason is that word processing windows provide a format command option called **Plain Text** which removes any text enhancements and returns the selected text to plain text. In a spreadsheet window, removing a format from a cell or block of cells must be done using the Style dialog box.

The first step is to select the cells you want to change. In this example those cells are currently highlighted already. Display the Style dialog box:

```
Click(left) on Format
Click(left) on Style
```

If you look closely at the check boxes under Styles: you will notice the instead of simply being blank, [ ], the boxes contain a dash, [-]. The reason for the dash is that these check boxes operate differently than most of the check boxes in Works. The typical check box has two settings: [ ]-blank for off and [X] for on. The check boxes in this dialog box are different in that they have a third state, [-], which stands for no change. The no change option means that when you close the dialog box no change will be made to the highlighted cells with respect to the option.

For example, suppose that the highlighted range contains some cells that are bold and some that are plain. If you close the dialog box with [-] for the Bold option, the cells will remain exactly as they are, that is, those with bold will continue to be bold and those that are plain will not be changed to bold. Conversely, if you close the dialog box with either a [X] or [ ] for the bold option, you will cause all of the highlighted cells to have the bold turned on or off, respectively.

The trick involved in removing an enhancement is to make sure that the option box for that enhancement contains a blank, [ ], instead of a [-] or an [X]. Because [-] stands for no change, options with this setting will not remove or add styles. Option boxes that display the dash, [-], will toggle between three(not two) settings, as shown in Table 7-1.

Table 7-1. Option Boxes.

Actions	Status
Default	[-]
Click once	[X]
Click twice	[ ]
Click three times	[-]

In order to remove the bold from the highlighted cells you must click twice on the Bold option. Note that clicking twice refers to two separate clicks on the same option, not a double click:

Click(left) on **Bold**
Click(left) on **Bold**

The option now shows a blank, [ ]. Closing the dialog box now will remove the attribute:

Click(left) on **<Ok>**

The cells are underlined but no longer bold.

FORMATTING WITH COLUMNS AND COLUMN WIDTH

By default all of the columns on the spreadsheet are set at a width of 10 characters. However, columns can be increased or decreased in size individually or in groups. Changes in column width are used for two reasons: to allow larger numbers and to improve appearance.

Allow Larger Numbers

When a format is applied to a cell you specify the number of decimal places to display. When the values become large the specified format may come into conflict with the column width. For example, a cell with a currency (2 decimal place) format can displays a values up to $9,999.99 in a 10 character column. If the value entered is larger than $9,999.99 Works displays ########## in the cell indicating that the current value cannot be displayed using the current format. You can solve the problem by changing the format or widening the column.

Improve Appearance

By manipulating the column widths you can improve the appearance of the spreadsheet by adding or removing space between columns.

Note that the total number of characters in a formatted value that can be displayed is always one fewer than the width of the column, e.g., 9 characters in a 10 character column. This is because the program reserves an extra character for a negative sign so that the smallest character, -$9,999.99, can be displayed.

Displaying Large Numbers

As an example of what happens when large numbers are added to a spreadsheet, change the number of people attending the party to a large value such as 10,000. While this value is unlikely for the model you are creating, it will serve to illustrate the point about formats and column widths:

```
Click(left) on cell B2(50)
```

Enter a large number:

```
10,000 [return]
```

Note that when you enter a large value, e.g., 10,000, only significant digits are recorded by Works. The large value in B2 causes the values in the rest of the spreadsheet to also increase. In the case of cells E4 and E8, the values exceed the size permitted by the current column width, as shown in Figure 7-5, causing the program to display the ########## symbol in those cells.

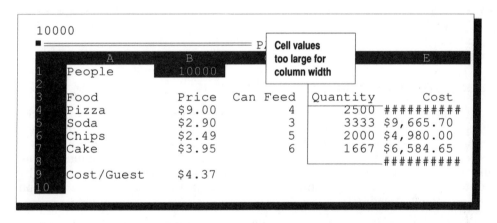

Figure 7-5. Shows Conflict between Format and Column Width.

Keep in mind that the ########## symbol does not mean that any data has been lost or the an error has occurred. Cells that reference E4 and E8 still calculate correctly. The only difference is that you cannot see or print the values for those cells unless you resolve the conflict between format and column width.

In this case change the column width to accommodate the larger values using the **Column Width** command located on the Format menu. Place the cell pointer in any cell in the column you want to change. For example, to change column E you could use E1, E10, E179, etc. Only the column letter is significant:

```
Click(left) on cell E1
```

Display the column width dialog box:

```
Click(left) on Format
Click(left) on Column Width
```

You can enter values from 0 (hidden column) to 80 characters. In this case widen the column to 12 characters by entering:

```
12 [return]
```

The column is now wide enough to display the large values in cell E4 and E8. Change the number of people back to a more usual value:

```
Click(left) on cell B1(10000)
```

```
50 [return]
```

Improving Appearance with Columns

A different reason for altering column widths is to improve the appearance of the worksheet. By increasing or reducing the size of various columns you can suggest various ideas. For example, the labels listed in column A actually represent two levels of row headings. Cell A3 has a major heading, Food, while A4 through A7 are subheadings. You can make the spreadsheet's appearance reflect this organization by altering the placement and size of columns. Begin by inserting a new column between column A and B:

```
Click(left) on Edit
Click(left) on Insert Row/Column
Click(left) on Column
```

A new column with a width of 10 is inserted between the former columns A and B. However, in this case you don't want to expand the width of the spreadsheet by a full 10 characters. Instead, a small increase of 3 characters is all that is needed. You can achieve this by reducing the width of column A to 3 characters:

```
Click(left) on cell A1(People)
Click(left) on Format
Click(left) on Column Width
```

```
3 [return]
```

Note that Works allows the text tables in column A to follow over into column B as long as the cells in B are empty. Complete the change by moving the labels in cells A4 through A7 into B4 through B7. This will indent the labels so that they appear to be subheadings of "Food":

```
Click(left) on cell A4(Pizza)
Drag(left) to cell A7(Cake)
```

Use the **Move** command found on the Edit menu:

```
Click(left) on Edit
Click(left) on Move
Click(left) on cell B4(blank)
```

```
[return]
```

Columns A and B now serve to display major and subheading row labels. Readers can now more clearly understand the ideas presented by the spreadsheet, as shown in Figure 7-6.

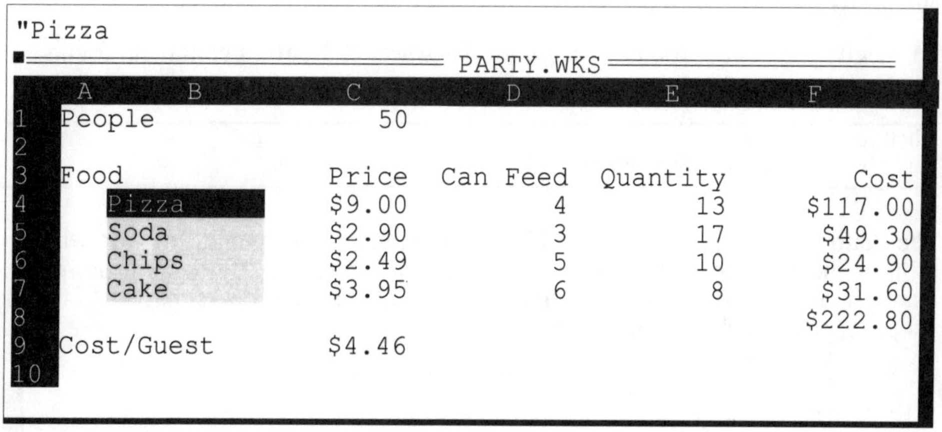

```
"Pizza
================================ PARTY.WKS ================================
        A         B           C         D          E             F
1  People                     50
2
3  Food                      Price   Can Feed   Quantity        Cost
4        Pizza               $9.00       4         13         $117.00
5        Soda                $2.90       3         17          $49.30
6        Chips               $2.49       5         10          $24.90
7        Cake                $3.95       6          8          $31.60
8                                                             $222.80
9  Cost/Guest                $4.46
10
```

Figure 7-6. Column Width used to Alter Appearance.

PRINTING SPREADSHEETS

At some point you will want to create a printed copy of the spreadsheet. Before you print you might want to save the current spreadsheet to a disk file in order to permanently store the changes you have made in this project:

```
Click(left) on File
Click(left) on Save
```

Because the spreadsheet window already is assigned a file name, PARTY.WKS, the save command does not display a dialog box but automatically uses the current window name to replace the existing version of PARTY.WKS with the modified version that appears on the screen.

Headers and Footers

When printing spreadsheets it is usually a good idea to place information at the top or bottom of each page that identifies the information. Usually this information consists of a title which identifies the spreadsheet, a date which tells when the information was printed, and a page number which numbers pages when spreadsheet are too large to fit onto a single page.

Works allows you to specify page headers (text that prints at the top of every page) and/or footers (text that prints at the bottom of every page). By default the header and footer text will print .5 inches from the top or bottom of the page.

To specify the header/footer text use the **Headers & Footers** command found on the Print menu:

```
Click(left) on Print
Click(left) on Headers & Footers
```

The dialog box displays two text boxes which are used to enter the text which will print as the page header or footer, as shown in Figure 7-7. By default the boxes are blank. In addition there are three options boxes: No header on 1st page, No footer on 1st page, and Use header and footer paragraphs.

```
Header: [................................]
Footer: [................................]

[ ] No header on 1st page    [ ] Use header &
[ ] No footer on 1st page        footer paragraphs

                              <  OK  >  <Cancel>
```

Figure 7-7. Header/footer Dialog Box.

No header on 1st Page

Turns off header printing for the first page of the spreadsheet.

No footer on 1st Page

Turns off footer printing for the first page of the spreadsheet.

Use header & Footer Paragraphs

Applies only to word processing documents. It is used to designate a multi-line paragraph as a page header or footer.

When you create header or footer text Works recognizes special *ampersand(&)* symbols that are used to insert information into the header/footer text. Four of the symbols insert information, as shown in Table 7-2.

Table 7-2. Ampersand(&) Information Symbols.

Insert current page number	&p
Insert current filename	&f
Insert current date	&d
Insert current time	&t

Three other symbols control the horizontal alignment of the items, as shown in Table 7-3.

Table 7-3. Ampersand(&) Horizontal Alignment Symbols.

Align on left margin	&l
Align centered between margins	&c
Align on right margin	&r

If you want to enter the **&** character itself as part of the text enter a double ampersand, **&&**, as shown in Table 7-4.

Table 7-4. Ampersand(&) as Text.

Entry	Results
Page -&p-	Page -1-
Printed on &d	Printed on 11/8/90

The alignment symbols are used in conjunction with text and text insertion symbols, as shown in Table 7-5.

Table 7-5. Ampersand(&) Text and Insertion Symbols.

Entry	Results
&cPage -&p- &rPrinted on &d	Page -1-(centered) Printed on 11/8/90 (flush on right margin)

In this case print the date on the right side of the page header and the page number in the center of the footer:

```
&rPrinted on &d [Tab]
&cPage -&p- [return]
```

Previewing the Printing

Works allows you to preview the printed page before you actually send it to the printer. The preview is a reduced size image of the printed pages. The purpose of this preview is to show you the overall layout of the page including header, footers, and margins—items which are not displayed in the spreadsheet window:

```
Click(left) on Print
Click(left) on Preview
```

The program displays a dialog box that has the same options listed as the Print dialog box. This means that you can use the Print specific pages option to print a selected range of pages, if you desire. This option would be relevant if spreadsheet had a large number of pages. Preview the current spreadsheet by selecting the **<Preview>** command button:

```
Click(left) on <Preview>
```

The program removes, temporarily, the desktop and window display and replaces it with the page preview display, as shown in Figure 7-8. The right side of the screen shows how the page will look when it is printed. The page shows the page headers and footers defined in the Header & Footer dialog box. You can see from the page display that Works automatically adds margins to the printed page. Note that some special effects, in this case underlines, do not appear as part of the print preview.

The **[Pg Up]** and **[Pg Dn]** keys are used to display the text or previous pages in a multipage spreadsheet.

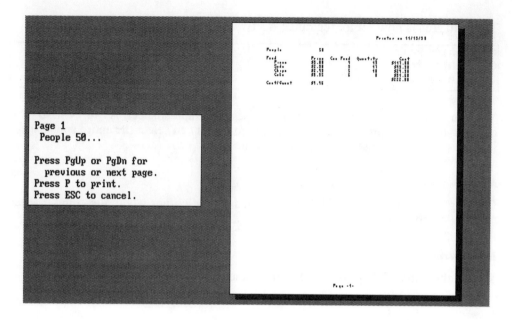

Figure 7-8. Print Preview Display.

Return to the normal desktop display by entering:

```
[Esc]
```

Printing Part of a Spreadsheet

Works will normally print the entire spreadsheet when you select the **Print** command. However, you may want to print only a specific section of the spreadsheet. You can accomplish this by setting a specific print area. Once you have set a print area, Works will print only the information in that range each time the **Print** command is used. For example, suppose that you wanted to print the food section of the spreadsheet—cells A3 through F7. Select the range that you want to print:

```
Point at cell A3(Food)
Drag(left) to F7
```

The command that sets the highlighted range as the print area is Set Print Area located on the Print menu:

```
Click(left) on Print
Click(left) on Set Print Area
```

The print area is now set for the range A3:B7. Print the spreadsheet again:

```
Click(left) on Print
Click(left) on Print
Click(left) on <Print>
```

You can return to the normal print area—the entire spreadsheet, A1 to IV4096—by defining the entire spreadsheet as the print area. You can select the entire spreadsheet in three ways: the mouse, the keyboard, or the menu.

Mouse

Clicking the mouse on the blank area framed by the corner where the column letter and row number bars meet.

Keyboard

The combination of [Shift-Ctrl-F8] selects the entire spreadsheet.

Menu

Choose the All command from the Select menu.

Use the menu command All to select the entire spreadsheet:

```
Click(left) on Select
Click(left) on All
```

Reset the print area by using the Set Print Area command while the entire spreadsheet is selected:

```
Click(left) on Print
Click(left) on Set Print Area
```

The print area is now designated as the entire spreadsheet. Keep in mind that when the entire spreadsheet is set as the print area, Works will only print the portion of the spreadsheet that actually contains information. That area extends to the cell in the lower right cell corner of the spreadsheet that marks the intersection of the last row and column in the spreadsheet that actually contains information. In this case that cell would be F9. Setting the print area to the entire spreadsheet will not result in the printing of blank pages. Save the spreadsheet as it is now set up:

```
Click (left) on File
Click(left) on Save
```

Making an Alternative Menu

In looking at the menu you have planned for this part, suppose you want to consider one or more alternative menus. You can accomplish this rather easily by making a duplicate of the main table within the spreadsheet—cells A3 through F9. To make this type of copy you will need to use the **Copy** command found on the Edit menu. The **Copy** command is used to make copies of ranges of cells in contrast to the Fill commands which makes duplicates of a single cell.

Begin by highlighting the range you want to duplicate:

```
Click(left) on cell A3(Food)
Drag(left) to cell F9(blank)
```

Place a duplicate of the range into the clipboard:

```
Click(left) on Edit
Click(left) on Copy
```

Place the duplicate table into the spreadsheet beginning at cell A11:

```
Click(left) on A11(blank)
```

```
[return]
```

The program inserts an exact duplicate of the previous table into a new location in the spreadsheet. But how does this help you create an alternative menu? At this point you have two menus that contain the exact same information. However, you can edit the independent values in the duplicate table allowing the formulas to calculate new values.

Editing within a Range

In order to actually create the alternative menu you will have to edit the information in cells B12 through D15. Recall that in the previous chapter you learned how to advance the cell pointer while entering data by using the arrow keys to end the entry rather than the **[return]**. However, it is far more instinctive to press **[return]** at the end of an entry than it is to press an arrow key. The best solution would be to be able to advance to the next cell each time you press **[return]**.

You can create exactly that type of situation in Works by entering data into a highlighted range of cells. For example, if you highlight cells B12 through D15, Works would automatically advance the cell pointer through the range each time [return] was entered. The cell pointer would start at B12. Pressing [return] would advance the cell pointer down the current column, B13, B14, and B15. When the cell pointer reaches the bottom of the highlight, the next [return] advances the cell pointer to the top of the next column—C12. The pattern continues until the last cell in the highlighted range is reached. If you continue to press [return] the cell pointer returns to the first cell in the range and repeats the cycle.

A highlighted range can be used to control the movement of the cell pointer with just the [return] key. This eliminates the need to think about which arrow key to use to advance the cell pointer making data entry, the most tedious part of spreadsheet operations, much simpler and faster.

You can put this technique to use while making the entries into the alternative menu. Highlight the range that requires entry:

```
Point at cell B12(Pizza)
Drag(left) to cell D15(6)
```

Enter the following data into these cells. Keep in mind that [return] automatically advances the cell pointer. Enter:

```
Burgers [return]
[return]
Fries [return]
Cookies [return]

2.95 [return]
[return]
1.50 [return]
2.95 [return]

1 [return]
[return]
2 [return]
12 [return]
```

The use of a highlighted range for data entry allows you to concentrate on entering data rather than having to think about advancing the cell pointer after each entry.

Revising a Formula

As you enter the new values, the costs for the alternative menu are automatically calculated. Recall that all of the formulas in both models are linked by formulas to the People cell, C1, because the reference entered into the formulas was an absolute reference, $People, which is not altered when a cell is copied.

244

Cell C17 is an exception. That cell currently displays the value $55.23 as the cost per guest for the alternative menu. Since the overall costs of the two menus is not very far apart, the value in C17 would appear to be an error. Place the cell pointer on C17:

Click(left) on cell C 17($55.23)

The formula on the edit line reads =F16/C9. The reference to F16, the total cost of the alternative menu, is correct. However, the reference to C9, as the denominator of the calculation, is not correct. Instead the reference should be to C1, the cell named "People". What caused this problem? The answer is that when the original formula was entered into C9, the reference for the cell named "People" was entered as a relative reference rather than an absolute one. When that formula was copied, Works adjusted both references resulting in a formula that did not use the value needed to calculate the cost per guest of the alternative menu.

You can correct the formula by editing the reference to C9. Activate the edit mode by entering:

[F2]

Use the [bkspace] key to delete the C9 reference:

[bkspace] (2 times)

If you want to point at the cell you want to reference with the mouse you can do so by clicking(left) on the cell you want to reference. If you want to use the keyboard to point at the cell, you must first toggle Works into the pointing rather than the edit mode. Note that the word "Edit" currently appears on the status line. You cannot point at a cell reference with the keyboard while that mode is active. Enter:

[F2]

Works removes the word "Edit" from the status line indicating that the pointing mode is active. Move the cell pointer to the cell you need to reference by entering:

[Ctrl-up] (6 times)

In order to avoid further problems you will want to change this reference to an absolute reference. The last time you entered an absolute reference you did so by typing in the $ along with the cell address or name, e.g., $People. When you are pointing, either with the keyboard or mouse, you can designate a reference as absolute by pressing the [F4] key rather than having to manually enter the $. Enter:

[F4]

245

Works inserts the $ in front of the cell name changing it to an absolute (non-adjusting) reference. Complete the formula by entering:

[return]

The formula now calculates the correct value for cost per guest, as shown in Figure 7-9.

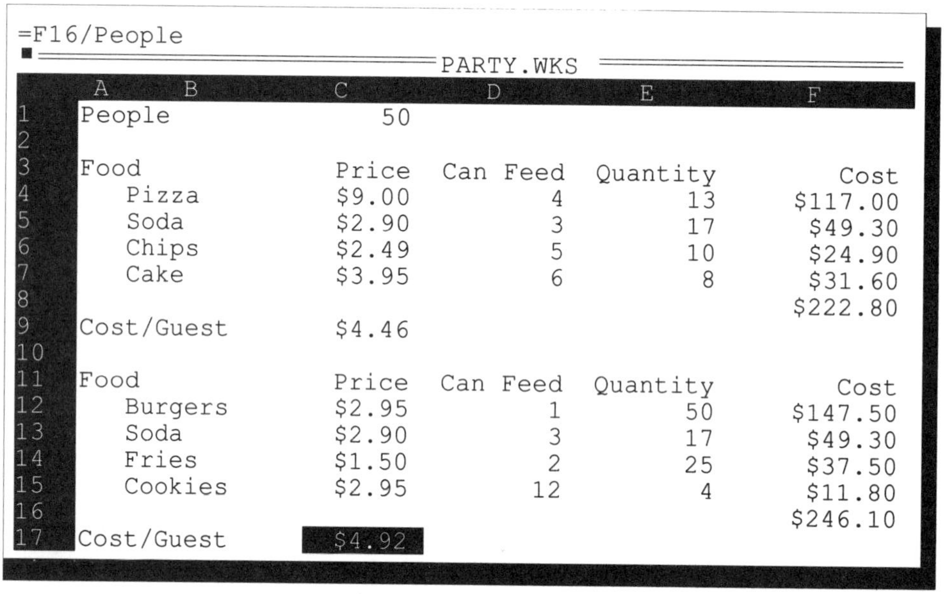

```
=F16/People
■ ══════════════════════════════ PARTY.WKS ═══════════════════════
        A        B          C       D          E              F
1   People              50
2
3   Food             Price   Can Feed  Quantity          Cost
4       Pizza        $9.00        4        13         $117.00
5       Soda         $2.90        3        17          $49.30
6       Chips        $2.49        5        10          $24.90
7       Cake         $3.95        6         8          $31.60
8                                                      $222.80
9   Cost/Guest       $4.46
10
11  Food             Price   Can Feed  Quantity          Cost
12      Burgers      $2.95        1        50         $147.50
13      Soda         $2.90        3        17          $49.30
14      Fries        $1.50        2        25          $37.50
15      Cookies      $2.95       12         4          $11.80
16                                                     $246.10
17  Cost/Guest       $4.92
```

Figure 7-9. Spreadsheet with Alternative Menu.

Inserting Rows

The two sections of the model both have menus that have exactly the same number of items. For example, a meal that consists of burgers and fries may also require condiments such as mustard and ketchup. In order to take into account the cost of these items you will have to insert a new row into the second menu.

To insert a new row you need to highlight the row in the spreadsheet just after the position where you want the new row to be inserted. Previously you highlighted the row by clicking on the row number in the row number bar. You can also highlight the current row or column using the Select menu.

Place the cell pointer on the row after where you want the insertion to take place, e.g., row 13. Note that when you insert a row, the column in which the cell pointer is positioned is not important:

Click(left) on cell C13($2.90)

Use the Select menu to highlight the row:

Click(left) on **Select**
Click(left) on **Row**

Row 13 is now highlighted. Insert a new row at that location:

Click(left) on **Edit**
Click(left) on **Insert Row/Column**

The program inserts a new, blank row in the spreadsheet. Your first instinct might be to begin entering the information into this row. However, it is important to remember that the new, blank row does not contain the cell formats and formulas that all of the other rows in the table contain. It would be more efficient if you first copied an existing rows and then edited the items that needed to be changed. You would avoid having to enter all of the formats and formulas on the new row. Select row 12 to be copied:

Click(left) on cell B12(Burgers)
Click(left) on **Select**
Click(left) on **Row**

Copy row 12 into row 13, the row you just created:

Click(left) on **Edit**
Click(left) on **Copy**
Click(left) on cell B13(Blank)

[return]

All of the values, formulas, and formats used in row 12 are copied into row 13. Fill in the information needed for the new item in row 13:

Point at cell B13(Burgers)
Drag(left) to cell D13(1)

With the cells highlighted you can use **[return]** at the end of each entry to advance the cell pointer:

```
Condiments [return]
2.95 [return]
25 return]
```

The alternative menu now uses a different number of items form the original menu. What is interesting is that the formula in cell F17, the one that totals the costs of the alternative menu, appears to include all five of the items even though the original formula used for that total has a cell range that cover only 4 rows. Place the cell pointer on F17:

```
Click(left) on cell F17($252.00)
```

The formula that appears on the Edit line, =SUM(F12:F16), adds the values from five rows—12, 13, 14, 15, and 16—to arrive at the total cost. Works has automatically expanded the range used in the formula because a new row was inserted within the original range—F12:F15—used in the formula. This means that you can insert rows and columns into tables without having to rewrite formulas that use range functions based on the original size of the table.

It is important to remember that this adjustment will take place only if the new row or column is inserted inside the range used in the formula. For example, you might want to add an item by inserting the new row at the end of the table, e.g., on this spreadsheet row 17. If you did insert a new row at row 17, the formula in F17 would remain =SUM(F12:F16) because row 17 is outside the range used in the formula F12:F16.

Dividing a Spreadsheet into Pages

When a spreadsheet is printed, Works automatically *paginates* the spreadsheet. Pagination is a process by which data which is not organized in pages, e.g., a row and column spreadsheet, is broken up into a series of printed pages. Works attempts to fit as many cells as possible onto the page set by default at 8.5 inches by 11inches.

However, it is sometimes desirable to be able to manually specify where pages should be broken rather than simply letting Work automatically paginate the spreadsheet. For example, suppose you wanted to print each of the alternative menus on a separate page. You could divide the spreadsheet in three pages by inserting manual page breaks before row 3 and row 11. You could then specify printing of pages 2 and 3 only in order to get the print out you desire.

Page breaks can be inserted at any row or column in the spreadsheet with the **Insert Page Break** command located on the Print menu. Insert a page break before row 3. Select the row (or column) at which you want to insert the page break before you enter the **Insert Page Break** command. Keep in mind that the row or column at which the page break is inserted will be the first row on the new page. For example, if you highlight row 3 and insert a page break, row 3 will print at the top of a new page ending the previous page with row 2.

Select row 3:

```
Click(left) on 3 in the row number bar
```

Designate that as a page break:

```
Click(left) on Print
Click9left) on Insert Page Break
```

Works places a symbol, >>, in the row number bar following the number 3 to indicate that this is a page break. Repeat the command for row 11:

```
Click(left) on 11 in the row number bar
Click(left) on Print
Click(left) on Insert Page Break
```

Printing Specific Pages

Now that the spreadsheet is divided into distinct pages you can print the pages of the spreadsheet which contain the two menus:

```
Click(left) on Print
Click(left) on Print
```

In order to print only some of the pages, select the Print specific pages option:

```
Click(left) on Print specific pages
```

The Pages text box changes from gray to black indicating that it is now an active option. Print pages are specified by entering the page numbers into the Pages box. You can enter page numbers in two ways: list and range.

List

A list is a series of page numbers separated by commas. For example, entering 5,8,12 will cause Works to print pages 5, 8, and 12.

Ranges

A range of pages is designated by separating the starting and ending pages with a colon or a dash. For example, entering 5:12 would print pages 5 through 12.

You can combine a list with a range, e.g., 1,5:12 would print page 1, then skip to page 5 and print 5 through 12. In this case you want pages 2 and 3. Enter:

```
Tab]
2:3 [return]
```

The program prints the specified pages, each of which contains a different menu.

You can remove a page break by placing the cell pointer on the row or column that currently contains the break and using the **Delete page break** command. Note that this command is active only when the cell pointer is positioned on a page break row or column. Remove the page breaks from the spreadsheet:

```
Click(left) on Print
Click(left) on Delete page break

Click(left) on cell A3(Food)
Click(left) on Print
Click(left) on Delete page break
```

Save the spreadsheet and exit Works:

```
Click(left) on the close button
Click(left) on <Yes>
```

If you are done working you can exit Works:

```
Click(left) on Exit Works
```

If you want to go on to the next project in Chapter 8, leave the program running. Chapter 8 will show you how to create charts and graphs from your spreadsheet information.

SUMMARY

In this chapter you learned how to enhance the appearance of your spreadsheet.

Cell Formats. Numeric formats are applied to cells in order to control the appearance of numbers. Formats allow you to specify a specific number of decimal places as well as other formatting attributes such as comma separators and leading dollar signs. Formatting creates a more uniform and consistent appearance which makes your spreadsheet easier to read and understand. If a value cannot be displayed using the assigned format, Works displays a special symbol, #########, in the cell. This symbol affects only the cell's appearance and not the value of the cell.

Formats and Rounding. If the value in a cell contains more significant decimal places than are specified in the cell format, Works rounds the displayed value of the cell to the number of decimal places specified in the format. However, this rounding affects only the appearance of the cell not its actual value in the spreadsheet. If the cell is referenced by a formula in another cell, Works uses the full decimal value regardless of how the value appears on the spreadsheet display. If your application requires that the appearance of the cell match exactly its actual value, e.g., bookkeeping, you must use the ROUND() function to alter the cell formula to round the value to the same number of decimal places specified in the cell format.

Erasing a Cell. The [**Del**] key will clear the label or value from a cell. Note that any cell format or style attributes assigned to the cell remain when the contents are erased. The **Clear** command on the Edit menu will erase the contents of a highlighted range of cells.

Cell Styles. There are three types of attributes that can be applied to cells: text enhancements (such as bold, italics, and underline), cell alignment-left, center, or right, and cell locking. Cell locking is used in conjunction with the Protect Data command on the Options menu to protect cell information from accidental alteration.

Column Widths. All spreadsheet columns are set initially at 10 characters in width. You can change the column width to between 1 and 80 characters. Widening a column is one solution for formats which cause ####### symbols to be displayed.

Headers and Footers. You can specify single lines of text that will print at the top or bottom of every page of the spreadsheet. Works recognizes special symbols which insert values into page headers and footers, e.g., &d inserts the correct date into a header or footer.

Range Entry. The [**return**] key automatically advances the cell pointer through a highlighted range of cells one cell at a time. This enables you to make a series of entries that end with the [**return**] key rather than having to use the arrow keys to advance the cell pointer following an entry.

Page Breaks. You can insert manual page breaks at the desired column or row in the spreadsheet. Works will begin a new printed page each time it encounters a page break in the spreadsheet.

EXERCISES

Exercise 1

Name cell E8 "Food Costs":

Click(left) on cell E8($233.65)

Click(left) on Edit
Click(left) on Range Name

Food Costs

Click(left) on **<Create>**

Chapter 8

Charts

I n this chapter you will learn how to transform spreadsheet information into charts and graphs. Charts convert columns and rows of numbers into a visual display that can communicate ideas quickly and powerfully. Before computers came along, creating charts was a tedious, time consuming, and inflexible task which required special skills and materials. Applications such as Works make charts easy, fast, and accurate. In this chapter you will use the PARTY spreadsheet created in Chapter 6 and modified in Chapter 7 as the basis for your charts.

CHARTS

The information contained in the spreadsheet can be presented by means of a chart such a bar, pie, or line graph. Charts and graphs help make numeric information easier to understand since the quantities used in the spreadsheet are translated to objects of different sizes in a chart. Works can create 8 different types of charts or graphs.

Bar Chart. A bar chart represents values by drawing vertical bars on the chart. Bar charts are good for showing the relative value of various items based on the height of the bars. All of the values that are contained in the same column (or row) of the spreadsheet appear as the same color bar on the chart. In Figure 8-1 a bar chart displays three different values for each month.

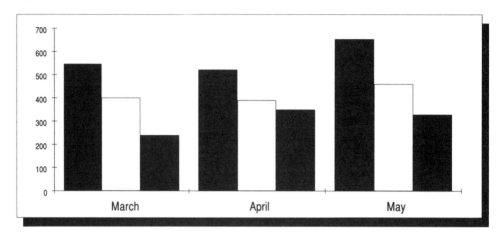

Figure 8-1. A Bar Chart.

Stacked Bar Chart. A stacked bar chart shows the combined effect of different categories of values added together. Use this chart when you want to illustrate the sum of several different series of values. In Figure 8-2 the chart shows the total value of three items for each month.

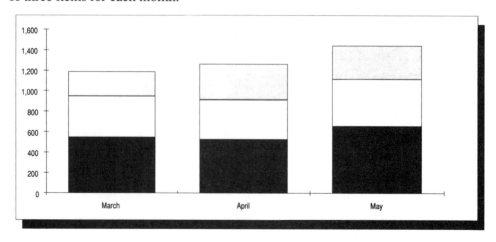

Figure 8-2. A Stacked Bar Chart.

100% Stacked Bar Chart. This chart converts values into percentages. It is similar in appearance to a stacked bar chart with the exception that all of the bars are the same height. What you are looking for in this chart is the relative size of each color within each bar. This chart should be used when you want to illustrate differences in percentages rather than actual values. 100% bar charts do not accurately show which bar is actually the largest since all the bars are scaled to be the same height. In Figure 8-3 the relative percentage of three different values is shown for each month.

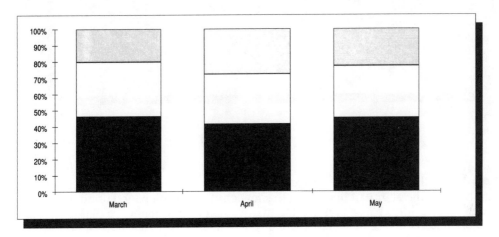

Figure 8-3. A 100% Bar Chart.

Line Chart. This chart shows the values of the spreadsheet as points on the chart connected by lines. While this chart does show the value of each of the items, it is designed to emphasize changes that occur over a period of time. Figure 8-4 shows the changes in three different values over a period of months. Line charts are almost always associated with charts containing date or time values in addition to numeric values.

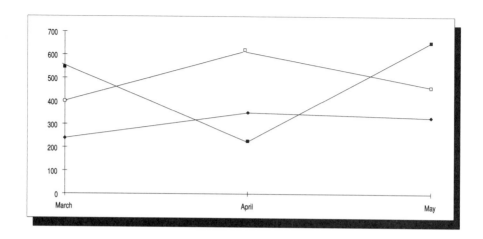

Figure 8-4. A Line Chart.

Area Line Chart. An area line chart combines the cumulative quality of a stacked bar chart and the ability of line charts to show changes over a period of time. The top line in an area line chart represents the total value of all of the items that fall on the date or time. Unlike a standard line chart, the lines on an area line chart will not cross since each the values for each date are added together rather than plotted individually. Figure 8-5 shows a line area chart with three series of data plotted.

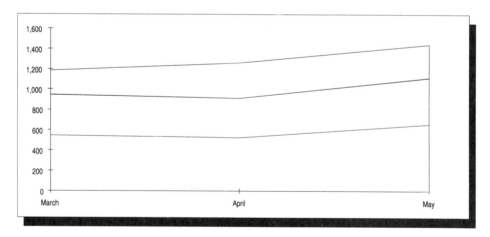

Figure 8-5. An Area Line Chart.

Hi-Low. A Hi-Low chart is a variation on the standard line chart. Instead of drawing the lines horizontally between different times and dates, the lines are drawn vertically between values at the same date or time. Hi-Low charts are used to illustrate changes that occur on the same date typically the changes in value of stocks or other traded commodity, as shown in Figure 8-6.

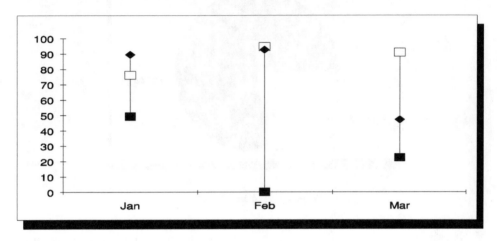

Figure 8-6. A Hi-Low Chart.

Pie Charts. Pie charts, like 100% bar charts, as used to show values as percentages of a whole, as shown in Figure 8-7. Because pie charts are circular, they can show only one series of values in which each slice of the pie represents one value in the series. Use pie charts when you want to emphasize part to whole relationships rather than the actual numeric values of various items.

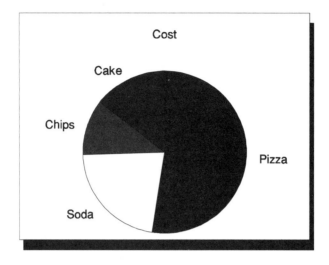

Figure 8-7. A Pie Chart.

X-Y Graphs (Scattergram). XY graphs are used in mathematical and scientific applications where it is necessary to plot points against two numeric axes, as shown in Figure 8-8. The resulting graph is used to illustrate the pattern, if any, that exists between the two series of values.

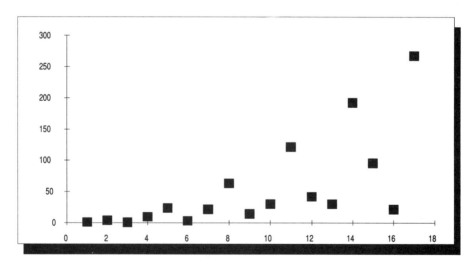

Figure 8-8. X-Y Graphs.

Charts are made up of a number of distinct parts, as shown in Figure 8-9.

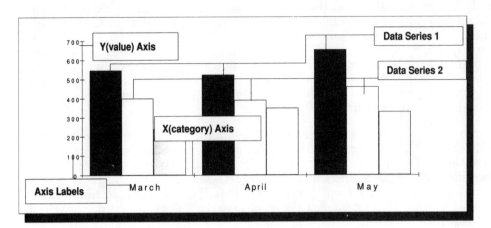

Figure 8-9. Chart Comprised of Distinct Parts.

Axes

The basis of all charts and graphs (with the exception of pie charts) are the horizontal and vertical axes. The vertical axis is called the value axis because it represents numeric values. Values increase as you move up the axis. In charts, such as bar and line charts, the horizontal axis, called the category, represents the categories which are not numeric values themselves. The exception to this rule are X-Y graphs in which both axes represent numeric values.

The axes are important because they determine the location of the items displayed on the chart. In a bar chart the value axis determines the height of the bars while the category axis determines the order in which the bars appear, from left to right.

By mathematical convention, the category axis is designated as the X axis and the value axis is designated as the Y axis. In many of the menus and dialog boxes, X is used to represent the category axis and Y the value axis.

Axis Labels

Each axis is labeled so that the person reading the chart can determine the meaning of the bar or lines that appear. The value axis will have a scale of numeric values while the category axis will have text labels. The numeric scale on the value axis is automatically calculated by Works to fit the range of values selected for the chart.

Data Series

The data series are the objects (bars, points, lines, pie slices) that appear on the chart to represent values stored in the spreadsheet cells. Data items are called table series because Works associates all of the items from the same row or column as a group of related values. For example, in Figure 8-7, all of the solid black bars represent values drawn from a single column or row. The order in which they appear from left to right on the chart is determined by their sequence in the spreadsheet cells. Works charts (with the exception of pie and X-Y graphs) can display between 1 and 6 different data series on a single chart.

You can create or modify a chart so that it draws information from any section of the spreadsheet. You can create many different charts associated with a given spreadsheet. This is important since it is seldom possible to present all the information from a spreadsheet in a single chart. One of the advantages of drawing information for a chart from a spreadsheet is that the chart is linked to the spreadsheet cells. This means that if you change the values in the spreadsheet, the chart will be re-drawn to match the new values. As with spreadsheet models, one chart can be re-drawn as many times as you desire simply by changing a few key values on the spreadsheet.

For example, suppose you wanted to create a chart that illustrated some aspects of the information contained in the current spreadsheet, such as the prices of the food items or the costs of the food items.

Charts are created in Works directly from the spreadsheet information. First, a section of the spreadsheet is highlighted. Then you use the **New Chart** command located on the Options menu to create a chart based on the highlighted information.

The crucial and sometime tricky part of charting is using the highlight to indicate to Works what information on the spreadsheet should be used for the chart. Works uses a built in set of rules to pick out from the highlighted cells the various parts of the chart, i.e., the category series, values series, the chart legend, etc.

Figure 8-10 illustrates how Works will construct a chart based on a selected range of cells. The figure shows cells B3 through C7 selected.

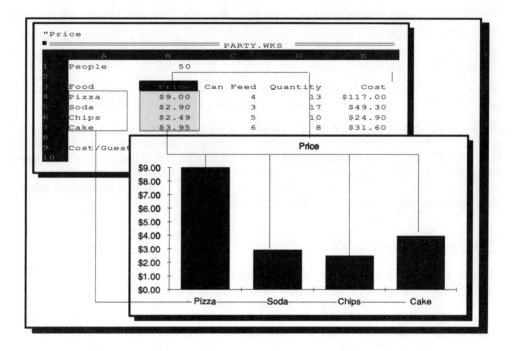

Figure 8-10. Spreadsheet Information Defines Chart.

Category Axis Items

Works assumes that the items in column B—the first column in the selected range—contain the information for the category axis. The labels written in column B appear along the horizontal axis of the chart.

Values Axis Series

Works uses the values found in column C as the values which should be displayed as bars on the chart. Works assumes that each column following the first contains a data series. If the selection had been the range B3:D7 then the chart would contain two value series: the first from column C and the second from column D. A chart select can contain up to seven columns, the first for the category axis followed by 6 columns of values.

Legend

Note that Works also assumes that the first item in each column is a label that functions as a column heading. These labels appear at the bottom of the chart as a

261

legend. The legend matches the column heading with the color pattern used for a given series of values.

Chart Type

All new charts are created as bar type charts. Once created you can use the commands on the chart menu bar to change the chart to pie, line, or other style of chart.

The rules for defining a chart hold true as long as the selected range contains more rows than columns. In Figure 8-10 the range contains two columns and four rows. However, if a range contains an equal or greater number of columns than rows then the roles of column and row as stated are reversed. For example, suppose the range highlighted was B4:F7. Works would then assume that each row represents a data series and that the labels in row 3 are the category axis items.

Creating a Chart

The previous discussion may have given you the impression that creating a chart is complicated. Just the opposite is the case, for the exact reason that most of the decisions required for charting are made automatically by Works using its set of charting rules. It is not necessary to even be aware of all of the rules Works uses since you can modify the chart generated by Works to suit your own needs after it has been generated. Start the Works program in the usual way. Load the PARTY.WKS spreadsheet from the disk:

```
Click(left) on Open Existing File
Double click(left) on PARTY.WKS
```

The first chart you create will use the information in the range of cells starting at B3 through C7. The chart will illustrate the prices of the items on the first menu in the spreadsheet.

The first task in creating a chart is to highlight the range of cell that contains the data for the chart. In this case that range is B3:C7. Highlight that range using the mouse:

```
Click(left) on cell B3(blank)
Drag(left) to cell C7($3.95)
```

Chart operations begin with the View menu. Display the View menu:

```
Click(left) on View
```

The View menu lists three commands: **Spreadsheet, New Chart,** and **Charts**.

Spreadsheet

This command is used to change from the chart mode back to the spreadsheet mode.

New Chart

This command generates a new chart based on the currently highlighted range of cells. Note that if you choose this command without highlighting a range of cells, a message is displayed that read "Series not selected." However, what the message does not indicate is that Works defines a new chart with no settings at all. You can use a blank chart to build a chart manually, part by part, if you desire.

Charts

This command displays a dialog box that lists all of the charts, if any, generated for the current spreadsheet. You can use the command buttons on this menu to delete, copy, or assign names to any of the existing charts.

Create a new chart:

Click(left) on New Chart

When Works generates the new chart it temporarily suspends the desktop view and displays a full screen image of the new chart, as shown in Figure 8-11. The bar type chart displays bars that represent the prices of the food that will be purchased for the party. The legend at the bottom of the screen shows that the black bars are price items.

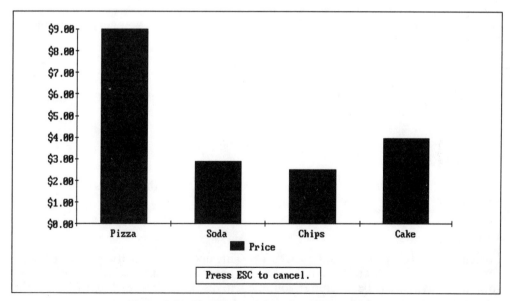

Figure 8-11. Chart Created from Spreadsheet Range.

Note that the message at the bottom of the screen, "Press ESC to cancel" is not part of the chart. Continue by entering:

```
[Esc]
```

The Chart Menu Bar

When you exit the chart display it appears that you have returned to the spreadsheet display. This is not quite true. While you can now see the normal desktop view some things have changed. The menu bar at the top of the window shows eight items instead of the nine items on the standard spreadsheet menu. The current menu is the Chart menu. The Edit and Select options have been removed and the Data option added. Note that the word CHART appears on the status line indicating that the chart mode is active. Display the View menu:

```
Click(left) on View
```

If you look closely at the menu you will notice two changes since the last time you displayed this menu:

Chart Name

A new item, Chart 1 has been added to the bottom of the menu. Works will add chart names, e.g., Chart 1, Chart 2, and Chart 3, for each new chart you generate from the current spreadsheet.

Selected Item

A black dot appears next to the name Chart 1. This indicates that Chart 1 is the active chart. Any commands issued from the chart menu will affect chart 1.

Chart Text

Part of the chart display consists of text. A Works chart has three types of text which are as follows:

Titles

You can create five text titles on a chart. The Title and Subtitle will appear at the top, center of chart. The X and Y axis titles will appear along side the X and Y axis. A second Y axis title can be entered if you select to display a second Y axis on the right side of the chart.

Legends

The legend text appears in the chart legend to identify the meaning of each seres on the chart. Legend text is selected from the first cell in a row or column series. You can change or eliminate that text.

Data Labels

Data labels are text (or numbers) that appear next to each data item on the chart. Typically, data labels are used to show the exact value of a chart item. You can also use data labels to place text next to one or more items on the chart.

Chart text is added by using the Titles, Legends or Data Labels commands found on the Data menu. For example, suppose you want to add a title to the chart. Select Titles from the Data menu:

Click(left) on **Data**
Click(left) on **Titles**

The titles dialog box, as shown in Figure 8-12, lists text boxes for the entry of the chart's titles. You can create a title by typing the text directly into the text box or entering a reference to a cell which contains a label or value you want to use as a title.

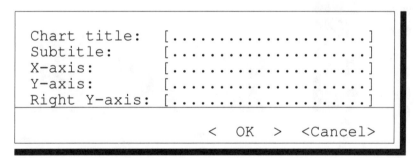

Figure 8-12. Chart Titles Dialog Box.

Enter the following titles for the chart:

Party Food Menu
[Tab] (2 times)

The X-axis title is used to describe all of the items that appear on the category axis. In this case they are all food items. Since the word "food "already appears in cell A3 you can enter the cell address instead of entering the text:

```
a3 [Tab]
```

The Y axis is the value axis. In this case the values show the cost for each item:

```
Cost per item [return]
```

Display the modified chart. You can use a keyboard shortcut, **[Shift-F10]**, to activate the chart display:

```
[Shift-F10]
```

The chart now displays the titles you added, as shown in Figure 8-13.

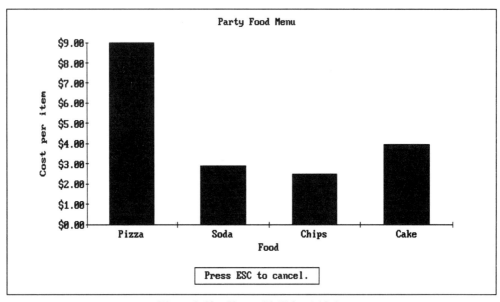

Figure 8-13. Chart with Titles Added.

Return to the desktop display by entering:

```
[Esc]
```

Since this chart contains only a single data series, the legend that appears at the bottom of the chart is unnecessary. You can use the **Legends** command on the Data menu to eliminate the legend from the chart:

```
Click(left) on Data
Click(left) on Legends
```

The Legends dialog box lists the six Y axis series in a list box. At the bottom of the dialog box the legend option shows the text or cell reference currently used for the selected series. In this case the selected series is the 1st Y series which uses the contents of cell C3 for its legend. You can eliminate the legend from the chart by deleting the cell reference from the Legend box. Enter:

```
[Tab] [Del]
```

```
Click(left) on <Done>
```

Display the chart again:

```
[Shift-F10]
```

The legend, Price, has been removed from the chart. When you are done with the chart you can return to the spreadsheet window by exiting the chart display and then selecting Spreadsheet from the View menu:

```
[Esc]
```

```
Click(left) on View
Click(left) on Spreadsheet
```

You have now returned to the normal spreadsheet operations mode.

MANUAL SELECTION OF CHART RANGES

Creating a chart is very simple when the information you want to chart is entered into an area of the spreadsheet that can be highlighted as a single block. Chart 1 used information from two adjacent columns, B and C. Suppose that you now wanted to create a chart that uses information from ranges that were not next to one another on the spreadsheet. For example, suppose that you want to chart the cost of each of the items on the menu. That would require using two separate ranges—cells B3:B7 as the category series and F3:F7 as the value series—as the basis of the chart.

There are two ways in which you could create this chart: manual selection of ranges and delete ranges.

Manual Selection of Ranges

This approach begins with a blank chart. Using the commands on the chart menu bar, you manually select each of the ranges needed for the chart. This method allows you complete control over the elements used in the chart.

Delete Ranges

A different approach to solving this problem would be to create a chart that includes all of the data in between the two ranges you want to use. For example, highlighting B3:F7 would create a chart with 4 values series, one for column C, D, E, and F. You would then use Chart commands to delete the data series you don't want (C,D, and E), leaving only the category series B3:B7 and the value series F3:F7.

The Delete Ranges method is probably a bit faster but it will only work if the total number of columns in the highlighted range is 7 or less since Works charts are limited to one category and 6 value series. The Manual Selection method can be used to create a chart that uses any block of cell on the spreadsheet.

Creating a Blank Chart

The first step in the Manual Selection method is to create a blank chart. This can be done by issuing the **New Chart** command when there is no range highlighted. Move the cell pointer back to the top of the spreadsheet by entering:

[Ctrl-Home]

The cell pointer is now located on a single cell with no range highlighted. Create a new chart:

Click(left) on **View**
Click(left) on **New Chart**

Because there is no highlighted range of cells, Works displays the message "Series not selected." This message confirms what you have deliberately done, which is to create a chart without adequate information. It is important to understand that this message does not mean that no chart has been created. It simply tells you that no data series have been assigned to the chart, exactly the chart you meant to create.

You can confirm that a chart has been created by displaying the View menu:

Click(left) on < **Ok** >
Click(left) on **View**

The View menu shows a new item, Chart 2. The black dot indicates that this chart is the currently selected item. Close the menu by entering:

```
[Esc]
```

Adding Ranges to a Chart

Once you have created the blank chart you can manually assign spreadsheet ranges to the various data series by following a two step process.

Highlight Range

Even though the CHART mode is active you can still move the cell pointer and highlight ranges on the spreadsheet. Use the mouse or keyboard to highlight the cell range you want to include in the chart.

Define Series

Once the highlight has been placed on the correct range of cells you use the Data menu to define the highlighted range as the category (X) or value (1st Y through 6th Y) series in the current chart.

For example, the values that you want to chart are contained in cells F4 through F7. Those cells should be assigned to value series 1 (1st Y). Highlight the range:

```
Point at cell F4($117.00)
Drag(left) to cell F7($31.60)
```

The cells F4:F7 are highlighted as a range. Define this range as the first value series in the chart by using the Data menu:

```
Click(left) on Data
```

The program displays the Data menu in Figure 8-14. The top section of the menu lists the seven data series—six Y (value) series and one X (category) series—available on a chart.

Figure 8-14. Data Series Menu.

Designate the Current Range as the 1st Y-Series:

Click(left) on **1st Y-Series**

Once you have added a Y (value) series to the chart you have given Works enough information to create a chart. Display the chart you have defined by entering:

[Shift-F10]

Works displays a bar chart—the default chart type—using the values in the designated range, as shown in Figure 8-15. Of course, the chart lacks text such as labels for the bar because the category series have yet to be defined for this chart.

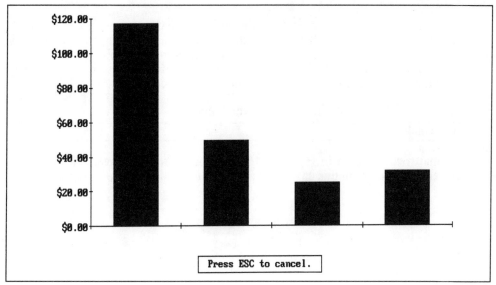

Figure 8-15. Chart Created by Manual Selection of Y (Value) Series.

Return to the desktop by entering:

[Esc]

You can use the same two step method—highlight and define—to add a category series to the chart. Highlight the labels in B4 through B7. Note that the number of cells in each range added to the chart should be the same so that each item in the Y (value) series matches an item in the X (category) series:

Point at cell B4(Pizza) Drag(left) to cell B7(Cake)

Define these cells as the X (category) series:

Click(left) on **Data** Click(left) on **X-Series**

Display the modified chart:

[Shift-F10]

The bars are now labeled with the text from cells B4 through B7. Return to the desktop by entering:

[Esc]

Changing the Chart Format

Chart Format refers to the basic style of the chart, i.e., bar, line , pie, etc. By default, all charts begin as bar charts. You can use the Format menu to change the style of the chart to one of the other styles available in Works. For example, the current chart might be changed to a pie chart. The pie chart would emphasize which items comprise the largest or smallest portion of the total food costs.

To change the chart format, display the Format menu:

Click(left) on **Format**

The Format menu, shown in Figure 8-16, lists the chart styles available in Works. The current chart style, in this case Bar is indicated by a dot next to the style name.

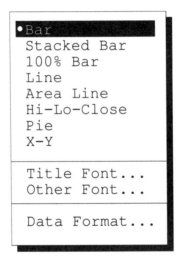

Figure 8-16. Chart Format Menu.

Change the chart to a pie chart by selecting Pie from the menu:

Click(left) on **Pie**

[Shift-F10]

The chart is now displayed as a pie chart in Figure 8-17. Note that Works automatically calculates and displays a percentage next to each slice of the pie. The percentages are calculated by dividing the value of each slice by the total value of all of the slices.

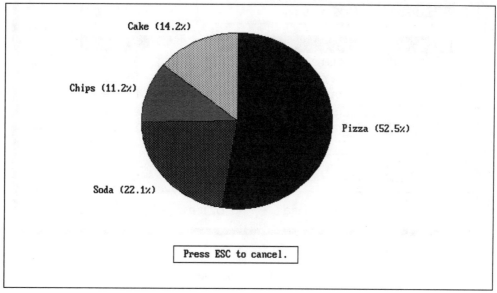

Figure 8-17. Chart Formatted as a Pie Chart.

Return to the desktop display by entering:

[Esc]

Exploding a Slice

An *exploded* slice is a pie slice that is separated from the rest of the pie. Exploding a slice is a technique used to emphasize the role of one particular part of the pie. For example, in the current chart, the cost of pizza is greater than all of the other items combined. You can emphasize this point by exploding that slice from the rest of the chart.

The option to explode a slice of the pie is found on the Data Format command dialog box found on the Format menu:

Click(left) on Data **Format**
Click(left) on **Data Format**

The Data Format dialog box contains options that allow you to control the details of the chart such as color and pattern of the objects displayed on the chart, as shown in Figure 8-18. You can format individual items, such as pie slices, or apply a given format to all of the objects (slices) on the chart.

273

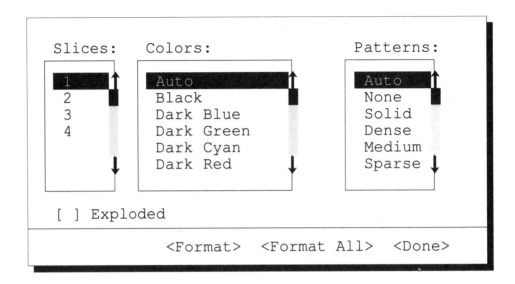

Figure 8-18. Data Format Dialog Box.

By default, the color and pattern of the items designated for all of the objects is Auto. The Auto setting allows Works to automatically select the colors and patterns used for the chart. If you desire to have certain items appear in a specific color or pattern you can manually select those colors or patterns from the list boxes.

The Exploded option controls whether or not a slice will be exploded from the main section of the pie. In this case you want to explode the slice that represents "pizza." Which number is that slice? The answer requires you to recall the order in which the items appear in the spreadsheet. In this case, the first item in the value series is "pizza " which tells you that slice one should be exploded. Since slice one is currently highlighted, any actions taken will apply to that slice:

Click(left) on **Exploded**

An X appears in the Exploded check box. Apply this option to the selected slice by using the **Format** command button:

Click(left) on **<Format>**

Close the dialog box:

Click(left) on **<Done>**

Display the modified chart by entering:

[Shift-F10]

The chart now shows the Pizza slice exploded from the rest of the slices, as shown in Figure 8-19.

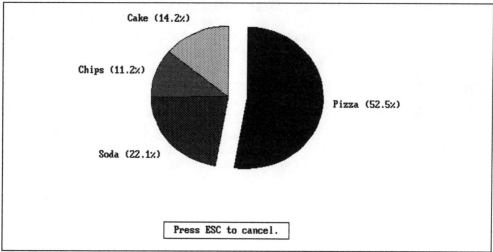

Figure 8-19. Pie with Exploded Slice.

Return to the desktop display by entering:

[Esc]

Adding a Chart Border

A chart border is a rectangle drawn around the chart so that it appears to be framed on the page. You can add a border to any chart by using the **Show Border** command location on the Options menu:

Click(left) on **Options** Click(left on **Show Border**

Display the chart by entering:

[Shift-F10]

The chart is now enclosed in a border. Return to the desktop display by entering:

[Esc]

Return to the spreadsheet mode:

Click(left) on **View** Click(left) on **Spreadsheet**

NAMING CHARTS

When you create a new chart for a spreadsheet, Works will automatically generate a name for the chart by numbering each chart consecutively, Chart 1, Chart 2 and so on. These names can be changed to more descriptive names by using the Charts command found on the View menu. Descriptive names for the charts help you recall what each chart represents much better than names like "Chart 1". Display the Charts dialog box:

Click(left) on **View**
Click(left) on **Charts**

The Charts dialog box contains a list of all of the charts currently defined for the spreadsheet, as shown in Figure 8-20. You can use the command buttons in the dialog box to rename, delete, or copy any of the existing charts.

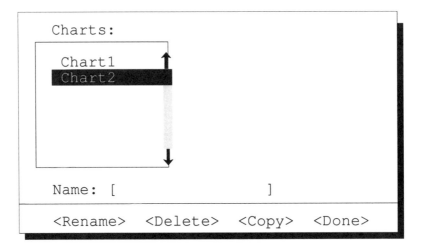

Figure 8-20. Charts Dialog Box.

In this case you want to change the names of the charts so that they reflect the contents of the charts. Change the name of Chart1 to Prices (bar):

Click(left) on *Chart1*

[Tab]
Prices(bar)

Click(left) on **<Rename>**

The name of the chart changes in the list box. Rename Chart2 to Costs (pie) by entering:

```
[Down] [Tab]
Costs(Pie) [return]
```

Exit the dialog box by selecting the **<Done>** button:

```
Click(left) on <Done>
```

Display the View menu:

```
Click(left) on View
```

The View menu shows the names you assigned to the charts instead of the default names, as shown in Figure 8-21.

```
•Spreadsheet
 New Chart
 Charts...
 1 Prices(bar)
 2 Costs(pie)
```

Figure 8-21. View Menu Shows Chart Names.

Return to the spreadsheet mode:

```
Click(left) on Spreadsheet
```

Charts with Multiple Data Series

Both of the charts you have created contain only one value series. However, Works charts can plot up to six different data series on a single chart. For example, suppose that you highlighted the values in the alternate menu B11 through F16. That range would include 5 columns. The first column will become the X (category) series while the next four columns would be assigned as Y (values) series 1 through 4.

Highlight the alternate menu information:

```
Point at cell B11(blank)
Drag(left) to cell F16($11.80)
```

Create a new chart based on this information:

```
Click(left) on View
Click(left) on New Chart
```

Works creates and displays a chart that has four different value series plotted on a single bar chart, as shown in Figure 8-22. Each value series places one bar at each of the category items on the X axis. The groups of bars are called cluster. Within clusters the bars are differentiated by order in which they appear, e.g., price, number that can be fed, quantity and cost, and color. The legend at the bottom of the chart matches series labels with the colors of the bars.

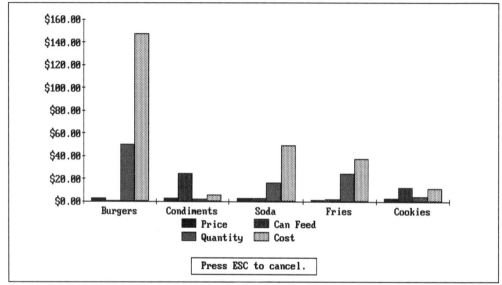

Figure 8-22. Chart with Multiple Value Series.

Return to the desktop display by entering:

[Esc]

Deleting Series

The new chart contains a data series for each of the value columns in the highlighted range. While Works will chart any values included in the range, this does not necessarily mean that these values make a meaningful chart. The chart would probably have more significance if only the Quantity and Cost series were charted.

The **Series** command on the Data menu allows you to delete series from the chart. You can use this option to eliminate the 1st and 2nd value series, C12:C16 and D12:D16, from the chart. The series ranges begins with row 12 not row 11. Works automatically assigned the items in the top row of the highlighted range as labels for the chart legend:

Click(left) on **Data**
Click(left) on **Series**

The Series dialog box displays a list box which shows the cell ranges assigned to each of the six value and one category range in the chart, as shown in Figure 8-23.

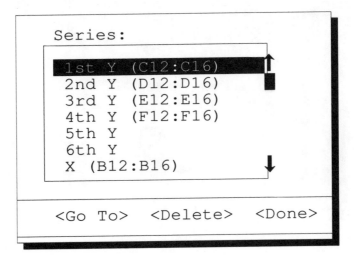

Figure 8-23. Series Dialog Box.

The **<Delete>** command button can be used to delete a series from the chart. In this case you want to remove series 1 and 2:

Click(left) on **<Delete>**

The 1st series is eliminated:

Click(left) on **2nd Y (D12:D16)**
Click(left) on **<Delete>**

Complete the series editing and display the new chart:

Click(left) on **<Done>**
Click(left) on **View**
Click(left) on **Chart1**

The chart now displays only two value series, Quantity and Costs, as shown in Figure 8-24.

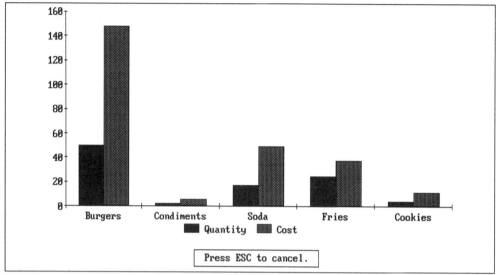

Figure 8-24. Unwanted Series Deleted from Chart.

Dual Scale Charts

If you examine the chart currently displayed on the screen you will notice that the bars for the quantity series are all smaller than the bars for the cost series. Some of the bars are so small that it is hard to estimate the differences between them. This type of problem will frequently arise when the chart contains two series that have quite a different range of values. In this example, the quantity series ranges from 2 to 50 while the Costs series ranges from $5.90 to $147.50. In order to accommodate all of the values in both series, Works must scale the Y axis to fit the largest value include in the chart. The main disadvantage of this is that the series with the smaller values is squeezed at the bottom of the chart. One solution is to add a second Y axis on the right side of the chart. You can assign each series to a different axis. Works can then scale each axis to more closely fit the values being charted.

The **Two Y-Axes** command located on the Options menu adds a second Y axis to the right side of the current chart:

Click(left) on **Options**
Click(left) on **Two Y-Axes**

When you select this option Works opens a dialog box that displays a series of option buttons. Each of the value series, 1 through 6, can be assigned to either the left or right axis. By default all of the value series are charted on the left Y axis, as shown in Figure 8-25.

280

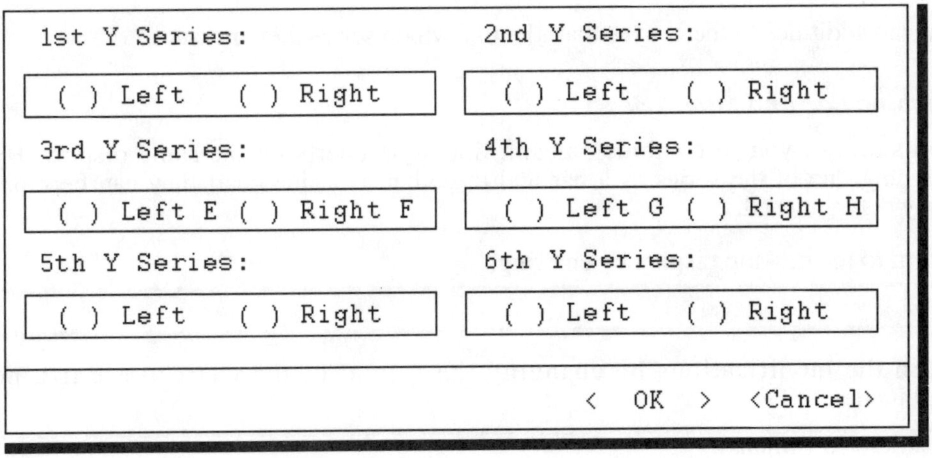

```
┌──────────────────────────────────────────────────────────┐
│  1st Y Series:              2nd Y Series:                  │
│  ┌──────────────────────┐   ┌──────────────────────────┐  │
│  │ ( ) Left   ( ) Right │   │ ( ) Left     ( ) Right   │  │
│  └──────────────────────┘   └──────────────────────────┘  │
│  3rd Y Series:              4th Y Series:                  │
│  ┌──────────────────────┐   ┌──────────────────────────┐  │
│  │ ( ) Left E ( ) Right F│   │ ( ) Left G ( ) Right H  │  │
│  └──────────────────────┘   └──────────────────────────┘  │
│  5th Y Series:              6th Y Series:                  │
│  ┌──────────────────────┐   ┌──────────────────────────┐  │
│  │ ( ) Left   ( ) Right │   │ ( ) Left     ( ) Right   │  │
│  └──────────────────────┘   └──────────────────────────┘  │
│                                                            │
│                          <  OK  >   <Cancel>               │
└──────────────────────────────────────────────────────────┘
```

Figure 8-25. Two Y-Axes Dialog Box.

Assign the 4th series to the right Y axis. To simplify select, Works places a letter, A through L next to each option button, since all of the buttons are labeled either left or right:

```
Click(left) on H
Click(left) on <Ok>
```

Display the modified chart:

```
[Shift-F10]
```

The chart now has two axes: one scaled from 0 to 50 and the other scaled from 0 to $160. Works uses the numeric format associated with the first data series on each axis to determine the format of the axis labels. The quantity axis uses the general format while the costs axis uses the currency format.

Bar and Line Combinations

Because the chart uses two different Y axes, one on the left and one on the right, it is not altogether clear which scale is related to which data series. There are two changes that can be made to this chart in order to clarify its meaning: y axis titles and combine bar and line styles.

Y Axis Titles

You can add titles to the Y axes that identify which series they measure.

Combine Bar and Line Styles

Works allows you to combine bar and line style charts on the same display. By assigning one of the series as a bar and the other as a line chart they can be more easily distinguished.

Return to the desktop display by entering:

```
[Esc]
```

Begin the modifications by changing the format of the chart to a Bar/Line combination:

```
Click(left) on Options
Click(left) on Mixed Line & Bar
```

Works displays a dialog box similar to the Two Y-Axes dialog box. This box allows you to select which style, line or bar should be used for each series. Change series 4 to a line chart:

```
Click(left) on G
Click(left) on <Ok>
```

Next, add titles to the two Y axis:

```
Click(left) on Data
Click(left) on Titles
```

Since the words "quantity "and "costs" already appear on the spreadsheet you can take a shortcut and enter the addresses of the cells instead of the text:

```
[Tab](3 times)
E11[Tab]
F11 [return]
```

Display the chart:

```
[Shift-F10]
```

Works displays a chart that has both bar and line elements as well as dual Y axes, as shown in Figure 8-26.

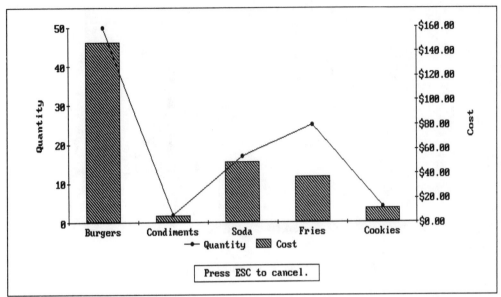

Figure 8-26. Mixed Bar and Line Chart.

Return to the desktop display by entering:

[Esc]

PRINTING A CHART

When the CHART mode is active (CHART appears on the Status line) you can print the currently active chart using the **Print** command found on the Print menu. You also have the option of previewing the chart with the **Preview** command. By default, Works prints charts in landscape orientation, as shown in Figure 8-27. This is in contrast to the spreadsheet print operation which defaults to portrait printing. Because most charts are wider than they are tall, the chart will fit better when printed in landscape orientation. When rotated into portrait orientation, printing will create a distorted appearance as if the chart were being stretched vertically.

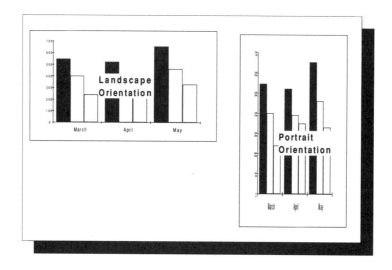

Figure 8-27. Charts Usually Fit Better in Landscape Orientation.

Choosing Print Density

Before you print a chart it is important to understand the difference between normal text printing, such as printing a word processing document or spreadsheet model, and printing charts and graphs.

Today, most computer printer use a dot matrix method of printing information. Dot matrix refers to a process by which characters are formed by printing a pattern of small dots. Even the best computer printers, such as laser printers, use dot patterns to create the images and character they print. Dot matrix printers function into two distinct modes which area as follows:

Text Mode

Most printing tasks are handled in the text mode. The text mode is the fastest and most efficient way for a printer to operate because text mode operations use built in fonts. A computer font is a set of pre-designed dot patterns that correspond to the basic set of characters found on the keyboard, e.g., A-Z, 0-9, plus special characters like @, #, etc. When text mode printing takes place the program in the computer sends instructions to the printer telling it which characters to print. For example, if the program want to print the word "CAT" it sends instructions to print the pre-defined dot patterns that correspond to those three characters.

Graphics Mode

Graphics mode allows printers to create images that are not part of a pre-designed font. In graphics mode the computer must instruct the printer as to the location of each dot that is required to create the desired image. Graphics printing is much slower than text printing because the computer must send a complete, detailed description of the image, dot by dot to the printer. The advantage of graphics printing is that the printer can reproduce an unlimited number of different images.

When you print a chart, you are printing in the graphics mode. The length of time required to print the image can increase dramatically. For example, an IBM Proprinter XL can print a page of letter quality text in 30 to 45 seconds. A full page chart may take 10 to 20 minutes.

One way to control the amount of time it takes to print a chart is to select the density at which the chart will be printed. Density refers to the number of dot the printed per square inch of paper. Most printers have two or more density settings. The higher the density, dot per inch, the sharper the image and the longer the print time. By reducing the density you loose image sharpness but shorten the print time.

You can determine or change the print density by using the **Printer Setup** command on the Print menu:

```
Click(left) on Print
Click(left) on Printer Setup
```

The dialog box shows information about the printer you have selected. Keep in mind that your screen may show different information depending upon what printer you are using. In Figure 8-28, the selected printer is the IBMPROXL for the IBM Proprinter II & XL. In this case the item you are interested in are the options listed in the Graphics list box. For the IBM Proprinter II there are three densities—240, 120 and 60 dp1—listed in the box. Dpi stands for dots per inch. This tells you that the printer can print graphs in three different density modes. The currently selected mode is 240 dpi. This selection will produce the highest quality chart but will take the most time to print. If you select HPLASER as your printer you can select among 300, 150 and 75 dpi settings. Keep in mind that your options will vary with different printer selections.

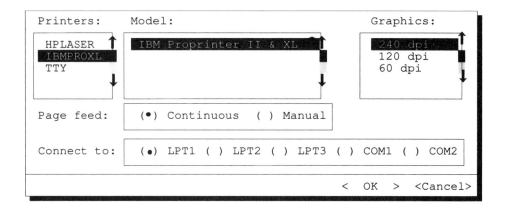

Figure 8-28. Printer Setup Dialog Box.

If you want to save time or simply want to get a draft quality version of the chart, you can change the Graphics setting to a lower density. The fastest printing will occur at the lowest available dpi, in this case 60 dpi:

```
Click(left) on 60 dp1
Click(left) on <Ok>
```

Once you have selected the density for graphics printing you can send the current chart to the printer:

```
Click(left) on Print
Click(left) on Print
Click(left) on <Print>
```

Works displays the percentage printed on the left side of the status line. When it reaches 100% the chart printing has been completed. Note that some printers have memory buffers. The buffers allow the printer to receive information from the printer at a higher rate of speed than the printer can print. The advantage of a print buffer is that the computer can complete transmission and go on to its next task while the printer is still printing the image. The result is that Works will reach 100% long before the actual chart printing is complete.

Recalculation of Charts

One of the advantages of creating charts based on spreadsheet information is that any changes in the spreadsheet information will be immediately reflected in the charts. As with spreadsheet formulas, once a chart has been defined, it will always reflect the latest changes made to any of the values in the spreadsheet. For example, suppose that you changed some of the values in the current spreadsheet. Change the number of people attending from 50 to 67:

```
Click(left) on cell C1(50)
```

```
67[return]
```

Note that you can edit the spreadsheet cells while the CHART mode is active. The only restriction placed on spreadsheet operations in the CHART mode is that you cannot access **Spreadsheet** command from the menu bar since the chart menu bar is currently active. Display the chart:

```
[Shift-F10]
```

While the chart retains the basic structure with which it was defined, the values in the chart have adjusted to the changes in the spreadsheet. In many ways, charts function as graphic spreadsheet models. A chart is not simply an picture but a dynamic graphical representation of the spreadsheet. A single chart can generate any number of images depending upon how the spreadsheet, from which it draws its data, is manipulated:

```
[Esc]
```

Saving a Chart

Charts are saved as part of the spreadsheet file. When you use the **Save** or **Close** command all of the chart and spreadsheet information is stored in a single disk file. The **Save** or **Close** command can be issued from either the spreadsheet or chart mode. Since all of the information is stored in one file it makes no difference what mode is active when you save:

```
Click(left) on File
Click(left) on Close
Click(left) on <Yes>
```

If you are done working you can exit Works:

```
Click(left) on Exit Works
```

SUMMARY

In this chapter you learned how to use spreadsheet information to create bar, pie, and line charts with Works.

Charts. Charts are graphic displays that represent values by objects of varying size. Charts are based on data entered or calculated in a spreadsheet model. A single spreadsheet can have a number of different charts associated with it. The charts are linked to the spreadsheet data so that any changes in the spreadsheet will be reflected in all of the charts associated with it.

Chart Types. Works supports bar, line and pie charts. Bar charts can be formatted as standard bar, stacked bar, or 100% bar charts. The line charts can be formatted as point/line, area line, high-low or point only (X-Y) type charts. The **Data Format** command allows you to control details of the charts formats such as colors, patterns, point marker, or exploded pie slices.

Data Series. A data series is a range of cells that contain information used on the chart. There are two types of series: the X series contains the category information while the Y series contains the values for the chart. A chart must have at least 1 Y series and it can have as many as 6 Y series. In X-Y charts both the X and Y series contain values.

Axes. All charts, with the exception of pie charts, have a category (X) axis and one or two value (Y) axes. The category axis lists the categories of data shown in the chart. The Y axes display a scale of values against which the value of the objects (bars, points, lines, etc.) that appear on the chart can be measured.

Chart Text. Text can be added to the chart display as title (main, subtitle, axes titles) and legends that identify data series or data labels which identify each object or point on the chart. The text can be entered directly as part of the chart definition or drawn from cells in the spreadsheet that contain text or values.

Selection Rules. Charts can be created automatically based on the a highlighted range of cells. Works follows a set of rules by which the contents of a highlighted range are converted into a chart. The **New Chart** command creates a chart based on the currently selected range, if any, using the Works rules for charting.

Manual Selection. Not all charts can be created by highlighting ranges. If no range is highlighted Works creates a blank chart. The blank chart can then be filled out with information about data series ranges, chart format and text on a manual basis using commands found on the Chart mode menu in order to add each desired element.

Names. Works assigns each chart a name, Chart1, Chart2, etc., when the chart is created. The **Charts** command allows you to change the chart name from the default name to a descriptive name of you own choosing. The descriptive name replaces the original name in the Charts menu.

Printing. The **Print** command on the chart menu bar prints the current chart. Charts are set by default to print in a landscape orientation. Graphics printing takes significantly more time that text printing. You can control the length of time required to print a chart by using **Printer Setup** to change the density setting for your printer. Note that density options are specific to the printer you have selected. Not all printers support the same set of density options.

Chapter 9

Text, Spreadsheets, and Charts

I n Chapters 4-8 you learned how to create text using the word processing window, spreadsheet models using a spreadsheet window, and charts using the View menu of the spreadsheet windows. Each of these elements were created and printed as separate items. However, it is possible to combine all of these elements into a single document and create a report that contains word processing text, spreadsheet data, tables, and charts. In this chapter you will learn how you can integrate all of these elements in Works, along with special word processing techniques such as the creation of footnotes and the use of multiple fonts within a document. Begin by loading the Works program in the usual manner.

Integration of different types of information into a single document is done through the word processing window. The word processing document created in this window will combine information from the spreadsheet windows which contains information in two forms: spreadsheet model tables and charts.

When the word processing window is printed, the document will combine all of the elements into a single document.

Create a new word processing document:

```
Click(left) on Create New File
Click(left) on New Word Processor
```

Works displays a new, blank document window.

STYLES AND SIZES

Suppose that after creating the spreadsheet and charts discussed in chapters 6, 7, and 8, you want to present the information contained in the spreadsheet and charts as a formal report. For example, imagine that the party that you were planning in the PARTY spreadsheet was being sponsored by a club or organization to which you belonged. You created the PARTY spreadsheet because you were asked to organize this event. Now you want to create a report that you can present to the organization so that they can decide what type of menu should be used for the party which is being planned.

While it might be adequate to simply print the spreadsheet data and the charts separately, bringing together all of the information in a single document would make a much clearer presentation. You also have the opportunity to add text that explains something about the meaning of the spreadsheet tables and the charts.

The first step in this process will be to create a heading for the report. Begin by selecting center alignment:

```
Click(left) on Format
Click(left) on Center
```

The cursor is centered between the margins. Enter the following text:

```
ANNUAL CLUB BANQUET
```

Since this is to be the title of the report, how can you make this text stand out? One way is to use the text enhancement options of bold, italic, or underlined text. A second possibility is to change the font of the text. The term font comes from the field of printing and typesetting. When you read a newspaper or magazine you will notice that the size of the letters and the style of print for the letter will vary. Headlines appear in a variety of sizes. The text in ads appears in a variety of lettering styles. A font refers to the size of the letters and the style of lettering used to print the characters. In Works you can use the **Font & Style** command located on the Format menu to change the style and size of the character in your printed document.

About Fonts

Before you find out how to use the **Font & Style** command it is important to understand some concepts related to the use of different fonts.

Printer Dependent

The idea of being able to choose letters of different sizes and styles is very exciting because it can add a professional quality to your documents. However, the options that are available to you are limited by the specific model of printer you are using. Suppose that you wanted to create letters that were 1 inch tall. You would have to have a printer that was capable of creating those letters in order to accomplish this goal.

Screen vs. Printed Image

When you change the style and/or size of the characters you will find that the characters on the screen remain the same size and style. The actual changes in font will appear only on the printed page. The Print Preview option will give you a close approximation of the final product but in many cases you must print the document in order to see exactly how the fonts will appear.

Keep in mind that because font operations are printer specific the instructions that follow may not match your computer. In this book the assumption is made that the selected printer is an IBM Proprinter XL. If you do not use this printer you will have to adjust your selections based on the fonts available for your printer.

Selecting a Font

If you want to change the font used for a section of a document you must first highlight the text you want to change. In this case you want to change the text in the current paragraph. Use a **[Shift]** key short combiantion—**[Shift-Ctrl-up]**—to select the current paragraph. Enter:

```
Shift-Ctrl-up]
```

With the text slected displays the dialog box for the **Font & Style** command. Enter:

```
Click(left) on Format
Click(left) on Font & Style
```

Works displays a dialog box, as shown in Figure 9-1, which contains four options: styles, fonts, size, and position.

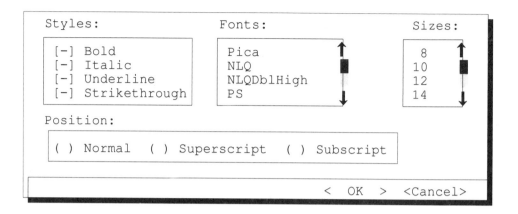

Figure 9-1. Fonts & Style Dialog Box.

Styles

This box contains options which correspond to the Format menu commands **Bold, Italics**, and **Underline**. The style options allow you to pick bold, italics, or underline at the same time as you are selecting the font and size. In addition, the box adds *Strikethrough* as a style option. Strikethrough text prints a dash character over the text indicating text that should be struck out of the document. Strikethrough is generally used during an editing process in which someone needs to approve proposed deletions from a document.

Fonts

This list box contains the names of the fonts (styles of lettering) available on your printer. The fonts listed in Figure 9-1 are for the IBM Proprinter XL. If you have selected a different printer, the font list will be different. One problem with font lists is that the names used to represent the fonts do not tell you very much about what the lettering for that font will look like. For example, Pica or Courier fonts produce text that looks like text printed with a standard typewriter. The letters like LQ (letter quality), PS (proportional spacing), or NL (near letter) may give you some hint as to the appearance of the font. If you are unsure about the appearance of a given font check the printer's manual to see if they show samples of the printer's fonts. Many printers can produce a text print which shows samples of the fonts. Your printer manual should explain how to generate this font text sheet.

Size

The size box lists the sizes available for each font. The values that appear in this list tell you the height of the characters as measured in *points*. A point, a measurement borowed from printing, is equal to 1/72 inch (0.014 inch). Standard typewriter text is usually 12 point text. By default, all text in Works is set at 12 point size.

Position

This option allows you to position text half a line up or down in the document. Superscript and subscript character are often used in mathemetical expressions. Keep in mind that if you select super or subscript, those characters may run into characters on the line above or below the current line. You may need to reduce the size of the character, if possible, to avoid this problem.

It is important to understand that not all of the possible combinations suggested by this menu can be implemented by your printer. For example, while italic and bold print are shown as styles that can be applied to any font and size, many printers cannot print these combinations. In order for a printer to print italic printing it is necessary for the printer to have a full set of italic characters in the specified font and size, something that is not always true. This means that you can make selections from this menu that will not be fully implemented by the printer.

In this case you will want to choose the 14 point bold Pica:

```
Click(left) on Bold
Click(left) on Pica
Click(left) on 14
Click(left) on <Ok>
```

The word processing window does not show much change. This is because Works cannot show changes in font and size on the screen as they will appear on the final printed page. However, the status line at the bottom of the screen shows B PIC14 representing bold text plus the new font.

Continue the text by starting a second line:

```
End] [return]
```

Note that the new line continues the new font, B PIC14. To return to normal text you must use the Font & Style menu again to change back to the original font, Pica 12. Note that the Plain Text option does not change font or size. It only removes the text enhancements bold, underline, italics, or strikethrough.

Display the Font & Style dialog box:

```
Click(left) on Format
Click(left) on Font & Style
```

Change the text back to normal, Pica 12 point text:

```
Click(left) on Bold
Click(left) on Pica
Click(left) on 12
Click(left) on <Ok>
```

When you return to the document window the status line shows PIC12, indicating that you have returned to the default text for this printer. Enter a subheading:

```
Proposed Menu and Cost Analysis [return]
```

Change the paragraph attributes to a left aligned paragraph with a single line of space before each new paragraph. Use the command short keys to issue the necessary commands:

```
[Ctrl-l](the letter L)
[Ctrl-O](the letter O)
```

Enter the following paragraph into the document:

```
Based on the discussion of the committe, cost estimates have
been made for two alternative menus. The first menu is based
on the use of pizza as the main course. This menu has a cost
advantage because a single pizza can feed as many as four
people. [return]
```

SPELL CHECKING A WORD

In Chapter 4 you learned how to use the spell check feature to proof a document after it has been entered. The spell check feature can be used in a more specific way so that you can quickly check a word or a phrase for correct spelling. For example, in the paragraph that you just entered the word "committe" was entered. Suppose that you want to check the spelling of just that word. You can select a specific word or phrase for checking by highlighting that word or phrase before you enter the Spell Check command. Highlight the word "committe" using the mouse:

```
Click(right) on committe

Click(left) on Utilities
Click(left) on Check Spelling
```

Have Works suggest the correct spelling by using the **Suggest** command:

```
Click(left) on Suggest
```

Replace "committe" with the word "committee" from the list of suggestion using the mouse:

```
Double click(left) on committee
Click(left) on <Ok>
```

This technique allows you to quickly check a suspect word without having to go through the entire document. Note that if, when you check a word or phrase, the program responds by displaying a box with the message "Spelling Check Finished" instead of the Check Spelling dialog box, you can infer that the word or words are spelled correctly. Works always displays this message when there is nothing more to correct. There is no message that actually tells you a word is spelled correctly.

COPYING SPREADSHEET TABLES

At this point in your document you may want to insert some of the data stored in your PARTY.WKS spreadsheet file. For example, the table that shows the costs of the menu that include pizza would be approprite at this point in the document. Instead of manually entering that table you can simply copy the information from the spreadsheet directly into the word processing document.

Enter a heading that will come before the spreadsheet table:

```
[Ctrl-End]
MENU #1: Pizza [return]
```

Load the spreadsheet file from the disk:

```
Click(left) on File
Click(left) on Open Existing File
Double click(left) on PARTY.WKS
```

The program loads the information from the file and displays the information in a spreadsheet window. The window covers all but the title bar of the word processing window. Note that the cell pointer is positioned on cell C1, exactly where it was positioned when you stored the spreadsheet at the end of Chapter 8.

Before you copy the spreadsheet data you can make any adjustments that are necessary. For example, suppose that between the time you saved the spreadsheet and the time at which you are preparing this report, the estimate of the number of people that will attend has changed from 67 to 72. Revise the spreadsheet by entering:

```
72 [return]
```

The data in the model is now updated to reflect the latest information available to you. The section of the spreadsheet that you want to copy is the range of cells from B3 to F8. Highlight that range:

```
Point at cell B3(blank)
Drag(left) to cell F8($313.86)
```

Copy this range into the clipboard using the function key shortcut command:

```
[Shift-F3]
```

Switch to the word processing window before you complete the copying process. You can accomplish this by clicking on any part of the word processing window that is currently visible:

```
Click(left) on WORD1.WPS
```

Insert the spreadsheet table into the word processing document by entering:

```
[return]
```

The table, with the data formatted and aligned in columns, is inserted into the document window, as shown in Figure 9-2.

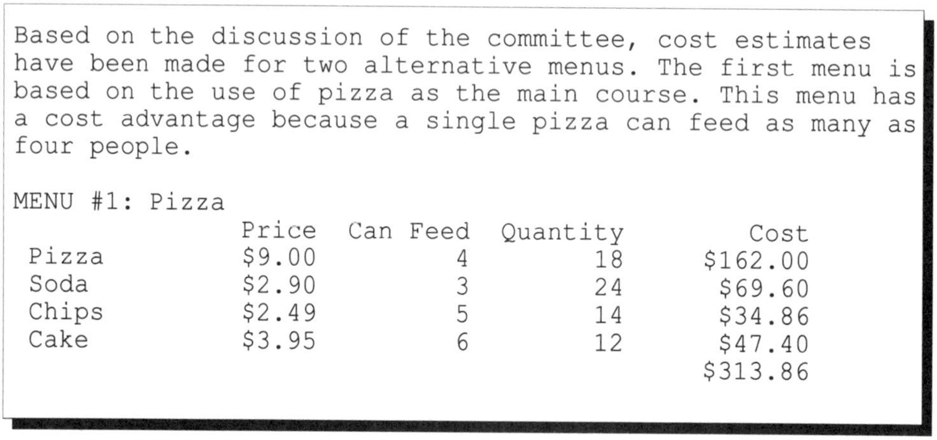

```
Based on the discussion of the committee, cost estimates
have been made for two alternative menus. The first menu is
based on the use of pizza as the main course. This menu has
a cost advantage because a single pizza can feed as many as
four people.

MENU #1: Pizza
                Price   Can Feed   Quantity        Cost
    Pizza       $9.00        4        18        $162.00
    Soda        $2.90        3        24         $69.60
    Chips       $2.49        5        14         $34.86
    Cake        $3.95        6        12         $47.40
                                                $313.86
```

Figure 9-2. Spreadsheet Text Inserted in Word Processing Document.

Add a line of space between the beginning of the table and the heading:

```
[Ctrl-o](the letter O)
```

If you look at the ruler line at the top of the window you will see that the letters L and R appear at various location on the ruler. These letters represent the location of tabs which align the next in columns. Works automatically sets the necessary tab stops when you copy spreadsheet data into a word processing document.

While it is possible to create tab-based tables directly in the word processing window, it is much easier to work in a column in a spreadsheet than it is in a word processor. Word processing is oriented towards paragraphs that flow left to right.

Spreadsheets make column operations much simpler than word processing. Since Works makes it so simple to copy information between windows, the best way to handle column tables is always in a spreadsheet window.

INSERTING A CHART

Works also allows you to print a chart along with the text of the document. Charts are integrated with a word processing document in a different manner than data from a spreadsheet.

Spreadsheet data is copied from the specified range in the spreadsheet to the word processing document. Once copied, the data becomes normal word processing text. This means that you can alter the spreadsheet text by editing it just as you would any text you manually entered into the word processing document. Conversely, a chart is not copied into the word processing document at all. Instead, Works inserts a code into the word processing document that links it to the selected spreadsheet chart. When the document is printed, or previewed, Works draws the chart image from the spreadsheet and prints it in the word processing document.

The chart will always reflect the latest changes made to the spreadsheet. The same may not be true of spreadsheet data copied into the document since once the copy is made, no link between the document and the spreadsheet is maintained. It is possible to alter the spreadsheet data and not have those changes reflected in the document.

Because charts are linked to word processing documents, the spreadsheet from which the chart is drawn must be open in a window when you print the document in order for the chart to print.

Move the cursor to the location in the document where you want the chart to be inserted. In this case that is the bottom of the current text. Enter:

[Ctrl-End]

Display the Edit menu:

Click(left) on **Edit**

In the third section of the menu you will find the command **Insert Chart**. This is the command that is used to insert a chart code into a word processing document. Select this command:

Click(left) on **Insert Chart**

Works displays a dialog box that lists all of the open spreadsheet windows. In this case there is only one spreadsheet window open, PARTY.WKS.

Next to the Spreadsheet list is a list box labeled Charts. When you select one of the spreadsheets, the charts list will show all of the charts that have been defined for that spreadsheet:

Click(left) on *PARTY.WKS*

The charts box lists the three charts that you defined for the spreadsheet in Chapter 8, as shown in Figure 9-3.

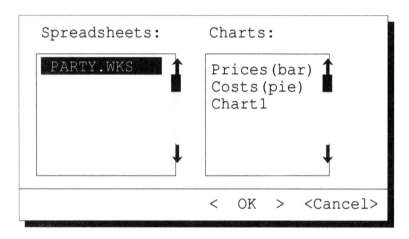

Figure 9-3. Insert Chart Dialog Box.

In this case you want to insert the chart entitled "Costs(pie)". Select that chart from the list:

Double click(left) on *Costs(pie)*

The insertion of the chart caused Works to scroll the document window's display down one screen. To see the code that was entered, scroll the display in the word processing document up a screen by entering:

[Pg Up]

At the bottom of the text is the chart code, *chart PARTY.WKS:Costs(pie)*. This code will cause Works to insert the specified chart image onto the printed. Add a caption line below the chart image. Make the caption center aligned and italics text:

[Ctrl-down]
[Ctrl-c] [Ctrl-i]
Costs of food item from first menu.

Begin a new paragraph by resetting the format to a normal paragraph:

```
[Ctrl-x] [Ctrl-space]
[Ctrl-o](the letter O)
```

FOOTNOTES

Footnotes are used to add information which may be useful to the reader but is not required in the main body of the text. Footnotes appear at the bottom of the page, separated from the main body of the text. In order to indicate what section of the document relates to the footnote a footnote reference is inserted into the text and at the beginning of the footnote text at the bottom of the page. This system allows you to have several footnotes on a single page, if necessary, because each footnote will have a unique number as its reference mark.

For example, you might want to add a footnote that explains something about the graph. In this case you might want to stipulate that the chart and table are based on the attendance of 72 people, the current estimate of attendence for the date the report was prepared. Instead of placing this information into the body of the report, place it into a footnote.

To insert a footnote, place the cursor at the location in the document where you want the footnote reference to appear. In this case that location is the end of the previous line of text. Move the cursor back one character by entering:

```
[left]
```

Footnotes are created with the **Footnote** command located on the Edit menu:

```
Click(left) on Edit
Click(left) on Footnote
```

Works displays a dialog box that has two options, as shown in Figure 9-4. The options allow you to choose the type of reference that is inserted into the text for the footnote. The default settings is Numbered which inserts a number, 1, 2, 3, etc., numbering each footnote that appears on the page. The alternative setting, Character mark allows you to use a character, *, as the footnote reference.

```
Footnote:

( ) Numbered
( ) Character mark
     Mark: [.....]


   <  OK  >  <Cancel>
```

Figure 9-4. Footnote Dialog Box.

In this case allow the program to use automatic footnote numbering. Enter:

[return]

When you select to insert a footnote, the program opens a special window pane at the bottom of the document window. The program also inserts the footnote reference number in the document at the previous cursor location and as the first character in the footnote window pane, as shown in Figure 9-5.

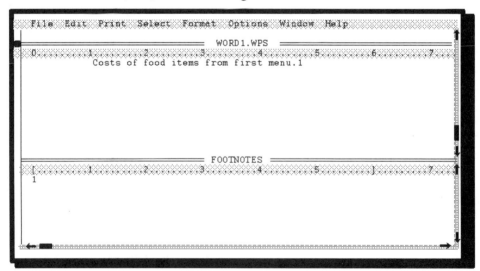

Figure 9-5. Footnote Window Pane Opened.

The purpose of the footnote window pane is to allow you to enter text of the footnote using all of the same editing and formatting abilities of the Works word processor. Works stores the footnote text at the end of the word processing document. Footnotes in Works are printed at the end of the document. Works does not support printing footnotes at the bottom of the same page on which the reference appears. (If printing footnotes on the bottom of the same page as the footnote reference is required you may need to purchase a stand-alone word processing program such as Microsoft Word or WordPerfect.)

Enter the footnote text into the footnote window. Keep in mind that you can use all of the same commands in this window as you can in the document window which allows you to add text enhancements such as underline or italics:

```
Table and figure based on attendance estimate of
[spacebar]
```

Use the keyboard shortcut command, [Ctrl-;], to insert the current system date into the text:

```
[Ctrl-;][spacebar]
of 72 people.
```

You can switch back and forth between the two panes by clicking the mouse in the pane in which you want to work or pressing the [F6] function key. Enter:

```
[F6]
```

The cursor returns to the main document window next to the footnote reference. Keep in mind that the footnote reference number is the link between the footnote text, stored in the footnote window pane and the text of the document. If you delete the footnote reference number from the document, Works will delete the footnote text related to that reference automatically.

Repeating the Process

In order to complete the document you need to repeat the three procedures discussed in this chapter for the information and chart related to the second menu in the spreadsheet. Move the cursor to the end of the document and insert the following text:

```
[Ctrl-End]
An alternative menu, which uses burgers as the main course,
has also been proposed. The data and chart below shows that
this menu would cost a bit more than the first proposal. [return]
MENU #2: Burgers [return]
```

Copy the data from the second menu from the spreadsheet. Switch to the spreadsheet window:

```
[Ctrl-F6]
```

Highlight the desired range of cells:

```
Point at cell B11(blank)
Drag(left) to cell F17
```

Place a copy of this information into the clipboard using the **Copy** command:

```
Click(left) on Edit
Click(left) on Copy
```

Switch back to the word processing window:

```
Click(left) on WORD1.WPS
```

Insert the copied data into the document by entering:

```
[return]
```

The table is inserted as text into the word processing document. Next, insert a copy of the charts—Chart1, from PARTY.WKS—which illustrates the costs involved with the second menu. Place the cursor at the end of the document:

```
[Ctrl-End]
```

Use the **Insert Chart** command to enter a chart code for the Chart1 chart:

```
Click(left) on Edit
Click(left) on Insert Chart
Click(left) on PARTY.WKS
Click(left) on Chart1
Click(left) on <Ok>
```

Finally, enter a caption for this chart:

```
[Ctrl-c] [Ctrl-i]
Costs of burger menu.
```

Insert a footnote for this caption:

```
Click(left) on Edit
Click(left) on Footnote
Click(left) on <Ok>
```

Works inserts a new footnote reference, 2, into the document and into the footnote window pane in which the cursor is now positioned. In this example you will want to insert a footnote with exactly the same text as you used for the previous chart. You can save time by copying that text from the previous footnote. Since a footnote window pane operates just like a document window you can use the same approach to copy text. Position the cursor at the beginning of the previous footnote:

```
[Pg Up]
```

Select the paragraph:

```
[Shift-Ctrl-down]
```

Copy the text into the clipboard:

```
[Shift-F3]
```

Insert the text into the second footnote:

```
[down] [return]
```

You have now assembled all of the elements needed to print a document. One other element that might improve the report would be the addition of a page footer that prints the page numbers. Page headers and footers can be added to word processing documents in just about the same way as they were added to spreadsheets:

```
Click(left) on Print
Click(left) on Headers & Footers
```

Recall from Chapter 7 that the code &p is used to insert the page number in a header or footer. The code &c is used to center text horizonatally in the header or footer. Create the centered page number footer by entering:

```
[Tab]
&cPage -&p-
```

Save the footer:

```
Click(left) on <Ok>
```

Now that you are done entering and editing footnotes, you might want to close the footnote window pane and allow the word processing window to return to full size. The **Show Footnotes** command located on the Options menu toggles the display of the footnote window pane on or off. Close the footnote pane with this command:

```
Click(left) on Options
Click(left) on Show Footnotes
```

Works closes the footnote window. If you need to access the footnotes simply repeat the command to toggle the footnote pane display on again.

Inserting a Page Break

Keep in mind that Works prints the footnotes at the end of the document. You might want to ensure that the footnotes begin on a separate page at the end of the document. You can make sure that this is the case by inserting a page break at the end of the document text. Page breaks are special codes inserted into the text to make sure that the text that follows the page break always starts at the top of a new page.

Page breaks can be inserted into a word processing document through the **Insert Special** command located on the Edit menu or directly with the shortcut keystroke [**Ctrl-return**]. Enter:

[Ctrl-return]

Scroll the displays up one screen by entering:

[Pg Up]

The page break appears in the document as a dotted line. You can delete a page break by placing the cursor at the beginning of the dotted line and enter [**Del**].

Before you print (or preview) the document, save the new document in a file called REPORT. This ensures that if you encounter any problems during the printing process, your document will not be lost:

Click(left) on **File**
Click(left) on **Save**

report [return]

The title bar now reflects the file name, REPORT.WPS, which you have assigned to this document. Preview the document using the **Preview** command found on the Print menu.

Return the cursor to the beginning of the document:

[Ctrl-Home]

Begin the document preview:

Click(left) on **Print**
Click(left) on **Preview**
Click(left) on **<Preview>**

The page preview shows that the document combines the word processing text, the spreadsheet table data, and the spreadsheet chart on a single page, as shown in Figure 9-6.

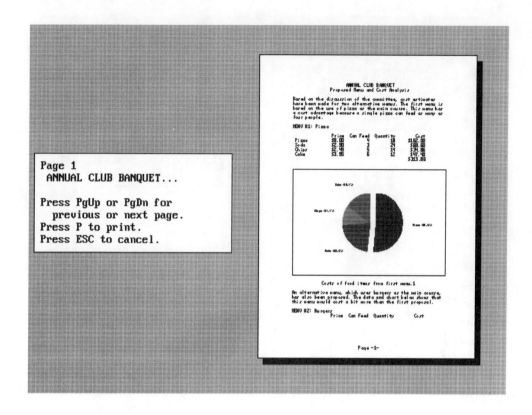

```
Page 1
ANNUAL CLUB BANQUET...

Press PgUp or PgDn for
  previous or next page.
Press P to print.
Press ESC to cancel.
```

Figure 9-6. Document Preview Shows Text, Table Data, and Chart Integrated.

Display the next page by entering:

[Pg Dn]

Page 2 shows more of the integrated document including the second chart, as shown in Figure 9-7.

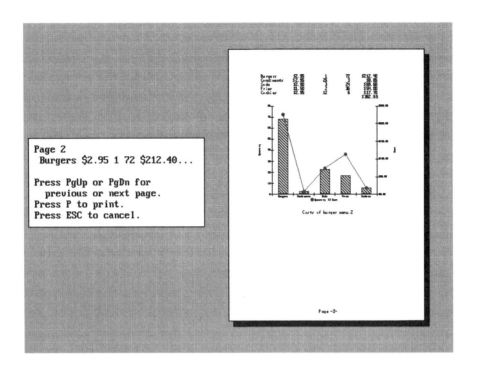

Page 2
  Burgers $2.95 1 72 $212.40...

Press PgUp or PgDn for
  previous or next page.
Press P to print.
Press ESC to cancel.

Figure 9-7. Second Page of REPORT.WPS.

Display the last page by entering:

[Pg Dn]

This page contains the footnotes. The page break inserted at the end of the document causes Works to print the footnotes at the beginning of a new page, as shown in Figure 9-8.

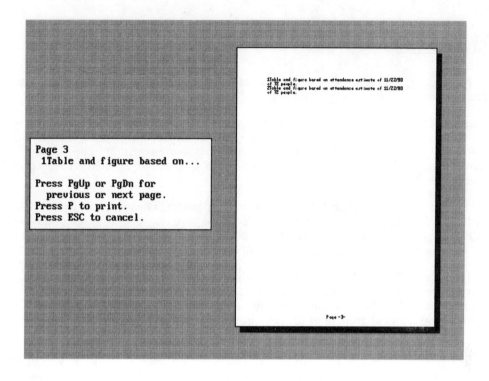

Figure 9-8. Third Page of REPORT.WPS.

If the preview of the pages looks OK, you can print the document directly from the Preview display by typing the letter p. Enter:

```
p
```

Works sends the entire document to the printer. When you print the document you will see that Works transferred the cell attributes, in this case underlining, to the corresponding text in the word processing document. One difference is that in word processing the underline is a continuous one which extends across the entire line of text in contrast to the series of short lines that appear when the same information is printed as part of a spreadsheet.

Close the open windows. You can use:

```
Click(left) on File
Click(left) on Close
```

If you are done working you can exit Works:

```
Click(left) on Exit Works
```

SUMMARY

In this chapter you learned how text, spreadsheet table data, and spreadsheet charts can be combined into a single document.

Fonts. Works supports the use of different print fonts in a single document. The font selection options are displayed in the Fonts & Style dialog box. The options displayed in this dialog box depend upon the selected printer. The font names represent different styles of lettering. The status line shows an abbreviation of the font name, Pica PIC.

Size. The size of the characters is measured in points. One point is equal to 1/72 inch. The Size option in the Fonts & Style dialog box allows you to select the point size of the text. Text which has been assigned different point sizes text will all appear as the same size text on the screen, but will be printed correctly.

Copy spreadsheet data. You can copy the information that appears in a block of spreadsheet cells into a word processing document. The cells are converted to text separated by tabs. The location of the tabs is automatically set by Works to match the column width and alignment of the cells in the spreadsheet range. Text enhancements such as underlines are also copied into the document.

Insert Charts. The **Insert Chart** command inserts a code into the document that specifies the spreadsheet and the chart name that should print at that location. In order for the charts to print, the spreadsheet to which tch code refers must be open on the desktop.

Footnotes. Footnote references can be inserted anywhere in the document. The references are automatically numbers. The text of the footnotes are entered into a footnote window pane. All footnotes print at the end of the document.

Page Breaks. Page breaks are inserted in the document when you want to ensure that the text following the break begins on a new page. The shortcut keystroke [**Ctrl-return**] inserts a manual page break in the document at the current cursor position. A dotted line appears across the window to indicate the presence of a page break.

Chapter **10**

Keeping Accurate Records

T he subject of this chapter is how to use Works to keep track of information accurately and efficiently. This type of activity is called *database management.*

Database management is used for storing data such as lists of names and addresses, financial transactions, or other types of record keeping. Of course, you have already learned how to store information without having to use a database.

A *database* is a computer file in which information is stored in a highly organized form. To understand what a database is, contrast its concept of organized storage with the way information is stored in the word processing or spreadsheet files.

When you store information in a word processing document there is no particular structure to data in the document. While there are lines and paragraphs, the information can be placed in any order. The only way to use or to locate information in a word processing document is to read through the document. For example, suppose you wanted to find the date of the letter. The date might appear on line 1 or line 10, or be missing entirely.

Spreadsheets are a bit more organized since the information in the spreadsheet is divided into individual cells, each with a unique address. In spreadsheets you can pick out individual items of data such as a cell or a range of cells. But even in a spreadsheet you cannot know what type of information will appear in a given cell. For example, cell A2 may contain a label. Cell B2 may contain a number. But knowing this cannot tells you what type of information might be in A4 or C2 since spreadsheets allow you to place any type of data into any cell.

Unlike word processing and spreadsheets, databases begin with a particular pattern or structure. All the information in the database follows the original pattern. This means once you know the pattern or structure of a database you know what type of information can be found in what locations in the database file.

For example, suppose the database you want to create is designed to keep information about the members of a club or organization to which you belong. What type of information would you want or need to keep? Typically, you would want to record the names, addresses, and phone numbers of the members. You might also want to keep track of the dates of birth, special interests or even payment of dues or other fees. In thinking about the information, you will notice that you begin the process not by thinking about individual members, but about qualities or items of information that all of the members have or potentially have. While the specific information will vary for each person, all the members will share a common set of qualities that will be the same for each person.

If you were to write down a list of each quality or piece of information that you needed for each member you would be creating the structure of the database. The structure would determine the organization of the database which would simply repeat for each individual member.

In computer terms, you could create a database in a spreadsheet by deciding right at the beginning that all the first names would be in column A and all the last names in column B, and so on. In this way you would know in advance that if you were looking for information about a particular person, you would search column B to find his/her last name.

Because of the highly structured nature of databases, they can provide special features that are appropriate and very helpful when your task involves record keeping. You will also learn in the next chapter how database information can be integrated with word processing and spreadsheet information.

Keeping records in a computer database has a number of very significant advantages over manual record keeping in file folders, journals, rolodex files or index card files. In fact, manual record keeping is so inflexible that often you are unable to get any advantage out of most of the information you store. Computer-based databases offer many important advantages over manual record keeping. You will find that databases make the information you store much more valuable because it can actually be put to use with very little extra effort. This is the exact opposite of the way manual records work—the more information you have, the harder it is to get any useful data pulled together. Computer databases can extract and reorganize large amounts of data with a very small amount of effort and a large degree of accuracy.

CREATING A DATABASE

Creating a database differs from word processing or spreadsheets in that the process can be divided into two distinct steps that must be carried out in a particular order: creating the database structure and entering records.

Create the Database Structure

Before you can enter any information into a database you must create a database structure. The structure is a list or pattern that describes the type of information you want to record, e.g., last name, street address, social security number, balance due, etc. Each item from which you want to enter information is called a *field*. The name field may seem odd since it is derived from the way information was entered on paper punch cards used for data storage before disk drives came into general use 15 to 20 years ago.

Enter Records

Once you have created the structure you can fill in information. All the fields that have information about the same person, place, or thing are called a record. If your database is keeping records about people, there will be one record for each person in the database.

Begin a new database by opening a new database window on the desktop:

Click(left) on **Create New File**
Click(left) on **New Database**

The new database window is displayed on the desktop. The window is completely blankjust like a word processing window with the window title set to the default for a database, DATA1.WDB.

At the bottom of the window the status line shows information unique to the database window. The left end of the line shows the current field number and name. Because this is a new database, the number is set for 1, the first field. There is no name, however, because this field is not created yet.

The next set of numbers to the right is a fraction. The top number tells you the current number of records available in the database, while the bottom shows the total number of records in the entire database. Since you have not created any records the fraction reads 0/0.

In the center of the status line is information about the current display mode. By default Works displays database information in the Form view. You will learn more about the Form view and its alternative, the List view, when you are ready to enter information.

Form Text

The Form view is designed to duplicate the way information is recorded when working with paper forms. Works allows you to enter text on any part of the form. For example, you might want to begin the form by entering a title or a heading that explains something about the form. Enter:

```
Organization Membership Information [return]
```

Move the cursor down two lines:

```
[down] (2 times)
```

Keep in mind that text entered onto the form has no functional purpose in the database. It merely serves to improve the appearance of the form itself. Since you can print database records, this extra text will be useful to other people who are reading the output and who may not be familiar with the purpose of the information on the form.

FIELDS

Before you can enter information in a database you must create a database *form*. The form consists of at least one field of information. Keep in mind that fields can be added and deleted from the form after its initial creation but you must begin with at least one field.

As stated at the beginning of this chapter, each field is used to store one piece of information you want to record. A field consists of two parts: field label and field entry area.

Field Label

The field label is the name you assign to the field. Works allows you to enter text into any part of the database form. However, a field label is distinguished from other text by the fact that it ends with a colon.

Field Entry Area

The field entry area is a block, similar to a spreadsheet cell, in which information is actually entered.

Creating fields is, on the surface, quite a simple matter since all you need to do is type in the field name followed by a colon. However, the fields you create are very significant in terms of how the information will be organized. For example, since this database is about members of an organization you will probably want to enter the names of the members. But how will you enter those names? Should you have one field for the name or separate fields for the first name and last name? How about titles, like Mr. or Ms? What about middle initials?

The choices you make are significant. If you think ahead you will realize that you might need to get an alphabetical list of the members. If you place the full name into a single field, e.g., "John Smith", the computer will not realize that when you sort the names it is the "Smith" portion of the entry that should determine its location in the list not the "John" portion. Most programs would use the first letter in the field, i.e., J as the key for sorting. It would be much better to separate the first name from the last name in two different fields so that the program can access the last names separately from the first names.

Of course, you cannot know in advance all of the implications of the decision you make about fields. That knowledge will come only with experience. However, one general rule about fields can be stated. It is always best to break up information into fields that contain as small a unit of information as possible. The reason is that database programs such as Works can usually assemble or combine fields when necessary but they have a hard time breaking up the contents of a field. In the case of names, you will find that Works could print the first and last name fields in several different ways, e.g., "John Smith" or "Smith, John", by combining to fields in different ways. If you had created a single field, "John Smith", you would not be able to take advantage of the program's features.

A similar consideration would apply to addresses. Instead of entering street, city, state, and zip code as part of a single address field, you would probably benefit by creating separate fields for each part of the address so that you could pick out all of the persons from a specific city or zip code.

Adding Fields

The actual process of adding a field to a database form is quite simple. In this database begin by entering a field for the first name and the last name:

```
First Name: [return]
```

When you enter **[return]**, Works will display a dialog box if the entry ends in a colon, as shown in Figure 10-1. The dialog box allows you to specify the width in characters and the height in lines of the field. The default values are 20 for the width and 1 line for the height.

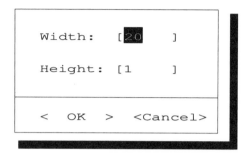

Figure 10-1. Field Size Dialog Box.

Accept the default values by entering:

[return]

The field entry area, indicated by a thin dotted line, is placed next to the field name. The cursor advances to the next line on the screen. Create a field for the last name:

Last name: [return] [return]

Skip down a few lines and begin entering the address field:

[down] (3 times) Home Address [return] [down] Street: [return]

This time enlarge the size of the field to 35 characters since many street addresses will require more than 20 characters:

35 [return]

The next line will hold the city, state, and zip code information. While it is simplest to place each of these fields on a separate line, people are used to reading address blocks in which these items appear in a block form. In this case you will place all these items on the same line. Begin with the city field:

City: [return] [return]

The cursor automatically moves ahead to the next line. Before you enter the next field you will need to reposition the cursor to the previous line. Enter:

```
[up]
```

When the arrow moves up it expands to a highlight that covers the entire field name. Once you create a field, the label and the field area function like cell in a spreadsheet. This means that if you want to change the name of the field you must do so by activating and edit mode (Press **[F2]** or click on the edit line) in order to alter the name. Move to the right by entering:

```
[right]
```

The highlight covers the entire field entry area. Move again to the right by entering:

```
[right]
```

The cursor returns to its normal size and it is positioned to the right of the entry area. Move right one more character and create a state field. Limit this field to a width of 2 characters:

```
[Right]
State: [return]
2 [return]
```

Change the cursor position and insert the zip code field:

```
[up]
[right] (3 times)
Zip: [return]
5 [return]
```

Note that Works is set to position the cursor on the next line at the at the same column as the beginning of the last field name. This makes it easy to enter a column of fields. Add a section for phone number:

```
[Home] [down] (2 times)
Phone: [return]
12 [return]
```

It is not necessary to have all of the fields begin at the left side of the form nor do they have to appear on a single screen. If necessary, you can continue to add fields filling as many pages as you like. However, placing your fields on a single screen where possible allows you to view all of the data at one time.

Hidden Field Names

The next section of the form is supposed to contain information about assessment and payment of dues. In this organization dues are assessed four times a year. One way to record the assessment and payment would be to have eight fields, four for

315

each assessment and four for each payment. The best way to arrange these fields would be in the form of a table with row and column headings, as shown in Table 10-1.

Table 10-1. Assessment and Payment of Dues.

	Dues	Payment
1st	0	0
2nd	0	0
3rd	0	0
4th	0	0

However, the layout of a table does not leave room for field names for each field. The solution in this case is to hide the actual field names and display only the entry areas. The text that appears as row or column headings are not the actual field names but simply text added to the form.

Begin by entering a series of text labels for the rows of the table:

```
[Down]
1st [return] [down]
2nd [return] [down]
3rd [return] [down]
4th [return]
```

Move the cursor back towards the top of the table and over to the right so that you can insert a column heading, Dues, for the first column of fields:

```
[up] (4 times)
[right] (8 times)
Dues [return]
```

The fields will be inserted next to the row labels. In this case the fields will have very simple names, e.g., D1 for 1st quarter due, D2, D3, and D4.

```
[left] (5 times)
```

Create the D1 field. Set the width of the field at 6 characters:

```
d1: [return]
6 [return]
```

Create three more fields, D2, D3, and D4 for the remaining dues fields:

316

```
d2: [return]
6 [return]
d3: [return]
6 [return]
d4: [return]
6 [return]
```

The field names make the table rather confusing to read. You can eliminate the unwanted field names by using the **Show Field Name** command on the Format menu. Normally this command, a toggle command, is set on by default. You can suppress the display of field names by placing the highlight on a field entry area and toggling this option off.

Highlight the D4 field by entering:

```
[up] [right]
```

```
Click(left) on Format
Click(left) on Show Field Name
```

The field label is removed from the form. Note that the status line still shows the actual name of the field, D4, so that you can always find the field name without having to display it on the form.

Keystroke Macros

In order to complete the table you will eventually need to repeat the **Show Field Name** command seven more times. Recall that many of the commands in Works have keystroke shortcut commands that allow you to complete a command with a single keystroke. Unfortunately, the **Show Field Name** command does not have a shortcut keystroke. However, Works includes a feature called keystroke *macros* which allows you to create keystroke shortcut commands of your own.

A macro is a series of two or more keystrokes that Works records while you are entering them. Once recorded Works can play back the keystrokes as many times as you like. Macro sequences can be assigned to **[Ctrl-letter]** combinations creating your own personal system of keystroke shortcuts.

In this case you might want to create a macro shortcut for **Show Field Name**. While this command is not very complicated, it is a convenient example of how to create a simple macro.

Macros are created by entering the keystrokes needed for the macro while macro recording is active. You can activate macro recording by entering a combination of **[Alt]** with the **[+=]** key. Note the [+] key on the numeric keypad cannot be used; it must be the [+=] from the top of the keyboard. Enter:

```
[Alt-+]
```

The macro dialog box contains two text boxes. The first box is used to enter the shortcut key to which the macro you are about to record will be assigned. In this case assign the macro to [**Ctrl-f**] for field. Enter:

[Ctrl-f]

Note that Works records the keystroke with its own notation for keystrokes, **<ctrlf>**. Next enter a descriptive title for the macro. This title can be used to explain what the [**Ctrl-f**] command is used for:

[Tab] Hide Field Name [return]

The dialog box is removed from the screen and the recording mode is activated. Note the word RECORD that appears in the message bar at the lower right corner of the screen.

The next step is to record the keystrokes needed to carry out the command. Note that you cannot record mouse operations so that you will have to make all entries which you want to be part of the macro with the keyboard. Enter:

[Alt-t] [Alt-n]

The command toggles the display of the field label on again. In this case these are all of the keystrokes you want to record as part of the macro. To end macro record enter:

[Alt-/]

Works displays a dialog box with macro recording commands and options. The first option, End Recording, stops keystroke recording and saves the macro. Cancel Recording stops macro recording and discards any keystrokes record. In this case save the macro:

Click(left) on **End Recording**

Put the macro to use by toggling the field label off once again. Enter:

[Ctrl-f]

Hide the labels for the rest of the field in this column. Enter:

[up] [Ctrl-f]
[up] [Ctrl-f]
[up] [Ctrl-f]

Fixed Input Macros

The next task is to repeat the basic process used in the dues column for a parallel column of fields for payments. Begin with the heading for that column:

```
[up]
[right] (5 times)
Payments [return] [down]
```

Before you begin the creation of the field for the payments—fields P1 through P4—you might consider whether or not a macro could help you speed up the process. Each field that you create will require exactly the same keystrokes each time with the exception of numbers 1 through 4 which were used in the field name. Since macros replay the same keystrokes each time, the fact that one of the keystrokes ought to be different would stop you from using a macro shortcut.

Works includes a special option which you can use to insert keystrokes during the playback of a macro. This enables you to create more generalized macros that have greater flexibility. Works allows two kinds of pauses for entry during a macro: fixed and variable input.

Fixed Input

In this type of pause the macro allows you to enter a fixed number of keystrokes after which it resumes playback.

Variable Input

This type of pause allows you to enter an indefinite number of characters. The macro resumes only after you press [**return**].

In this case, a fixed input pause for one character would create a macro that could be used for all of the fields. Turn on the macro recording:

```
[Alt-+]
[Ctrl-1] [Tab] Make Payment Field [return]
```

Enter the first letter of the macro:

```
p
```

It is here that you need to pause the macro for the entry of the number. Display the macro options dialog box:

```
[Alt-/]
```

Select a fixed input pause:

```
Click(left) on Fixed Input
Click(left) on <Ok>
```

The fixed input pause is activated. The word "FIXINPUT" appears in the message bar in the lower right hand corner of the screen. When the fixed input pause is selected, Works keeps track of the number of keys you enter but does not record the keystrokes themselves. When the macro is replayed, you will be able to enter the same number of keystrokes before the playback resumes. Enter:

```
1
```

From this point on, the rest of the keystrokes will be the same for each field and should therefore be recorded as part of the macro. To resume, enter [**Alt-/**] again:

```
[Alt-/]
```

The dialog box confirms that you are about to end the input:

```
[return]
```

The mode changes to RECORD once again, as indicated on the right end of the message bar, so that you can complete the recording of the macro:

```
: [return]
6 [return]
```

The field has been created. End the recording and save the macro by entering:

```
[Alt-/] [return]
```

To create the second payment field, use the [**Ctrl-1**] macro. Enter:

```
[Ctrl-1]
```

The macro types in the letter p and then stops for a fixed input. Note the FIXINPUT indicator appears on the right side of the message bar. Enter:

```
2
```

The macro completes the creation of the field. Complete the column by entering:

```
[Ctrl-1] 3
[Ctrl-1] 4
```

Use the [**Ctrl-f**] macro to hide the field names:

```
[up] [Ctrl-f]
[up] [Ctrl-f]
[up] [Ctrl-f]
[up] [Ctrl-f]
```

The database form, as shown in Figure 10-2, is now ready for data entry.

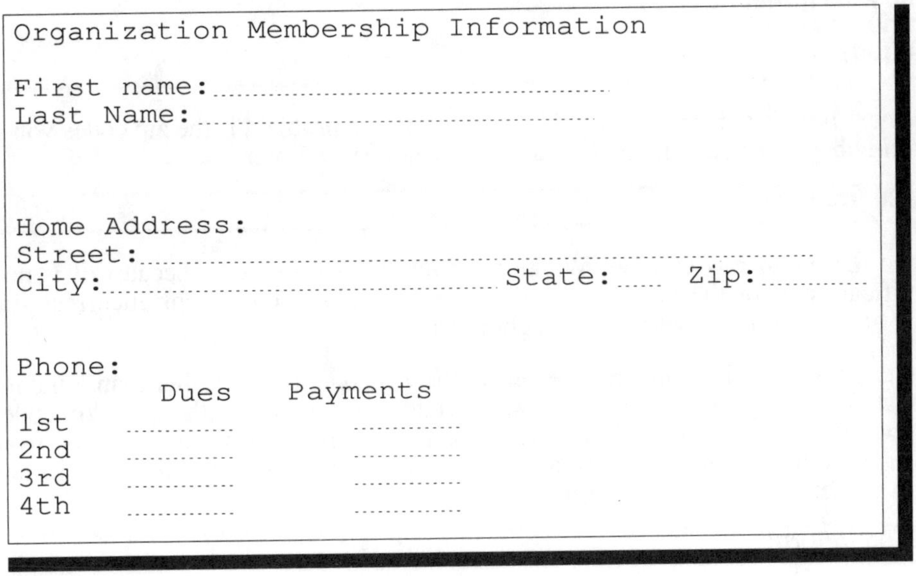

```
Organization Membership Information

First name:.................................................
Last Name:................................................



Home Address:
Street:...........................................................................
City:...................................... State:..... Zip:.............


Phone:
         Dues    Payments
1st      .............    .............
2nd      .............    .............
3rd      .............    .............
4th      .............    .............
```

Figure 10-2. Database Form.

DATA ENTRY

Once you created a form (even if there is only a single field) you can begin data entry. You can begin data entry by placing the highlight on a field entry area and entering text or numbers.

Begin with the first name field:

Click(left) on *First name*

The field label is highlighted. To move into the field entry area enter:

[right]

Fill in this record by entering:

```
Walter [tab]
LaFish [tab]
1250 Pine Street [tab]
Walnut Creek [tab]
CA [tab]
```

The next field is the zip code field. Zip codes pose a problem if the zip codes you are entering begin with a non-significant value, i.e., 09190. Enter:

```
09190 [return]
```

When the number is entered, Works removes the leading zero because it is not a significant part of the value 9190. This means that the entry look incorrect since there are only 4 digits when there ought to be 5.

You can resolve this problem by entering the zip code as text rather than a number. In fact, from a database point of view zip codes are text, i.e., although a zip code is composed of numeric digits it does not function as a numeric value since you would never perform mathematical operations such as addition or multiplication. To enter digits as text precede the first digit with a ":

```
"09190 [return]
```

This time the full 5 digit code appears in the field. Of course, if all of your zip codes begin with 1 or greater you would not encounter this problem. Complete the record by entering the phone number:

```
[tab]
415-372-6767 [return]
```

Adding More Records

The database form can be used to enter as many records as you desire into the database. The commands [Ctrl-PgDn] and [Ctrl-PgUp] display the next or previous commands, respectively. Display record #2 by entering:

```
[Ctrl-Pg Dn]
```

The form appears with all of the field empty. If you look on the left end of the status line you will see the number 2 indicating that this is the second record in the database. Note that the fraction reads 1/1. This fraction will not reflect the addition of a second record until data entry for this record is complete. Enter:

```
[Ctrl-Pg Up]
```

The screen moves back to record 1 showing the data that you have just entered. Another way to display a record is to use the **[F5]** key to go to a specific record. Enter:

```
[F5]
```

The program displays a dialog box with two items. The text box at the top allows you to enter the number of a record to display. The list box shows the names of the fields in the database. You can move your highlight to a field by selecting its name from this box. This option is useful when you want to locate a field which has its label hidden.

In this case move to record 2 by entering:

```
2 [return]
```

Activate the first field by entering:

```
[tab]
```

Fill in the next four records as shown below. Remember that **[Ctrl-Pg Dn]** will display the next record screen:

```
Organization Membership Information

First name: Judy
Last Name: Hirsch

Home Address
Street: 21 Springwood Drive
City: Reno                    State: NV Zip: 89007

Phone: 315-908-7721
        Dues    Payments
1st
2nd
3rd
4th
Organization Membership Information

First name: Diane
Last Name: Kamrin

Home Address
Street: 57 Wellman Court
City: Modesto                 State: CA Zip: 94301

Phone: 421-987-5656
        Dues    Payments
1st
2nd
3rd
4th
Organization Membership Information

First name: Heather
Last Name: Hart

Home Address
Street: 765 Providence Lane
City: Martinez                State: CA Zip: 94553

Phone: 415-777-9090
        Dues    Payments
1st
2nd
3rd
4th
```

You should now have four records in the database. The fraction on the status line should show 4/4 indicating that there are four current records available in the database and four records total in the database.

SEARCHING, SELECTING, AND SORTING

In a very small database (such as the sample) you can probably locate all of the information by simply leafing through the records with **[Ctrl-Pg Up]** or **[Ctrl-Pg Dn]**. However, as the database grows in size you will need the help of the program to manage the data. Once you have created a database there are three common activities that you will likely want or need to perform in order to locate and work with specific parts of your database file: searching, selecting, and sorting.

Searching

Searching refers to locating a particular record within the database by searching for a specific item in a field such as a last name or a street address.

Selecting

Selecting is used to create groups of records that have some quality in common. For example, you might want to select only these records from a certain state or city.

Sorting

Sorting is used to change the order of the records within the database based on the value in one or more fields. Sorting rearranges the records so that you can leaf through the database in alphabetical order or numeric order based on specific fields. For example you might want to sort the database according to last name or city location.

The simplest operation is the **Search** command located on the Select menu. This command locates records in the database that contain specific information. For example, suppose you wanted to locate the record for "Judy Hirsch". Move to the beginning of the database by entering:

[Ctrl-Home]

You are now located at the first record in the database. To search for the record you want to find, display the Search dialog box:

Click(left) on **Select** Click(left) on **Search**

The dialog box shown in Figure 10-3 allows you to enter the text you want to locate. The text should be a segment of text that can be found in one field. For example, if you want to find "Judy Hirsch" you need to pick the part of the name that you think is most unique. Since the first name and the last name are in different fields you cannot actually search for "Judy Hirsch" but either "Judy" or "Hirsch".

```
┌─────────────────────────────────────────────┐
│                                              │
│   Search for: [....................]         │
│                                              │
│   Match:                                     │
│   ┌──────────────────────────────────────┐  │
│   │ ( ) Next record   ( ) All records    │  │
│   └──────────────────────────────────────┘  │
│                                              │
├──────────────────────────────────────────────┤
│                                              │
│                      <  OK  >  <Cancel>      │
│                                              │
└─────────────────────────────────────────────┘
```

Figure 10-3. Search Dialog Box.

Enter:

hirsch [return]

The program locates the text in record 2 and displays that record on the screen. The highlight is positioned to the field in record 2 that contain the search text. Note that the search is not sensitive to differences in case, i.e., hirsch would match hirsch, HIRSCH or Hirsch.

Selecting with Search

Selection is a process by which you temporarily suppress the display of any records that do not fit a certain criterion. Simple searching is useful when you are looking for a particular record within the database. For example, when you search for a last name you are looking for one particular record out of all of the records in the database. When you find that record you have no need to go further with that search.

On the other hand you may want to search for a less specific criterion which may occur in more than one record. In that case you would want the search process to select as well as search. Selection is an important tool in database management because it does more than locate a single record. When selection is used the program picks out all of the records in the database that match the search text and creates a working group of records. In this group only the matching records are displayed when you leaf through the database with [**Ctrl-Pg Up**] or [**Ctrl-Pg Dn**].

Selection makes it easy to examine a group of records because all of the records that do not match the search text are temporarily hidden from display. When you want to return to the full database you would select the **Show All Records** command located on the Select menu.

The key to selection is to pick the All Records option in the search dialog box. For example, suppose you wanted to examine only the records that had 415 as the area code. Since more than one record is likely to meet this criterion you can use the All Records option to create a selection as part of the search:

```
Click(left) on Select
Click(left) on Search
```

```
415
```

Select the All Records option:

```
Click(left) on All Records
Click(left) on <Ok>
```

This time the search displays record 1 since 415 appears in the phone number. If you look at the status line you will notice that the fraction reads 2/4. The 2 tells you that 2 of the 4 records in the database have been included in the selection. Enter:

```
[Ctrl-Pg Dn]
```

When you move to the next record in the database Works skips to record 4. Because you are working in a selection, the next record is not simply the next record in the database, i.e., record 2, but the next record that matches the search text. In this case that means records 2 and 3 should be skipped and record 4 should be displayed.

When you have established a selection, the database behaves temporarily as if the selected records are the only one in the database.

The selection will remain active until you specifically deactivate it with the **Show All Records** command:

```
Click(left) on Select
Click(left) on Show All Records
```

What has changed? The change is subtle but significant. The fraction on the status line has changed to 4/4 indicating that all of the records in the database are now available for display. The database has returned to normal operation.

Sorting

Sorting a database is another way to improve its organization. When you keep records manually, such as in rolodex files or index cards, you will usually keep them in alphabetical order. There are two major drawbacks to manual organization of this type that often prevent you from getting useful data from the stored information. In manual record keeping you are usually locked into the original sequence. If you arrange your mailing list in alphabetical order it is very difficult to rearrange it in order by city, state, or zip code. Because the computer can sort hundreds of records in a few seconds, you can rearrange your records as often as you desire in order to get the best use out of the data for the purpose you have in mind. Since different sort orders are useful for different tasks you will find that sorting records in different ways can reveal interesting facts about the data in the database.

The sorted order of the database depends on the fields specified as the sort keys. You can have up to three levels of sort keys in Works. Why would you need more than one sort key? The answer is that multiple sort keys are necessary when the values in the first sort key are not unique. For example, in sorting by last name it is possible that more than one record contains the same last name. In that case, you might choose to use the first name field as second sort key. If two or more records have the same last name, then those records are sorted by first name. You can add a third key to handle records in which the first two fields have identical contents. If you do not specify all of the keys, records that have the same sort values will appear in the order in which they were entered.

Sort the current database by last and first name. The **Sort Records** command is located o the Select menu:

Click(left) on **Select** Click(left) on **Sort Records**

The sort dialog box shown in Figure 10-4 has three text boxes in which you can enter the names of the fields that will be the sort keys.

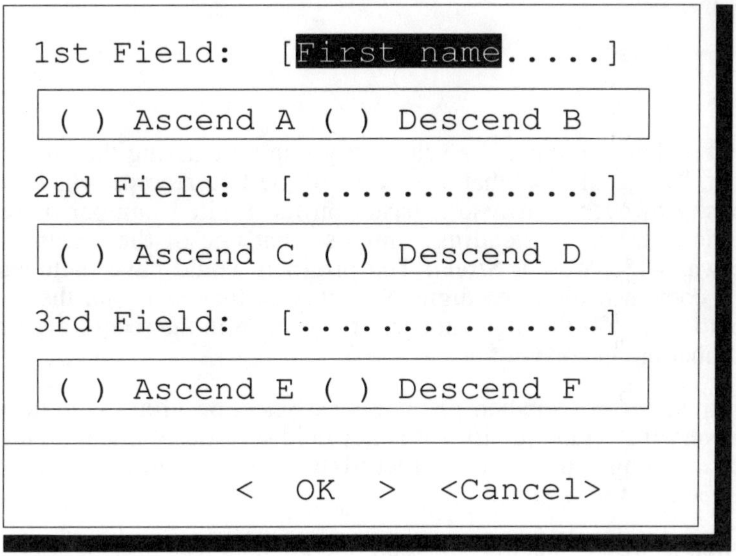

```
1st Field:   [First name.....]

 ( ) Ascend A ( )  Descend B

2nd Field:   [...............]

 ( ) Ascend C ( )  Descend D

3rd Field:   [...............]

 ( ) Ascend E ( )  Descend F


     <  OK  >  <Cancel>
```

Figure 10-4. Sort Dialog Box.

The dialog box for sorting automatically inserts the name of the first field in the database structure—first name. In this case that is not the correct field. Enter:

last name [tab]

Each key can be designated as ascending sort order (low to high) or descending order (high to low) independently so that you can have different sequences for different keys, if desired. The default is ascending sort order. Enter the second key, first name:

[tab]
first name [return]

The records are sorted by Works. What has changed? At first when you look at the screen nothing seems to have been accomplished. However, upon close examination you will see that the record number for the current record, "Heather Hart", has changed from 4 to 1. That is because "Hart" is the first name in the alphabetical order by last name. Enter:

[Ctrl-Pg Dn]

The next record is "Hirsch", which is the next record by alphabetical order. Change the order of the database so that the records are in zip code order. Try this on your own. You will find the correct command under Exercise 1 at the end of the chapter.

When you finish, Walter LaFish will be the first record because of the zip code in this record.

Queries

Recall that earlier you created a selection group by entering the number 415 as the search text. The result was that you selected the two records which contained 415 area codes. However, that result, based on the limited number of records in the example database, is misleading. Suppose that one of the street address in the database was 4150 Walnut Street. The program would have included that record because it contained the three digits even though they were not the area code. The same would be true if the digits appeared anywhere in the record even as part of the phone number or zip code.

The search all records method of creating a selection group is quite simple but it lacks one very important quality—it is not field specific. While search is useful, it is not specific enough to select the records you have in mind in databases with a significant amount of records.

The solution is a field-specific selection operation called a *query*. A query is a blank record form. Instead of filling in data, you place into the field on that form the information that you want to use as the selection criteria. If you want to find all of the records that have a state value of "ca "you would enter "ca" in the state field. The selection would pick out only those records with "ca" in the state field. Because the selection is field-specific the "ca" would not pick up unwanted matches such as in the last name field, e.g., "Carter".

In addition, you can narrow the selection by placing criteria in more than one field. For example, you could select for all of the "smith" last names in the state of "ca" by entering "smith" into last name and ca in state. Keep in mind that making the selection too restrictive may result in no records being selected. Of course that is not a bad thing because it will tell you that none of the records meet those criterion. For example, you might select for all of the members who owe dues. If none are selected you can conclude that all of the members are up to date.

To create a query form select the Query option from the View menu:

```
Click(left) on View
Click(left) on Query
```

The screen displays what looks like a blank record. In the center of the status bar the word "Query" appears indicating that the database is in the query mode. Suppose that you wanted to select record in which the last name begins with the letter H and the state is CA.

Place the highlight on the last name field:

```
Click(left) on the entry area next to Last Name:
```

In this case you are going to select by only the first letter of the last name. You can use the * character as a *wildcard*. The wildcard tells Works to match any characters. Entering H* as the search text will pick out any name that begins with H:

h*

Move the highlight to the state field:

Click(left) on the entry area next to **State:**

ca [return]

You have now set up the query specification to extract the record you are looking for. Return to the Form view:

Click(left) on **View** Click(left) on **Form**

The record that appears is record 4, "Heather Hart". This record was selected because the last name, "Hart", begins with an H and the State is CA. The status line fraction, 1/4, indicates that this is the only record in the database that qualifies under the current query.

To remove the query and return to the full database use the **Show All Records** command:

Click(left) on **Select** Click(left) on **Show All Records**

FORMATS AND STYLE

As with word processing and spreadsheet information, you can apply various formats and styles to the text, field names, and fields in order to enhance the appearance of the form.

For example, you might want to make the heading of the form bold text:

Click(left) on *Organization*

Text enhancements such as bold are found on the Style dialog box located on the Format menu:

Click(left) on Format Click(left) on **Style** Click(left) on **Bold** Click(left) on **<Ok>**

The text is changed to bold. You can also apply styles to field labels or field contents. You might want the last name of the member to appear in bold so that it stands out as you leaf through records:

```
Click(left) on entry area next to Last Name:
Click(left) on Format
Click(left) on Style
Click(left) on Bold
Click(left) on <Ok>
```

Move to the first record in the database:

```
[Ctrl-Home]
```

The text and field in this record are also bold. This is because changes made to the database form flow through all of the records in the database. When you add a text enhancement such as bold to a field, field label, or form text it will appear on all of the records no matter which record was displayed when you made the change.

Number Formats

In addition to text enhancements, you can apply numeric formats, such as those used in spreadsheet models, to fields that contain numeric information. Move the cursor down to the D1 field that is part of the dues and payments table:

```
[tab] (6 times)
```

Enter the amount of dues owed for the 1st quarter of the year:

```
12.50 [return]
```

The field shows 12.5 as its contents. Why didn't the 0 appear? The answer is that when numeric values are entered into fields Works, by default, stores only the significant figures and discards any numerically insignificant values. This is the same style of numeric display used in spreadsheets. Enter the dues for the 2nd quarter:

```
[down] 10.00 [return]
```

In this case both zeros to the right of the decimal point were discarded. The display, while numerically accurate, is difficult to read because the decimal places in the two values do not align vertically. The solution to this problem is to use a numeric format for the field. Numeric formats allow you to designate a specific style, including the number of decimal places required for the display of the values (See Chapter 7 for details about numeric formats).

The format menu lists the formats that can be applied to numeric values. In this case format the D2 field as a fixed field with 2 decimal places:

```
Click(left) on Format
Click(left) on Fixed
Click(left) on <Ok>
```

The value in the field now changes to 10.00. The format, which specified 2 decimal places, adds the two zeros to fill out the appearance of the value on the form. Apply the same format to the D1 field using the repeat action command, [**Shift-F7**]:

```
[up] [Shift-F7]
```

Continue by applying the format to all of the fields in the table—D3 and D4—plus P1 through P4. Try this on your own. You will find the correct command under Exercise 2 at the end of the chapter.

Enter a payment into the P1 field:

```
12.5 [return]
```

The format displays the entry as 12.50. Note that when you enter values it is not necessary to bother entering the extra zeros since the program will automatically add them. This can speed up your data entry.

Move to the next record by entering:

```
[Ctrl-Pg Dn]
```

Enter a payment:

```
12.5 [return]
```

The format operates on this record as well. As with text enhancements, a format applied to a field will flow through all of the records in the database.

Date Formats

Works provides special formats that can be applied to date or time information. Suppose that you wanted to add the members' dates of birth to the database. Insert a field called Date of Birth below the last name field. Enter:

```
[Home]
[up](10 times)
Date of Birth: [return] [return]
```

Note how simple it is to add a field to an existing database. Enter the date into the new field:

```
[up] [right]11/20/62 [return]
```

Once you have entered a date into field, you can apply a date format to the field in order to change the way that the date appears:

Click(left) on **Format**
Click(left) on Time/Date

The Date/Time dialog box, as shown in Figure 10-5, displays the options for the display of dates or times. The default setting is to display the month, day, and year for the date. The long option for dates changes the display from a numeric display to one that uses a text abbreviation for the month name and full 4 digit year value.

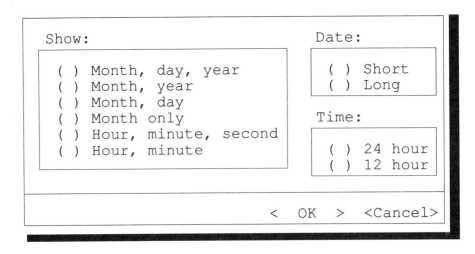

Figure 10-5. Date/Time Format Dialog Box.

Change the format to a long date format:

Click(left) on **Long**
Click(left) on **<Ok>**

The date changes to read Nov 20, 1962. Use the Style dialog box to center the date within the field:

Click(left) on **Format**
Click(left) on **Style**
Click(left) on **Center**
Click(left) on **<Ok>**

The date is centered in the field. Move back to record 1 and enter a date of birth for that record:

[Ctrl-Pg Up]
6/7/59 [return]

Even though you entered the date in numeric format, the format assigned to the field changed the style of the display to match the other records.

FIELD FORMULAS

Most of the information in a database record is entered directly by the user. However, it is possible to create fields that use formulas to calculate a value. For example, you might want to create calculate fields that sum the total value of all of the dues fields, the payments fields, and one that shows the current balance between dues and payments for each record.

Move the cursor to an open area on the form:

```
[right](10 times)
```

Create a field called Dues Owed by entering:

```
Dues Owed: [return]
7 [return]
```

Add two more fields for the Payments and Balance:

```
Payments: [return]
7 [return]
Balance: [return]
7 [return]
```

Move the highlight back to the Dues Owed field:

```
[up] (3 times)
[right]
```

The value for this field is the total of the D1, D2, D3, and D4 fields. Writing a database formula is similar to writing a spreadsheet formula with the exception that you must type in the names of the fields instead of using cell references. As with formats, when a formula is entered into any record, it is applied to the same field in all of the other records in the database.

Works recognizes 5 basic mathematical operators and uses the following symbols in formulas to represent them, as shown in Table 10-2.

Table 10-2. Mathematical Operator Symbols.

Operation	Symbol
Addition	+
Subtraction	-
Multiplication	*
Division	/
^	exponential

A formula can contain field names, arithmetic operators, or numeric values, such as percentages or other values that are constant values in a formula. All formulas begin with an =. Enter:

```
=d1+d2+d3+d4 [return]
```

The field shows the total, 22.5, which is the correct total of the dues fields for this record. Use the format command to set the format of this field as currency:

```
Click(left) on Format
Click(left) on Currency
Click(left) on <Ok>
```

Place a similar formula in the payment field that sums the fields P1 through P4:

```
[down]
=p1+p2+p3+p4 [return]
```

Repeat the last formatting command by entering the repeat command:

```
[Shift-F7]
```

Move down to the balance field:

```
[down]
```

In this field you will subtract the payments from the dues owed. Enter:

```
=dues owed-payments [return]
[Shift-F7]
```

This field correctly shows a balance of $10.00, as shown in Figure 10-6.

```
Organization Membership Information

First name: Walter
Last Name: LaFish
Date of Birth:        Jun 7, 1959              Dues Owed:    22.50
                                               Payments:     12.50
                                               Balance:      10.00

Home Address
Street: 1250 Pine Street
City: Walnut Creek              State: CA Zip: 09190


Phone: 415-372-6767
        Dues      Payments
1st     12.50          12.50
2nd     10.00
3rd
4th
```

Figure 10-6. Database Form with Calculated Fields.

Moving Fields

The three calculated fields do not align their values in a straight vertical columns. This is the result of the fact that each of the field names is a different number of characters. Now that the data has been entered you can see that the form would look better if the fields were moved so that the decimal points would align in a vertical column.

You can change the position of a field on the form by using the **Move Field** command located on the Edit menu:

Click(left) on **Edit**
Click(left) on **Move Field**

The entire field, both label and entry area, are highlighted. You can change the position of the highlight by using the arrow keys or clicking the mouse. For example, the Balance field should be moved two characters to the right. This means that the beginning of the field should be at the position now occupied by the letter l in Balance:

Click(left) on the letter *l* in *Balance*

The highlight shows the new location of the field. To place the field at that new location enter:

[return]

The decimal points in the Balance and Dues Owed fields lines up in the same vertical column. Move the Payments field one column to the right to align all three fields:

```
Click(left) on Payments
Click(left) on Edit
Click(left) on Move Field
```

Enter:

```
[right] [return]
```

You might want to improve the appearance of the form by drawing a line between the Payments and the Balance fields. In order to make room for this line you need to insert a blank line into the form. This can be done with the **Insert Line** command found on the Edit menu. Enter:

```
[down]
```

```
Click(left) on Edit
Click(left) on Insert Line
```

Draw a line of "=" between the two fields:

```
[left](2 times)
= (12 times)
[return]
```

The calculated fields will immediately update when you make changes to the fields. For example, suppose you recorded that Walter LaFish has just paid his second quarter dues. Enter:

```
[tab] (10 times)
10 [return]
```

As soon as you enter the payment, the values in the calculated fields update to show that there is currently a zero balance.

Setting Default Field Values

Move to the next record in the database:

```
[Ctrl-Pg Dn]
```

The calculated fields appear in this record and all other records in the database and perform the same calculations. This record shows a balance of -12.50. That is because there has been a 12.50 payment entered but the dues column is empty.

You can use a formula to create a *default* value for a field. In terms of a database the default value is automatically entered into the field when ever a new record is added to the database or the current record have no entry in the field. The default can be replaced with a different value if desire. The value that replace the default value formula effects only the current record.

This type of default can be quite useful. In the example of the Dues column, you can post a dues charge to all of the records in the database by entering a single formula. In this example you can automatically insert the 12.50 charge for first quarter dues into records 2 through 4, and also any new records added to the database by entering the value as a formula. Recall that a formula begin with an = sign. That means that entering =12.5 instead of simply 12.5 will create a default value in that field for all of the records.

Move the highlight to the D1 field by entering:

```
[Shift-tab] [up]
```

Enter a default value formula:

```
=12.5 [return]
```

The value causes the calculated fields to update resulting in a zero balance. Display record 3:

```
[Ctrl-Pg Dn]
```

The 12.50 charge appears in this record automatically since no entry had been made into that field. Add a second default value formula in D2 that updates all records (except record 1 that already has an entry in that field) with a 10.00 second quarter dues charge:

```
[down]
```

Move to the next record:

```
[Ctrl-Pg Dn]
```

This record shows the default values for both D1 and D2 and a balance due of 22.50.

Note that default values can work for text fields also. Enter the formula =CA [return] would insert the letters CA in the field in each empty or new record. This type of default might be useful when all or most of your address are from the same state, i.e., California.

Overriding a Default

While default values are useful because they enter the same value into all of the empty fields or the fields in any new records added to the database, there may be some records for which these values are not correct. Suppose that "Heather Hart" was not a member during the 1st quarter of the year. The dues charge for that quarter should not appear in her record. You can override a default value by replacing it with a value, not a formula. In this case place a value of zero into field D1 by entering:

```
[up] 0 [return]
```

Heather is now charged only for second quarter dues. Enter a 10.00 payment for "Heather":

```
[tab] [down] 10 [return]
```

This record now has a zero balance.

Selecting with Inequalities

The calculated fields provide important information about the records in your database. For example, suppose you wanted to know which members had an outstanding balance, that is, which record contains a balance greater than zero. When you use terms such as greater than or less than you are using inequalities. In this case you want to select records based not on their match a value, e.g., zero or 10.00, but on the fact that they are greater than zero.

Works allows you to write formulas in a query form that use standard math symbols for greater and less than relationships, as shown in Table 10-3.

Table 10-3. Greater and Less Than Symbols.

Relationship	Symbol
greater than	>
equal or greater than	>=
less than	<
equal or less than	<=

If you wanted to select those records that has a balance greater than zero, begin with the query form display:

```
Click(left) on View
Click(left) on Query
```

340

Note that the query values from the last query selection are still stored in the query form. To start with a blank query form use the **Delete Query** command on the Edit menu:

```
Click(left) on Edit
Click(left) on Delete Query
```

The query form is cleared of all old values. Highlight the balance field:

```
Click(left) on entry area next to Balance:
```

Enter the inequality formula:

```
>0 [return]
```

Return to the form display:

```
Click(left) on View
Click(left) on Form
```

The database shows record 2. If you look at the status line it shows the fraction 2/4 indicating that two of the four records in the database have a balance greater than zero. Return to the full database:

```
Click(left) on Select
Click(left) on Show All Records
```

Move to the first record in the database:

```
[Ctrl-Home]
```

THE LIST VIEW

The Form view allows you to view all of the fields in the database for one record at a time. The List view changes the display to a column (fields) and row (records) table similar to the display format of a spreadsheet. The advantage of the List is that you can see the data from more than one record at a time. The disadvantage is that because of the column and row format, not all of the fields can be visible at the same time. Change to the List view:

```
Click(left) on View
Click(left) on List
```

The screen changes to a spreadsheet-like display, as shown in Figure 10-7, in which each of the columns is a field and each row a record.

```
 File  Edit  Print  Select  Format  Options  View  Window  Help
"Walter
■══════════════════════ C10.WDB ══════════════════════╪
│    First nameLast Name   Street    City     State    Zip    Phone     =
│ 1  Walter    LaFish    1250 Pine Walnut CreCA    09190    415-372-67  ↑
│ 2  Judy      Hirsch    21 SpringwReno      NV          89007 315-908-77
│ 3  Diane     Kamrin    57 WellmanModesto   CA          94301 421-987-56
│ 4  Heather   Hart      765 ProvidMartinez  CA          94553 415-777-90
│ 5
│ 6
│ 7
│ 8
│ 9
│10
│11
│12
│13
│14
│15
│16
│17
│18                                                                      ↓
║←                                                                      →■
 1 First name    4/4       LIST                              <F1=HELP>
Press ALT to choose commands, or F2 to edit.
```

Figure 10-7. List View of Database.

You can perform all of the same operations in the List view as you can in the Form view including data entry or query operations. The primary disadvantage of the List view is that you can see many fewer fields on the screen than you can in the Form view. Each column width is set to 10 characters, which is smaller than many of the field width so that only part of the field can be displayed.

On the other hand, you can perform selections on ranges of fields from several records or fields as you would in spreadsheet operations. In fact, each field, in the List view, can be treated like a spreadsheet cell in many respects. Perhaps the best way to use the List view is to limit the display to small fields, typically the numeric values. This allow you to view the numeric data in your database in a spreadsheet like display. In order to achieve this type of display you must hide all of the fields you do not want to display.

For example, it might be useful to display in the list mode the three calculated fields: dues owed, payments, and balance. This means that you need to hide all of the other fields. Hiding a field is accomplished by setting its field width to zero. Keep in mind that this change affects only the List display. If you change back to the form display the field will appear unchanged on the form.

You can select a block of fields (columns) by dragging the mouse across the field names in the field name bar at the top of the window. In the following instruction the screen display will scroll horizontally as you drag the mouse towards the field which is currently off the screen:

| Click(left) on the field name *Street* |
| Drag(left) to the field name *Date of Bi* |

With all of these fields highlighted, set their width to zero:

Click(left) on **Format** Click(left) on **Field Width**

0 [return] **[Ctrl-Home]**

The List now shows only the first name, last name and calculated fields, as shown in Figure 10-8. The spreadsheet-like view is a quick way to review the financial status of the organization.

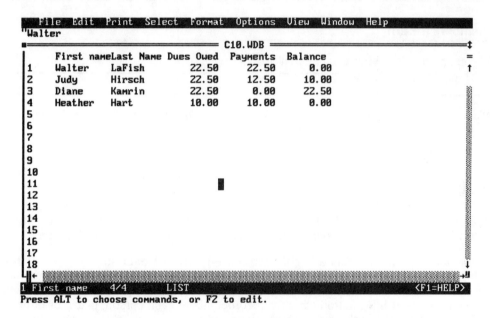

```
  File  Edit  Print  Select  Format  Options  View  Window  Help
"Walter
===================================== C10.WDB =====================================
     First nameLast Name Dues Owed   Payments   Balance                          =
 1   Walter    LaFish      22.50      22.50      0.00                             ↑
 2   Judy      Hirsch      22.50      12.50     10.00
 3   Diane     Kamrin      22.50       0.00     22.50
 4   Heather   Hart        10.00      10.00      0.00
 5
 6
 7
 8
 9
10
11                                 █
12
13
14
15
16
17
18
1 First name     4/4        LIST                                    <F1=HELP>
Press ALT to choose commands, or F2 to edit.
```

Figure 10-8. List View with Hidden Fields (Columns).

You can use query forms in the List view just as you do the Form view. Apply the current query, balance greater than zero, to the list:

Click(left) on **Select** Click(left) on **Apply Query**

The List view now shows the two records with outstanding balances. Return to the Form view:

Click(left) on **View** Click(left) on **Form**

Note that the changes made to the field widths in the List view do not affect the display of the fields in the Form view. Release the query selection and return to the full database:

```
Click(left) on Select
Click(left) on Show All Records
```

Save the database:

```
Click(left) on File
Click(left) on Close
Click(left) on <Yes>
```

```
members [return]
```

If you are done working you can exit Works:

```
Click(left) on Exit Works
```

If you want to go on to Chapter 11, leave the program running. The next chapter will deal with printing records and reports from your database.

SUMMARY

This chapter dealt with the basic skills needed to create a database form, enter information, perform selections, sort, and make calculations on the database data.

Databases. A database is a highly structured form of data storage. All of the information in a database belongs to two types of groupings. All of the items that relate to information about a particular person, place, or thing form a record. Each different piece of information which is recorded about each person, place, or thing is a field. Each record in the database has the exact same set of fields which repeat for each record.

Fields. Before you can create records, you must define the fields of the database. A field consists of a field name and a field data entry area. Fields are created by entering the field name followed by a colon and a **[return]**. You then specify the size of the field entry area. If you do not want the name of the field to appear on the form you can hide the field name.

Views. Works allows you to view the database as a series of forms in which all of the data for one record at a time is presented in a full screen display. You can switch to a list view in which the fields appears as spreadsheet columns and the records as spreadsheet rows. The List view enables you to view data from more than one record at a time.

344

Searching. You can locate information by searching the database for specific words, phrases, or values. This type of search is not field specific and will locate the information in any field in the database.

Selecting. The All Records option of the **search** command converts the search process into a selection process. In a selection process, the program displays only those records that contain data that matches the search text. The other records are temporarily hidden until you release the selection with the **Show All Records** command.

Queries. A query is a field specific selection. A query is created by filling in a query form with values that you want to match within the database. The matching values are specific to individual fields and will match data only in those fields. Queries can also operate on inequalities so that records can be selected for greater than or less than relationships.

Sorting. Sorting changes the sequence of the records within the database by arranging the records in order according to sort key fields. You can have up to three levels of sort keys which can be independently set for ascending or descending sort order.

Formulas. A formula is an arithmetic calculation that uses information in the database fields to arrive at a value for another field. If a formula is entered into a field it is automatically applied to all of the records in the database. Formulas that insert values or text create default values for empty field and new records.

Macros. You can speed up repetitive operations by using macro recording and playback to create your own personal shortcut keys. You can insert variable or fixed input pauses in macros to increase their flexibility.

EXERCISES

Exercise 1

Sort records by zip code:

```
Click(left) on Select
Click(left) on Sort Records
```

```
zip [tab]
[tab] [Del]
[return]
```

Exercise 2

Apply the currency format to the table fields:

```
[down] (2 times)
[Shift-F7] [down] [Shift-F7]
[right](7 times)
[Shift-F7] [up]
[Shift-F7] [up]
[Shift-F7] [up]
[Shift-F7]
```

Beyond the Basics

Chapter 11

Database Printing and Reports

T his chapter will show you how to use a database to create documents. Databases have two primary uses. First, they serve a direct purpose in helping you store and retrieve data and provide analysis of information by performing calculations, sorting records according to key values, and selecting groups of related records based on logical qualifications.

The second purpose of a database is as a source of data for reports, documents, and labels. In these procedures the database fields supply data which fill out a pre-defined document form with specific information. Many of the analytical tools provided by the database are shared indirectly by these documents. For example, you might want to send a form letter to all those members whose balance is greater than zero. The database would supply the form letter with information from a specific set of records which meet the query specification. The database determines who the form letters go and how many are printed, based on the logical criteria included in the query form.

In this chapter you will learn how a database can be used to create two different types of documents.

Record Printouts. A record printout is a printed copy of the information that appears in the database form. Each record is printed on a separate page. Or, in cases where there is a large number of fields each record is printed on a separate set of pages you can select to print the field names or only the data in the fields.

Reports. A report is a column-oriented document in which field information is printed in columns. Each row of the document contains data from one record. The overall appearance of a report is similar to a spreadsheet. Reports also provide a means by which you can generate summary information about all of the records included in the report. For example, you could use a report to list information about dues and payments, and summarize totals for the entire database at the end of the report. In Works reports, are created from the View menu in the database window. Begin this project by loading the Works program from the startup screen in the usual manner. Once loaded, retrieve the MEMBERS database file:

| Click(left) on **Open Existing File** |
| Double click(left) on *MEMBERS.WDB* |

The MEMBERS database displays the last record with which you were working when you saved the file. Note that many of settings such as the List view layout, the last query form and the last selection, if any, are stored along with the file. This means that when you return to the database you can continue working from the point at which you last left off.

PRINTING RECORDS

The simplest type of output that you can generate from a database is record printing. This type of printing sends one or more records to the printer. Each record is treated as a separate document so that they print on individual pages. If the form is too large to fit on one page, Works prints a separate set of pages for each record in the current selection.

One important consideration in printing records are the page margins, in particular the left and right margin settings used by Works when a document is printed. When you lay out a form on the screen you have a tendency to use the width of the screen window as the frame of reference for your layout. This makes sense because most of the work you do with databases involves reading information on the screen. However, the width of the screen window is wider than the width of the text—Works usually prints on an 8.5 inch by 11 inch page of paper. This is because the default margins of 1.3 inches on the left and 1.2 inches on the right sides of the page leave a print width area of 6 inches. In word processing these margins are not of great concern because Works automatically wraps long lines of text to fit inside the margins. In spreadsheet application, Works automatically paginates the spreadsheet into multiple pages when there are two many columns to fit on a single page. In database record printing you probably want to ensure that all the text from a given record form prints on the same page. In the current example, the Dues Owed, Payments and Balance field extend past the 6 inch print width area.

How should the margins be set in order to accommodate the current form? You can calculate the width of the current form by using the X-Y display that appears on the status line. The X value tells you the distance from the left edge of the paper (including margins) of the cursor while the Y measures the vertical distance from the top edge. Move the cursor to the left edge of the window:

```
[Home]
```

If you look at the status line you will see that it shows the X value as 1.30 inches confirming that the default page margin is 1.3 inches from the left edge of the paper. To determine the width of the form, move the cursor to right so that it is positioned just beyond the last column on the form that contains information. Enter:

```
[End]
```

The cursor will stop just to the right of the Dues Owed field, an X position 7.50 inches. The default limit would be 7.30 inches (1.3 inches margin plus 6 inches print width area). This tells you that the current form is too wide to fit on the standard page. You need to reduce the left and/or right margins by at least .2 of an inch. The margins can be set using the **Page Setup & Margins** command on the Print menu:

```
Click(left) on Print
Click(left) on Page Setup & Margins
```

The page setup dialog box, as shown in Figure 11-1, displays the current values for all of the margins on the page.

```
Top margin:      [1"......]   Page length:   [11".....]
Bottom margin:   [1"......]   Page width:    [8.5"....]
Left margin:     [1.3"....]
Right margin:    [1.2"....]   1st page number: [1....]
Header margin:   [0.5"....]
Footer margin:   [0.5"....]

                              <  OK  >  <Cancel>
```

Figure 11-1. Page Setup and Margins Dialog Box.

Change the left and right margins to one inch each by entering:

```
[tab] (2 times)
1 [tab]
1 [return]
```

Use the **Print Preview** command to display the record as it will print on the page:

```
Click(left) on Print
Click(left) on Preview
```

In database operations the print and print preview dialog boxes, as shown in Figure 11-2, offer options that relate specifically to database printing.

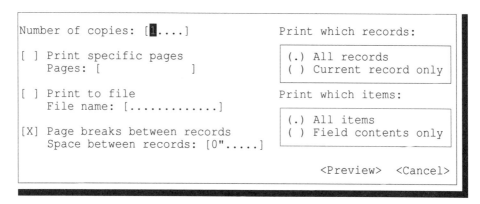

Figure 11-2. Preview Dialog Box.

Page Break between Records

This option determines if each new record will begin at the top of a new page which is the default selection. If you turn this option off, Works will print as many records as can fit onto the same page. When this option is off, you have the option of entering a value in inches of the amount of additional space, if any, that should be inserted between the end of one record and the beginning of the next.

Print which Records

This option is set to print only the current record on the screen. You can print all of the records in the current selection by changing the setting to All records.

Print which Items

The record is normally printed exactly as it appears on the screen. You can select Field contents only to print only the data in the entry areas without the field names.

This option is useful if you want to match the layout on the screen to positions on a pre-printed form. The X-Y location indicator on the status line enables you to match up screen locations with locations on pre-printed forms so that the data can be inserted into the correct locations. Most office supply stores or printers can supply you with standard preprinted forms for invoices, billing statements and packing slips. Pre-printed forms save time because they reduce the amount of printing done by your printer.

In this case, preview the printing of the current record using the default settings:

Click(left) on **<Preview>**

The preview in Figure 11-3 shows that the form fits into the page margins correctly.

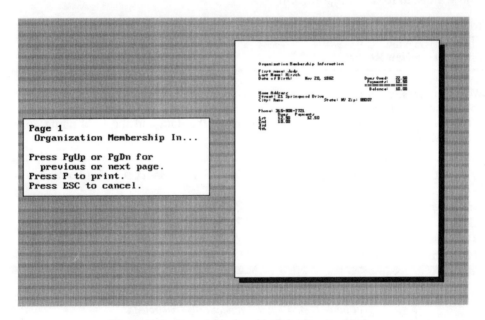

Figure 11-3. Record Displayed in Print Preview Mode.

Return to the desktop view by entering:

[Esc]

REPORTS

While printing one or more records can be useful for documentation purposes, database reports provide a means by which information from database records can be printed in a row and column format similar to the appearance of a spreadsheet.

Works database reports are automatically generated based on the current layout of the List view. Recall that the List view was a spreadsheet-like row and column display that showed database fields as columns and database records as rows.

Activate the List view:

```
Click(left) on View
Click(left) on List
```

The List view shows only five of the fields in the database because in Chapter 10 you hid all of the other fields by changing their column width to 0. When a new report is created, Works uses the current layout of the List view, in particular the field widths, to format a report form.

To create a new report use the **New Report** command on the View menu:

```
Click(left) on View
Click(left) on New Report
```

Works automatically creates the report based on the List view. The report displayed on the screen in Figure 11-4 looks exactly like the List view displays with the exception that a blank line is inserted between the data and the field name column headings.

First nameLast Name	Dues Owed	Payments	Balance
Walter LaFish	22.50	22.50	0.00
Judy Hirsch	22.50	12.50	10.00
Diane Kamrin	22.50	0.00	22.50
Heather Hart	10.00	10.00	0.00

Figure 11-4. Report Automatically Generated.

Return to the desktop display by entering:

```
[Esc]
```

When you return, Works displays the Report mode, indicated by the nature of the display and the fact that REPORT appears on the status line. The columns in the report form display match the columns shown in the List view display. Note that the column letters skip for A,B to Q,R,S because all of the other field columns were hidden in the List view.

The Report display, as shown in Figure 11-5, is a special type of row and column display. Its purpose is to serve as a model of the way the database information should be transformed into a report. While it is similar in appearance to the List view display there are some significant differences.

The report form display is divided into a series of rows that have special names, such as Intr Report, Record, or Summ Report. Each of the rows represents a report band.

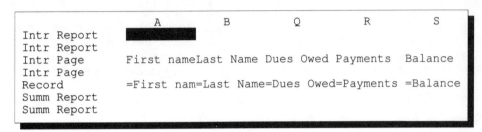

```
                          A          B         Q         R         S
Intr Report       ████████████████
Intr Report
Intr Page         First nameLast Name Dues Owed Payments   Balance
Intr Page
Record            =First nam=Last Name=Dues Owed=Payments =Balance
Summ Report
Summ Report
```

Figure 11-5. Report Form Display.

Reports bands are used to determine what information prints on the report. A band is different form a row or record in that different types of bands behave in different ways on the report. Bands differ with respect to two factors: where and when the band prints.

Where Does the Band Print?

Report bands differ with respect to the location on the page at which they print. Some bands print at the top of the page while other always print at the bottom of the page. Other bands print at different locations depending on what has preceded that band.

When Does the Band Print?

The printing of a band is also affected by special conditions. Like page headers and footers, some bands print only after or before a page break. Other bands are affected by the printing of records, for example, a summary band would print only after all of the record in the database have been printed.

When a new report is generated, Works creates a default set of report bands that include the following types: intr report, intr page, record, and summ report.

Intr Report

The bands with this label print at the top of the first page of the report only. These bands are used for the major title or heading of the report. Two of these bands are inserted by default.

Intr Page

This band is designed to function like a page header in that it prints at the top of each page of the report including the first page. Note that on the first page of the report both the Intr Report and the Intr Page print, while only the Intr Page prints on all subsequent pages.

Record

This band prints after the Intr Report and the Intr Page bands. However, it will repeat printing on the page until the page is full or there are no more records to print. It is this band that inserts the detailed information in the report. By default a single report band is inserted into the report form. However, you may create reports in which there are more than one report band if desired.

Summ Report

These bands will print only once during a report, following the printing of the last record in the current database selection. This band is used to print summary information such as field totals or averages.

Note that in Works reports still have page headers and footers in addition to all of the report bands. This means that standard page items such as page numbers still use the page header or footer lines. Remember to use the Header & Footer dialog box to number pages.

The purpose of the report display is to allow you to add to or modify the report that was generated automatically from the List view. Since the report so closely resembles the List view you may wonder what reports are necessary. First, reports can contain additional information such as field totals which cannot be generated in a List view of the database. Second, Works allows only one List view of a database. However, you can have many reports. This means that you can use the List view to generate different reports and keep all of them stored with the database for later usage.

Layout Modifications

When you generate a report from a list view there are usually three areas in which you want to make modifications: add hedings, adjust column widths, and add summary calculations.

Add Headings

You should add any headings, or titles you want to the report form. You should also use the Print Header & Footer dialog box to establish page numbering for the report. You can also edit the column headings that have been automatically inserted if you find that different headings would improve the meaning of the report.

Adjust Column Widths

All column widths are set to the same size as the column widths in the List view, which by default is 10 characters in width. Since field size can vary significantly between fields you will probably have to adjust the width of some of the fields.

Add Summary Calculations

If you have numeric fields in the report you may need to add formulas to in the Summ Report bands that calculate totals, average, or other statistical information.

Begin by adding a title for the report in the first Intr Report band. Enter:

Membership Dues Report [return]

Note that there are two Intr Report bands in the report. The purpose of the second band, which is empty, is to print a blank line between the report title and the column headings that appear in the Intr Page band. If you wanted more blank space you could insert another blank Intr Report band into the report or delete the space by deleting the blank band.

Create the page numbering by using the Header & Footer dialog box accessed through the Print menu. This is the same option that appears on all Works Print menus:

Click(left) on **Print**
Click(left) on **Headers & Footers**

Print the date of the report in the header and the page number in the footer:

&rReport Printed on &d [tab]
&cPage -&p- [return]

Next widen columns A and B(first and last name) to show 12 characters each:

Point at column letter **A**
Drag(left) to column letter **B**
Click(left) on **Format**
Click(left) on **Column Width**

Change the width from 10 to 12 for these two columns:

12 [return]

The program uses the field names as the column headings. You have the opportunity to change those names to something that better fits the nature of the report, if you desire, by simply editing the text in the Intr Page band. Note that the headings have no effect upon what data prints in the columns since that is controlled by the formulas that appear in the Report band. Enter:

```
[down] First [return]
```

You can use the Style dialog box to add style enhancements to the text such as bold, underline, or center alignment. Center the heading in the column:

```
Click(left) on Format
Click(left) on Style
Click(left) on Center
```

Continue editing the column headings:

```
[right] Last [return]
```

Repeat the alignment format with the **[Shift-F7]** repeat command:

```
[Shift-F7]
```

Change the Dues Owed heading to Charges:

```
[right] Charges [return]
```

Note that the field in columns Q, R, and S contain numeric information. Column headings above numeric data look best when they are aligned to the right edge of the column rather than the left since the numeric values are aligned to the right so that their decimal places match up vertically. Change the headings for these three columns to right alignment by entering the following. Note this time the **[F8]**—extend highlight command—is used to expand the highlighted column:

```
[F8] [right] [right]
```

```
Click(left) on Format
Click(left) on Style
Click(left) on Right
Click(left) on <Ok>
```

Column Summary Formulas

The last step in completing the report form is the creation of totals for the report. Move the highlight to the second Summ Report band. The first Summ Report band is left blank so that there will be a blank line between the last record and the total values:

```
[down] (4 times)
```

Sum formula scan be entered manually or insert by using the Insert Field Summary command located on the Edit menu. In most cases the menu option is preferred because the program will automatically insert write the correct formula. Manual entry is necessary only when you want to enter an unusual formula that is more complicated than a simple field total or average.

To calculate the total of the Dues Owed field insert a summary formula using the menus:

Click(left) on **Edit**
Click(left) on **Insert Field Summary**

The dialog box, as shown in Figure 11-6, lists the database field on the left side and the summary calculations on the right. Works can perform in a database report. The SUM() function is the default calculation. Table 11-1 lists summary calculations and their functions.

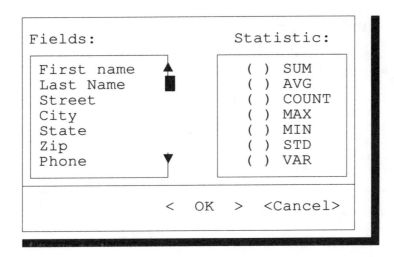

Figure 11-6. Summary Calculation Dialog Box.

Table 11-1. Summary Calculations and Their Functions.

Calculation	Function
Sum	SUM
Average	AVG
Number of records	COUNT
Largest value in the field	MAX
Smallest value in field	MIN
Standard deviation	STD
Mathematical variance	VAR

Create the sum of the Dues Owed field by entering:

```
[down] (17 times)
[return]
```

Works inserts the formula =SUM(Dues Owed) into the report. Create a total for the Payments and Balance fields. In this case you will enter the formulas directly:

```
[right]
=sum(payments) [right]
=sum(balance)
```

Move to column A and enter a heading for this row:

```
[Home] Totals [return]
```

Adding Another Band

Suppose that you wanted to list the total number of records printed at the end of the report. This can be done by inserting a COUNT() function. Note that for a count function it doesn't matter which field is counted. In order to add this additional summary item you will need to insert a new band into the report. The **Insert Row/Column** command on the Edit menu operates in a band specific mode in the database form mode. This means that when you insert a row a dialog box appears from which you must select the type of band you want to insert. Move the highlight below the current last band in the report:

```
[down]
```

Designate this row as a Summ Report band:

```
Click(left) on Edit
Click(left) on Insert Row/Column
Click(left) on Row
Click(left) on <Ok>
Click(left) on Summ Report
Click(left) on <Ok>
```

Enter the information in this new band:

```
Number of records [right]
=count(last name) [return]
```

Display the report on the screen:

```
Click(left) on View
Click(left) on Report1
```

The report is shown below:

Report Printed on 11/28/90				
Membership Dues Reports				
First	Last	Charges	Payments	Balance
Walter	LaFish	22.50	22.50	0.00
Judy	Hirsch	22.50	12.50	10.00
Diane	Kamrin	22.50	0.00	22.50
Heather	Hart	10.00	10.00	0.00
Totals		77.5	45	32.5
Number of Records			4	

Note that the values in the summary band did not print with the same format as the field from the records. This tells you that you need to apply formats to any new formulas that you add to the report form if you want them to print in a specific style. Return to the report form mode by entering:

```
[Esc]
```

Format the summary formulas as comma style with 2 decimal places:
Display the report again:

```
Point at =SUM(Dues
Drag(left) to =SUM(Balan
Click(left) on Format
Click(left) on Comma
Click(left) on <Ok>
```

```
Click(left) on View
Click(left) on Report1
```

This time the report displays the totals with the same format as the record data as shown below:

Report Printed on 11/28/90				
Membership Dues Reports				
First	Last	Charges	Payments	Balance
Walter	LaFish	22.50	22.50	0.00
Judy	Hirsch	22.50	12.50	10.00
Diane	Kamrin	22.50	0.00	22.50
Heather	Hart	10.00	10.00	0.00
Totals		77.50	45.00	32.50
Number of Records		4		

Return to the report form by entering:

```
[Esc]
```

Printing Reports From a Selection

Once you have defined a report you can print or display the report with all of the records or only a select. To print the report with only a selected group of records change to either the Form or List view and apply the current selection, if that meets your needs, or create a new selection. In this case use the current query which selects records with balances greater than zero:

```
Click(left) on View
Click(left) on List
```

Apply the query to the database:

```
Click(left) on Select
Click(left) on Apply Query
```

Display the report:

```
Click(left) on View
Click(left) on Report1
```

The report applies to only the selected records, as shown below:

Report Printed on 11/28/90				
Membership Dues Reports				
First	Last	Charges	Payments	Balance
Judy	Hirsch	22.50	12.50	10.00
Diane	Kamrin	22.50	0.00	22.50
Totals	45.00	12.50	32.50	
Number of Records		2		

To get a printed copy of the report exit the display and return to the REPORT mode:

```
[Esc]
```

Send the report to the printer:

```
Click(left) on Print
Click(left) on Print
Click(left) on <Print>
```

REPORTS WITH GROUPS

Another feature that can be implemented through the report form is group summaries. A group summary breaks up the records in the database into groups based on a particular field. For example, suppose that you wanted to print the membership report but have separate totals for each state. The State field would be the group field. A report with a group will have additional bands which will print headings and totals for each group in addition to the report summary bands that summarize the entire report.

Groups are added to a report by adding a report sort order. If you want to organize the members by state you would set the State field as the sort field:

```
Click(left) on Select]
Click(left) on Sort Records
```

Enter the primary sort field:

```
state
```

The option labeled Break G is used to designate whether or not the sort key should be used to break the report into groups or simply to sort the records. In this case you want to create sorted groups:

```
Click(left) on Break G
```

The 1st Letter option is used to limit the group breaks to changes in the first letter of the group field only. This option is used to create breaks for fields, such as Last Name, that have a large number of unique entries. In a case such as last name, the 1st Letter option would create groups for each letter in the alphabet, that is, an A group, a B group, and so on. Without this option each unique name, e.g., Anderson and Arnold, would be treated as a separate group. In the case of state you do not need to use this option.

You can add a second sort key to arrange all the records within the same state in order by last name. Note this sort key is used for sequencing only and should not be designated as a break key:

```
Tab] (2 times)
last name [return]
[
```

Works automatically inserts a new band called Summ State. The band contains counting formulas for the last name and first name fields and sum formulas for the three numeric fields. This band will print after each state group calculating totals for that group alone.

In this case two counting function are not necessary. Replace the formula in column A of the Summ State with a heading:

```
[down] (5 times)
State Totals [return]
```

In order to add some spacing to the report, insert a blank Summ State band into the report below the Record band:

```
Click(left) on Edit
Click(left) on Insert Column/Row
Click(left) on Row
Click(left) on <Ok>
Click(left) on Summ State
```

This new band will insert a blank line between the last record of the group and the group totals. Another type of band you might want to insert is a Intr State band. This band will print a heading before each group:

```
Click(left) on Edit
Click(left) on Insert Column/Row
Click(left) on Intr State
Click(left) on <Ok>
```

Add two more of these bands so that there will be extra space before and after the heading:

```
Click(left) on Edit
Click(left) on Insert Column/Row
Click(left) on Intr State
Click(left) on <Ok>
Click(left) on Edit
Click(left) on Insert Column/Row
Click(left) on Intr State
Click(left) on <Ok>
```

To insert the state name create a formula that specifies the field name, e.g., =state. Enter:

```
[down] State: [right]
=state [return]
```

The report form, including the new group bands, is shown in Figure 11-7.

```
                       A              B            Q           R           S
Intr Report    Membership Dues Reports
Intr Report
Intr Page          First          Last        Charges     Payments     Balance
Intr Page
Intr State
Intr State     State:         =State
Intr State
Record         =First name =Last Name   =Dues Owed=Payments =Balance
Summ State
Summ State     State Total =COUNT(Last =SUM(Dues =SUM(Payme=SUM(Balan
Summ Report
Summ Report    Totals                   =SUM(Dues =SUM(Payme=SUM(Balan
Summ Report    Number of Records        =COUNT(Las
```

Figure 11-7. Report Form with Groups.

For this report you will want the entire database to be included. Release the current selection:

Click(left) on **View**
Click(left) on **List**
Click(left) on **Select**
Click(left) on **Show All Records**

Display the report:

Click(left) on **View**
Click(left) on **Report1**

The report will look like the one shown below. Note that on your screen displays (by default 25 lines long) you will have to press **[return]** to see the bottom section of the report since all of the text shown below will not fit on a single screen:

Membership Dues Reports				
First	Last	Charges	Payments	Balance
State:	CA			
Heather	Hart	10.00	10.00	0.00
Diane	Kamrin	22.50	0.00	22.50
Walter	LaFish	22.50	22.50	0.00
State Total	3	55.00	32.50	22.50
State:	NV			
Judy	Hirsch	22.50	12.50	10.00
State Total	1	22.50	12.50	10.00
Totals		77.50	45.00	32.50
Number of Records		4		

The group report summarizes each state and then the entire database. Return to the report mode by entering:

```
[Esc]
```

Save and close the database:

```
Click(left) on File
Click(left) on Close
Click(left) on <Yes>
```

If you are done working you can exit Works.

```
Click(left) on Exit Works
```

If you want to go on to the next project, leave the program running. The next project will show how databases can be used to create form letters and mailing labels by combing database information with word processing documents..

SUMMARY

In this chapter you learned how to print database records and how to create analytical reports based on the database information.

Printing Records. When you print from the Form view the records are printed as they appear on the form screen. By default each record is printed at the beginning of a new page. You have the option of printing the current record or all of the records in the current selection. You can also choose to suppress the page breaks between records and to suppress the printing of the field names when you want only the field contents to be printed.

Reports. Reports are column-oriented printouts that can be used to summarize the data in the database. Reports are automatically generated from the current layout in the List view mode. Fields that are hidden in the List view mode will not be included in the automatic report form.

Bands. The reports created by Works are constructed from bands. A band is a special type of row which prints at specific locations and times during the report process. The details of the report are printed through the Record band which repeats until all of the records in the current selection are printed.

Summary Bands. Summary bands allow you to add calculations that summarize the data in the report. The band prints only after all of the records have been printed. It can contain any number of formulas calculating sums, averages, and counts to other mathematical values supported by Works.

Groups. Group allow you to divide the records included in the report into groups based on the contents of a specific field. The report generates one group for every unique value in the specified field. If there are too many unique values in that field you can select to create a group only when there is a change in the first letter of the group field value. Groups are specified by selecting the Break option in the Sort Records dialog box. Sort fields designated as Break fields cause Works to insert a group Summary band into the report. The formulas on this band summarizes the values in each group which print after the last record in each group. You have the option of adding a group introduction band that prints a heading, usually the break field value, before each group.

Chapter 12

Form Letters and Labels

I n Chapter 11 you learned how to output database information in the form of printed records and column reports. In this chapter you will learn how database information can be used indirectly to create special word processing documents that create a series of form letters or that printing mailing labels.

Form Letters. Form letters are word processing documents that combine word processing text with data drawn from individual records. The form letter process prints one form letter for each record in the current database selection.

Mailing Labels. Mailing labels are a special form of word processing document oriented to print database information on special types of forms such as mailing labels.

Begin this chapter by loading the Works program from the startup screen in the usual manner.

Once loaded, retrieve the MEMBERS database file:

```
Click(left) on Open Existing File
Double click(left) on MEMBERS.WDB
```

In Chapter 10 you printed information directly from the database itself. One type of output was a printed copy of the database form. The other type of output was a column oriented report which summarized database information.

However, there are certain types of output which can be better formatted using facilities of a word processor. For example, while it is possible to create a list of addresses using the report facility or by simply printing all of the forms, the most common way to read addresses is in the block format that appears on envelope or at the top of a letter.

The trick is to get the data out of the database and into the word processor. The Works word processor contains a command which links sections of a word processing document to the fields in a database. These links allow the records in the database to insert data into word processing documents as they are printed. In effect, the word processing document functions as a framework into which database information can be inserted.

In this chapter you will see that Works provides a number of different ways in which database information can be combined with and printed through word processing documents.

Suppose that you want to create a list of the addresses of all the people in the MEMBERS.WDB file. Begin not by creating a report in the database, but by opening a word processing document window:

```
Click(left) on File
Click(left) on Create New File
Click(left) on New Word Processor
```

The key to combing word processing with database management is the **Insert Field** command found on the Edit menu. This command inserts a link between the word processor and a field in any of the open database files. When the document is printed the field link is filled in with data from the current record.

Unlike a normal print operation in which the number of copies is determined by the number of copies you enter, printing documents with database links causes Works to repeat the printing until each record in the current selection has been substituted in the field link.

Works recognizes two types of database/word processor printing operations: form letters and labels.

Form Letters

Form letter printing assumes that the word processor will generate one entire document for each record in the current database selection. It is called form letter printing because this assumption makes sense when you want to produce a series of letters to be sent to different people. You would need a separate document for each person in the database. Keep in mind that even though this feature is called form letter printing it can be used for any type of form document, e.g., invoices, report cards, invitations, etc., in which each record in the database requires a separate document to be printed. Printing form letters is similar to printing individual database forms.

Labels

Label printing refers to a link between a database and a word processing document in which more than one record can be printed on the same page. Works will print as many records as can fit on a single page based on the size of the area designed for each record. This type of printing is very useful for printing database information on mailing labels. However, you can apply the principle of label printing to a number of different types of documents.

PRINTING AN ADDRESS LIST

In order to print a list of addresses you will need to link the word processing document to the first name, last name, street, city, state, and zip fields. Each of the fields requires the insertion of a database link with the **Insert Field** command. Begin with the first name field:

Click(left) on **Edit**
Click(left) on **Insert Field**

The Insert Field dialog box displays a list of the open database files. In this case the name of the MEMBERS.WDB file is listed. Select that database:

Click(left) on *MEMBERS.WDB*

When selected, the database lists the names of the field in that file, as shown in Figure 12-1.

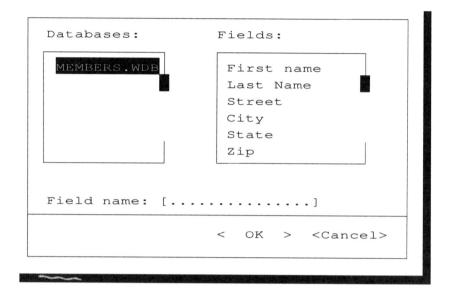

Figure 12-1. Insert Field Dialog Box.

You can select any of the fields from the list into the document at the current cursor position:

```
Click(left) on First name
Click(left) on <Ok>
```

The program inserts a code <<First name>> into the document. When the document is printed as a form letter or a label the field code will be replaced with the contents of the first name field in the first record of the MEMBERS database. Enter a space:

```
[spacebar]
```

When you format a document that uses field codes you must treat the field code exactly as you would treat an actual word or phrase. If you normally type a space between the first name and the last name then you would put a space between the first name field code and the last name field code so that when the field data is substituted the result looks as if they had been manually typed into the document.

Insert the Last Name field:

```
Click(left) on Edit
Click(left) on Insert Field
Click(left) on Last Name
Click(left) on <Ok>
```

Start a new line so that you can place the street address below the first and last names. Enter:

```
[return]
```

```
Click(left) on Edit
Click(left) on Insert Field
Click(left) on street
Click(left) on <Ok>
```

Start a third line for the city, street, and zip code field:

```
[return]
```

Insert the code for the city field:

```
Click(left) on Edit
Click(left) on Insert Field
Click(left) on city
Click(left) on <Ok>
```

Enter:

```
,
[spacebar]
```

Next the state field:

```
Click(left) on Edit
Click(left) on Insert Field
Click(left) on state
Click(left) on <Ok>
```

Enter:

```
[spacebar]
```

Insert the zip code field:

```
Click(left) on Edit
Click(left) on Insert Field
Click(left) on zip
Click(left) on <Ok>
```

The document looks like this:

```
<<First name>> <<Last Name>>
<<Street>>
<<City>>, <<State>> <<Zip>>
```

LABEL PRINTING

Label printing refers to the method of output that places as many records on the page as will fit. It is called label printing because it is generally the method used to print mailing labels. However, it can be used for printing on pages as well. In this case you want to print a list of the names and addresses stored in the MEMBERS database. This means that you want to place as many of the name and address blocks as possible on the same page.

Begin the Label printing by selecting Print Labels from the Print menu:

Click(left) on **Print**
Click(left) on **Print Labels**

The dialog box that appears is used to define the database that should be used to fill in the fields and the size and frequency of the labels, as shown in Figure 12-2.

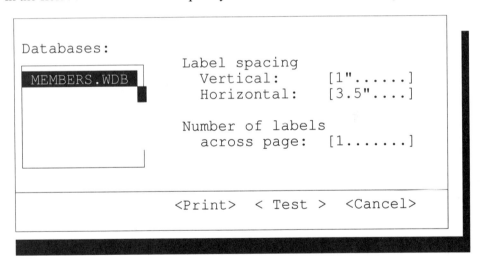

Figure 12-2. Print Label Dialog Box.

The Label spacing settings section contains two values—vertical and horizontal—that define a rectangle that makes up the size of one label. It is important to keep in mind that in this case the idea of a label is more of an abstract concept than an actual physical item.

The document you are printing contains only three lines. If Works simply printed one record after another, the second name and address block would begin on the fourth line immediately following the last line printed.

However, Works was designed to take into consideration the fact the you might want to place each printed block into an area of a definite length and width. For example, if you print on a sheet of pre-pasted labels it is important that the second record printed begin at the beginning of the next label rather than after the last line of the previous address block.

The vertical measurement under Label spacing sets the distance between the first lines of each block of fields. By default Works sets that distance at 1 inch. This means that the labels will begin one inch apart vertically.

The horizontal measure is significant if you would like to print more than one record across the page. Since address blocks are less wide than standard paragraph you might want to place more than one across instead of simply leaving the right side of the page blank. In this case you can probably print two labels across.

Of course, you need to remember that Works has automatically set page margins, left 1.3 inches and right 1.2 inches. This means that at the present margins you only have 6 inches in which to print labels. This means that you need to change the width of the label so that it fits the page width. Change the horizontal measure to 3 inches. Enter:

```
[tab] (2 times)
3
```

Set the number of labels across at 2:

```
[tab] 2 [return]
```

The next dialog box is the page margins and setup dialog box which would also appear if you selected the **Page Setup & Margins** command. For now leave the margins at the default settings:

```
Click(left) on <Ok>
```

This displays the Print dialog box:

```
Click(left) on <Print>
```

Note that the record numbers 1/4, 2/4, 3/4 an 4/4 flash on the status line as the printing is taking place. The printed page should look like this:

```
Heather Hart              Diane Kamrin
765 Providence Lane       57 Wellman Court
Martinez, CA 94553        Modesto, CA 94301
Walter LaFish             Judy Hirsch
1250 Pine Street          21 Springwood Drive
Walnut Creek, CA 09190    Reno, NV 89007
```

Continuous Form Labels

The report you have created for printing a list of address blocks can be used to print the addresses on mailing labels. The only difference is that you need to adjust the page margin settings to reflect the actual dimensions of the labels you are using.

If you have a dot matrix printer, such as IBM Proprinter XL, you will be using continuous form labels. These labels do not come on a sheet but on a continuous roll or series of perforated sheets. They rolls come in 1, 2, and 3 across styles. The most common form is 1 across labels that are 1 inch high and 3.5 inches wide.

Set the label size dialog box options to 1 inch vertical, 3.5 inches horizontal, and 1 across. If you have forms with two or three labels across, check the width of each label (correct the 3.5 inches setting if necessary) and change the number across to match your labels.

When the margin setting dialog box appears during the label printing process, set the top, bottom, left, and right margins at 0. When you print the labels the result will be a continuous series of labels space so that the beginning of each label is 1 inch from the beginning of the next.

Form Letters

Form letters are database/word processing printing that print one complete document for each of the records in the current database selection. Suppose that you wanted to send a statement about what members owe to each of the members who has a balance greater than zero. The first step is to apply a query to the database to select just those records:

```
Click(left) on MEMBERS.WDB
```

Apply the query to the database:

```
Click(left) on Select
Click(left) on Apply Query
```

Return to the word processing document:

```
Click(left) on Window
Click(left) on WORD1.WPS
```

Continue the document by entering a date:

```
[return]
[Ctrl-o](the letter O)
[Ctrl-d] [return]
```

Create a personalized salutation by inserting the first name field in the salutation:

```
Dear
[spacebar]
```

```
Click(left) on Edit
Click(left) on Insert Field
Click(left) on First name
Click(left) on <Ok>
```

```
, [return]
```

The next section of the document is paragraph text. However, you can still insert fields when specific items are needed. Enter:

```
In checking our records we find that your dues assessment
for this year is
[spacebar]
```

Insert the Dues Owed field:

```
Click(left) on Edit
Click(left) on Insert Field
```

Since the Dues Owed field requires you to scroll the list box down, you can scroll the box by clicking the mouse on the down scroll arrow or simply type in the field name. Enter:

```
[tab](2 times)
dues owed [return]
[spacebar]
but we have received only
[spacebar]
```

Insert the Payments field:

```
Click(left) on Edit
Click(left) on Insert Field
```

```
tab](2 times)
payments [return]
. [return]

This leaves a balance of
[spacebar]
```

Insert the Balance field:

```
Click(left) on Edit
Click(left) on Insert Field
```

```
[tab](2 times)
balance [return]
[spacebar]
due. Please remit this amount so that we may continue to serve
you and our other members. [return]
Thank you!
```

The entire form letter looks like this:

```
<First name> <Last Name>
<Street>
<City>, <State> <Zip>

*date*

Dear <First name>,

In checking our records we find that your dues assessment
for this year is <dues owed> but we have received only
<payments>.

This leaves a balance of <balance> due. Please remit this
amount so that we may continue to serve you and our other
members.

Thank You!
```

To create the actual form letters use the **Form Letter** command on the Print menu:

```
Click(left) on Print
Click(left) on Print Form Letters
```

A dialog box appears so that you can select the database for the form letters. In this case there is only one database, MEMBERS.WDB:

```
Click(left) on <Ok>
Click(left) on <Print>
```

The form letters are printed. They will look like the following letters:

```
            Diane Kamrin
            57 Wellman Court
            Modesto, CA 94301

            11/29/90

            Dear Diane,

            In checking our records we find that your dues assessment
            for this year is 22.50 but we have received only 0.00.

            This leaves a balance of 22.50 due. Please remit this amount
            so that we may continue to serve you and our other members.

            Thank you!

            Judy Hirsch
            21 Springwood Drive
            Reno, NV 89007

            11/29/90

            Dear Judy,

            In checking our records we find that your dues assessment
            for this year is 22.50 but we have received only 12.50.

            This leaves a balance of 10.00 due. Please remit this amount
            so that we may continue to serve you and our other members.

            Thank you!
```

Save the form letter document in a file:

```
Click(left) on File
Click(left) on Close
Click(left) on <Yes>
```

```
formltr [return]
```

Close the database:

```
Click(left) on File
Click(left) on Close
```

WORKS SETTINGS

The Works settings screen contains options and settings that control the way that Works operates. You can access it can from any Works mode with the **Works Settings** command located on the Options menu:

Click(left) on **Options**
Click(left) on **Works Settings**

The settings screen, as shown in Figure 12-3, contains 8 options that control various aspects of using Works.

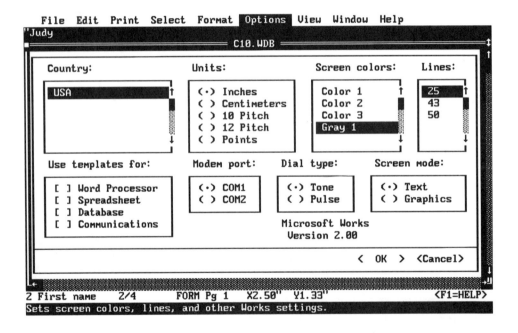

Figure 12-3. Works Settings Screen.

Country

This setting determines the default settings for such items as page length and width, currency symbol, date and time display format, month names, and other items where Works uses preset options that vary in different parts of the world.

Units

This setting determines the basic unit of measure used by Works. For example, when inches are selected the top page margin would be set at 1 inch by default. Selecting points would change the display to read 72 pt (points). Note what has changed as the unit of measure is not the measurement itself, since 72 points equals 1 inch.

Screen Colors

Works has four built in sets of color combinations. You can select one of the four. However, you do not have direct control over the colors used in Works.

Lines

The VGA screen display used in the PS1 allows you to select the number of lines of text that appear on the screen. By default the screen shows 25 lines of text total on the screen, including window borders and bars. You can select 30, 34, 43, or 60 line displays in graphics mode or 25, 43, or 50 line displays in text mode. Keep in mind that when you increase the number of lines you reduce the height of the characters displayed in each line. You may find that you want to use 50 or 60 line modes only when you need to review a large document or spreadsheet display. Also, because more information is displayed on each screen, 50 or 60 line mode will scroll a bit slower than the standard 25 line mode.

Screen Mode

The VGA display supplied with the PS1 (either color or black and white) can operate in two modes: text or graphics. In the text mode all of the characters on the screen are drawn from a set of 255 built-in characters called the IBM extended character set. This means that certain special effects, such as italic or underlined text, cannot be represented on the screen directly. Instead, the text mode shows text assigned to these characteristics in different colors or shades of gray. The mouse pointer appears as a solid block and the entry areas in database forms blend into the background when the highlight is not positioned on a field. In graphics mode underline and italics appear on the screen as they will print—the mouse pointer is an arrow shape and database fields are marked by a dotted line. You can switch between modes to determine which you find most pleasing. The PS1 is set for graphics mode by default.

Modem Port

This option is used to select the communications port for the modem. On the PS1 this setting should always be COM1.

Dial Type

If you use a push button phone this option should be set on Tone. If you use a rotary dial phone change this to Pulse.

Templates

The last item on the Settings dialog box is for templates. You have found that Works has defaults settings for all of the options in the program. You may find that in your situation you must change the default settings each time you begin a new document, spreadsheet, or database.

You can create your own personalized default settings for word processing, spreadsheet, or database documents by creating a template application.

For example, suppose that you want to use 1 inch left and right margins as the default for your word processing instead of the 1.3 inch and 1.2 inch margins Works defaults to. Select a word processor template and leave the Settings dialog box:

```
Click(left) on Word Processor
Click(left) on <Ok>
```

Open a new word processing document:

```
Click(left) on File
Click(left) on Create New File
Click(left) on Word Processor
```

Change the margin settings for the page:

```
Click(left) on Print
Click(left) on Page Setup & Margins
```

Change the left and right margins to 1 inch:

```
[tab](2 times)
1 [tab]
1 [return]
```

Instead of saving this document, use the **Save as** command:

```
Click(left) on File
Click(left) on Save As
```

In the lower right corner of the dialog box you will see the Save as template option. Selecting this option creates a template for all new word processing documents that use the current margin settings and as the default for all future word processing documents. The file will be called TEMPLATE.PS:

```
Click(left) on Save as template
Click(left) on <Ok>
```

The template is now created. Discard the current document:

```
Click(left) on File
Click(left) on Close
Click(left) on <No>
```

Create a new document:

```
Click(left) on File
Click(left) on Create New File
Click(left) on Word Processor
```

Display the margin settings for this document:

```
Click(left) on Print
Click(left) on Page Setup & Margins
```

The margins are automatically set according to the template values. Discard this document and Exit Works:

```
Click(left) on <cancel>
Click(left) on File
Click(left) on Exit Works
```

You can restore the factory default settings by deleting the TEMPLATE.PS or other template files from the disk.

TELECOMMUNICATIONS

The PS1 is designed and set up for telecommunications using the Prodigy service. In fact, you receive a free 3 month subscription to the service when you buy your PS1.

However, that is not the only way that you can perform telecommunications on the PS1. Works also includes a full Communications module. Although a full discussion of this module is beyond the scope of this book (since the primary focus of the PS1 is on Prodigy), this section will briefly sketch how and why you would want to use the communications module in Works.

Dialing Numbers

One of the most handy features of Works is the **Dial this Number** command, located on the Options menu. This option will use the built-in modem in the PS1 to dial a phone number. For example, in a database that has phone numbers, place the highlight on the phone number field and select the **Dial this Number** command. Works will dial that number automatically for you. Note that the phone number must be complete, i.e., if you need to dial a 1 before the number that must be included in the field, e.g., 1-415-372-5729.

The primary problem with using this command is technical. The PS1 modem is constructed so that you cannot have your telephone hand set plugged into the phone jack when you have it attached to the PS1. You can get around this problem by using a line splitter, which you can purchase at an electronics store. One you have both the hand set and the modem feeding into the splitter you can pick up the hand set once the computer has dialed the number.

The **Dial this Number** command can be used from word processing, spreadsheet, or database windows so long as you have highlighted a valid phone number.

Other Services

While Prodigy is supplied with the PS1, it is not the only service available to you. You can use a variety of different services with the PS1 modem and Works. The largest service is called CompuServe, but there are many others.

If you want to log onto a service you need to know have three very important pieces of information: password, phone number, and communications settings.

Password

Most services require a password before you can log on. When you contact a service such as CompuServe they will give you a temporary password so that you can get started. Note that you cannot just dial up services like CompuServe. You must first acquire a CompuServe startup kit that contains your password.

Phone Number

The startup kit will have a list of the network nodes. Choose the closest available node that communicates at 2400 baud. Note that many services offer network nodes with different communications rates. Always choose the highest rate available up to the maximum speed for your modem—2400 baud.

Communications Settings

In order to communicate using Works you need to know three settings in addition to the baud rate: data bits, stop bits, and parity. The data bit value is either 8 or 7. The stop bit value is either 1 or 2. The parity setting can be either none, odd or, even. If you are told to set your communications to 71E it means 7 data bits, 1 stop bit, and even parity. CompuServe uses 71E. Other services or bulletin boards may differ.

Setting Up a Communications Window

Suppose that you wanted to communicate with a service such as CompuServe. Assuming that you knew the required information (the password if any, the phone number and baud rate, and the communications settings) you have to set up a communications window correctly to use those settings in order to communicate.

The first step is open a new communications window:

```
Click(left) on Create New File
Click(left) on New Communications
```

The second step is the Communication dialog box:

```
Click(left) on Options
Click(left) on Communication
```

By default, Works uses the setting 1200 baud, 8 data bits, 1 stop bit, and none for parity. If your settings do not match these, as is the case if you want to use CompuServe, you will need to change the settings. For CompuServe you would do the following:

```
2400 [tab]
7 [tab]
[tab] (2 times)
e [return]
```

Next insert the phone number:

```
Click(left) on Options
Click(left) on Phone
```

Type in the phone number:

```
111-2233 [return]
```

Access the service by using the **Connect** command:

```
Click(left) on Connect
Click(left) on Connect
```

If you want to terminate communication, repeat the **Connect** command. Note that **Connect** acts as a toggle since there is no hang up command on the Works menus.

Once you have established this window, save it and use it for communications with that service in the future. You may want to make this window the communications template file so that every new communications window uses these settings by default.

Accessing CACHE.DAT

In Chapter 3 the basic operations of the Prodigy service were discussed. As designed, the Prodigy service does not support copying text directly to the disk. Features in Prodigy, when available, will print to the printer only. However, part of the Prodigy software operations text, which appears on Prodigy screen, is often stored in a file called CACHE.DAT. The purpose of this file is to speed up operations in Prodigy when an article is several pages long. Prodigy will store the entire article in the

CACHE.DAT file so that it does not have to go back to the original each time you leaf through a page.

When you have completed a Prodigy session you may find that the information which you read is still contained in the CACHE.DAT file. This file can be opened as a Works word processing window, viewed, printed, or copied to another word processing window. Note that the CACHE.DAT file is not organized for use with Works. You will find that the sections of text are scrambled up with blocks of what seem to be nonsense characters which have use to Prodigy but not to Works.

To open this file do the following:

```
Click(left) on File
Click(left) on Open Existing Fil
Click(left) on Open Read Only
```

```
c:\prodigy\cache.dat [return]
```

```
Click(left) on Word Processor
Click(left) on <Ok>
```

Most of this file will not make much sense. However, you will find by leafing page by page, [Pg Dn], you will encounter text that had appeared on the Prodigy screen in past sessions. You can use the **Copy** command to cut out useful sections and transfer them to a separate word processing window where you can store them for future review or printing. Note that the Open Read Only option protects you from making any changes in the file.

You must exercise the same care in using information copied from the CACHE.DAT file as you would for information read or printed from Prodigy. For example, if you have an article from the on line encyclopedia, you can use it in a report only if you correctly cite the source of the information. To submit that information without such a citation is plagiarism. This is also true of copyrighted articles and other Prodigy information which you print.

SUMMARY

This chapter dealt with combining word processing and database information.

Insert Fields. The **Insert Field** command enables you to link a word processing document with a field in an open database. The command inserts the field name into a code inside the word processing document. When the document is printed as a label or form letter, the code is replaced by the actual data stored in the current record of the database.

Print Labels. This type of output prints as many records as possible on the page using the current label size.

Print Form Letters. This type of output prints one complete document for each record in the current database select.

Words Settings. The Works Settings dialog box contains settings options that control the screen display and other options. You can also select which Works modules will use your personalized default values as contained in template files. A template is created by using the Save as template option in the Save As dialog box when saving a word processing, spreadsheet, or database file.

Chapter **13**

DOS Operations
and Techniques

C hapter 1 discussed the function and basic operation of IBM DOS 4.00. In this chapter you will learn about what DOS is and how it can be used to organize, modify, and maintain your PS1. Three main areas of DOS operations are discussed in this chapter:

File System and Basic Operations. This section covers the use of the commands built into the PS1 DOS shell. These operations include the File System program, formatting, and copying disks.

DOS Prompt Operations. This section explores the powerful but often forbidding world of the DOS command prompt. You will learn how to carry out powerful operations by directly entering DOS command sentences and creating DOS batch files.

The DOS Shell Menu System. The heart of the DOS shell is its menu system. In addition to the menus included with the PS1, you can use DOS to modify and expand the menus to include a variety of options that allow you to customize your PS1 to your own needs and preferences.

389

THE DOS SHELL PROGRAM

As discussed in Chapter 1, a shell program is one that presents basic information about your computer system in a special form. Shell programs are typically used to present the operating system of the computer to the user in a particular manner and style. The first question you might ask is why are shell programs needed? Why is the operating system so important?

The answer to these questions revolves around finding the best way to organize a computer system. There are two basic approaches to this problem: application specific operating and application independent operating.

Application Specific

An application specific approach assumes that the manufacturer of the computer knows in advance exactly what you will be doing with the machine. With this assumption in mind the entire computer system is organized around the one task, the application, for which the computer will be used. A good example of this approach are machines that are sold as word processors. In fact, all word processing machines are computers. The major difference between a word processing machine and a computer is that the word processor's operating system cannot be separated from its application, e.g., word processing. While in theory the word processing machine could perform other computer based tasks, e.g., calculate spreadsheet formulas, you cannot put this into practice because the machine and its application software are implemented as a single unit. This means that word processing machines have the disadvantage of being less flexible than computers. On the other hand, since the machine's function is defined in advance, it can be sold a bit below the cost of a computer since it is not expandable and cannot be customized the way a computer system can.

Application Independent

Machines sold today as personal computers have in common the fact that they are application independent in design. The design of the machine allows the user to perform any type of operation they desire so long as they can locate a software program that meets their needs. (Of course, if you have the knowledge and time you can create your own software applications and run them on the computer.) In order to make this approach practical the computer is supplied with a program that controls and organizes its basic operations, e.g., data storage and retrieval, transfer of data from screen, to disk to printer, etc. This general program, called the operating system, then allows you to run all sorts of applications, e.g., word processing, spreadsheet, etc. Because the operating system takes care of the basic operations, the applications need only concentrate on the specific task they are required to perform, word processing, etc. Application independent computers offer an unlimited horizon of applications. In the long run they have far greater potential than any dedicated machine like a word processor.

390

The application independent computer has built the personal computer industry. However, there has been a nagging problem with this approach. The operating system supplied with the original IBM PC, called IBM or Microsoft DOS, was modeled after the type of operating system found on older and larger computer systems. While the application software for personal computers was designed for the ease of use of the customer, the operating system, since it was the lowest common denominator, maintained its sparse and confusing character.

The solution to this problem is the shell program. The current version of DOS, 4.00 or higher, allows for the use of different shell programs. This means that user can select different approaches to the operating system without having to actually the change the operating system in their computer. Shells allow you to maintain compatibility with existing software programs while you have some variety in the way that the system appears and operates.

The PS1 is supplied with three different operating system shell programs: the PS1 folder system, the DOS 4.00 Shell, and the DOS Prompt Command Interpreter.

PS1 Folder System

The Folder system is a special shell unique to the PS1. As discussed in Chapter 1 the folder system allows you to select programs to execute from a file folder type display.

DOS 4.00 Shell

DOS version 4.00 and higher supports a menu driven shell which allows you to perform a variety of operations by making selections from various menus. The PS1 includes a number of pre-defined menus that operate under the DOS shell. You can expand and modify the shell menus to include your own operations in addition to the shell menus supplied with the PS1.

DOS Prompt Command Interpreter

This approach to DOS operation is command driven in contrast to the other shells that are menu driven. The DOS prompt mode is one in which you control DOS operations by entering in command sentences. These sentences are complete instructions about what task you want to perform and how it should be carried out. Command driven operations and generally faster and more powerful than menu operations. They also offer flexibility since operations are not limited to the choices on the menu. On the other hand you must know in advance the commands and options available through the DOS command interpreter since no menu displays are provided to guide you through operations.

In this chapter you will learn about the use and modification of the DOS 4.00 shell program and the use of the DOS prompt mode. The techniques and concepts explained can apply to any computer system running DOS 4.00 or higher.

Starting the DOS Shell

The PS1 is set up to start the DOS shell program when you select IBM DOS from the startup screen:

```
Click(left) on IBM DOS
```

The shell program displays the Main Group menu. There are 11 options on this menu (they were discussed in Chapter 1).

Disks and Directories

As mentioned in Chapter 1, computers used disks to permanently store information because the internal memory of the computer will be automatically erased when the power is turned off. A single computer disk can contain many files. A hard disk has several thousand files. Disk storage is organized so that each file can be stored and retrieved without interfering with any of the other files of information on that disk. In order for this system to work, each file must have a unique location called a path. The path name of a file consists of three parts which are as follows:

File Name

This is the name that you assign to the file when you create it using a program such the word processor in Works. The file name can be 1 to 8 characters with a one to three character file extension.

Directory

DOS stores files in directories. When a disk, hard or floppy, is first formatted for use in the system, a directory is created for listing files stored on that disk. This directory is called the root directory since any additional directories begin at the root. Additional directories are defined in order to group files on a given disk. The purpose of a directory is to create groups of related files which are easier to handle than a long list which contains every file on the floppy or hard disk.

Drive

Each drive in the computer is assigned a single letter, A-Z, to identify the drive. The path name consists of the file name, the name of the directory in which the file is contained and the drive letter. DOS uses special punctuation to distinguish the elements. The drive letter is always followed by a colon. The directory name is enclosed in \ (backslash) characters. By placing all of the elements together you can arrive at the path of the file. For example, the file PARTY.WKS, which is stored in the WORKS directory of the hard disk would have the path name C:\WORKS\PARTY.WKS, C: = drive, \WORKS\ = directory and PARTY.WKS = file name.

THE FILE SYSTEM PROGRAM

The most important single part of the DOS 4.00 shell is the File System program. The File System provides two important functions. They are as follows:

Visual Representation of Disk Storage

The File System displays a diagram that shows how the files are stored on the disk. File storage is relatively simple on a floppy disk since the total number of files is limited by the capacity of each disk. However, hard disks have such a large capacity, e.g., 30 million characters, that the filing system takes on added complexities. The diagram shown by the DOS shell helps the user quickly grasp the organization of any disk, hard or floppy, that is in the computer system.

Menus of File Commands

In addition to displaying a diagram of the disk, the shell provides menus which present operations that are commonly required for maintenance of the computer system such as deleting, renaming, or copying files. To access the File System, select File System from the Main Group menu:

Double click(left) on **File System**

The file system display appears on the screen, as shown in Figure 13-1. The display consist of several distinct parts: drives, the current directory, and the directory tree.

Drives

This box lists the drives in the system by letter. DOS assigns each drive a letter. The first floppy drive is always A and the first hard drive is always C. Note that the PS1 shows to drives, B and D, that are not part of the system. DOS shows a letter B even though there is no floppy drive B in the system. The D drive is how DOS see the ROM (Read Only Memory) chip that contains the startup screen information. On a floppy system drives A though C are listed where C is the ROM drive.

Current Directory

This shows the path name of the current drive and directory. Note that a \ by itself refers to the root directory of the disk.

Directory Tree

This section of the screen shows a diagram of the directories contained on the current disk. The PS1 hard disk is supplied with 4 directories that branch from the root: WORKS, DOS, SYSTUTOR, and PRODIGY. The WORKS directory contains a subdirectory called PROGRAM as indicated by the diagram. Note that one of the directories is always highlighted. The highlight indicates that this is the current or active directory.

393

File List

To the right of the directory tree is a list of files contained in the directory that is currently highlighted. If the file list is empty that means that the current directory is empty. The list shows the file's size and the date that the file was last saved. Figure 13-1 shows the file system screen display.

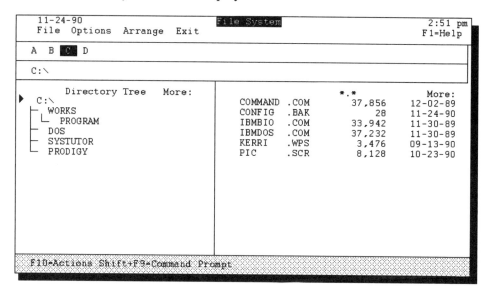

Figure 13-1. File System Screen Display.

Changing the Active Directory

You can display a file list for any of the directories or subdirectories on the disk by moving the highlight through the directory tree diagram. You can move the highlight with the arrow keys or by clicking on the directory name with the mouse. For example, suppose that you wanted to display the list of files contained in the PRODIGY directory:

Click(left) on PRODIGY

The file list on the right side of the screen changes to show the files contained in the newly selected directory. In this case the list is too long for all of the files to appear at one time. You can use the scroll bar to scroll the list down if necessary. Select the DOS directory:

Click(left) on **DOS**

Display Options

You can control the list of files that appear on the file system display in two ways: by filter and sequence.

Filter

You can list the file displayed to those that match a specific pattern. Pattern matches use a wildcard specification to select matching files. A wildcard is created by entering one or more characters, which must be matched by the file names in order for them to appear on the list, plus a wildcard symbol, * or ?, that indicates the position in the file name that any character can appear. For example, suppose that you want to list only those files which have names that begin with F. The wildcard f*.* would select those files. On the other hand, suppose you wanted only those files with a WKS extension. The wildcard *.wks would select those files. The more character you add the more restrictive criterion is created, For example, the wildcard f*.wks would list only WKS files that begin with the letter F. Note that the wildcard *.* appears at the top of the file list. *.* refers to all of the files in the current directory.

Sequence

The select files are normally listed in alphabetical order. You can select to sort the list according to extension, date, size or the actual order in which they are stored on the disk.

Change the sort order of the file list to size order:

```
Click(left) on Options
Click(left) on Display Options
Click(left) on Size
Click(left) on Enter
```

The file names are rearranged in size order beginning with the largest file in the directory, probably SHELLC.EXE and moving down towards the smaller files.

Selecting Files

You can use the Options menu to select a group of files based on a file wildcard. Suppose that you wanted to limit the files displayed to those with a COM file extension:

```
Click(left) on Options
Click(left) on Display Options
```

Enter the wildcard for the files you want to select, in this case *.COM to select all COM files:

```
*.com [return]
```

The list of files now displays only the files in the current directory that match the wildcard. The sort order and selection settings will continue no matter what disk or directory you displays. Display the PRODIGY directory.

```
Click(left) on PRODIGY
```

The program displays the message "No files match file specifier" to indicate that the selected directory does not contain any COM files.

Adding a New Directory

You can perform operations on the directories and files by using the menu bar at the top of the display. You can activate the menu bar by pressing [**F10**] or by clicking on the menu bar item you want to use.

You can add a new directory to the disk using the **Create Directory** command found on the File menu. When you use this command it is very important to first position the highlight on the directory tree to the level at which you want to place the new directory. The PS1's hard disk is divided into three levels: the root directory, four first level directories (WORKS, DOS, SYSTUTOR and PRODIGY) and one second level directory (PROGRAM). You should place the highlight on the level below the level of the directory you want to create. For example, to create a directory called PRACTICE at the same level as DOS you would highlight the root directory, C:\. To make PRACTICE a subdirectory of DOS you would highlight DOS.

In this case create a new directory on the same level as DOS:

```
Click(left) on C:\
```

Select the **Create Directory** command from the File menu:

```
Click(left) on File
Click(left) on Create Directory
```

The file system program displays a dialog box that asks you to enter the name of the directory you want to create. Enter:

```
practice [return]
```

The new directory appears in the directory tree display.

FILE OPERATIONS

The most important part of the file system operations are those that operate on files and groups of files. You can use the file system commands to copy, rename, delete, move and change file attributes. The current directory, C:\, will list two files that begin with the letters IBM, IBMDOS.COM and IBMBIO.COM. The IBMDOS.COM file is highlighted because it is the selected file for any operations. Select IBMDOS.COM:

Click(left) on *IBMDOS.COM*

File Information

You can obtain information about the file, directory, and disk with which you are working by using the **Show Information** command on the Options menu:

Click(left) on **Options**
Click(left) on **Show Information**

The program shows information about the current file, current directory, and disk, as shown in Figure 13-2.

```
        Show Information
File
   Name  : IBMDOS.COM
   Attr  : rhsa
Selected            C
   Number:          1
   Size  :     37,232
Directory
   Name  : ROOT
   Size  :    120,662
   Files :          6
Disk
   Name  : MAIN FOLDER
   Size  : 30,976,000
   Avail : 23,496,704
   Files :        311
   Dirs  :          7

Esc=Cancel    F1=Help
```

Figure 13-2. Show Information Box.

One of the most interesting pieces of information displayed in the box are the file attributes listed next to the Attr label. DOS maintain 4 different types of file attributes. They are: read-only, archive, and system/hidden.

Read-Only (r)

If a file has this attribute it is protected from changes or erasure. A read-only file can be listed, printed or displayed but it cannot be removed or modified until the read only attribute is removed.

Archive (a)

The archive attribute is used to keep track of which files have been backed up to floppy disks and which have not. Each time a file is created or modified, DOS assigns it the archive attribute. When a backup operation is performed the attribute is removed. You can easily determine if a file needs to be backed up by checking its file attributes.

System(s)/Hidden(h)

These two attributes are similar in their effect. When either of these attributes is selected, the file names of the file will not appear when lists of files are displayed such as in the file selection boxes in Works. Files are hidden to protect them from accidental erasure. While the read-only attribute would also protect a file from erasure, read-only files appear in directory listings.

The currently selected file is assigned all of the attributes. Most file use only the a attribute. Remove the information display by entering:

```
[Esc]
```

Copying and Deleting Files

The two most commonly used file operations are copying and deleting files. Suppose that you wanted to copy some of the files that are in the DOS directory into the PRACTICE directory. Display the DOS directory:

```
Click(left) on DOS
```

The file list shows all of the COM files in the DOS directory. Select the BACKUP.COM file:

```
Click(left) on File
Click(left) on Copy
```

To copy the file, select the **Copy** command found on the File menu:

```
Click(left) on File
Click(left) on Copy
```

The program displays a dialog box with two options, From and To. The name of the highlighted file is automatically placed in the From box. The name of the current directory is placed in the To box. If you want to place a copy of the file in a different directory with the same name you must enter the name of the directory to which the file is to be copied. On the other hand if you want to place the copy in the current directory you must enter a new file name.

In this case you want to place the copy into the PRACTICE directory. Enter:

```
c:\practice [return]
```

Check the results of the command. Display the PRACTICE directory:

```
Click(left) on PRACTICE
```

The file BACKUP.COM appears in the PRACTICE directory.

Copying Groups

You can work with more than one file at a time. For example, you might want to select a group of files and copy them all to the same location with a single command. This is much faster and less confusing than copying the files one at a time.

Return to the DOS directory:

```
Click(left) on DOS
```

Select the first file in the group:

```
Click(left) on BASICA.COM
```

If you want to add another file to the selection and not make a different selection, you must press down and hold down the **[Shift]** key while you click on the next name. This mouse operation is called a Shift-Click. Shift-Click on file DEBUG.COM to add it to the selection:

```
Shift-Click(left) on DEBUG.COM
```

Note that even though the full highlight moves to DEBUG.COM, the symbol next to BASICA.COM is still highlighted indicating that it is still part of the selection. Add a third file to the group:

Shift-Click(left) on *EDLIN.COM*

There are now three files in the selection. Copy all three to the PRACTICE directory with a single copy command:

Click(left) on **File** Click(left) on **Copy**

The From box lists all three of the selected files. Enter the destination directory:

c:\practice [return]

A dialog box appears and show the name of each file as it is copied.

Multiple Directory Listings

Copying operations require two locations: from and to. In its simplest form the copy command requires you to manually enter the name of the directory or disk to which the files are being copied. Another approach uses a dual directory display in which you can select the destination directory and avoid any manual entry at all during the copying process.

The Multiple file list command located on the Arrange menu, splits the screen so that you can display two directories at the same time:

Click(left) on **Arrange** Click(left) on **Multiple file list**

The screen is now divided into two smaller versions of the original screen display. The advantage of the split screen displays is that you can display tow different directories at the same time. Change the directory of the lower list to PRACTICE:

Click(left) on *PRACTICE*(lower list)

In order to use the two lists as source and destination directories you must select a special file operation option called Select across directories found on the File Options dialog box:

Click(left) on **Options** Click(left) on **File Options**

Activate Select across directories:

Click(left) on **Select across directories** Click(left) on **Enter**

You can now use the mouse to perform an entire copy operation. First, select the file you want to copy from the upper list:

Click(left) on *FDISK.COM*

Next, select the directory in the lower window into which you want to copy the file:

Click(left) on *PRACTICE*

Select the **Copy** command:

Click(left) on **File**
Click(left) on **Copy**

Note that the name of the destination directory, PRACTICE, is automatically filled in by the program. Complete the command:

Click(left) on **Enter**

The file is copied to the PRACTICE directory.

Deleting

You can delete single or groups of files with the file system program. Select the EDLIN.COM file in the PRACTICE directory:

Click(left) on *EDLIN.COM*(lower directory)

Delete the file with the **Delete** command on the File menu:

Click(left) on **File**
Click(left) on **Delete**
Click(left) on **Enter**

The program displays a dialog box asking you to confirm your decision to delete this file:

Click(left) on **Delete this file**

You can select all of the files displayed in a directory with the **Select All** command:

Click(left) on **File**
Click(left) on **Select All**

Delete the files using the mouse:

Click(left) on **File**
Click(left) on **Delete**
Click(left) on **Enter**
Click(left) on **Delete this file***(4 times)*

You can also delete directories from the disk. Note that only a directory that contains zero files can be deleted. If a directory contains a file, attempts to delete the directory will be rejected by the operating system. Remove the PRACTICE directory:

Click(left) on **File**
Click(left) on **Delete**
Click(left) on **Delete this directory***(4 times)*

Exit the file system by entering:

[F3]

The screen changes to the Main Group menu display.

Finding a File

The file lists that appear in the File System display show the contents of the disk in a directory by directory manner, as shown in Figure 13-3. The multiple file list option displays two directories at the same time. However, suppose that you wanted to look for a file but did not know which directory in which it was contained.

One solution is to use the System file list option in the File System. This option displays a single list that contains all of the files on the disk regardless of the directory. Select the File System option from the Main Group menu:

Double click(left) on **File System**
Click(left) on **Arrange**
Click(left) on **System file list**

The file list displayed is different than the normal file list in several respects. No directory tree is displayed because the file list is drawn from all of the directories on the disk. In place of the directory tree the file information box is displayed. The information box shows the directory location of the selected file.

```
 11-25-90                      File System                    2:12 pm
   File  Options  Arrange  Exit                    |          F1=Help

 A  B  C  D

 C:\DOS

 File                                     *.*                 More:   ↓
   Name  : 0BZE0A38           0BZE0A38        9,158   11-24-90  11:46am
   Attr  : ...a               0C103551       13,448   10-18-90  12:16pm
 Selected            C        4201    .CPI    6,404   12-02-89  12:00am
   Number:           0        4208    .CPI      641   12-02-89  12:00am
   Size  :           0        5202    .CPI      402   12-02-89  12:00am
 Directory                    ADDRESS .WDB    4,858   12-02-89  12:00am
   Name  : DOS                ANSI    .SYS    9,172   12-02-89  12:00am
   Size  :   2,240,398        APPEND  .EXE   11,186   12-02-89  12:00am
   Files :          97        ARC-E   .COM    7,168   10-25-90  11:29pm
 Disk                         ARC     .TXT    1,536   10-25-90  11:24pm
   Name  : MAIN FOLDER        ASSIGN  .COM    5,785   12-02-89  12:00am
   Size  :  30,976,000        ATTRIB  .EXE   18,247   12-02-89  12:00am
   Avail :  23,498,752        BACKUP  .COM   33,818   12-02-89  12:00am
   Files :         311        BACKUP  .MEU    3,552   12-02-89  12:00am
   Dirs  :           6        BACKUP1 .BAT      487   12-02-89  12:00am

 F10=Actions Shift+F9=Command Prompt
```

Figure 13-3. System File List Shows all Files on Disk.

You can combine the system file list with file section to locate the file or files you are looking for. In this case you are looking for a file called VDISK.SYS:

```
Click(left) on Options
Click(left) on Display Options
```

Enter the file name:

```
vdisk.sys [return]
```

The display shows the name VDISK.SYS. The information box indicates that this file can be found in the DOS directory. System listing plus file selection can locate any file on the hard disk even when you are unsure of its directory location.

Return to the Main Group menu by entering:

```
[F3]
```

DOS PROMPT OPERATIONS

The DOS prompt mode is used to directly enter DOS commands. The advantage of this mode is that you can perform a wider variety of DOS operations than you can from the DOS shell menus. The disadvantage is that you need to know in advance about the commands you want to enter. A complete discussion of all of the commands that you can execute at the DOS prompt is beyond the scope of this book. However, it might be useful to duplicate the operations you have just performed in the File System module of the DOS shell through the DOS prompt mode so that you can see how the two approaches differ. Note that you cannot use the mouse in the DOS prompt mode.

You can access the DOS prompt by entering the combination **[Shift-F9]**:

[Shift-F9]

All of the menus are removed from the screen. The DOS prompt appears, C:\DOS>, and the cursor is placed next to the prompt. What is the DOS prompt? A prompt is a message displayed by the computer that tells you the program is ready to accept a command. The DOS prompt is the specific prompt that DOS displays in order to let you know that you can enter a DOS command. The typical DOS prompt shows the current directory name followed by a >. In this case the prompt C:\DOS> tells you that the active directory is the DOS directory on drive C and that DOS is ready for a command. Where does it tell you that DOS is ready? The answer is that it does not explicitly tell you it is ready. When you see the prompt you can infer that DOS is ready for a command.

What kind of commands do you enter at the DOS prompt? DOS commands are actually sentences which you compose that describe the action that you want DOS to perform. A DOS command sentence always begins with a DOS command word. That word is usually followed by specifications required to complete the command.

The DIR command lists the files in the current directory. Enter:

dir [return]

You can alter the style of directory display by using the /W option. Enter:

dir/w [return]

You can list the files in a directory other than the current directory by adding the directory name to the command. For example, the command below lists the contents of the PRODIGY directory:

dir c:\prodigy [return]

Suppose that as in the previous section you wanted to create a new directory on the disk called PRACTICE. The DOS command for creating a directory is **MKDIR** or **MD** (make directory) for short. However, just entering **MD** is not enough for DOS since all DOS commands must contain all of the information needed to complete the command. In the case of the **MD** command you will need to add to the command sentence the name of the directory you want to create. The full command is **MD**

C:\PRACTICE. This command tells DOS to make a new directory called PRACTICE. The C:\ indicates that the directory should be placed on the level just below the root directory of the disk. Enter:

```
cd c:\practice [return]
```

The DOS prompt returns. What has happened? The answer is that you have created a new directory. But how do you know? Once again the conclusion that you have created the directory is inferred. When you enter a DOS command and the DOS prompt returns without an error message you can conclude that your command was successful. The **COPY** command is used to copy files. In the previous section you copied the file BACKUP.COM to the PRACTICE directory. You can use the **COPY** command to accomplish this same task. The **COPY** command requires two parameters, the file you want to copy and the location (disk or directory) or new name for the file. Enter:

```
copy backup.com c:\practice [return]
```

DOS displays the message "1 File(s) copied" that confirms the copy operation. You can use wildcards to copy groups of files. To copy all of the COM files in the DOS directory to the PRACTICE directory use the wildcard *.COM with the **COPY** command. Enter:

```
copy *.com c:\ptarctive [return]
```

This time DOS copies 28 files into the specified directory.

XCOPY

One of the advantages of the DOS prompt mode is that you can access a variety of DOS commands and utilities. For example, in addition to the **COPY** command, DOS provides an alternative method of copying called **XCOPY**. **XCOPY** is a more powerful version of **COPY**—it uses more available memory to copy files resulting in faster copying. Repeat the previous group copy command but substitute **XCOPY** as the command:

```
xcopy *.com c:\ptarctive [return]
```

DOS copies the 28 files but at a slightly faster speed. The **COPY** command copies each file by reading and writing each file individually. **XCOPY** reads as many files as it can at one time and then write all of those files to the new location. This makes **XCOPY** generally faster than COPY. The **DEL** command can be used to erase files from the disk. You should exercise great caution when using **DEL** since the DOS prompt mode does not confirm each deletion. If you wanted to erase the copy of the BACKUP.COM file you have just placed in the PRACTICE directory enter:

```
del c:\practice\backup.com [return]
```

The command deletes the file. However there are no messages displayed on the screen that either warn you about the deletion or confirm its success. You can use wildcards with the **DEL** command. For example, to erase all of the files in the PRACTICE directory enter the following:

```
del c:\practice\*.* [return]DOS
```

DOS asks you to confirm this deletion. This message is an exception to the rule that DOS does not warn you or display messages. If you request to delete all of the files from a directory, *.*, this question will appear. Enter:

```
y [return]
```

The files are deleted. The directory can be removed use the **RMDIR** or **RD** command. Note that a directory must be empty in order to remove the directory:

```
rd c:\practice [return]
```

Printing From DOS

You can send the information that is output by a DOS command to the printer by adding the suffix >PRN after the command. The suffix >PRN means redirect the output of the command to the printer. For example, adding this to the **DIR** command will print a copy of the file list:

```
dir >prn [return]
```

Since the file list will probably not end at the bottom of a page you can eject the rest of the page by using a special DOS command called **ECHO**. The character created when you press [**Ctrl-l**](the letter L) when sent to a printer will cause the printer to feed the rest of the current form. Enter:

```
echo
[spacebar] [Ctrl-l](the letter L)
> prn [return]
```

Note that when you press the combination [**Ctrl-l**] DOS displays ^L, the symbol for [**Ctrl-l**] on the command line.

Exiting the DOS Prompt Mode

The **EXIT** command terminates the DOS prompt mode and returns you to the application or program that started the DOS prompt session, in this case the DOS shell program. Conclude the current DOS prompt session by entering:

```
exit [return]
```

The DOS shell returns to the screen display.

RUNNING BASIC

BASIC refers to the BASIC programming language. The PS1 is supplied with a program called BASICA.COM that can be used to run, create or modify programs written in the BASIC language. BASIC is not very important in business computing where applications such as word processing, spreadsheet or database dominate computer usage. However, BASIC has many educational and recreational applications. Most school math books, even those for early grades, will include BASIC programs at the ends of the chapters as special exercises. Many magazines will publish BASIC programs and there are many books that contain listing of BASIC programs.

You can create BASIC programs of your own by learning the BASIC language or simply entering in the programs you find in books or magazines. A full discussion of BASIC is beyond the scope of this book. However, if you have a listing of a BASIC program there are a few things you need to know.

You can start BASIC from the Main Group menu of the DOS shell by selecting BASIC Programming Language:

Double click(left) on **BASIC Programming Language**

Before the DOS shell runs the BASIC language it displays a dialog box that tells you how to exit BASIC by using the SYSTEM command. Load BASIC:

Click(left) on **Enter**

Like the DOS prompt mode, BASIC is a command driven environment with no menus or help screens. BASIC displays a prompt that reads Ok. The prompt means that BASIC is ready to accept an instruction. The Ok prompt does not mean that everything is OK, that is, you haven't made an error. It simply means that BASIC is ready to continue.

In order to write a BASIC program you must know the commands you want to enter or have an listing of a program you want to type in.

All lines in a BASIC program are numbered. Enter the following BASIC program:

10 cls [return]
20 print "Hello [return]

You have just entered a two line basic program. This program clears the screen (CLS) and then prints the word Hello on the screen. To execute a program enter the **RUN** command:

run [return]

The program executes, the word Hello is printed, and then it returns to the OK prompt.

IBM BASIC assigns commonly used commands to the function keys. That is the meaning of the bar at the bottom of the screen. The [F1] key lists the contents of your program. Enter:

```
[F1] [return]
```

The two lines of your program are displayed. The [F2] will run the program:

```
[F2]
```

The program executes again.

Printing a Program

You can print a program by adding the [F6] command to the [F1], LIST command. Enter:

```
[F1][F6]
```

You may need to feed the rest of the current form through the printer. This can be done though BASIC by sending the BASIC equivalent of [Ctrl-l] to the printer. The command is LPRINT which sends output to the printer in contrast to PRINT which sends it to the screen. Enter:

```
lprint chr$(12) [return]
```

The remainder of the page is feed through the printer.

Saving BASIC Programs

Once you have created the program you will need to save on the disk so that you can use it again at another time. Any program lines entered into BASIC and not saved in a disk file will be lost when you exit BASIC and return to the DOS shell.

BASIC programs can have file names between 1 and 8 characters without spaces. BASIC adds a BAS extension to all BASIC programs.

To save the current program on the disk enter:

```
[F4]
example [return]
```

You can display a list of the files on the disk by using the **FILES** command:

```
files [return]
```

You should see EXAMPLE.BAS at the bottom of the file list.

To exit BASIC enter the SYSTEM command. The system referred to by the command is the DOS operating system. Enter:

```
system [return]
```

The DOS shell Main Group menu reappears.

Loading BASIC Programs

To retrieve a BASIC program stored on a disk begin by loading BASIC:

```
Double click(left) on BASIC Programming Language
Click(left) on Enter
```

List the current program by entering:

```
[F1] [return]
```

The screen will show no program lines because you have not entered or loaded a program. Load the EXAMPLE program using the **[F3]**, **LOAD**, command:

```
[F3]
example [return]
```

List the program by entering:

```
[F1] [return]
```

The lines of the EXAMPLE program are now listed exactly as they were when you saved the program.

Exit BASIC by entering:

```
system [return]
```

THE DOS SHELL MENU SYSTEM

The Main Group menu that appears when you activate the DOS shell program can be modified and extended to include additional commands or menus of your own design. It is important to understand that all DOS shell menu options perform their functions by executing DOS prompt commands such as those discussed in this chapter under using the DOS prompt mode.

This means that knowledge of DOS determines the sophistication of the functions assocatied with your menu options. However, even with a limited understanding of your system and DOS you can customize and personalize the DOS shell menu system.

In this section you will learn how to add commands or entire menus to the DOS shell menu system.

The DOS shell menu system works with two kinds of elements: groups and programs.

Groups

A group is a list of options that appear as a menu in the DOS shell program. Each group stores the information that created and operates the menu in a file with an MNU extension. The Main Group menu is stored in a file called SHELL.MNU. A group menu contains programs which can be executed from the menu or references to other group files which will display menus of their own.

Programs

A program is a list of DOS prompt commands that should be executed if that menu option is selected. The purpose of a menu program is to provide a simple way of carrying out a given operating system task.

Adding a Program to a Group

The most basic tasks involved in customizing a DOS group menu is the addition of a program to the current menu. For example, DOS 4.00 contains special commands that return statistics about the systems memory and disk storage. The **MEM** command summarizes memory while the **CHKDSK** command summarizes both disk space and memory usage. Suppose that you wanted to add these commands to the Main Group menu.

To add a program, select the **Add** command from the Program menu:

```
Click(left) on Program
Click(left) on Add
```

A dialog box appears with four text boxes: title, commands, help text, and password.

Title

The title is the text that will appear on the menu representing the program.

Commands

The information entered into this text box is a series of valid DOS commands which carry out the operation you want assocatied with the menu option. You can enter one or more DOS commands in this box. Each command is separated by a special character inserted when you press [F4].

The last two items are optional. They only have an effect if you use a dialog box as part of the program. You will learn later in this chapter how to add dialog box displays to your menu selections.

Help Text

You can enter text that will be displayed in a help box if the use selects help, [F1] while viewing the dialog box for the current programs.

Password

You can add password protection to a program with this option. Only users who correctly enter the password can execute the program.

In this example, begin by entering the title of this option:

Check Disk and Memory [tab]

The command which executes this DOS operation is **CHKDSK**. Enter:

chkdsk

Save the program specification using the [F2] key:

[F2]

The new program appears at the bottom of the Main Group menu. Execute the command by selecting the title from the menu:

Double click(left) on **Check Disk and Memory**

The **CHKDSK** command is executed. The shell automatically executes the command. The information about the disk and memory usage is displayed on the screen. When the command is complete the DOS shell reappears.

One problem with the current program is that the information generated by **CHKDSK** command does not stay on the screen but is immediately erased by the DOS shell when it reappears. Since the purpose of the **CHKDSK** command is to display information on the screen, you need to find a way to pause the program after the **CHKDSK** command so that the user can have an opportunity to read the information. The DOS command **PAUSE** will halt execution of commands until the user presses a key. You can modify the program by using the Change command on the Program menu. Note that the program you want to change must be highlighted when you use this command:

```
Click(left) on Program
Click(left) on Change
```

Move the cursor to the end of the command **chkdsk** in the Commands box:

```
[tab] [End]
```

In order to add a second command to this program, enter the command separator symbol by pressing **[F4]**:

```
[F4]
```

The key inserts a I in the text box. Enter the next command:

```
pause
```

Save and then execute the modified program:

```
Click(left) on Save
Double click(left) on Check Disk and Memory
```

This time the message "Press any key to continue" appears at the end of the CHKDSK display. The screen remains paused until you press a key. This is the effect of the **PAUSE** command. Complete the command by entering:

```
[return]
```

Programs with Dialog Boxes

The DOS shell allows you to create programs that use customized versions of the DOS shell dialog boxes. A Dialog box is necessary when you want to execute a command that requires, or permits optional, parameters. For example, in the DOS prompt section the use of the **XCOPY** command, which is faster than **COPY**, was discussed. You might want to add this command to your Main Group menu.

Unlike **CHKDSK**, any command that uses **XCOPY** will require the entry of parameters each time it is used. It is necessary for this program to display a dialog box which will have a text box into which parameters can be entered. Create a new program for the **XCOPY** command:

Click(left) on **Program**
Click(left) on **Add**

Enter the title for this program:

Advanced Copy(XCOPY) [return]

You can cause the display of a dialog box by adding [] following the command. The shell program will automatically format the contents of the dialog box with generic text that can apply to any dialog box. Enter:

xcopy []

Save and execute the program:

Click(left) on **Save**

The program displays the default dialog box (generated by the DOS shell) that asks you to enter the parameters for the program, as shown in Figure 13-4. This is the default dialog box which is generated by the DOS shell.

```
 11-25-90                    Start Programs                     7:53 pm
 Program  Group  Exit                                         | F1=Help
                              Main Group
              To select an item, use the up and down arrows.
            To start a program or display a new group, press Enter.


 Set Date and Time...
 File System
 Format (Prepare a diskette for use)...
 Disk Copy (Copy a diskette)
 Copy a File
 Backup and Restore Your Fixed Disk...
 Command Prompt
 Change Colors                    ┌──────────────────────────────────┐
 Customize How System Start       │        Program Parameters        │
 Change Hardware Configurat       │                                  │
 BASIC Programming Language       │  Type the parameters, then press Enter. │
 Check Disk and Memory            │                                  │
 Advanced Copy(XCOPY)             │  Parameters . . [_            >  │
                                  │                                  │
        ▓                         │ <─┘=Enter  Esc=Cancel  F1=Help   │
                                  └──────────────────────────────────┘

 F10=Actions            Shift+F9=Command Prompt
```

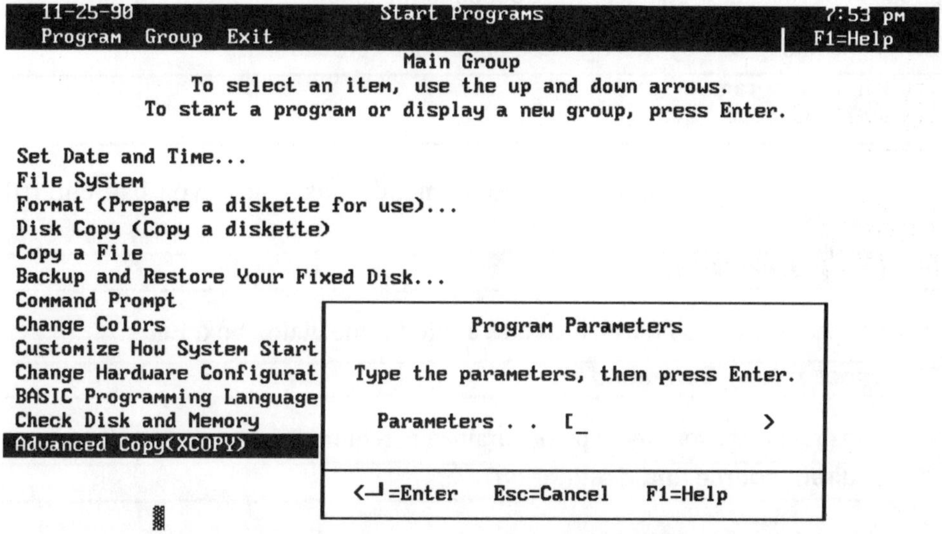

Figure 13-4. Dialog Box Displayed for New Program.

413

The parameters needed for the **XCOPY** command are a file name to copy and a destination for the copied file. Enter the following parameters which copy the BACKUP.COM file to the root directory of the C drive:

```
backup.com c:\
```

The **XCOPY** command completes its task and you return to the Main Group menu.

Dialog Box Options

You can customize the display of the dialog box by specifying special parameters inside the [] that appear in the programs command text box.

/T. This option displays a title at the top of the dialog box.

/I. This option displays an additional 40 characters of text that can serve as instructions. The instructions appear below the title.

/P. This option specifies the text of the prompt that appear next to the text box.

/D. This option allows you to insert default values into the text box.

/R. This option control the editing style for the text box. If used, the current contents and the default values in the text box are removed when a new entry is made. If this option is not used, new characters are added to the default parameters, if any.

Change the dialog box by adding these optional specifications:

```
Click(left) on Program
Click(left) on Change
```

Move the cursor to the place in the commands box where you can enter the specifications:

```
[Tab] [End] [backspace]
```

The first specification is /T which creates a title for the dialog box. Enter:

```
/T"Advanced Copy Command"
```

Specify instructions about the type of parameters required:

```
/I"2 Required: source and destination"
```

Next add a prompt for the text box:

```
/P"Enter From & To"]
```

414

Save and run the modified program:

```
Click(left) on Save
Double click(left) on Advanced Copy(XCOPY)
```

The dialog box now displays the text specified by the command option settings, as shown in Figure 13-5.

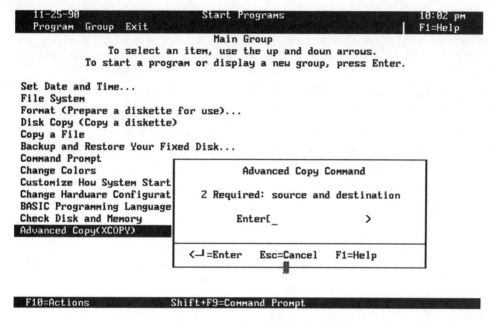

Figure 13-5. Custom Text Appears in Dialog Box.

Cancel the command by entering:

```
[Esc]
```

Creating a New Group

In addition to adding new programs to existing menus you can create a new group menu. A new group must always be attached to an existing group menu. For example, you might want to create a group that has commands related to Works. While you can start Works from the PS1 startup screen, you can use the DOS shell to run Works and automatically load specific files at the same time. Creating a new group is similar to creating a new program in that you must create a title for the group on the menu. Select the **Add** command from the Group menu:

```
Click(left) on Group
Click(left) on Add
```

The group dialog box is the same as the program dialog box except that instead of having a text box for the commands it has a text box for the name of the file which will hold the menu specifications. The name can be any combination of one to eight characters as long as there is not already a group file on the disk with the same name. Enter:

```
Microsoft Works [return]
MW
[F2]
```

The new group appears on the menu. The "... " indicate that this item is a group. If you want to add programs to the new group you must first select and activate that group:

```
Double click(left) on Microsoft Works
```

The title now appears as the group name. The message "Group is empty" appears where the menu for the group should be. This message will disappear when you add programs to this group.

The first program will be one that runs Works and automatically loads the ADDRESS database file. Works is supplied with this file, ADDRESS.WDB. Create the first program for this group:

```
Click(left) on Program
Click(left) on Add
```

Enter the title of the program:

```
Name and Address Database [return]
```

The next entry will be the commands that actually execute when this option is selected. Begin with the CD (change directory) command. This command is used in the DOS prompt mode to select a directory as the active directory. Enter:

```
cd c:\work
```

Place a command separator after the command by entering:

```
[F4]
```

The next command is the one that starts the Works program. That command is WORKS because the file that contains the Works program is called WORKS.EXE. Files that end in EXE or COM extensions are program files and can be executed from the DOS prompt mode by entering the name of the file. It is not necessary to enter the EXE or COM extension since DOS assumes that any file name you enter must refer to one of those types of files. Enter:

```
works
```

At this point your program will start the Works program in exactly the same way that the startup screen Works option does. In order to start Works and automatically load a particular file you can place the name of the file as a parameter following the **WORKS** command. For example, to load a database called ADDRESS you would use the command works address. Many programs allow you to load a file along with the program by specifying the file name as a parameter. Complete the command by entering:

```
[spacebar]
address
[F2]
```

The Microsoft Works menu shows the new program. Execute the program:

```
Double click(left) on Name and Address Database
```

Works loads and displays the specified database as a single operation. Exit the program:

```
Click(left) on File
Click(left) on Exit Works
```

Note that the program takes you back to the startup screen rather than the DOS shell menu. The reason has to do with the way that Works is installed on the PS1 hard disk. The Works program is not stored in the WORKS directory. You will recall from the directory tree display of the File System that the WORKS directory contains a subdirectory called PROGRAM. The Works program files are stored in this directory so that your data files, stored in WORKS will be separated from the program files.

If this is the case why did the program start when you tried to access it through the WORKS directory? The answer is that in the WORKS directory is a file called WORKS.BAT. BAT files are called batch files. A batch file is a text file that contains DOS prompt commands. Batch files contain the same type of commands that you are entering into the commands text box. The only difference is that in a batch file, each command is on a separate line eliminating the need for the **[F4]** command separator.

The WORKS.BAT file is what actually execute when your program runs Works. How does that related to the problem of going back to the startup screen? The answer here has to do with the programming concept of a subroutine. Briefly stated, when you want to use a batch file (BAT) as part of a menu program you must precede the batch command with the **CALL** command. **CALL** causes DOS to return to the program that started the batch file. Without **CALL,** as you have seen, when the batch file is done, you will return to the startup screen instead of the DOS shell program.

Fix this problem by adding the **CALL** command to your program:

```
Click(left) on IBM DOS
Click(left) on Program
Click(left) on Change
```

```
[return]
[right] (12 times)
```

Turn on the insert mode:

```
[Ins]
```

Add the **CALL** command:

```
call
[spacebar]
```

The command should now read "cd \works|call works address." Save and execute the program:

```
Click(left) on Save
Double click(left) on Name and Address Database
```

Works loads and displays the specified database as a single operation. Exit the program:

```
Click(left) on File
Click(left) on Exit Works
```

This time you return to the menu— Microsoft Works— from which you executed the program. Note that the DOSHELL keeps track of which menu was the last one used and returns to that menu when you restart the DOS shell program.

Dialog Box Entry

Another variation on this idea would be to create a Works startup option with a dialog box. The box would allow you to enter the name of any of the Works files you wanted to start automatically.

Create a new program:

```
Click(left) on Program
Click(left) on Add
```

Enter the title:

```
Start Works with File [return]
```

Begin the command section with the **CD** command:

```
cd c:\works
[F4]
```

Next enter the works command. Recall that in this case the works command refers to the WORKS.BAT batch file not the WORKS.EXE program file. This means that it is necessary to use **CALL** rather than directly execute the program. In order to display a dialog box begin the option section with a [character:

```
call works [
```

Add a title for the dialog box:

```
/T"Microsoft Works"
```

Add an instruction:

```
/I"Enter file or files to load"
```

Define the prompt for the text box:

```
/P"Filename:"
```

You can set a default file, e.g., the BUDGET spreadsheet, if you desire using the /D option. Enter:

```
/D"BUDGET"
```

Add the /R option which will remove the default file name BUDGET as soon as a new character is entered. The /R option ensures that any entries made into the text box will begin with a blank box. The] closes the options section:

```
/R] [return]
```

419

In this case add help text to the dialog box by filling in the Help Text box. Enter:

> **This program starts Works and loads the specified files in one step. Enter the name of the Works file. If more than one is entered, separate each with a space.**

Save and execute the new program:

> Click(left) on **Save**
> Double click(left) on **Start Works with File**

The program displays a dialog box with the text specified in the program commands. The name BUDGET appears in the file name box as a default:

Display the help text by entering:

> **[F1]**

The program displays the user defined help in the help dialog box, as shown in Figure 13-6.

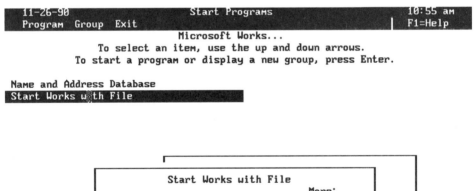

Figure 13-6. Customized Help Display.

Remove the help dialog box and execute the command with the default value:

> **[Esc] [return]**

The Works program loads and displays the BUDGET spreadsheet. Return to the DOS Shell menu by exiting Works:

```
Click(left) on File
Click(left) on Exit Works
```

Return to the Main Group menu and then exit the DOS shell program by entering:

```
[Esc] [F3]
```

You are now back at the startup screen. Note that you can delete any of the groups or programs in the DOS shell by using the **Delete** command on either the Program or Group menus.

SUMMARY

This chapter discussed the ways in which you can execute programs and DOS operations that are not included in the options displayed on the startup screen.

The DOS Shell Program. The DOS shell program is provided as part of the DOS 4.00 system. The shell program is created to provide a menu driven means of executing standard operations such as copying and deleting files.

The File System Program. The main section of the DOS shell program is the File System program. This program, supplied with the DOS shell, allows you to view and operate on the files, directories and disks in the system. The program displays a directory tree diagram that shows the organization of the directories on a disk plus a list of the files contained in the selected directory. The program can display two different directories at the same time. The File menu contains standard operations such as copying, deleting and renaming of files.

File Operations. The File menu on the File System menu bar contains commands which operate on the selected file or files in the current directory. You can move, copy, rename, change file attributes, create or delete directories using this menu.

The DOS Prompt Mode. The DOS prompt mode allows you to directly access DOS commands and utilities without being limited by the options on the DOS shell menus. The **[Shift-F9]** keystroke activates this mode from the DOS shell program. In order to use this mode you must already know what commands you want to enter and the names of the files and directories you want to work with. Commands entered in this mode are command sentences that list the command and any parameters needed to carry out the command. Once in the DOS prompt mode you will remain in that mode until you enter the **EXIT** command to return to the previous application, in this case the DOS shell program.

BASIC. The BASIC programming language can be used to create BASIC programs. It can be accessed from the Main Group menu. Once activated you must enter the command SYSTEM to return to the DOS shell program.

DOS Shell Menus. You can modify and expand the DOS shell menus by adding programs or groups of your own. A program is a option that will be displayed on a menu. A group is a menu option that leads to a separate menu of programs. All new groups begin at the Main Group menu.

Programs. A program is an item that appears on a group menu. When you create a new program you must supply a program title, which appears on the menu, and a list of DOS prompt type commands that tell the DOS shell program what to do when the menu item is selected. Programs that have more than one command use the [**F4**] key to insert a separator symbol between each command.

Dialog Boxes. You can add custom defined dialog boxes to programs by inserting [] following a program command. The dialog box allows you to display information about the program and also to allow the user to enter parameters for the program before it executes. If the [] are empty the DOS shell program displays a default dialog box. You can use special options, e.g., /T, /I, /D, etc., to define the text that appears in the dialog box. You can also create an optional help display or add password protection to a program.

Chapter **14**

Customizing Your
PS1

O ne of the ironies of computers, in particular the family of personal computers that trace their origin to the original IBM PC, is that they are far easier to use than they are to set up. Of course, if you can't get your computer set up properly to begin with, you will never find out that it is not as hard to use as you think. This chapter shows you how to customize you PS1 by installing programs and modifying the setup of the PS1 system.

The PS1 is designed to eliminate the frustrations associated with the set up of a personal computer as much as possible. This is accomplished by setting up the machine for you, i.e., installing all the software in advance so the computer is ready to operate as soon as you plug it in.

However, one of the advantages of a computer is its versatility. The software included with the PS1, Prodigy, and Microsoft Works are good products but they are not the only products available. In fact there are thousands of programs that can run

423

on the PS1, including major best selling applications such as Windows, WordPerfect, Paradox, Lotus 1-2-3, Quatro Pro, Harvard Graphics, and more.

You can also change the set up of your PS1. These changes are required in order to run certain applications. Other types of changes are personal preferences you might choose to implement. In this chapter you will learn how to install popular software programs such as WordPerfect and Windows, and how to modify the set up of the PS1 system.

THE BOOTING PROCESS

Customization of the PS1 revolves around altering the way the computer starts. When you turn on your computer you begin a process called booting. In the PS1 this process takes place invisibly during the few moments that occur between turning on the computer and the display of the startup screen.

When you add a new program to the PS1 system you may need to change the actions taking place during the boot process. In order to understand how and why these changes are necessary you should have an understanding of what is going on during those first few seconds of each session.

The key to understanding the booting process lies in two concepts: volatile memory and maximum flexibility.

Volatile Memory

As discussed in Chapter 1, the majority of the memory in the computer cannot retain information when the system is shut off. In order to retain information between sessions, data is stored on a disk, hard or floppy. However, while this system seems quite logical, if you think about it for a moment you will realize that there is a paradox involved. The paradox is that the operating system, which tells the computer how to read and retrieve information from the disk, is also lost each time the computer is turned off. Of course, a copy of that information is stored on the disk. But when you first turn on the computer it does not have that copy in memory so it doesn't know how to read the disk in order to get the operating system information. The situation would be similar to a person who does not know how to read, being asked to read about learning to read. The information they need, instructions on how to read a book, are stored in the pages of the book. But if they cannot read, the book is of no use to them. To get the computer system up and running requires an extraordinary process by which the operating system is moved from the disk to the memory without having to use the operating system to do it. This process is called booting because of its analogy to the expression pulling yourself up by your own boot straps, a difficult task for human and computer alike.

Maximum Flexibility

The complexity of the paradox that requires the extraordinary step of booting is also an opportunity. Since the operating system is loaded each time you start the computer, you have an opportunity to alter the configuration of the computer each time you restart it. The PS1 and all DOS computers have options available that will change the way the operating system performs. Many programs require special settings or the loading of special information during the boot process in order to function properly. The PS1 is set up to run the applications with which it is supplied. However, when you add other programs such as Windows or WordPerfect, the startup configuration will need to be changed. You may also want to change the startup configuration to suit your own personal needs.

The booting process consists of three distinct stages: CMOS setup data, system configuration, and automatic execution commands.

CMOS Setup Data

In order to get around the paradox discussed previously, the PS1 is supplied with a small amount of battery powered CMOS memory. CMOS memory will operate on the very small amount of power supplied by the battery for many years. This memory is used to hold information about the hardware and software options in the system. When the computer is first turned on, it reads the CMOS data and uses those settings to start the booting process. Note that the CMOS data should match the actual system hardware. For example, if the CMOS is set for a hard disk and no hard disk is installed (or the hard disk fails to operate properly) a special system error screen will appear which displays an error code number that tells you about the problem. The information on this screen is designed for the use of a repair specialist so that it is unlikely that you will understand the meaning of the code numbers; furnishing that number however, can help you get aid from someone over the phone.

System Configuration

When the CMOS information has been read, the computer can then begin looking for information stored on the hard or floppy disk. Note that one piece of information stored in the CMOS is the location in the system from which the System Configuration should be read. The factory setting is to read the System Configuration from the configuration file built into the PS1 at the factory. The configuration file determines how much memory and what information will be used by the operating system. The configuration information is always stored in a file called CONFIG.SYS (configure system).

Automatic Execution Commands

After the configuration file has been loaded, the computer searches for an Automatic Execution file. This file contains a list of DOS commands that should be automatically executed each time the computer is turned on. This file determines what program or programs should be automatically loaded and executed. The PS1 is set up at the factory to run a program that displays the startup screens. You have the

425

option of changing that process. For example, you might choose to start the IBM DOS shell program each time the computer is turned on, rather than the startup screen. The Automatic Execution information is always stored in a file called AUTOEXEC.BAT (automatic execution batch file).

When you want to customize your PS1 system there are three questions that you are dealing with.

Where to Look for Boot Information?

You must decide where the PS1 should look for the configuration and automatic execution data. This is very important because the information in those files determines how the PS1 behaves after it has been booted. This also means that it is possible to have more than one CONFIG.SYS and AUTOEXEC.BAT file in the system. However, only one of these can be read when the computer boots. The one that you designate for reading at boot time is the one that actually controls the computer system.

Configuration Commands

The configuration commands do two important tasks. First, they set the size and use of memory for the operating system. For example, the total number of files that can be open at any one moment is set at the time the computer boots. The PS1 sets this value at 12. Some applications such as WordPerfect require a higher setting, 20 or more files. Note that the number of files used by a program has a technical meaning. WordPerfect can only edit two documents at once even though it has a higher file requirement than Works. The second important function is the loading of programs that enhance DOS functions. These programs are called device drivers since they are often required in order to integrate a special hardware addition into the computer system. DOS is supplied with some device drivers and many hardware product supply device drivers for their products.

Automatic Execution

The contents of the AUTOEXEC.BAT file determines what it is that appears on the screen at the end of the booting process. The PS1 is set to display the startup screen. However, by changing this file you can switch the startup to the DOS shell menu or even some specific application, i.e., Works or Prodigy.

INSTALLING ADDITIONAL PROGRAMS

Almost all of the computer programs designed for MS DOS computers can run on the PS1. The only software that cannot are those programs designed for a computer with a 386 processor. The PS1 uses a 286 processor and is not compatible with those applications. This means that you can expand the PS1 by adding applications such as WordPerfect, Windows, or Lotus 1-2-3.

When installing new software onto the PS1 there are three considerations that have to be taken into account. They are as follows: automatic or manual installation, changes to configuration files, and starting the program.

Automatic or Manual Installation

Most of the major applications are furnished with automatic installation programs. These programs will automatically create a directory for the new program, copy all of the required files from one or more floppy disks and create or modify the CONFIG.SYS and AUTOEXEC.BAT files if necessary for the application. If the program does not have automatic installation it will be necessary to perform manual installation where DOS commands are used to create the directory, copy files, and make any configuration changes that are required.

Changes to Configuration Files

Some applications require special values or device drivers to be installed in the CONFIG.SYS file and/or the AUTOEXEC.BAT. This may be done automatically through install programs or might be required to be manually done. In the PS1 there are special considerations that do not apply to most MS DOS computers in this regard. They will be discussed later in this chapter.

Starting the Program

When you add programs to the PS1 you need to decide how you would like to start the programs. Programs can be started from the folder system, the IBM DOS shell or at the DOS prompt mode. If you want to add these programs to the DOS shell you can do so using the techniques discussed in Chapter 13.

In the rest of this chapter the details of installing popular programs will be discussed. If the program you want to install is not specifically mentioned it will probably fall into one of the same classifications as the programs discussed.

THE D DRIVE

It was mentioned in Chapter 1 and the beginning of this chapter that the PS1 is supplied with built in settings that are used during the boot process. These settings are stored in ROM (read only) memory. This means that these items are built into the system and cannot be erased or changed.

The built in settings appear to DOS as if they were a disk. In hard disk systems the letter D is assigned to the ROM information, while on floppy disk systems it is drive C.

You can list the files in this drive just as you would any floppy or hard drive. Activate the IBM DOS file system:

Click(left) on **IBM DOS**
Double click(left) on **File System**
Click(left) on **D**

Drive D lists 5 files: AUTOFEXEC>BAT and CONFIG.SYS, COMMAND.COM, MOUSE.COM, CHECK.COM, SHELLSTB.COM, AND ROMSHELL.COM.

AUTOEXEC.BAT and CONFIG.SYS

These files are the automatic execution and system's configuration files that DOS reads when it boots the computer.

COMMAND.COM

The COMMAND.COM file is the DOS command interpreter. When you activate the DOS prompt mode you are actually running the COMMAND.COM program. It is this program that displays the DOS prompt and executes the commands that you enter. When you enter EXIT you terminate the COMMAND.COM program. All MS DOS machines have this file.

MOUSE.COM

When this program is executed it enhances the operating system of the PS1 to allow for programs that use mouse operations and commands. Without this file many programs would not recognize the presence of the mouse. Note that MOUSE.COM is different than most programs in that once it is loaded it remains in memory while other programs, e.g., Works, run. This type of program is called a TSR (terminate and stay resident) type program.

CHECKC.COM

This is a special utility that informs DOS if a hard disk drive is present in the computer. This enables the AUTOEXEC.BAT file to figure out which drive it should start working off of, A or C.

SHELLSTB.COM

This file is a device driver used for running the startup screen.

ROMSHELL.COM

This file contains the information that creates and operates the startup screen. The only difference between drive D and a normal drive is that you cannot delete, change or add information. You can read the information or even copy the files to another disk if you desire.

The PS1 CONFIG.SYS and AUTOEXEC.BAT Files

With the files on drive D listed you can use the **View** command on the File menu to examine the contents of the CONFIG.SYS and AUTOEXEC.BAT files:

```
Click(left) on CONFIG.SYS
Click(left) on File
Click(left) on View
```

The CONFIG.SYS file contains two commands: **files** and **install.**

FILES

This command sets the number of DOS file handlers at 12.

INSTALL

This command loads the SHELLSTB.COM program used by the DOS shell program.

Display the AUTOEXEC.BAT:

```
Click(left) on Cancel
Click(left) on AUTOEXEC.BAT
Click(left) on File
Click(left) on View
```

This file contains the following commands: **@ECHO OFF**, **MOUSE>NUL**, **PROMPT &P&G**, **CHECKC.**, **A:**, **IF errorlevel 1 C:**, and **IF errorlevel 1 PATH C:DOS.**

@ECHO OFF

This command suppresses the display of the commands as this batch file executes. Normally, batch files display each command on the screen before the command is executed. This aids in locating errors in new batch file programs. The @ECHO OFF is added to suppress this display which is no longer needed once the program is complete. This command has no functional significance since the batch file will operate exactly the same if it is removed.

MOUSE >NUL

This command loads the mouse driver. The >NUL is a suffix that suppresses the message normally output by the driver. If the >NUL is removed the message will appear on the screen.

PROMPT PG

This command sets the style of the DOS prompt. $P displays the current drive and directory, and $G displays the > character, e.g., C:\DOS>. If this command were not executed, the prompt would show only the drive letter, e.g., C:>.

CHECKC

This is a special program that tests for the presence of a hard disk. If it finds a hard disk, it sets a value called ERRORLEVEL to 1. If not, ERRORLEVEL remains at zero.

A:

This switches operations from the D or C ROM drive to the A drive.

IF errorlevel 1 C:

This command checks the ERRORLEVEL setting. If it is 1a hard disk is present the active disk is switched to C: If ERRORLEVEL is not 1, nothing takes place.

IF errorlevel 1 PATH C:\DOS

This command also uses the ERRORLEVEL value to determine whether a search PATH should be set to the DOS directory on drive C. A PATH allows you to execute programs located in the specified directory, e.g., DOS, no matter what directory you happen to be using. This is a rather common technique that most hard disk users should employ to allow access to their DOS commands from anywhere in their hard disk system. Without PATH you can only execute programs in the current disk or directory.

Exit the DOS shell program. Enter:

```
[Esc] [F3] [F3]
```

MAKING A SAFETY DISK

Before you begin to alter the configuration of the PS1 you should create a disk that has certain important files on it. This disk is important even if you have backed up the entire hard disk with the **Backup** command on the DOS shell menu. That is because the backup disks created with the DOS shell command cannot be used unless you run the RESTORE program. RESTORE is one of the files you want to place on this safety disk.

The first step is to format the disk. Place a new, unused floppy disk (or an old disk which does not contain information that you want to save) in drive A.

Activate the IBM DOS program:

```
Click(left) on IBM DOS
```

Select the Format option on the menu:

```
Double click(left) on Format(Prepare a diskette for use)
```

Select the type of diskette from the menu. If your disk is labeled as double density, DD or 2S DS choose the option labeled 720 KB. If the disk is high density or HD select the 1.44MB option:

```
Double click(left) on Format a 31/2
```

Enter:

```
[return]
```

The program shows you the percentage of the disk that is formatted until it reaches 100%. When the format is complete return to the DOS shell by entering:

```
[return]
n [return]
```

The next step is to make the diskette a bootable disk. This means that you can use this disk to start the IBM PS1 if there is a problem with the hard disk. This command will be executed at the DOS prompt. Enter:

```
[Shift-F9]
sys a: [return]
```

When done, the message "System transferred" will appear. Next copy the following files to drive A:

```
copy command.com a: [return]
copy format.com a: [return]
copy configur.exe a: [return]
copy customiz.exe a: [return]
copy restore.com a: [return]
copy mouse.com a: [return]
```

Return to the shell menu by entering:

```
exit [return]
```

431

Return to the Startup screen:

[Esc] [F3]

INSTALLING AUTOMATIC INSTALLATION PROGRAMS (WINDOWS)

In this section you will learn about installing programs that have automatic install programs included. The main example that will be used is Microsoft Windows 3.0. This is one of the most popular programs for MS DOS computers and it raises most of the problems associated with installing new programs on the PS1.

Note that all programs purchased for use with the PS1 or other MS DOS compatible computers are supplied on one or more floppy disks. However, if you have only a 3 1/2 inch floppy disk for your PS1, you must make sure that 3 1/2 inch disks are included in the program that you purchase. Some programs contain both 5 1/4 and 3 1/2 inch disks. Others have two different packages with different disk sizes. A third solution, used by some manufacturers that have only 5 1/4 inches is to include a coupon that can be sent to the company in exchange for a 3 1/2 inch version of the software.

Running an Install Program

Most software programs that come with automatic installation programs designate one disk as the Install or Setup disk. WordPerfect, dBASE IV, and Lotus 1-2-3 are among the programs that use the name INSTALL. Microsoft products such as Word, Windows, Works, and Excel use the name SETUP. In either case the advantage of the INSTALL or SETUP program is that it will perform all the operations needed to install the program once you start the install or setup program.

Keep in mind that on the PS1, because of its initial factory configuration, additional steps not accounted for by most INSTALL programs are necessary to complete the installation.

To begin installing a program place the INSTALL or SETUP disk into drive A. If the disks are numbered, disk #1 usually contains the Install program.

In order to execute the install program you must activate the DOS prompt mode:

Click(left) on IBM DOS

[Shift-F9]

432

Activate the floppy disk by entering the drive designation—a letter followed by a colon:

```
a: [return]
```

In the case of Windows you would enter SETUP to start the setup program. With Lotus 1-2-3, WordPerfect, or dBASE IV you would use INSTALL. If you are not sure what to enter, list the disk directory:

```
dir [return]
```

You should look for a file name that seems similar to INSTALL, SETUP, etc. The file name should have a BAT, COM or EXE extension. File names with one of these extensions will not function as an install program. This may indicate that you need to perform manual installation, discussed later in this chapter.

In the case of Windows 3.0 enter:

```
setup [return]
```

When the program loads, a screen appears that explains you are about to install windows on your computer. To continue, enter:

```
[return]
```

The next prompt asks you where in your system you want to install the program. The setup procedure suggests C:\WINDOWS. This means the program will create a new directory called WINDOWS into which it will install the new application. Unless you have some special reason it is usually best to accept this default designation. Enter:

```
[return]
```

The next step is to specify the hardware in your system. The install program will generally try to automatically detect your hardware and list what it has found. The PS1 display is a VGA display. Select VGA when selecting screen type with programs that cannot detect screen types during installation.

In most cases you can accept the hardware specifications:

```
[return]
```

Windows will proceed to copy information onto the hard disk. Change disks when prompted to do so by the setup program.

When disk #2 has been copied, Windows loads its graphic display. To continue with the setup click on continue:

```
Click(left) on Continue
```

Note some setup programs ask you about installing various features. In most cases you should install all of the features. The only disadvantage of this approach is that many features take up large amounts of disk space. WordPerfect's clip art graphics images take up a lot of space. You might want to skip those and add them later if you feel you need them.

Towards the end of the installation process most of the setup programs will ask you whether or not you want to allow the program to make changes to the CONFIG.SYS and AUTOEXEC.BAT files. In most cases you should allow these programs to make the changes unless you have a specific reason why you do not want changes made. You will learn in the next section how to read and change these files yourself.

In Windows make these changes by selecting CONTINUE:

```
Click(left) on Continue
Click(left) on Ok
```

When you are asked to select your printer, select your printer from the list by double clicking the name of the printer. For example:

```
Double click(left) on IBM Proprinter XL24
```

Place the correct printer disk in the drive and continue.

Windows, unlike most applications, can run other programs, since Windows is a type of shell program itself. Windows will ask if you want to automatically set up any programs you have on your hard disk to run under windows. Allow this to take place:

```
Click(left) on Ok
```

Windows will recognize Works and BASIC:

```
Click(left) on Add all
Click(left) on Ok
```

Windows will also display text files for you to read, which contain additional information not included in the printed manuals. When you have finished reading these files, exit the notepad:

```
Click(left) on File
Click(left) on Exit
```

Exit the Windows setup:

| Click(left) on **Exit to Dos** |

At the end of the installation program you will be at the DOS prompt again. You have now completed the automatic portion of the installation program. However, due to the structure of the PS1 there are some additional steps you must take in order to complete the installation.

Return to the startup screen by entering:

| **exit [return]**
[F3] |

Editing CONFIG.SYS and AUTOEXEC.BAT Files

If the application you have installed told you that changes were made to the CONFIG.SYS file it means that this application requires some special settings in the system's configuration in order to operate properly. You will need to perform some editing in order to get your PS1 to create the desired environment.

Why do you have to do this extra work? Didn't the install or setup program make the necessary changes? The answer is related to the use of the D or ROM drive built into the PS1. The install program expected that the system's CONFIG.SYS and AUTOEXEC.BAT files would be found in the root directory of drive C. Since no files were found there, the program created new CONFIG.SYS and AUTOEXEC.BAT files.

The problem is that when you start your PS1, it will ignore all of the files on drive C and read the built-in files on drive D instead. Thus the changes made by the install program will not have any effect on the configuration of the PS1.

You need to perform two tasks: change boot location and edit files.

Change Boot Location

In order to get the PS1 to read the CONFIG.SYS and AUTOEXEC.BAT files from the hard disk, drive C rather than drive D, you must make changes in the data stored in the PS1 CMOS. This can be done using the CUSTOMIZ.EXE program. This program is set up to run from the Main Group DOS shell menu under the title "Customize How System Starts."

Edit Files

The install programs are designed to modify the existing CONFIG.SYS and AUTOEXEC.BAT files. This means that the new commands or settings are added to the one you have already established for your system. However, in the PS1, the install programs couldn't find (and even if they could they couldn't modify) the existing CONFIG.SYS and AUTOEXEC.BAT files on drive D. This means that the files on drive C may lack some of the instructions found on drive D. You need to edit the new CONFIG.SYS and AUTOEXEC.BAT files to make sure they include the commands from drive D. If you don't perform this task the system will no longer boot to the startup screen since instructions to do so are contained only on drive D at this time.

Begin with the editing tasks first. The CONFIG.SYS and AUTOEXEC.BAT are text files. This means that you can make all of the necessary changes using the Works word processing module.

Load Works:

Click(left) on **Microsoft Works**

Loading CONFIG.SYS

In order to resolve the differences, if any between the new CONFIG.SYS file and the drive D CONFIG.SYS you can load both files into Works word processing windows. Start with the drive D CONFIG.SYS file:

Click(left) on **Open Existing File**

Change the file selector display to drive D:

Double click(left) on **D** in the Directories box

The D drive files appear in the File box. Load the CONFIG.SYS file:

Double click(left) on *CONFIG.SYS*

Works displays a box that warns you that you cannot modify this file because it is a read-only file. This is OK since you want to use this file for reference only:

Click(left) on <Ok>

Works then displays a dialog box that asks you to identify the type of file. This is because Works can load text word processing, spreadsheet or database files. Select word processing:

```
Click(left) on Word Processor
Click(left) on <Ok>
```

The window shows the commands you saw when you viewed the file from DOS. The next step is to load the CONFIG.SYS from drive C. However, there is something you must do before you attempt that operation. Works cannot have two windows open with the exact same name. Since window titles do not have room for drive or directory designations, if you open another CONFIG.SYS the current window will be automatically closed. To avoid this, save a copy of this file on drive C with a different name, e.g., CONFIG.PS1:

```
Click(left) on File
Click(left) on Save As
Double click(left) on C in the Directories box
```

Enter the new name for the file:

```
config.ps1 [return]
```

Close the current window and then load CONFIG.PS1:

```
Click(left) on File
Click(left) on Close
```

```
config.ps1 [return]
[return]
```

You can now load the CONFIG.SYS from the root directory of drive C without conflict:

```
Click(left) on File
Click(left) on Open Existing File
Double Click(left) on C in the Directories box
```

Since you know the exact location of the file you want you can type in the path name of the file directly instead of navigating around to different directories:

```
c:\config.sys [return]
[return]
```

Use the Arrange All command to show both files at one time:

```
Click(left) on Window
Click(left) on Arrange All
```

The CONFIG.SYS file created for windows lists the following commands:

    files = 30
    buffers = 30
    device=C:\himem.sys
    device=C:\WINDOWS\mouse.sys /Y
    device=C:\WINDOWS\smartdrv.sys 320

The Windows CONFIG.SYS file sets the FILES at 30. It also allocates memory for BUFFERS. Buffers can improve the performance of disk-to-memory transfers by allocating memory so that more data is read or written each time. Windows also loads three device drives: one which expands the memory available to DOS beyond 640K by another 64K HIMEM.SYS; one which loads a mouse driver, and one which uses 320K of extended memory (memory that is not used in the PS1) for a disk caching program which is also designed to speed up disk operations.

In this case you will want to remove the mouse driver since the PS1 already has a mouse driver, and add the **INSTALL** command for the SHELLSTB.COM program, which does not appear in the Windows CONFIG.SYS.

Remove the line that contains MOUSE.SYS:

Click(left) on in the margin next to *mouse.sys.*

[Del]

Add the following command to INSTALL the SHELLSTB.COM program:

[Ctrl-End] [return] **INSTALL=D:\SHELLSTB.COM**

The modified CONFIG.SYS should read:

    files = 30
    buffers = 30
    device=C:\himem.sys
    device=C:\WINDOWS\smartdrv.sys 320
    INSTALL=D:\SHELLSTB.COM

Note that it was necessary to designate the drive location of SHELLSTB.COM since the CONFIG.SYS file will not be on the same drive as SHELLSTB.COM.

Save the modified CONFIG.SYS:

Click(left) on **File** Click(left) on **Close** Click(left) on **<Yes>** Click(left) on **File** Click(left) on **Close**

Editing the AUTOEXEC.BAT

You need to perform the same type of operation with the AUTOEXEC.BAT files. You can use DOS as a shortcut way to make a copy of the original PS1 AUTOEXEC.BAT file:

```
Click(left) on Run Other Programs
Double click(left) on DOS prompt
Click(left) on <Ok>
```

Enter the following DOS command that creates a file called AUTOEXEC.PS1 that is a copy of the D drive AUTOEXEC.BAT:

```
copy d:\autoexec.bat autoexec.ps1 [return]
```

Return to Works by entering:

```
exit [return]
```

Load both files so that you can compare their contents:

```
Click(left) on File
Click(left) on Open Existing File
```

```
autoexec.ps1 [return] [return]
```

```
Click(left) on File
Click(left) on Open Existing File
```

```
c:\autoexec.bat [return] [return]
```

```
Click(left) on Window
Click(left) on Arrange All
```

The AUTOEXEC.PS1, the original file reads:

```
@ECHO OFF
MOUSE >NUL
PROMPT $P$G
CHECKC
A:
IF errorlevel 1 C:
IF errorlevel 1 PATH C:\DOS
```

The AUTOEXEC.BAT, the one created by Windows, reads:

    PATH C:\WINDOWS;
    set TEMP=C:\WINDOWS\TEMP

To understand the differences between the files requires some knowledge of DOS. It is probably best to start at the beginning of the current file AUTOEXEC.BAT and write the commands that are actually needed.

```
[Ctrl-Home]
```

The **@ECHO OFF** command is a good one to have since it suppresses the display of the commands as they execute. Enter:

```
@ECHO OFF [return]
```

Next enter a **PROMPT** command to set the system's prompt. This command is also the same as it appears in the original D drive autoexec:

```
PROMPT $P$G [return]
```

The next command loads the mouse driver. In this case the mouse command must be modified to indicate that the MOUSE.COM program is found on drive D. Enter:

```
D:\MOUSE >NUL
```

Note that the **PATH** command appears in both files but specifies a different directory in each. You can resolve this by opening a PATH to both directories. Add on a PATH to C:\DOS by entering:

```
[End]
C:\DOS;
```

The AUTOEXEC.BAT file now executes all of the commands needed to get the system running properly for all the software, including Windows. Note that the **ERRORLEVEL** commands are not needed since the assumption is that you are using a hard disk. Save the new AUTOEXEC.BAT and exit Works:

```
Click(left) on File
Click(left) on Exit Works
Click(left) on <Yes>
```

Changing the Start Up Settings

All of the modifications you have made to the AUTOEXEC.BAT and CONFIG.SYS files will not make any difference in the way that the system operates unless you change the settings stored in CMOS memory, that tell the PS1 where to locate the files when the system is booted. The PS1 is installed at the factory to use the built-in drive D AUTOEXEC.BAT and CONFIG.SYS files. The CUSTOMIZ.EXE program allows you to alter the settings in the CMOS and change the way the system gets configured during booting.

The CUSTOMIZ.EXE program can be executed from the DOS prompt or through the DOS shell menus. Use the DOS shell menu:

```
Click(left) on IBM DOS
Click(left) on Customize How System Starts
```

This screen controls how the system starts. The first setting you want to change is under the heading "Choose where the computer looks for the operating system." The default setting is "Start From Built-in DOS." Change this setting to "Try Diskette First (otherwise Start From Built-in DOS)." This is done in case you make a mistake and create information on the hard disk that hangs up the computer, you can recover control by using the safety floppy disk you created at the beginning of this chapter. That disk contains a copy of the operating system as well as the CUSTOMIZE program which will allow you to change all settings back to built-in, and then correct **your mistake:**

```
Click(left) on Try Diskette First (otherwise...
```

Note that the third option in this section, "Try diskette first, then Try Fixed Disk," will disable the D drive (ROM drive) so that you cannot use the files stored in this drive, specifically the MOUSE.COM and SHELLSTB.COM. If you want to use this option, you can copy the files you need from drive D to drive C and have your CONFIG.SYS and AUTOEXEC.BAT use the copied rather than the original files in the D drive.

The next settings are found at the bottom of the screen listed under Read Config.sys and Read Autoexec.bat. The default setting are both for Built-in. Change both settings to From Disk so that the PS1 will read the CONFIG.SYS and AUTOEXEC.BAT files you have created instead of the built in files on drive D:

```
Click(left) on From Disk next to Read Config.sys
Click(left) on From Disk next to Read Autoexec.bat
```

The Disk to read from options should be set for drive C. Save the changes you have made to the start up options. Enter:

```
[return]
```

You can restart the system by pressing down and holding the [Ctrl] and [Alt] keys and then pressing [Del]. You can then release all keys. This keystroke causes the computer to go back and execute the boot routine. Make sure that you remove any disks in the floppy drive before you enter the key combination. Enter:

```
Ctrl-Alt-Del]
[
```

You will notice that the Windows device drivers display messages that flash on the screen as they load. These messages are not significant so you need not be concerned about reading them.

Note that when Windows 3.0 is installed in a PS1 with 1 megabyte of memory. The program will have about 590K of usable memory left once it has loaded. Note that this is in contrast to a usable memory size of 567K for the PS1 when it is running from the built-in configuration. The additional memory is furnished to Windows by means of the HIMEM.SYS driver that makes additional memory above 640K available to applications designed to work with HIMEM.SYS such as Windows.

Note that the two applications found by Windows, BASIC, and Works are stored in the group icon labeled "Non-Windows Applications."

Running New Programs

Windows (or any other new application) is now installed on the PS1. But how do you access the program? There are three ways: the folder system, DOS Shell, and DOS Prompt.

The Folder System

You can add the new program to the main folder of the folder system.

DOS Shell

You can add a program to the DOS shell menu.

DOS Prompt

You can execute the program from the DOS prompt.

Begin with the folder system option. Display the folder system by selecting Your Software from the startup screen:

Click(left) on **Your Software**

The folder system display will show the new directory or directories created for the new programs that you installed. In this example there will be a directory folder called WINDOWS. Open that folder:

Click(left) on **Windows**

The Windows folder will list a large number of program names. Most of these names are programs that should be executed only from Windows. The program that starts Window is WIN. If you installed WordPerfect the WP file would be the one that starts Wordperfect. To start Lotus 1-2-3 the program would be 123.

Select the program you want to start:

```
Click(left) on WIN
Click(left) on Add to List
Click(left) on Ok
```

WIN is added to the Main Folder. Execute Windows by selecting the command:

```
Double click(left) on WIN
```

Windows executes and loads. Exit from Windows:

```
Click(left) on File
Click(left) on Exit Windows
Click(left) on Ok
```

You return to the Main Folder Display. Exit the folder system:

```
Click(left) on Exit
```

The second method of running an application is by adding a program to the DOS shell menu. This procedure was detailed in Chapter 13 using existing PS1 programs as examples. The procedure remains basically the same when you have added a new program.

Activate the DOS shell from the Start screen:

```
Click(left) on IBM DOS
```

Create a new program for the Main Group menu:

```
Click(left) on Program
Click(left) on Add
```

Enter the title:

```
Microsoft Windows 3.0 [return]
```

The program needs two commands: **CD** to change to the WINDOWS directory and **WIN** to run window. Enter:

```
cd c:\windows
[F4]
win
[F2]
```

Run Windows by selecting the new program from the menu:

```
Click(left) on Microsoft Windows 3.0
```

Windows executes and loads. Exit from Windows:

```
Click(left) on File
Click(left) on Exit Windows
Click(left) on Ok
```

The last method is to use the DOS prompt directly. Enter:

```
[Shift-F9]
cd\windows [return]
win [return]
```

Windows executes and loads. Note that Windows (or any other application) will have about 6K less available memory when it is loaded with the DOS prompt method. This is because memory is reserved for continuation of the DOS prompt session while the application is running. Exit from Windows:

```
Click(left) on File
Click(left) on Exit Windows
Click(left) on Ok
```

You return to the DOS prompt mode exactly at the point where you loaded Windows. Return to the start up screen by entering:

```
exit [return]
[F3]
```

Note on Batch Files

Some applications, such as Ventura, use batch files to start the application from DOS. Ventura Desktop Publisher uses batch files called VP.BAT or VPPROF.BAT. If you want to install these programs in the DOS shell menus you must use the CALL command if you want the program to go back to IBM DOS after it is terminated.

Without CALL the programs will return to the Startup screen instead. For details on the CALL command see Chapter 13 under "Installing Works in the DOS shell menu system."

Keep in mind that once you have switched the PS1 to using the AUTOEXEC.BAT and CONFIG.SYS from drive C, any other programs that you install can modify those files as they would on a PC that did not use the PS1 start up system.

Manual Installation

Manual installation has the same considerations as automatic installation with the exception that you must manually enter commands that create the directory for the new program and copy the files to the hard disk. For example, suppose that you have an application which does not have an setup or install program included. Begin by accessing the DOS prompt:

```
Click(left) on IBM DOS
```

Enter:

```
[Shift-F9]
```

Use the **MD** commands to create a new directory. For example, create a directory called PRACTICE. Enter:

```
md c:\practice [return]
```

Place the disk which contains the program files in drive A and use the **XCOPY** command to copy all of the files to the new directory:

```
xcopy a:*.* c:\practice [return]
```

If the program uses more than one disk, Repeat the command for each disk. Note that when you are in DOS you can repeat the last command by pressing **[F3]** followed by **[return]**. Note this works only for the last command executed at the DOS prompt.

Once you have reached that point, installation is pretty much the same. Of course, during manual installation no modifications are made to the CONFIG.SYS or AUTOEXEC.BAT files. You will need to examine the programs documentation to determine if the default configuration, FILES=12, is adequate for the application.

If you need to change the configuration, follow the method shown in the section on installing Windows.

STARTING WITH WINDOWS

The PS1 startup screen is designed to make getting started with the PS1 simpler than getting started with a standard PC. However, at some point you may find that you may want to change the way the system starts. The DOS shell program and the Windows 3.0 program both provide shell programs that enable you to load software programs by pointing at objects on the screen. Unlike the Startup screen, the DOS shell or Windows can be modified to include many different applications.

Suppose you would like to have the PS1 boot directly into Windows rather than the Startup screen. This can be done by making modifications in the CONFIG.SYS and AUTOEXEC.BAT files, assuming you have already setup the PS1 to read those files from the hard disk.

Disabling the Startup Screen

The first modification is made to the CONFIG.SYS file and it is made in order to disable the startup screen. Load the CONFIG.SYS into Works as described earlier in the chapter:

Click(left) on **Microsoft Works** Click(left) on **Open Existing Document**

c:\config.sys [return] [return]

Delete the line in the CONFIG.SYS file that reads:

INSTALL=D:\SHELLSTB.COM

Save the file:

Click(left) on **File** Click(left) on **Close** Click(left) on **<Yes>**

Load the AUTOEXEC.BAT:

Click(left) on **Open Existing Document**

c:\autoexec.bat [return] [return]

Add two lines at the end of the file that read:

cd c:\windows [return] win

Save and exit:

```
Click(left) on File
Click(left) on Exit Works
Click(left) on <Yes>
```

Reboot the system by entering:

```
[Ctrl-Alt-Del]
```

The PS1 will boot directly into windows with no startup screen display.

Integrating Prodigy into Windows

If you do decide to use Windows as your startup program you will need to integrate Prodigy into Windows since Prodigy is the only one of the supplied programs not automatically picked up by Windows when it is installed.

Begin by displaying the Non-Windows applications group:

```
Double click(left) on the Non-Windows Applications icon
```

Add a new application to the group:

```
Click(left) on File
Click(left) on New
Click(left) on Ok
```

Enter the description of the new item:

```
Prodigy Service [Tab]
```

The next line is used for the commands that run the Prodigy service. The name of the program is RS.EXE and it is located in the Prodigy directory. The RS program must be started with a parameter, the letter P. Enter:

```
c:\prodigy\rs p [return]
```

A new icon appears in the window. Start Prodigy:

```
Double click(left) on the Prodigy Service icon
```

The Prodigy program loads in the usual manner. Exit Prodigy:

```
e [return]
```

You can add a second icon for the IBM User Club. The only difference is that the parameter for the RS program is A instead of P:

```
Click(left) on File
Click(left) on New
Click(left) on Ok
```

```
IBM User Club [Tab]
c:\prodigy\rs a [return]
```

A new icon appears in the window. Start Prodigy:

```
Double click(left) on the Prodigy Service icon
```

The Prodigy program loads in the usual manner. Exit Prodigy:

```
e [return]
```

SUMMARY

This chapter dealt with the installation of additional software programs into the PS1 system. The chapter included information on: the booting process, PS1 startup, and CONFIG.SYS and AUTOEXEC.BAT files.

Index

Index

X

Y

Z